EIGHT VOICES
OF THE EIGHTIES

UQP AUSTRALIAN AUTHORS

General Editor: L.T. Hergenhan
                  Reader in Australian Literature
                  University of Queensland

Also in this series:

In preparation:

EIGHT VOICES
OF THE EIGHTIES

Stories, journalism and criticism by Australian women writers

EDITED BY GILLIAN WHITLOCK

University of Queensland Press

First published 1989 by University of Queensland Press
Box 42, St Lucia, Queensland 4067 Australia

Typeset by University of Queensland Press
Printed in Australia by The Book Printer, Melbourne

Distributed in the USA and Canada by
International Specialized Book Services, Inc.,
5602 N.E. Hassalo Street, Portland, Oregon 97213-3640

Arts for
Australians
Australia Council

Creative writing program assisted by the
Literary Arts Board of the Australia Council,
the Federal Government's arts funding
and advisory body

Cataloguing in Publication Data

National Library of Australia

Eight voices of the eighties.

 Bibliography.
 Includes index.

 1. Australian literature — Women authors. 2. Australian
 literature — 20th century. I. Whitlock, Gillian Lea,
 1953- .

A820'.8'09287

ISBN 0 7022 2225 9

Contents

HELEN GARNER

Acknowledgments

This project was aided by a research grant from the Division of Humanities, Griffith University and the research assistance of Joy Doherty. I should like to thank Alrene Sykes, Helen Tiffin, David Carter, Judith Allen and Stephen Slemon for their encouragement and also Laurie Hergenhan, who discussed this selection at length on a number of occasions. Thanks also to Kay Ferres, who made her unpublished thesis on the short story available to me. On the home front, thanks to Theo, who took care of Sam, and to my parents and Gerry who, as always, were a source of constant support.

For permission to reproduce the material in this anthology, acknowledgment is made to Thea Astley for "Being a Queenslander", *Southerly* 36 (1976); and for "The Teeth Father Naked At Last", *Three Australian Writers*, Foundation for Australian Literary Studies, Monograph no. 5, James Cook University; to Australian Literary Management for Beverley Farmer, "Letter to Judith Brett", *Meanjin* 43 (1986); for Kate Grenville, "A Time of Hard", *Scripsi* 4 (1987); and for Elizabeth Jolley, "The Well-Bred Thief", *South Pacific Stories*, ed. C. and H. Tiffin (St Lucia: SPACLALS, 1980); "The Fellmonger", *Times on Sunday*, 22 February 1987; review of Helen Garner's *The Children's Bach*, *Scripsi* 3 (1985); and review of Kate Grenville's *Lilian's Story*, *Sydney Morning Herald*, 29 June 1985; to Curtis Brown (Aust.) Pty Ltd for Barbara Hanrahan, "Annie M." and "Dream People", *Dream People* (London: Grafton, 1987); "Weird Adelaide", *Adelaide Review* 49 (March 1988); "Beginnings"; and "Childhood", interview with Jenny Palmer in *Bulletin*, 21–28 December 1982; to the Estate of Olga Masters for Olga Masters,

2222222

22222222

222222222

"The Lang Women" and "Leaving Home", *The Home Girls* (St Lucia: University of Queensland Press, 1982); "The Christmas Parcel", *A Long Time Dying* (St Lucia: University of Queensland Press, 1987); "War Gave Women a First Taste of Liberation", *Sydney Morning Herald*, 13 August 1985; and "Monet: *The Meadow*", *Sydney Morning Herald*, 15 June 1985; to McPhee Gribble Publishers for Beverley Farmer, "Place of Birth", "Home Time" and "A Woman with Black Hair", *Home Time* (Fitzroy: McPhee Gribble/Penguin, 1985); and for Helen Garner, "Postcards from Surfers" and "Civilisation and its Discontents", *Postcards from Surfers* (Fitzroy: McPhee Gribble/Penguin, 1985); to Barbara Mobbs for Helen Garner, "What We Say", *Sydney Morning Herald*, 6 January 1987; introduction to Eleanor Dark, *Lantana Lane* (London: Virago, 1986); "Elizabeth Jolley: An Appreciation", *Meanjin* 42 (June 1983); review of Thea Astley's *An Item from the Late News*, *National Times*, 17–23 October 1982; and "A Woman's Word", *National Times*, 24–30 October 1982; to Pan Picador Books for "Writing as a Neuter", from interview with Thea Astley by Candida Baker, *Yacker: Australian Writers Talk About Their Work* (Sydney: Picador, 1986); to Penguin Books Australia Ltd for Thea Astley, "Heart Is Where the Home Is", *It's Raining in Mango* (Sydney: Viking, 1987); and "A Northern Belle", *Hunting the Wild Pineapple* (Melbourne: Nelson, 1979); for Jessica Anderson, "Under the House" and "Against the Wall", *Stories from the Warm Zone* (Ringwood: Penguin, 1987); for Jennifer Ellison, interviews with Jessica Anderson, Thea Astley, Beverley Farmer, Helen Garner and Elizabeth Jolley from *Rooms of Their Own* (Ringwood: Penguin, 1986); and for Elizabeth Jolley, "Hilda's Wedding", *Woman in a Lampshade* (Ringwood: Penguin, 1982); to Gerry Turcotte for interview with Kate Grenville, *Southerly* 47 (1987); to the University of Queensland Press for Kate Grenville, "Federation Story", *Joan Makes History* (St Lucia: University of Queensland Press, 1988); and "The Test Is, If They Drown", *Bearded Ladies* (St Lucia: University of Queensland Press, 1984).

Introduction

Elizabeth Jolley has dubbed the 1980s a "moment of glory" for the woman writer, a phase in the national literary history when women writers and readers have entered the mainstream.[1] Thea Astley takes a more general view when she typifies it as a "decade of the minorities".[2] It is no accident of course that these should coincide. The prominence of women writers causes a move to heterogeneity rather than homogeneity and stable definition. National mythologies are undermined as, to adopt the title of Kate Grenville's latest novel, Joan makes history; the traditional centres and oppositions are displaced to allow space not only for the experience of women but also a marked sense of regional, ethnic and class based difference. As readers cast their eyes over the writings here there may be an impression of affiliation amongst these Australian women writers. However Astley is quick to speak as a Queenslander; Hanrahan pursues the obscured working class voices of Thebarton, South Australia; Jolley is careful to be faithful to the peculiarities of the West, and Garner goes forth from an urban Carlton which is far removed from Master's Cobargo, on the far south coast of New South Wales, "a terribly dull place in 1935".[3] These women spin local mythologies rather than national or sexual stereotypes.

The prominence of women's writing this decade has been such that the WACM (as Elizabeth Webby dubs the white Anglo-Celtic male who has been the icon of Australian literary traditions and patronage)[4] has suffered considerable anxiety. It is striking then that, as we look to previews of the decade, we find little in the way of precursors for this surge. For example in her review of Australian women's novels of the 1970s, Margaret Smith ruefully concludes that, whereas some of the earlier twentieth century literature by women can be seen as a product of first wave feminism, "as yet in Australia there has not been a groundswell fully emerging with the second wave".[5] At about the same time, Stephen Torre observes a dramatic increase in the publication of short stories in Australia and a "new wave" of writers coming into view.[6] Although Torre's bibliography of the Australian short story 1940–80 includes entries for Thea Astley, Kate Grenville, Helen Garner, Barbara Hanrahan, Elizabeth Jolley and Olga Masters, their presence is a slight ripple, easily subsumed into the category of "new writing" capacious enough to accommodate them alongside the likes of Peter Carey, Michael Wilding and Murray Bail. That the short story would emerge as a particularly suitable vehicle for women's voices could not be foreseen.

This literary landscape changed dramatically during the eighties; a decade when women writers came "out from under" to be labelled variously as feminist, woman-centred or, most notoriously, as sacred cows.[7] In a recent appraisal of directions in Australian fiction Brian Matthews identifies three surges in Australian writing; in the 1890s with the impetus to write nationalist literature; in the 1970s with the pressure to write protest literature; and the 1980s when "probably the greatest single and coherent pressure is the voice of second-wave feminism, whose tones many women writers convey with great assurance despite the fact that such an adoption still, in our time, commits them to confrontationist stances of some degree or another. It is a voice which . . . has become a dominant note in our literary culture. It is one of the elements in the current exciting mix which could change the rules."[8]

This anthology presents a selection of stories, criticism, reviews, interviews and commentaries from the most recent work of eight Australian women writers: Jessica Anderson, Thea Astley, Beverley Farmer, Helen Garner, Kate Grenville, Barbara Hanrahan, Elizabeth Jolley and Olga Masters. Together these stories and prose writings present an array of different kinds of writing and different perspectives upon women's writing in Australia now. In interview extracts these writers discuss feminism, colonialism, regionalism and what it means to them to be thought of as a "woman" writer and as an "Australian" writer. They also comment upon the situation of writers in Australia in terms of relations with publishers, readers, critics and funding agencies. In the reviews we can perceive a sense of community amongst these women. This is most obvious between Elizabeth Jolley and Helen Garner, for example, who clearly influence each other's writing. It is also apparent in comments Astley and Garner, Jolley and Grenville have to make about each other's work. The reviews, interviews and commentaries by these writers are not merely a background to their fictions; rather they set out a series of issues and considerations which are frameworks within which the stories can be read.

Together these writers have been typified as the "crest" of the current wave of women's writing, the "prize blooms in the perfumed garden".[9] Recently Carmel Bird objected to women writers such as Hanrahan, Garner and Farmer being routinely represented as "eclipsed" or obscure on the basis of their gender; these women, she argues, cast a good deal of light.[10] If this is so, and certainly women writers are by no means equally or necessarily marginalised, who or what put an end to the dark ages for women's writing? What brought women's writing and gender-based readings of Australian writing generally onto the agenda? Why is the spotlight cast on these writers in particular?

These large questions need to be addressed in the process of reviewing this past decade of Australian writing as something of a literary phenomenon for women writers and readers. The context which is sketched in the following introduction will begin by focusing not so much on these individual writers, though differences between them will not be overlooked, but on their place in a process of feminisation. From looking to the larger arena of cultural politics we can then move on to consider ways of locating this particular group of writers as a community. Notions of a women's room or a female tradition will be deliberately avoided here, for the choice of this group of writers, and the quite specific context of this anthology — eight women writers in the eighties — suggests a different framework for interpretation. Finally, given that the focus of this edition is short fiction by Australian women writers, we need to ponder issues of gender and genre and gender and nation. Why might the short story be particularly useful for the woman writer? To what extent does the national context remain a useful frame for thinking about their work?

Cultural Politics

One should not underestimate just how substantial a shift in cultural politics has occurred for feminism to emerge as a powerful force in Australian cultural and literary affairs, given its potential "to change the rules of the game" and displace well-established interests. By a shift in cultural politics I have in mind changes and reorientations in various institutions (academic, journalistic, publishing) over the past decade. Although the sense of the passage of text from author to reader is often cherished as a direct and quite personal relation, it can be useful to turn to a different paradigm and think about texts as commodities which are, in some respects, produced and marketed and consumed like much less hallowed objects. This is not to impugn the quality of the writing itself or the status of each of these writers individually; the labelling of the reasons for the success of these women writers as merely "sociological" has quite rightly been recognised as a slur.[11] In her recent discussion of the commodity status of culture, Judith Brett points out that books are commodities, bought and sold in the marketplace; authors are workers trying to make a living. However books are also bearers of culture, writers are also artists and thinkers in a system of exchange quite other than that of the market.[12] In this particular instance, as we consider the emergence of women's writing as something of a phenomenon of the decade, it is useful to begin by looking not only to the author but also to the publishers, readers and critics who have played a significant part in this reorientation.

From this perspective, we can see that the emergence of women's writing in Australia (and elsewhere) has been related to a series of effects produced by the re-emergence of feminism. Feminist politics have shaped both the production and reception of what women have to say. In "A Woman's Word" Helen Garner ponders the question of who makes a book a feminist book, suggesting that finally "perhaps it is the reader, and not the writer . . ." [13] What we see over the past ten years or so (perhaps AMG, or "After Monkey Grip", as some critics have suggested!) is a number of factors which have come together to alter significantly the range of books available to a growing woman-centred audience who have become increasingly aware of the politics of reading.

The establishment and success of, for example, a number of small and specialist presses has been a significant part of this process. Sybylla, Redress Press, Fremantle Arts Centre Press, McPhee Gribble and Sisters have attempted to "upset the economy" by fostering women's writing in particular. Larger publishers, such as Penguin and Collins, have also greatly expanded the amount of women's writing on their publishing lists. The significance of women as editors in publishing houses and their close relationship with writers is a hidden yet vital part of the emergence of a female voice. Helen Garner asserts that women publishers have been "crucial" to her success; "A Time of Hard", the additional chapter to Grenville's *Lilian's Story*, was produced by editor and author working closely together; Olga Masters likewise has paid tribute to her very close relationship with editors at UQP. [14]

Important too is the discussion of ways of reading women's writing. Reviewing and criticism determine what texts get read, and how, and by whom. I shall return shortly to the issue of how we read writings by women; it is sufficient to say at this point that the success of women writers has been facilitated by the emergence of sympathetic feminist reviews and criticism. Helen Garner has spoken of the value of the critic "who will come and put their elbows on the desk with you metaphorically . . . they're marvellous, real jewels." [15] Although, as Beverley Farmer's "Letter to Judith Brett" reveals, this meeting of critic and writer is not always harmonious and constructive, second-wave feminism has helped to shape a receptive audience for women's writing. If we look at the antagonistic reviews of those early examples of women's writing, such as *Monkey Grip* (McPhee Gribble, 1977) or *Country Girl Again* (Sisters, 1979), we can gauge how fundamental this shift has been in the ways we receive women's writing. This has been effected by feminist journals such as *Hecate, Refrac-*

tory Girl, Scarlet Woman and *Australian Feminist Studies*, and especially by the "feminisation" of *Meanjin* and *Australian Book Review* during the editorships of Judith Brett and Kerryn Goldsworthy respectively. To some extent this has percolated through to the review pages of major weekend papers such as the *Australian, Sydney Morning Herald* and the *Age*.

Significant too is the emergence of a number of academic women who are able to publish and teach about women's writing; although their place tends to be tenuous rather than tenured, they too have helped to rupture a male preserve. A small group of feminist critics, and the work of Carole Ferrier, Kerryn Goldsworthy, Sneja Gunew, Bronwen Levy and Susan Sheridan comes to mind in particular, have constructed the groundwork for an ongoing commentary focused on Australian women's writing quite specifically. Furthermore the influence of feminist criticism and the sheer volume of women's writing recently has percolated through mainstream journals and criticism to the extent that it is by no means a specifically female or feminist preserve. Most importantly — given, as Beverley Farmer (following Barthes) reminds us, that "literature is what is taught" [16] — women's writing has found a specific place on undergraduate and other curricula and has become an increasingly respectable topic for postgraduate study. When these writings are taught and researched with a notion of their potential to "change the rules", and it is by no means the case that women's writing is necessarily read with a mind to its oppositional potential, literary canons and orthodoxies of the national literature are open to debate and redefinition.

Finally, economic considerations need to be noted. The feminisation of Australian literature has been facilitated by new federal programs of support for both writers and publishers. The Literature Board has been under considerable pressure to increase funding of women's writing in particular. There has been some acrimonious debate about sexual politics in the funding process — Margaret McClusky, for example, has argued that women writers routinely ask for and get less support. [17] However a number of the writers included in this collection have benefited from a wider array of sources of funding, from federal and state grants, to writer in residence schemes to literary prizes.

A Community of Women

These shifts in the cultural economy are both a pleasure and a danger for women writers. Does incorporation compromise the potential of women's writing to "change the rules of the game" and upset the balance? [18] Certainly the celebration and canonisation of particular writers deserves close scrutiny. Although the cultural shifts outlined above have enabled a structural shift so that, as Kerryn Goldsworthy remarks, there is a "trend in Australian writing — and publishing — away from the dominance of people called John, Peter, Alan, Patrick, Hal and Frank and towards a more equitable representation of people with names like Serge and Angelo and Ania, and Marian and Elizabeth and Kate", it is not the case that ethnic, Aboriginal and women writers have been favoured equally. [19]

For example, Gina Mercer has commented on the promotion of women writers in a "star" system. She notes how the particular acceptability of Helen Garner seems to go hand in hand with the presentation of a "small", "modest", "housewifely" person. [20] Ever since Jane Austen, the miniature and the domestic have been acceptable and neutralising categories for the woman writer. They allow her a "place".

It seems both disingenuous and misleading to deny notions of a canon when dealing with these eight writers who have so obviously represented the acceptable and popular face of women's writing in Australia. To some extent this canonisation must amuse writers such as Beverley Farmer, whose work has been declared offside according to some feminist criteria, or to Thea Astley, for whom the term "woman writer" has often been cast as a form of thinly veiled abuse, and who wrote for years "in the wilderness". The "star" system has not been without its costs for Garner also. "Star" billing can trigger a process of neutralising the oppositional potential of this writing and taming it to coffee table status.

Garner correctly identifies this as a way of silencing and denigrating the woman writer: "I read in a review of Barry Humphries' new show that on Edna Everage's coffee table 'Helen Garner and Doris Lessing have replaced the *Women's Weekly*'. This information provokes a flinching, of course, and an urge to protect myself from mockery either by vanishing completely or by pretending I was never really serious about anything much when I wrote the books." [21]

However, given the lesser attention paid to the writings of black, migrant and avant-garde women writers, we need to consider why the writings of these women have been paid particular attention. Putting to one side judgments on the basis of that slippery notion of "quality", we can see that this most recognised and celebrated community of women writers are not disadvantaged by class and ethnic background; a white Anglo-Celtic culture is maintained. All have had access to tertiary education of one kind or another; all speak English as their first language, although Jolley is a migrant. Jolley and Farmer have written about lesbian relationships (most notably in *Palomino* and *Alone*), but neither is a Radclyffe Hall or a Jane Rule, raising issues of lesbian sexuality in a way which forces critics to acknowledge it as a major feature of their writing (as did, for example, Elizabeth Riley in *All That False Instruction*). Even so, Jolley's *Palomino* and Farmer's *Alone* have caused some discomfort and been regarded less favourably by critics. It is also noteworthy that writings about party politics tend to be put to one side. The best known example of this kind of marginalisation is the lack of attention paid to Amanda Lohrey's novel, *The Morality of Gentlemen*; however as Astley points out in her conversation with Jennifer Ellison, the political content of *An Item from the Late News* is rarely noticed. [22] Lohrey has alleged recently that the quarantining of women to the domestic sphere has the consequence that they have to fight anew to write about work, sport, war and politics. [23] To some extent this comment ignores feminist reconceptualisations of "work", "war" and "politics"; when we turn to the stories included in this collection there is no dearth of politics. However, given traditional notions of "politics", it is true that in the stories that follow here (and in the wider array from which they were

selected) there is little attention to trade unionism or the committee room, or to explicit ideologies.

No doubt the eminence of these writers is due largely to the fact
that they have provided women readers, many middle class and
urban, with a powerful representation of their own experience;
they have also written a style of fiction which is amenable to the
most common varities of feminist criticism: the experiential and
thematic modes of reading. Together, readers and critics have
constituted an interpretive community receptive to this kind of
writing in particular. There is a powerful shock of recognition
when details of women's lives and conversations are presented
intimately and naturalistically. Although this has sometimes been
dismissed as domestic trivia, readers have found in recent
women's writing a powerful authentication of their own
experience.

This, in itself, lends to the writings the oppositional status
which Matthews has commented upon. However the tendency to
place all women writers in shared opposition on the margins, with
the implication that all are equally oppressed, needs to be
questioned. Recently a number of editors have introduced their
selections in the context of a trans-historical tradition of
Australian women's writing. This approach tends to yoke
together writings from different historical and sociological con-
texts on the basis of a quite fixed "eclipse", a fixed and immutable
binary opposition between the masculine and the feminine which,
it is suggested, produces amongst women a common con-
sciousness and a distinctive literary tradition.[24]

It may well be that anthologies are generically given to this kind
of generalisation; that they tend to homogenise. Furthermore, as
an editor, one sends an anthology out to sea with little control
over what cargo it will bring back to port; it is more the case now
than ever that there is no single way of reading a text with an eye
to gender. Certainly some of the extracts selected here could be
used to develop notions of a transcendent Australian female tradition. For example Thea Astley's comments on Barbara Baynton's
work, "The Teeth Father Naked at Last", and Kate Grenville's
return to history through her characters Joan and Lilian could be

used to bring these contemporary writers into a kind of con-
tinuous relation with earlier counterparts in terms of their concern
with masculinity and the national mythology.

However a quite different approach might argue that, although
all women have been oppressed by their gender status, they have
not been oppressed equally. Furthermore, masculinity and
femininity are not fixed prescriptions but varying scripts. So, for
example, although Australian women writers in general have
written within a national culture in which the recurrent icons have
been masculine, ideologies of masculinity have varied. For
instance Marilyn Lake's study of the *Bulletin* and the writings of
William Lane discern quite opposing yet contemporaneous
notions of manhood and masculinity.[25] Likewise Susan Sheridan's
analysis of romantic fiction in this same period discerns a specific
alignment of democratic and nationalist politics, realist and ver-
nacular writing and masculinity. Sheridan is careful to avoid
generalisations and to locate this alignment within the particular
cultural and sociohistorical debates of the 1890s.[26]

To take another example, it has been argued that one of the
continuities of the female tradition has been a sensitivity to race,
an ongoing sense of affinity with the Aborigine. However a closer
and historically specific analysis reveals a more complex relation.
In her study of women writers of the 1930s and 1940s Susan
Sheridan argues that at this time the writing of women played a
central role in the projection of an Anglo-Celtic nationalist
identity. From their place within this the dominant culture,
Sheridan discerns that white women tended to represent
Aboriginal women as objects or symbols, the "other" woman.[27]
She goes on to draw parallels between the women's writings of
this period and the kind of justificatory myth that Nadine Gordimer writes about among white liberal writers in South Africa in
the 1960s. Again Sheridan's approach focuses upon an identifiable
group and a specific sociohistorical context.

All of the above suggest that the kind of socio-economic con-
textualisation we have been exploring for the eight writers
selected for this anthology is not merely a sketching in of local
colour, a set of considerations which the writings themselves
transcend, but a network of relations in which these writings are

embedded. In describing these eight writers as a community of women who are located quite specifically in the terrain of white, middle class feminism, we are not negating the transforming power of their desire but we are bypassing a tendency to subsume women into one sisterly category of "woman" despite real differences of race, class and historical condition. These considerations do not necessarily divide women, but they do demand a sense of multiplicity. Women at different moments in history have been both oppressed and oppressive, submissive and subversive, victim and agent, allies and enemies both of men and one another.[28]

If this seems far removed from the stories which follow, turn to Thea Astley's "A Northern Belle" for a fictional study of the tangled relations between gender and race, victim and oppressor, power and domination. Or turn to her "Home Is Where the Heart Is" as a statement of the limitations of white middle class liberalism in relation to the Aborigine. Astley's stories demonstrate powerfully the limitations of placing women and, in this case, Aborigines, as similar victims of a unified white patriarchal power. She shows white middle class women to be located instead in an ambiguous relation to dominant power structures, both oppressor and victim at one and the same time. Grenville's "Federation Story" and "A Time of Hard" make a similar point, although here the power relations are those of gender and class. In thinking about these writers and their work we can and should avoid the fallacy of an overarching and immutable schema of masculinity and femininity which places these women in the position of speaking for all women and scripts their stories into a continuing and transhistorical Australian female aesthetic. Rather, we can choose to see women's writing not as a monolith but as a series of clusters which address issues of gender and sexuality from the perspective of different historical, economic, social and generic placings. In the stories and commentaries of Anderson, Astley, Farmer, Garner, Grenville, Hanrahan, Jolley and Masters we can isolate one such cluster and address quite specifically the question of how they represent their difference.

Gender and Genre: The Short Story

A good deal of the burden of a distinctively Australian literary ethos has been placed on the back of the short story. If, as Kerryn Goldsworthy asserts, short fiction written before the 1890s is "rather a sort of throat-clearing before the short story beings to speak",[29] it is equally the case that what has come after has been cast in the shadow of Henry Lawson's voice and its yoking of the short story to the Australian legend. There is nothing new then about the association of gender and genre here; the short story has been guardian of a strong and masculinist sense of identity. In the 1970s "new" fiction was characterised by a break from realism and nationalist preoccupations in the stories of Bail, Carey, Moorhouse, Wilding and Lurie most notably. However, the masculinism remained intact if not resurgent, as a number of these sexually frank stories appeared in "girlie" magazines.

It goes without saying that women writers in the eighties have used the short story to quite different purposes, and the question arises as to why a broadly feminist impetus might find this genre especially appropriate. One reason which immediately seems relevant is Valerie Shaw's association of the short story with an audience thought of as an intimate group or community and the tendency to the instinctual rather than the intellectual, the speaking voice rather than the literary.[30] This suggests a particular appropriateness of the short story for the kind of close experiential and associational reading which feminist writing often evokes. Shaw also notes the traditional association of the short story with submerged population groups and "frontier experiences" of all kinds,[31] again suggesting that this form of writing may be especially suited to oppositional views and so the woman writer may find it appealing as a means of questioning and reinventing womanhood; a way of asserting a different voice and a different view. Elsewhere the short story is described as generically predisposed to representing experiences "not considered normative or authoritative in society", such as childhood, the non-heroic, the fantastic.[32] This too suggests that it may be an especially congenial form for the woman writer.

Language: A Different Voice

These general observations suggest numerous points of entry relevant to the stories gathered here. Perhaps the first that should be taken up is the general problem of women and language which has preoccupied feminist critics. There are a number of ways in which the short story seems especially suited to representing women as a muted or silenced group. For instance one of the strategies which its form allows is the muting of a female character. This can have striking effects. One of the best examples is Beverley Farmer's short story "A Woman with Black Hair", which presents the woman entirely from the male point of view; however it is not merely "male" but masculinist in its ugliest and most violent form. The absolute passivity, silence and helplessness of this woman, as opposed to the power, authority and all-knowing perspective of the rapist, is a representation of the masculine and the feminine taken to horrific proportions. This is the kind of story which has caused the feminism of Farmer's work to be questioned from a prescriptive approach, a criticism which caused Farmer to write the "Letter to Judith Brett" included here. However rather than reading such stories as this with male and female characters in mind, it seems more appropriate to think of their roles more abstractly, in terms of masculinity and femininity. There is an alarmingly slight gap between the violent and distorted playing out of these roles in rape and the socially approved projection of masculine and feminine qualities. In this story the masculine and the feminine have been driven to destructive, mutually exclusive extremes. These kinds of distortion and falsification are, as Farmer herself points out, designed to distort the real, to be "just that little bit wrong [and] make an impression, and produce a friction".[33]

There is a sharp contrast between the characteristically authoritative and self-centred masculine discourse and the tentative "exalted gossip" of women, as Garner labels it in "What We Say". For example in "Postcards from Surfers": "The women are knitting. They murmur and murmur. What they say never requires an answer"; "My mother and Auntie Lorna, well advanced in complicated garments for my sister's teenage children, conduct their monologues which cross, coincide and run parallel." In "The Lang Women" Olga Masters creates a wonderful tableau of a "female world of love and ritual".[34] The lack of punctuation and the fluency of the prose in the first part of this story are part of the projection of a female language, in which conversation between women is like "frolicking together in the sea". Significantly this female ritual is spied upon and known to the rest of the town as the "cock show", which immediately recontextualises the ritual in terms dictated by the male gaze. The deterioration of the conversation between the women and the destruction of the language of this nightly ritual is an inevitable corollary of the intervention of the appropriately named Arthur Mann.

The search for other kinds of language for speaking proliferates in women's stories. So the semiotics of the postcard enters Garner's "Postcards from Surfers"; given the inappropriateness of words the narrator looks for pictures without words, only to find postcards in which a bikini-clad, big-breasted young girl poses seductively, her whole head covered by a latex mask representing a witch. In *Lilian's Story* Lilian's bulk is in itself an attempt to speak outside the terms of the conventionally feminine; her other strategy is to turn to a master text, the plays of William Shakespeare, so she can make herself heard. Finally the mother in Anderson's "Under the House" conveys her affection and concern through giving food.

Throughout the stories the women are in various ways smothered, and the most articulate and perceptive female characters tend to be children. It is here that the writer finds what Barbara Hanrahan calls "an other-worldly view"; "someone who isn't labelled", in Valerie Shaw's terms. This use of the child's perspective is another way in which the short story tries to escape the "authoritative view" and enter the world of fantasy.

Childhood, the Non-Heroic, the Fantastic

A sustained study of childhood and language occurs in Jessica Anderson's stories "Under the House" and "Against the Wall".

These stories are clearly inflected with a strong regional note, and Astley's "On Being a Queenslander" is a useful backdrop for grasping the specific qualities not only of the Mango region of North Queensland which Astley herself chronicles but also for the "Warm Zone" of Anderson's childhood in Brisbane. A quite different and more contemporary image of the north is found in Garner's Surfers. Each of these women writers uses the region in quite gender specific ways.

The difference of Anderson's idea of the "warm zone" is immediately apparent if we contrast her story "Under the House" with David Malouf's representation of this archetypally Queensland space. In Malouf's fiction under the house is a dark, gothic space, a place where the subconscious looms along with the spectre of a suicide from the rafters, "a dream space, dark, full of terrors that lurk behind tree-trunks in the thickest forest . . ." [35] Anderson's version of this space is quite different. What hangs down there are relics of the grandparents' household and old dog collars, with the occasional hand of ripening bananas. Most significantly, Anderson's under the house is orientated in relation to the sound of mother's footsteps above. Bea always knows where her mother is, and what domestic rituals are underway, as the sound of footsteps above maps her movements. Here the wilderness is not under the house but away from mother's surveillance, by the creek, where she can meet children from the camp.

Language is the key issue in these stories. In an interview Anderson has admitted to a factual basis in her own childhood to the stammer which Bea develops.[36] However the translation of autobiography into story produces psychological and feminist resonances. Recent psychoanalytic feminist criticism has debated the question of women and language, and the relationship between the child's entry into language and sexuality. In the light of these debates the conjunction of incidents in "Against the Wall" is striking. Bea's stammer coincides with the dominance of an authoritarian female teacher at school and is curiously related to the onset of a deteriorating relationship with her father and the finding of condoms down at the forbidden creek. Bea is able to make a "lightning" connection between the "treasure" found at the creek, the ritualistic "showing" of the genitals, her mother's "frightening" disgust and her sister's speculation about what condoms are used for, "but the reminders, the allusions, [her] treasure bore" make her sink back again into silence. The conjunction of these various discoveries with the onset of Bea's inability to master the language invites us to read Anderson's story with recent French feminisms in mind. These suggest that women are required to suppress their female identity in order to speak in the discourse of a male-oriented language; as Adrienne Rich writes: "This is the oppressor's language/I need it to talk to you".[37] To speak about the difference of women's experience requires then that the writer find ways of subversion, of using this language differently, and of adapting it to represent the feminine — oppositional functions which, as we have already seen, the short story seems particularly suited to undertake.

Of course it is not only women who are cast as outsiders in the terms of the dominant discourse and it is too simplistic to assume that only women speak from what feminist criticism has conceptualised as a feminised or non-authoritative position. A decentred, non-heroic discourse allows room for a number of muted groups to speak and we can conceptualise Bea's awkwardness and inability to enter the language more broadly in relation to a number of stories included here.

In "Beginnings" Barbara Hanrahan points out that in her pursuit of the regional, working-class voice of Annie M. she was influenced by what black women writers of the United States were doing, "writing against stereotypes", getting "behind the silences". Annie's story is subjective, there are no climaxes or epiphanies and the medicinal properties of Fairy margarine loom large in her universe. War and Depression are represented through the day to day realities of Annie's existence and on a par with local marriages, accidents and illnesses. As David Parker suggests, what is chronicled in this kind of fiction is a conventionally unmemorable daily existence.[38] In "Annie M" and "Dream People" it is the ebb and flow and detail of a small and private life which calls the tune.

Annie is one example of a number of "non-heroic" speakers who find a voice in the short stories collected here. We might broadly conceptualise two speaking positions adopted by characters in these stories. Firstly there is the central, authoritative discourse which tends to characterise the father figures. Lilian's uniformed, brutal father is at the masculinist and authoritarian extreme of this spectrum, personification of Virginia Woolf's fascist figure that he is.[39] So too is the rapist narrator of "A Woman with Black Hair" and, to show that this speaking position can be appropriated by a woman, Jolley's Night Sister Bean, who is silenced for most of "Hilda's Wedding", so allowing carnivalesque, fantastic play. Less violent but no less authoritative are Garner's Father and Philip characters and the Academic, the narrator of "The Fellmonger", who almost silences but does not impregnate the surrogate female: ". . . he feels he wants a chance to talk with Rosie, to know and understand her. It is the excitement of offering her his intellect, which he wants and, for this, he needs to have time alone with her".

A feminised or non-authoritative speaking position is, quite clearly, expected of Rosie in "The Fellmonger". More generally it can be associated with women, especially the child and mother figures who, as we have seen, tend to seek other forms of communication. It is also the province of the poor, as in Masters's Depression stories, and working-class characters such as Annie M. This space, then, is determined not only by gender but also by region, race and class. Indeed there is some ambiguity here, as it is by no means always the case that women do necessarily enter these stories as non-authoritative and marginal speakers. In two of Grenville's stories, for example, we see different hierarchies drawn. Lil's attempts to appeal to a community of women in "A Time of Hard" are rejected because of her privilege in relation to them; the other prisoners refuse to speak to her. In "The Test Is, If They Drown" an act of betrayal hangs upon the choice of a girl, by use of a few words, to remain part of the gang and assert the labelling of an aged woman as a witch.

Thea Astley's stories are especially interesting in this respect. Astley's essay "Being a Queenslander" is a classic statement of the regional, decentred voice; it casts the Queenslander as speaking from a periphery. Writing about a space cast as "deep north", mango and wild pineapple territory, has allowed Astley, more than any other writer selected here, to grapple with the relations between different races and between race and gender. In "A Northern Belle" she experiments with translating a character type from the post-bellum United States of William Faulkner to the Australian north. In fact the story is as much about an Aboriginal man, Willy Fourcorners, a story which is difficult to capture, like "photographing in shadow". Finally the narrator gives "Willy's story, my words". As this short prologue suggests, it is Willie the Aborigine who is the non-authoritative speaker here. As the story goes on to present the history of the lonely spinster, the "belle" Clarice, who, as her body beings to seize up with age and rheumatism, turns to Willie for help, it is seemingly Clarice who is the outsider. However, in the space of a scream in the last line of the story, the hierarchy of gender over race is asserted and the power of the woman to impose the label of "sexually maddened blackfellow" makes Willie an outcast. Clarice becomes her mother's daughter.

The later story from the "Mango" collection again demonstrates the language gap between the races. In "Heart Is Where the Home Is" Astley attempts to represent Aboriginal English in her prose. Again the final stages of the story are crucial, with the seemingly anti-authoritarian settlers asserting their own dominance and normative view, as in "A Northern Belle".

These narratives of the child and the non-authoritative figure are paradoxical, marked as they are by hesitancy, obscurity and an overwhelming sense of the inadequacy of received narrative forms and language to represent the muted. Here the open-endedness and discontinuity of the short story form are exploited in a self-reflexive way to demonstrate the inadequacies of literary language and representation itself.

The fantastic is a third and quite different way that this non-authoritative perspective can find a voice in the story. Elizabeth Jolley's fiction frequently uses fantasy to trace the unseen and unsaid of culture: "that which has been silenced, made invisible, covered over and made absent". In recent criticism fantasy has been associated with the carnivalesque, subversion, disorder and illegality.[40] This is apparent in Jolley's "Hilda's Wedding", where the absence of Night Sister Bean causes the institution to explode in anarchy. Jolley frequently presents marginal characters; not only women but migrants, the aged, the "mad" and the solitary, who undercut the structures of power and authority in the most repressive type of institutions: asylums, prisons, hospitals. The grotesque and fantastic scenario of "Hilda's Wedding" culminates in an absurd inversion of man and wife, marriage and birth. The patterns of repetition and revision in Jolley's writing which are commented upon by Helen Garner, the frequent reference to literary and musical themes, the linguistic playfulness and carnival are all elements which have been linked to a specifically female language in Jolley's writing. [41]

Brush, Lens and Pen

As a final observation about the liaison between the short story and the language (or silence) of the feminine it is worth keeping in mind Valerie Shaw's comparison between the short story and other forms of visual art, such as the picture and the photograph, which focus on illumination through a single image. [42] A number of these writers comment upon the similarity between the techniques employed in their stories and impressionist painting in particular; for example Helen Garner finds vindication for her "small and domestic scope" in Van Gogh's painting of the chair in his bedroom. Beverley Farmer compares the abruptness of her narrative with a Cézanne painting — "impulsive", "awkward". The suggestion in this case is that literary language is being pushed to its limits. In her commentary upon the post-impressionist exhibition in Sydney, Olga Masters chooses Monet's "The Meadow" as especially attractive to her because Monet broke with the conventions and traditions of his art. As Masters describes this, Monet diverged from the "man-made" roads for straight and narrow feet, to include the familiar, the non-authoritative, the child-like.

In several stories here the narrative frame is expanded by inclusion of another artistic medium, and in each case this is related to a sense of the inadequacy of literary forms for the woman writer, the need to reach for another image to juxtapose against and supplement the literary. As we have seen, Astley prefaces Willie

Fourcorner's story with an allusion to "inspecting the negative" of the photograph, "framing and hanging its reversals". In "Home Time" the narrator "gives herself over to *Casablanca*". The plot of the film becomes a mastertext which is implicitly read against the experiences of the two women. The "innocence" and romance of the film is thrown into relief by their knowledge that love is not enough: "I wonder if Ilsa would have gone with Rick . . . would it have ended up with her on the floor with her nose smashed? You never know." In the final "frame" of the story the narrator's own authorship, her use of the personal and experiential, is cast as "scavenging" by her lover. The act of writing a different, far less romantic kind of narrative is deeply subversive, and one in which her lover refuses to be included: "I am not to figure in anything you write". Here the code of romantic love is found wanting, although the breakdown in communication between the sexes is to some extent compensated for by the closeness of the two women, who meet in the bar and acknowledge the gap between what they know from experience and what they see and respond to on the screen.

There is a similar effect in Helen Garner's story "What We Say". Here it is an opera, *Rigoletto*, which becomes the text against which different and gendered discourses are measured. With characteristic deftness Garner splices together the "small and domestic" — the comforting ritual of sharing salad and spaghetti, the close observation of bright light on grey walls — and the politically charged undercurrents which fragment the mealtime conversation. What women say and mean is conveyed in the sodden handkerchiefs, in quick glances, and in their responses to Barbara Baynton's "The Chosen Vessel". What women say is a "shadow tradition", "It's there, but nobody knows what it is"; The pattern "they" use strikes women dumb, renders them absent.

One is reminded of the narrator of Farmer's "Home Time", "Because she takes all the photographs, she won't find herself in any of them"; "Bare interiors of sun and shade and firelight, in which as always she appears absent". Here the shift to film, another form of representation, reinforces the sense of the difficulty of capturing woman's experience in the established and inherited conventions. In these very self-conscious stories the parameters of the short story itself are stretched, questioned, supplemented to include the personal and the feminine perspective; they also demonstrate the tensions which come into play when the woman chooses to write about intimate relations between the sexes.

The Politics of "Female Naturalism"

> This is an important book, the critic assumes, because it deals with war. This is an insignificant book, the critic assumes, because it deals with the feelings of women in a drawing room. A scene in a battlefield is more important than a scene in a shop . . .[43]

As we have seen, attention to the private and domestic sphere has caused women's writing to be both trivialised and dismissed. Although the gap between private and public worlds, and the corresponding dichotomy of the personal and the political, has been challenged by the politics of both first- and second-wave feminism, the difference of value which Woolf describes persists. War, depression and poverty, violence and fascism are no less "political" because they are cast in the framework of domestic life and female experience, and yet they seem so.

This may be so because of the way political concerns enter women's writing. Kay Ferres describes as "female naturalism" [44] that attention to domestic detail and rhythms that is one of the recurring characteristics of women's writing. It is one of the ways in which the influence of impressionism, with its stress on the perceiver and the subjective, is apparent. Elizabeth Jolley comments on this kind of detail in her review of Helen Garner's writing, "the details of daily living come to assume sacramental importance.[45] The language of such writing includes the careful and detailed reference to objects — food, clothing, furniture, the way the table is set and the kettle on the boil; the subjective impression which tends to resist any final conclusion or resolution; and a chronicling in relation to births, marriages and deaths: events of significance in private life.

Olga Masters's "The Christmas Parcel" is a fine example of this "female naturalism". The story is about a family confronting a Christmas in the midst of the Depression with no prospect of

Christmas dinner. Throughout the story images, metaphors and conversation focus upon food; landscape, character and plot are organised in terms of a language of commodities. So the boy Lionel's chest is "no bigger it seemed than a golden syrup can"; the setting sun fills the sky "with salmon and peach jam and beaten egg white"; the absolute poverty of the family is conveyed in the miracuously thin peel which Mrs Churcher pares from the peaches and the repeated references to Mr Churcher's hands, "the fingers spread as if a cigarette was there." This attention to food is not mere fetish or trivia but accurate sociohistorical detail; Masters herself argues that: "Food had more value then because of the scarcity, the tightness of the times, the hungry times . . . I think food's a story on its own".[46] It is of course precisely this attention to familiar detail which rarely impinges upon the "man-made roads" that Masters commented upon in Monet's painting. This technique achieves not only documentary detail but also an orientation in relation to a feminised or non-authoritative view. As Goldsworthy suggests, this is intensely political writing, mingling the emotional and material economy in a way that demonstrates how clothes, food, money, sexuality and love are all inextricably bound to one another; "the exchange, the giving, or the with-holding of money and goods become a substitute for language".[47]

From this perspective war and depression are translated in terms of local and personal meanings. It is a way in which the story is oriented to the concerns of social history, the representation of the experience of those traditionally "hidden from history". The same kind of close attention to detail and narrative technique is used by Barbara Hanrahan in "Annie M". Here is the war in Annie's narrative: "When it was the First World War Sammy Lunn was dancing on the steps of the Grand Picture Theatre with his walking-stick . . ."; "When it was the Second World War, I worked at Holdens and had full authority over a hundred and twenty girls and five blind men and five deaf and dumb women. Then I worked in the butter room at the Co-op." This is more in the nature of oral history than traditionally recorded history, it requires that we accept Lilian Singer's asser-tion: "I am history, and so are you." Kate Grenville's "Federation Story" from *Joan Makes History* likewise reshapes history in the light of the priorities and subjective view of a newly genteel mayor's wife. Here the "official history", the rhetoric of the newspapers and the books contrasts sharply with the woman's own experience of celebration; her description of the peau-de-soies and the crepe-de-chines, he etiquette for eating asparagus, the smell of feet and the Prince, "a pale puny sort of man . . . a small man with a cocked hat that seemed too large for his head . . ." and the devastating faux-pas with the glove. These are handed down to her granddaughter as a precious inheritance: "What we would be able to tell her was priceless, for it was all that no one else could tell her, all the things no book would ever mention."

Gender and Nation: Remaking the Legend

What happens to notions of national identity when we take the view from the obscured voice? When Joan makes history what happens to national mythologies and stereotypes? Processes of mythmaking and national identity in Australia have been and continue to be particularly masculinist; to draw upon Thea Astley's characterisation of this tradition, the characteristics of the peasant Teeth Father ("the Father of Ockers, the despiser of sheilas") are still respected as virtues. These "myths of oz" are difficult to displace.[48]

We have already seen a number of ways in which these stories by women do decentre this authoritative Father figure. The perspective from Mango, Thebarton and Carlton is local and particular rather than unified and homogenous. Annie M. and Lilian speak with a voice which is in the process of creating its own history and mythic existence. This is not to say that place is irrelevant when we hear woman's voice. To the contrary, most of the writers we are considering here find the adjective "Australian" a meaningful one. For example in "Beginnings" Barbara Hanrahan speaks of the nostalgia for Australia which fuels her books. Although the local is included in her sense of the national very strongly, Hanrahan is nevertheless not untypical when she speaks of being more comfortable with the description "Australian writer" rather than "woman writer".[49] For all the ambiguities of "home" in women's writing, features of landscape, such as the hot smell of tea-tree in Farmer's "Place of Birth", are signs of the Australian imprint, an elemental relation between what Astley calls "landscape and flesh".[50]

Kate Grenville's notion of two different levels of "place" is useful here: "There's the place you actually know from your own experience, and then there's the place that you know as cultural artefact — that's been built up from what you've read and which you know from art. So there are those two separate 'places', and one of the problems . . . with being Australian, is that there's a big dislocation between those two senses of place." [51] As she later makes clear, as colonial offspring of Albion all Australians to some extent share a sense of cultural dislocation. The ongoing effects of colonialism are represented in the exchange of letters in Jolley's "The Well-Bred Thief". However the relationship between Lilian and her father Albion in *Lilian's Story* places women, "the daughters of Albion", in the condition of being doubly colonised, as it were. Grenville's distinction establishes an important difference between the nostalgia for a personal experience, such as we find in "Home Time", and the representation of women's experience in Australian culture and national myth.

Women writers are still engaged in the task of wresting Australian mythologies from the maws of Astley's Teeth Father, protean figure that he is.[52] In the stories, commentaries and interviews gathered here a community of women find a voice. They may speak as the "prize blooms" of contemporary Australian women's writing, but they will defy any neat arrangement alongside the *Women's Weekly* on the coffee table. These tall poppies are not for cutting: "whoever tells the story wins in the long run. It's the ultimate revenge of those who've been rendered voiceless".[53]

Notes

1.   Elizabeth Jolley, *The Bulletin*, 27 May, 1986: 77.
2.   Thea Astley, "In the Decade of the Minorities", included in this volume.
3.   Olga Masters, *A Long Time Dying* (St Lucia: University of Queensland Press, 1985), p.1.

4. Elizabeth Webby, "Short Fiction in the Eighties: White Anglo-Celtic Male No More", *Meanjin* 2 (1983): 34-41.

5. Margaret Smith, "Australian Woman Novelists of the 1970s: A Survey", in *Gender, Politics and Fiction: Twentieth Century Australian Women's Novels*, ed. Carole Ferrier (St Lucia: University of Queensland Press, 1985), pp.200-221.

6. Stephen Torre, *The Australian Short Story 1940-1980: A Bibliography* (Sydney: Hale & Iremonger, 1984).

7. Gerard Windsor, "Writers and Reviewers", *Island Magazine* 27 (1986): 15-18.

8. Brian Matthews, "Directions in Recent Fiction" *Island Magazine* 28 (1986): 34-43.

9. James Hall, "Why Women Writers Crowd the Best Sellers List", *The Bulletin*, 27 May, 1986: 72-77.

10. Carmel Bird, "Speaking Volumes for Women", *The Age*, 2 August, 1988.

11. Kerryn Goldsworthy, "Dense Clouds of Language", *Island Magazine* 27 (1986): 2-27.

12. Judith Brett, "Publishing, Censorship and Writers' Incomes, 1965-1988", in *The Penguin New Literary History of Australia*, ed. Laurie Hergenhan (Ringwood: Penguin Books, 1988), p.464.

13. Helen Garner, "A Woman's Word", included in this volume.

14. See Helen Garner, "Showing the Flipside", in this volume; Olga Masters in *Rooms of their Own*, ed. Jennifer Ellison (Ringwood: Penguin, 1986), p.224.

15. Helen Garner, interview in *Yacker: Australian Writers Talk About Their Work*, ed. Candida Baker (Sydney: Picador, 1986), p.156.

16. Farmer, "Literature Is What Is Taught", included in this volume.

17. Margaret McClusky, "Biting the Hand that Feeds You", *The Sydney Morning Herald*, 29 October, 1988.

18. See Sneja Gunew's comments in the Introduction to *Telling Ways: Australian Women's Experimental Writing* (Adelaide: Australian Feminist Studies, 1988).

19. Kerryn Goldsworthy, "Short Fiction" in *The Penguin New Literary History of Australia*, ed. Laurie Hergenhan (Ringwood: Penguin Books, 1988) p.543.

20. Gina Mercer, "Little Women", *Australian Book Review* 81 (June 1986): 26-28.

21. Helen Garner, "A Truth Between Women", *The National Times*, 10-16 May, 1981.

22. Thea Astley, "In the Decade of the Minorities", included in this volume.

23. Amanda Lohrey, "The Dead Hand of Orthodoxy", *Island Magazine* 27 (1986): 19-21.

24. For example Dale Spender, ed., *The Penguin Anthology of Australian Women's Writing* (Ringwood: Penguin Books, 1988); Connie Burns and Marygai McNamara, *Eclipsed* (Sydney: Collins, 1988); Dale Spender, ed., *Writing a New World: Two Centuries of Australian Women Writers* (Sydney: Pandora Press, 1988).

25. Marilyn Lake, "The Politics of Respectability: Identifying the Masculinist Context", *Historical Studies* 22 (April 1986): 116-131; "Socialism and Manhood: The Case of William Lane", *Labour History* 50 (May 1986): 54-62.

26. Susan Sheridan, " 'Temper, Romantic; Bias, Offensively Feminine': Australian Women Writers and Literary Nationalism", *Kunapipi* 8 (1985): 9-58.

27. Susan Sheridan "Women Writers", in *The Penguin New Literary History of Australia*, ed. Laurie Hergenhan, pp.319-336.

28. Judith Newton and Deborah Rosenfelt, eds., *Feminist Criticism and Social Change: Sex, Class and Race in Literature and Culture* (New York: Methuen, 1985), p.xxvii.

29. Goldsworthy, "Short Fiction", p.537.

30. Valerie Shaw, *The Short Story: A Critical Introduction* (London: Longman, 1983), p.viii.

31. Shaw, *The Short Story*, p. 191.

32. L.K. Ferres, "Reflections and Revisions: The Representation of Woman in Short Stories by Four Women Writers", PhD thesis, Department of English, James Cook University of North Queensland, 1987, p.1; Mary Louise Pratt, "The Short Story: The Long and the Short of It", *Poetics* 10 (1981): 188.

33. Beverley Farmer, "Literature Is What Is Taught", included in this volume.

34. Carroll Smith-Rosenberg, "The Female World of Love and Ritual: Relations Between Women in Nineteenth-Century America", in *A Heritage of Her Own*, eds. Nancy Cott and Elizabeth Pleck (New York: Simon and Schuster, 1979).

35. David Malouf, *12 Edmonstone Street* (Ringwood: Penguin Books, 1986), p.47.

36. See Anne Chisholm, "The Australian Reality of Jessica Anderson", *The National Times*, 11-17 October, 1981.

37. Adrienne Rich, "The Burning of Paper Instead of Children", *The Dream of a Common Language: Poems 1974-1977* (New York: W.W. Norton, 1978).

38. David Parker, "Re-Mapping Our Suburbs", *Quadrant* (July-August 1986): 126-130.

39. Virginia Woolf, *Three Guineas* (New York: Harcourt Brace Jovanovich Inc., 1966).

40. Rosemary Jackson, *Fantasy: The Literature of Subversion* (London: Methuen, 1981), p.4.

41. Paul Salzman, "Elizabeth Jolley: Fiction and Desire", *Meridian* 5 (1986): 53-62.

42. Shaw, *The Short Story*, p.14.

43. Virginia Woolf, *A Room of One's Own* (Harmondsworth: Penguin, 1974), p.47.

44. Ferres, "Reflections and Revisions", p.98.

45. Elizabeth Jolley, "Rescuing Fragments: Review of Helen Garner's *The Children's Bach*", included in this volume.

46. Olga Masters interview in *Rooms of Their Own*, ed. Jennifer Ellison (Ringwood: Penguin, 1986), p.228.

47. Kerryn Goldsworthy, "Female Culture in a Small Town", *Island Magazine*, 25/26 (Summer-Autumn 1986): 116-117.

48. Tony Bennett, "Ozmosis. Looking at Pop Culture", *Australian Left Review* 10 (April-May 1988): 33-35.

49. Barbara Hanrahan, "Beginnings", included in this volume.

50. Thea Astley, "Singles", *It's Raining in Mango* (Sydney: Viking, 1987), pp.65-81.

51. Kate Grenville, "Daughters of Albion", included in this volume.

52. Thea Astley, "The Teeth Father Naked At Last", included in this volume.

53. Kate Grenville, "Daughters of Albion", included in this volume.

Kate Grenville

EDITOR'S NOTE

Kate Grenville established her reputation as a short story writer with the publication of *Bearded Ladies* (UQP, 1984). Since then she has published several novels: the award-winning *Lilian's Story* (Allen & Unwin, 1985); *Dreamhouse* (UQP, 1986) and, most recently, a novel funded by the Bicentennial Authority, *Joan Makes History* (UQP, 1988). Kate Grenville has held fellowships from the International Association of University Women, and from the Literary Arts Board of the Australia Council.

"The Test Is, If They Drown" was first published in *Bearded Ladies* (UQP, 1984), pp.24–36; "A Time of Hard" is a new chapter of *Lilian's Story* written for the American edition, and first published in Australia in *Scripsi* 4, iii (1987): 51–59; "Federation Story" is Scene Eleven from Kate Grenville's most recent novel, *Joan Makes History* (UQP, 1988), pp.249–62; and "Daughters of Albion" is an extract from an interview with Gerry Turcotte originally published in *Southerly* 47, iii (1987): 284–99. "Joan's History of Australia" (referred to on p. 45) was published as *Joan Makes History*.

Federation Story

In 1901 Australia ceased to be a colony of Britain and became a self-governing nation: the first federal parliament was opened in that year by the heir to the throne. It was an occasion of splendour such as Australia had not previously seen, and I, Joan, assumed a suitable form.

I was resplendent, comparatively, in the black charmeuse with the purple embroidered lisse jabot. To tell you the truth, I fancied myself at least as fine as any of these other women, although it had been a great disappointment not to be able to wear the peacock-blue mousseline-de-soie that did such a lot for me: but everyone was looking sallow in black for our dear departed Sovereign, so we were all in the same boat, and I was sure I was grand enough for the occasion, and for my position. After all, I, Joan, was the wife of the Mayor of Castleton, a mother of six, and grandmother of three, and none of that was to be sneezed at.

True, George and I had not arrived in our own carriage for the occasion of the Opening of Parliament, but in the hackney from Foyle's. I supposed too, that some of these peau-de-soies and crêpe-de-chines in the throng had cost more than my charmeuse, and some of them had no doubt been constructed in Paris or London by supercilious women who snapped their fingers and made minions run with pins. In spite of that, I swelled with pride within my purple embroidered lisse jabot, knowing that I was as good as any of those other pigeon busts. I had no doubt that some of theirs, like mine, were cunningly padded with horsehair and pongee to make up for what Nature had seen fit to be niggardly about.

The Exhibition Building was resplendent, too, with bunting and flags snapping and heaving against a breeze, and the trees of the grounds bowing and curtseying to each other as the fine gentlefolk were doing, milling on the paths. Behind the barricades, people in cloth caps pointed and stared and fat women in calico aprons held babies up to see history being made. There was a family of black folk there too, clustered together and watching without any kind of expression at all: but no one liked to give too much thought to them and what they might be thinking.

Carriage after carriage drew up and everyone craned to see who it was, and if it was someone whom everyone knew, such as Lord and Lady Tennyson, or dear Nellie Melba herself (what a cheer went up when she stepped out, and a hush fell as if we half-expected her to open her mouth then and there and let her voice soar out), a pleased bright murmur went through both crowds, the silk one and the calico one, for everyone likes to recognise the famous.

At the start of the day, I had congratulated myself for being a member of this nation, and I felt that it was truly the way they said it was, that this was a land of equality and justice for all, an example to the bad old lands with histories too long ever to be put right. It must be so, for here were George and I, folk from humble origins, up here rubbing shoulders with the highest in the land.

After all, I had grown up in a hut with a dirt floor and had shared a pair of boots with my sister, so we could never go into town at the same time: I had worn smocks made of flour bags and had filled up with plenty of damper and dripping in my time. And when George and I had married, and he had started up the business, we had had to count every penny. I had made the sheets of the cheapest unbleached calico, and made them last by turning sides to middle, and had spent my evenings darning George's socks and turning his collars, and patching the children's clothes and running string along the inside of hems for when they needed letting down: I had grated up carrot to make cakes stick together when eggs had been scarce, and knew how to make scrag end into a good meal. And now, when we had arrived by such hard work and thrift at a position of comfort, here I was, creaking in the best whalebone, sweating discreetly in my charmeuse, up here with the grandest.

George and I were not altogether comfortable among such fine clothes and genteel speech, such display and waste, but I knew we would not disgrace ourselves today, for we had learned, laboriously, what these grand folk had been born to and could do without giving it a thought.

We had not taken in etiquette with our mother's milk, and there were still small issues on which I had to keep my eyes open and see how others did it, and I still had to make discreet enquiries of folk I trusted, and had a small collection of books hidden away on the subject of manners in the best society. And for this day in particular I had prepared with the greatest care, because there would never again be a day like this one, and what if I should be presented to Nellie Melba or Lady Tennyson, and need to know how to address her? Should she be *Ma'am*, or *My Lady*, or *Your Ladyship*, or what should she be? The book was tantalising on this subject: *A knight's wife, is, of course, Lady Blank*, it told me smugly, *and is never addressed by her equals as Your Ladyship*. Not being an equal, that did not help me much, but I thought I would be safe with *Ma'am*: or would that make me sound like a servant girl? And what if I was (or *were*, as I tried to remember to say), confronted with the problem of an introduction: *Mrs X, may I present Mr Y*? And what of the controversy surrounding the curtsey, which some said was quite out of fashion, while others were adamant that it was still quite the thing, or *de rigueur*, as I had read but never dared to say? Even the handshake was a matter of anxiety: I had taken to heart the importance of avoiding the *flabby palm*, the *crushing grasp* and the *clinging clasp*, until I felt as stiff about it all as a plank.

I had practised eating asparagus with the fingers, had studied lists of who — or was it whom? — should precede through doorways, and had become deft in fan-manipulation: I had rehearsed in the cheval glass various expressions and movements, and the kind of elegantly long-winded ways of saying it was a fine day that were essential in good society. Preparedness had always been my forte: I had always carried a supply of safety pins and sal volatile in my reticule as a mark of my preparedness, and I was sure I had thought of everything for this day. I had even rehearsed the controversial curtsey, in case I should come face to face, somehow, with the Duke and Duchess themselves: I knew I would feel it *de rigueur* to curtsey then, whatever the fashionable said, and I had made little Alice squeal with the fun of seeing Gran practise, spreading my skirts in a deep teetering curtsey.

I had consulted with George on my only doubt: the propriety of taking opera glasses along. Would that be a mark of the proper enthusiasm, or would it be merely vulgar? The books were strangely silent on this matter, and George had submerged into a great deal of silent frowning thought, during which he fingered his watch chain in the way I knew so well, and loved for knowing that it meant serious thought and self-doubt: at last he said in his most mayoral tones, somewhat adenoidal in their seriousness: *Yes, that would seem an appropriate thing, Joanie, although in moderation.*

I had prepared so hard that I found myself purblind and half deaf on arrival at the building glittering and twinkling in the sun: so much finery and so many important men and their swaybacked wives! Everywhere I looked in the throng, I saw faces I knew from the illustrated papers, and I succumbed to a kind of daze in which the only solid thing was George's arm, keeping me upright and dignified.

I tried, though, to collect myself and take note, because Alice, that newest and best-loved of all our grandchildren, had demanded that I tell her every detail: to tell her *everything, Gran, every single thing, promise.* And it was no hardship to peer and crane at details of fichus and collarettes, for I had always been in-clined to be a bit of a stickybeak, and this was a stickybeak's treat, peering at everyone around us, slow-moving women cautious with their parasols in the crush, and their menfolk look-ing cross with the gravity of it all.

I stared and suddenly found myself exclaiming to George: *Why, there is Lady McNab,* and a woman next to us turned to stare at me. I was fool enough to feel proud of knowing Lady McNab, and it passed through my ignoble mind to say something that would make the woman know that not only did I recognise Lady McNab, but that I had dined in her company in Castleton, on the occasion of the laying of the foundation stone of the Castleton and District Hospital. George and I had enjoyed a haunch of good meat, and French wine in crystal glasses, and had laughed with everyone else at her husband's laborious tales of Surrey hunts, and at hers of the droll banter at Amblehurst, and I had even sympathised with the way you could not get good help, these days, and the way servants were beyond words grand and troublesome. George and I had sat and smiled, and been seduced by it all, although uneasy.

She is looking better than when we saw her last, I could not resist saying now to George, and he nodded without saying anything, for he had not enjoyed that day or that dinner, and had been made uncomfortable by Lord and Lady. George had too much natural honour to have thought of impressing the stranger in front of us with our intimacy with English aristocracy.

It was no great surprise to see Lady McNab here: she was higher gentry than we, after all. The surprise was that Lady McNab had seen us too, had caught my eye and was making her way towards us to speak. I was somewhat astonished: in such a crush it would have been easy for her to bow slightly and move on, and after all at that fine dinner the Mayor and his wife had been only minor guests, people of no real account: but I was pleased and flattered and proud, for this must truly be a day when *all hearts were joined, regardless of rank, to the same great goal*, as the papers had said that morning, and *all distinction of degree was forgotten*.

Well, Lady McNab advanced on us, huge in gleaming satin that made her look like a gigantic muscatel, and I waited confidently, knowing the right thing to do. I waited with one foot slightly behind the other, preparing to perform my vestigial bob, of which the exact degree of drop was a matter of fine judgment, regulating nicely the exact degree of deference. But even as I was on the point of performing my bob, Lady McNab beamed with all her fine teeth and made a grand gesture with her right hand, a gesture of bestowing, and I had to recognise that she had made a different decision on the matter of curtseys: she was offering me her hand to shake.

Frankly I panicked. At war within my horsehair and pongee chest were two imperatives: the one, that a hand proffered from aristocracy was never to be refused: the other, that a lady never shakes hands with her gloves on. Now, I am not a woman of pretension, and know I am no lady, and can only excuse myself by saying that in my panic there seemed only one possible thing to do. In the few seconds left to me while Lady McNab's hand was outstretched, I must remove, with all haste and decorum, the glove from my right hand.

It was panic, of course, or I would never have been so mad as to imagine all those tiny mother-of-pearl buttons could possibly be undone in time. It was panic, and I felt the raw blood bursting in my veins, engorging into a blush over my whole body, so the glove seemed to become part of my flesh, never to be removed in time for contact with the palm of Lady McNab. It was panic, and there was no time, and finally what those warring imperatives left me with was a glove only half-removed from the hand, so that it was empty fingers of black suede kid that were shaken by Lady McNab. Lady McNab, that smiling gracious grape, smiled all the more and seemed to linger endlessly over the business of shaking the hand, or the glove, of the lady wife of the Mayor of Castleton. I knew that many a marvellous Melbourne dinner party would rock with laughter, such as would alarm the maids sedate by their sideboards, as she told this story of a jumped-up shopkeeper's wife who thought she was as good as quality.

I was still swollen with the mortification of this when men in livery began to herd us to our allotted places. We all moved with a great silken rustling into the great hall, under the mighty arches and domes. At least there I could bow my blazing face down into my chest and try, in the change of place, to put behind me that grotesque moment of ill-judged etiquette, although even when we were shown to our places I was still hot and was starting to wish the day was over. We had been allotted a place in one of the high galleries, a long way up, and as far away from the dais as it was possible to be while still being actually in the hall, so that I was glad of my opera glasses: here it was easy to see a quite precise gradation of rank, from the most grand down close to the Prince, to the most humble up here, where the heat gathered in a smell of feet and we were packed in rather tightly together.

For Alice's sake, I stared and strained with the rest to catch sight of the heir apparent to the throne. I could see by glimpses a pale puny sort of man, covered in froggings and braid, with bits of coloured ribbon on his chest, and most of his face covered with hair. He stood in a great shaft of light from a window high up, a small man with a cocked hat that seemed too large for his head, and read his few words full of bombast, while we all strained to hear over the unceasing shuffle of feet on the wooden floors.

I counted the people on the stage and tried to remember the mousseline-de-soies and the ostrich feathers, the arrangements of bows and curls, and the way the Duchess stood leaning ever so slightly on her watered-silk parasol. Down there on the dais, the important people were doing their best to look solemn, and not to sway where they stood at attention: the men had become all chest, the women rigid under their stays, and the white plumes of the helmets of the men in uniform had gone limp in the heat.

The band blared and we shuffled our programmes: *All People That On Earth Do Dwell*, we sang, the echoes of so many voices blurring the song into a great droning muddle of sound like a melancholy beehive. Then the speeches began, and I did my best to hear what was being said. But up here and where the minor folk were situated, there was little to be heard, just a great breathing, the sighing of thousands of people present at history, and from up here the words ebbed and flowed like the sea, sometimes audible, sometimes not, so that it looked as though nothing much more important was happening than a lot of mouths opening and closing, and lips shaping themselves with hot air around grand phrases.

All those dark mouth-holes were making the history of their land, and making it in their own image, so that as far as I could hear, that history was one of pastures and acquisitions, pounds and acres: it was a history full of great men, men like themselves with whiskers and hats that concealed their eyes, and long ponderous sentences that concealed their souls. They spoke of *progress*, it was a word they seemed fond of, and which they uttered with enough conviction to bring it all the way up to us in our distant gallery. A few other words were robust enough to last the distance: words such as *enterprise* and *initiative*, and under these splendid words were others that no one quite uttered, but which we could all hear just the same: these unspoken words were ones like *cash* and *profit*, and the images were of gold things, of wads of banknotes, of fawning bankers, of diamonds against skin, of minions pandering. It was men in the leather armchairs of clubs admiring other men for making more *cash* and *profit*: it was tight-skinned pert children going to the best schools and having great things expected of them: it was an image of beating the other fellow, squeezing another few pounds out of a deal or labour out of a minion, or objects out of a heap of some raw material: it was pride in being sharp, and pleasure in paying some ferret-nosed gent to find a way of breaking the laws without the laws being able to do anything: it was riding along in a fine carriage and seeing men in caps look up as they trudged, or lined up in front of the Works at Christmas, cheering on a signal from the foreman and being grateful for their Christmas boxes. Above all it was the satisfaction of having more than nearly everyone else, and the feeling that they deserved it all, for having also been cleverer than everyone else.

My encounter with Lady McNab had punctured my pride somewhat, and I had been reminded all too brutally that I was not, in spite of my elegant charmeuse and the books about asparagus, on the same level as Lady McNab and her like. I was piqued and punctured, and as I stood growing weary of distant words, I found an argumentative frame of mind coming on. *What of the others, the ones who are not in this hall?* I became indignant and wanted to ask: *What of those who lived here before us? What of all the people who will melt away like mud when they die, remembered in no book of history?*

However, I, Joan, had no cause for complacency: it was true that George and I were not in the business of stripping this land of all it had, and wringing profit out of every transaction, and we did not think it clever to do a man out of a living wage: but here we were, standing stiff in our best, listening to such men as if we admired them: we were accomplices. We were happy enough to be Mayor and wife of Mayor: we stood, fleshy ourselves, listening to other fleshy folk speak of *opportunity* and *freedom*, when we knew it meant their own opportunity, their own freedom, to do nothing but make profit on profit and let the rest go hang.

Finally the last speech, prayer, hymn and blessing had gone floating up on its puff of hot air: the Duke had said his piece, and had pressed the button for the flags to be raised all over Australia, and we had all cheered and clapped until we did not quite know how to stop. Then the band put an end to it, blaring out a sort of march to get us on the move, and there was a hubbub of people pleased with themselves for having witnessed history, and glad it was over, so that they could find a place for a bit of a sitdown.

The books would have many a fine phrase for what we had seen: they would tell how the hearts of all had *swelled with tumultuous feeling*, how the Duke had stood in a beam of light as if *illumined by the Finger of God*: how the *thunderstorm of cheering* had shaken the building to its foundations, and how we had emerged into the *dawn of a new age of liberty and hope*.

In fact, George and I emerged into a din that made my ears ring, of people shouting and exclaiming: close by us on the steps two men boomed a lot of laughter out of their chests, and a woman called shrilly *Come ON, Percy, for heaven's sake!* and was drowned out by cheering from some group I could not see, over to the side. There was a din from the crowd beyond the barricades, of wooden rattles being whirled, and whistles blown: babies wailed, dogs barked, horses and carriages clattered on the road: I was made dizzy by the battery of noise, and by so much feeling running high.

I knew I should be wanting to join the exultation, but I could not find it in me to rejoice: I felt surly about it all now, and the more these other people believed in it, the more aloof I was. *It is all just so many fine words*, I called, made a little hysterical by the clamour. *Just words!* I heard my voice go shrill and strange, but in the din no one seemed to hear: a man in a topper next to us turned and seemed to stare at me, but then he waved and smiled and nodded at someone over my shoulder: even he had not heard. *Joanie, Joanie*, I heard George beside me, and felt him squeeze my hand: he at least had heard, but it was not George whom I wanted to make listen, but those others. *Do not believe them!* I shouted, or tried to, but I could hear how reedy, how thin, how puny my voice was, how the words were lost as soon as they left my lips, and all at once I was consumed with tears.

I recovered myself on the steps at the side of the crowd, sitting hiccupping and gulping while George fanned me with his programme and warded off a fat woman thrusting smelling salts into my face. *It is just the excitement*, George mumbled at her. *Just a short spell and she will be right*. The fat woman left and gradually the clamour died away. The rattles stopped one by one, or grew more distant as the crowd wandered away along the paths: boys got sick of blowing their whistles, everyone ran out of laughing and things to shout to each other, and the minds of most began to turn toward lunch. George and I sat on our step while the carriages all rolled away bearing the gentry off to their silver and damask, and the men in cloth caps and the women in aprons straggled back along the avenues, their babies asleep over their shoulders, looking forward to a plate of cold mutton and a glass of stout. Now we could hear the wind in the trees and a bird or two: we could hear doors slamming behind us in the hollow building where it had happened, and a broom somewhere else close at hand sweeping a path, and a pail of water being set down with a clank.

George stood up and I stood too, and took his hand. He tucked it up against him: I felt foolish and flat now, and there seemed nothing to have become so excited about. The bunting looked ragged, the grass was ugly and trampled where the barricades had been, and all the glory had evaporated from the scene. Everyone had gone, even the group of blacks was nowhere to be seen, unless a cluster of shadows under a distant tree might have been them. *It is silly*, I whispered, meaning myself as well as the pomp we had seen, but George squeezed my hand tighter. *But we were here, Joanie, and saw it with our own eyes*, he said. *We were on the spot*.

We did not say any more about my lapse, but walked in an agreeable silence along the avenues of trees. *Alice will nag us for every blessed thing*, I said at last, and George smiled and said, *By Jove, we had better not leave anything out or there will be strife!* We walked along smiling then, for Alice was at the age of questions, and we both knew the way she would pluck at my skirt and insist: *Then what, Gran, what happened then?*

What had happened? Well, some grand men had said some grand words, and those inclined that way had got a bit dewy of eye about it all. Other things had happened too: I would not shirk from telling Alice how my glove had made a fool of me, and how I had thought the Duke looked like an impostor in someone else's hat, and how I had got hot and bothered at the end, and made a spectacle of myself in a small shrill way. It would not matter that we would not be able to tell her the precise words that the Duke had used, or exactly how many notables had been on the dais, or just who they were, for she would be able to read that in any of the books. What we would be able to tell her was priceless, for it was all that no one else could tell her, all the things no book would ever mention. They were peculiar, lopsided, absurd sorts of things that we would tell her: they were things that would look silly in a book, and no one would be tempted to make a bronze statue of any of them. They mattered just the same, for they were the rest of the history, and without them it was all wrong. *Alice*, I would say seriously, so that she would become solemn and her eyes would grow very big, watching my face for what I would tell her: *Listen carefully now, for this is your inheritance.*

The Test Is, If They Drown

Miss Spear in number forty-two is a witch. From the street we can see her sometimes on her veranda, spreading her hair over a towel on her shoulders to dry in the sun. We gather at a safe distance and whisper across the sunny air — Witch! The hiss fades before it reaches her. She never looks around at us.

Behind her house, up on The Rock, my gang and Mick's gang meet. From high above we can look down into her garden, where the cat stalks among great clumps of vine-smothered rose bushes, and sometimes Miss Spear herself comes out and drags ineffectually at the consuming creepers.

Miss Spear is what happens to you if the orange peel doesn't make a letter when you drop it on the ground. It nearly always makes an S. That means you'll marry Steven or Sam or Stan. Sometimes it makes a C and you take a second look at Carl and Conrad. Miss Spear's what happens to you if you don't step on all the cracks in the footpath between the school gate and Spencer's shop. Miss Spear's what happens to you if the numbers on the bottom of the bus ticket don't add up to an even number. She's what happens when you lose a game of Old Maid.

When she leaves the house to shop, she wears a skirt that reaches her ankles, and sandshoes. She's never been seen without the unravelling straw hat with the feathers stuck in the band. The cat comes to the gate with her and sits with its front paws tidily together and its eyes narrowed waiting for her to come home.

Mum calls her *Poor Miss Spear*, and says there's a sad story there somewhere. Dad says that Miss Spear wasn't ever anything to write home about. Mum shakes her head and mashes the spuds with a great rattle, punishing them, her lips gone thin. She thumps the saucepan down on the table and says that it's a good thing Miss Spear's got her house and a bit of independence at least. Dad laughs as he pulls the potatoes towards him and says he reckons she's got a bob or two stashed away in there.

At the shops she buys fish and milk and according to Mr Spencer the grocer, more eggs than you'd believe. The butcher skilfully rolls the corned beef and ties it with string, living proof that no-one needs more than two fingers on each hand. He tells Mum that Miss Spear comes in once a month for a piece of best fillet. He doesn't see hide nor hair, he says, then regular as clockwork there she is wanting a bit of best fillet. The butcher says he supposes Old Spear's harmless, and Mum agrees with a sigh as she puts the corned beef in the basket.

Of course Miss Spear isn't really just an old maid whose dad left her the house when he died, like they say. She can't really be just an old stick whose cat gets fish every day while she makes do with eggs except for a treat once a month. An old lady wearing funny clothes living in a big house with a cat must be a witch. No way she can be anything else. A witch a murderer a gobbler of children a creature from another planet. An alien.

Up on the Rock we watch her cat stalking a butterfly through the long grass, sliding on its belly, ears flattened to its skull. My gang has just beaten Mick's gang at spitting. All us girls got it further than the boys. And in spite of her ladylike pucker, Sonia got it furthest of all.

Mick shifts round restlessly, looking for a way to impress us.

— Betchas don't know what she did, the Witch, he says. Betchas can't guess.

I lean back and pick a scab on my knee. I'm not worried, I can beat him at anything except indian wrestling and even then I can usually trick him into losing. I'm better at nearly everything than the boys. Pam and Sonia are hopeless the way they're always worried about getting dirty or being home late for tea. But they're my gang and I'm the only girl that's got one.

Mick hasn't done too well with the suspense so he hurries to the punch line.

— She murdered her mum. Got this carving knife see and chopped her in little bits.

Stewart and Ross are impressed. Ross wipes a fleck of saliva from the corner of his mouth and says avidly:

— Geez what she done with the bits eh Mick?

Mick hasn't thought that far.

— That's, um, a secret.

He purses his lips and pretends to be very interested in the way a bird is flying past above us.

— Aw come on Mick tell us tell us.

Pam and Sonia won't let him off the hook.

— Betcha don't know, come on tell us or that means you don't know.

An impressive pause from Mick. Stewart and Ross lean forward agog.

— She buried the bits in the garden. Right down there.

He points dramatically down into the tangles below.

— S'that all?

Pam and Sonia are openly contemptuous and even Ross and Stewart are disappointed. Mick's eyes dart around as he tries to come up with an embellishment. This is my moment.

— 'Fraid you've got it all wrong, I say casually.

They all look at me expectantly. Girl or no girl they know I always deliver the goods.

— It was her dad. She killed her dad.

Mick is beginning a shrug. Mum or dad, so what?

— With cyanide. One drop in his tea every day for six months. She mixed it with the sugar so when he put sugar in his tea he got the cyanide.

The awed silence seems to demand some more details.

— And then when he was dead . . . she stuffed him. Like Phar Lap. He's in a glass case in her bedroom. To keep the dust off.

Stewart's mouth is hanging open and he's breathing loudly through his nose as he always does when concentrating.

— Geez what a weirdo eh.

Mick jabs him with a sharp elbow and shouts:

— Oh yeah, sez who. You gunna believe a girl, fellas?

Stewart snaps his mouth shut like a carp and nods. But his eyes are still glassy with the idea of such a sweet and unsuspecting death.

Ross glances at Mick and mutters to me furtively:

— What did she stuff him with? She pull his brains out his nose like them Egyptians did? What she done with the guts?

I've got all the answers. But Mick's tired of having his thunder stolen.

— Shaddup stoopid, she doesn't know nuffin. What ja believe her for?

He hawks and spits the same way I've seen his father do.

— C'mon, I can't be bothered hanging round these sissy girls any more. C'mon gang, I've had it.

We sit in silence after they leave. Sonia blows a huge bubble with her gum and watches it cross-eyed before sucking it back in. She chews it and tucks it away in the corner of her mouth.

— That for real, she knocked off her dad? Howja know?

Leadership means having no fear of the next lie. I say immediately:

— I looked in the window. He's sitting up there in this glass case.

Pam stops sucking the end of her plait and tosses it back over her shoulder.

— He got clothes on? Or not?

She's watching me closely.

— Course he's got clothes on. His pyjamas.

— What colour, Sandy?

— Blue and white stripes.

Lies must always be switched truths. The glass case from the skeleton at the Museum. Dad's blue and white pyjamas.

Sonia blows a great flecked bubble and we all watch as it trembles, threatening to burst over her face. She deflates it masterfully and gets up.

— Time for tea.

Leadership is never being quite sure if they believe you.

— Oooaah Sandy you've got all moss on your shorts, your Mum'll kill you.

Her smooth pink face expresses satisfaction at this. Sometimes I hate girls.

I plan my raid carefully, and alone of course. Pam and Sonia would giggle at the wrong moment or get panicky about spiders. And although I almost believe now in the body and the glass case, I want to be alone when I make sure.

I watch from behind the oleander until Miss Spear comes out to go to the shops. She sets off without seeing me, her hair showing through the hole in the top of her hat. The cat slips through the bars of the gate and sits blinking. It yawns once and begins washing its ears.

I watch Miss Spear until she turns the corner, and wonder what she is. Women don't wear hats like that, that you can see hair through. Women don't wear sandshoes and no socks so their ankles show red and sinewy. And women don't chop the heads off dandelions with a stick as she's doing now. If Mrs Longman at school with her smooth chignon and her dainty handkerchiefs is a woman, where does that leave Miss Spear?

When she's disappeared I cross the road and pull aside a loose paling in the fence. I glance up and down the street before sliding through the hole and dragging the plank back into place behind me.

Straight away everything becomes terribly quiet. I can still hear the billycarts rattling down Bent Street, and a dog barking across the road, but all these sounds are very far away, and seem to fade as I stand listening, until I can only hear silence ringing in my ears. Miss Spear's garden has locked me into its stillness. Behind the thick bushes and the fence, the street is invisible and belongs to some other world. It may not even exist any more. A leaf gives me a fright, planing down suddenly onto my shoulder, and my gasp seems deafening. The windows of Miss Spear's house stare at me and the veranda gapes open-mouthed. The shadow of one of the tall chimneys lies over my feet and I step aside quickly. It's a few minutes before I can make myself tiptoe down the overgrown path towards the back of the house. Damp hydrangea bushes, as tall as I am, crowd over the path, holding out clammy flowers like brains. The leaves are as smooth as skin as I push through and some are heavy with the weight of snails glued to them. Sonia and Pam would be squealing by now.

In the back garden, the grass has not been cut for a long time, and blows in the breeze like wheat. I creep towards one of the windows on hands and knees, moving twigs out of the way so they won't snap noisily. I'm doing well, being very silent. I am feeling better about all this when a mild voice behind me says hello.

For a few mad seconds I think that if I stay quite still I won't be seen. My green sweater against the grass, the famous chameleon girl.

— I thought you were a little dog at first.

Since the earth does not seem about to open and swallow me, I stand up. Miss Spear is holding a carton of eggs and a bottle of milk. I see her teeth as she smiles, and her eyes under the shadow of her hat. I can see freckles across the bridge of her nose and a small dark mole beside her mouth. I've never been so close to her before.

— Exploring?

I stand numbly, waiting for a miracle. No miracle occurs and she moves closer and says:

— You live down the street don't you? I've seen you around.

She watches me in a friendly way while I wonder if I could pretend to be deaf and dumb. The cat comes and winds itself around her ankles, smoothing its tail along her shins.

— You want some milk, don't you? This is Augustus, she explains to me. He's greedy but he's good at catching mice. Augustus, say hello to our visitor.

She pushes her hat further back on her head so that I can see her whole face. It is a perfectly ordinary old face with wrinkles in all the usual places.

— I don't know your name, she says, and smiles so that the wrinkles deepen.

— Sandy, I hear myself say, and become hot in the face.

It is too late now to pretend to be deaf and dumb.

— Sandy, that's a boy's name, she says. I've got a boy's name too.

She looks at my hat.

— Your hat's a bit like mine, she says. And we both collect feathers.

I pull the hat off my head and crush it between my hands. My hat is nothing like hers.

— I've got something you might like, she says. I never use it, but someone should have it. Won't you come in for a moment?

Even Mrs Longman would not be able to be more genteel.

— Perhaps you'd like a glass of milk.

Anyone would think it's quite normal to be a mad spinster in sandshoes. I follow her into a kitchen more or less like most kitchens and watch as she pours some milk into a saucer and gives it to Augustus. She pours a glass for me and I sit down and drink it while she rummages in a drawer. I glance around between sips, feeling congested by this situation. But in this kitchen there's a stove and a lino floor and a broom in one corner. Just the usual things.

— Here we are.

She hands me a penknife and I open all the blades and look at it. It's a very good one. It even has a tiny pair of scissors. When I've inspected it I become aware of her watching me. I hand it back to her, but she won't take it.

— No, she says, it's for you. It used to be mine when I was a tomboy like you.

I turn the knife over in my hands, feeling clumsy. My hands seem to be a few sizes too big and I feel that I'm breathing noisily. Here I am, sitting talking to Miss Spear the alien, drinking the milk of Miss Spear the poisoner, accepting a gift from the witch.

She takes the knife and attaches it to my belt.

— Look, you can clip it on here, she says. Then it won't get lost.

She sits across the table and with both hands carefully lifts her hat off her head. When she sees me watching, she wrinkles up her eyes at me.

— Sometimes I forget I've got it on, she says.

Augustus jumps into her lap and whisks her cheeks with his tail. She brushes the tail away as if it's tickling her, sneezes, and says:

— He's very affectionate. As you can see.

She strokes the cat and smiles through the swishing tail at me. I can hear a tap dripping in a sink. The sound is peaceful and I find myself relaxing. I unclip the knife and while I'm having another look at it, I try to frame some impossible question. How come you're so normal? I could ask, or: What's it like being a witch?

— It's great, I bring out at last. Thanks a lot Miss Spear.

She goes on stroking Augustus and smiling. I can't think of anything else to say. I want to go, yet I like it here. I want to find the others and tell them all about it, and yet I don't want to say anything to anyone about it. Miss Spear puts the cat down and gets up.

— Drop in any time. Next time I'll show you the tree house.

Out on the street, the proper standards resume their place. Miss Spear is loony. I take the knife off my belt and put it in my pocket. I keep it in my hand, but out of sight.

Mick has decided he wants to hear about the brains being pulled down the nostrils, after all. But now I don't want to tell him.

Stewart glows with righteous indignation.

— We oughter tell the cops about her. She oughter be locked up I reckon. Them shoes she wears and that old hat like a . . . bunch of weeds.

Ross nods energetically, and his eyes bulge more than usual as he says:

— She's not normal my mum says. Oughter be locked up in the loony bin.

Mick says loudly:

— My dad says what she needs is a good fuck.

We all stare, shocked and admiring. Sonia giggles behind her hand. Mick takes courage from this and calls down into Miss Spear's backyard: What you need is a good fuck. The hydrangea bushes shift in the breeze and I feel the knife in my pocket. Sonia beside me shrills out: Silly old witch, and Pam joins in: Witchy witchy ugly old witchy. Ross takes up the idea: Witchetty grub witchetty grub. Mick stares at me.

— What's up Sandy, you scared of summing?

I want to push him over the cliff, ram moss into his mouth, stab him to the heart.

— She's just an old bird. Leave her alone.

Sonia stares at me making her blue eyes very wide and surprised.

— Oh yeah? Since when? You gone potty or summing?

Pam grabs my hat.

— They'd make a good pair, look at this dirty old thing just like
hers.

She stares, pretending to be frightened.

— She's turning into a witch, quick Sonia, look.

Sonia stares at me, her mouth in an artificial smile like the one
Mrs Longman uses when she explains silkily how girls don't shout
like that Sandra dear. Pam is staring at me too. I see them ready
to tear me limb from limb. I look at the boys and see them too,
waiting to pounce, waiting for me to go further and step out of
line. Their eyes are like knives, like packs of snapping dogs, like
slow poison, like sharp weapons raised to kill.

Miss Spear comes into her backyard and pulls at a few tendrils
creeping over a rose bush. Mick nudges me.

— Go on, say something. I dare you.

They're all watching me and waiting. Leadership means falling
into line. Miss Spear is directly underneath, her hair poking
through the hole in her hat, Augustus following a few yards
behind as she walks among the roses. I want to stab Mick and
Sonia and Pam and rip the smiles off their faces. Or is it Miss
Spear I want to stamp on and destroy? Below us, she looks small,
weak, hateful. I want to crush her like an ant, to be part of the
pack and hunt her down as she runs alone.

— Silly old witch, silly old witch, I yell.

My voice is carried away on the breeze. She doesn't look up.
Behind me the others are chanting:

— Ugly old witch, silly old witch.

Sonia uses some imagination.

— Red white and blue, the boys love you.

She laughs so hard she begins to dribble. We take up the chant,
laughing at Sonia's dribble and the way Miss Spear can't hear us.
Mick yells:

— Come on beautiful, give us a kiss!

I'm laughing, or something, so hard the tears are running down
my face and I can hardly breathe. I hear myself screaming:

— Nasty old witch, nasty old witch, I hate you!

The last words carry and she looks up at last. We all stare in silence across the air. I seem to be staring straight into her flecked hazel eyes. Mick nudges me.

— I dare you, tell her she needs a good fuck.

The tears rise in my throat and run down my cheeks and across the silent air I hear myself yell, yell straight into her eyes, see her face on a level with mine and see the freckles across her nose like mine and her smile as she says I was a tomboy like you are, I hear myself yell and see her face change across the distance as I screech, You need a good fuck, fucking witch, until my voice cracks, I see her look down and turn away and walk into the house.

It's very quiet. I look around for the others but they've already turned away. Sonia picks her way down the first part of the rocks and turns back to look up at me.

— You've got all dirt on your face, she says. You look real silly.

She turns away again and climbs down out of sight. Without looking at me, Pam follows her. Mick and his gang have already gone down the other way.

The hydrangeas, the house, the sky shudder and fracture and I stand with my hands in my pockets holding Miss Spear's knife and whispering, witch, ugly fucking old witch, until at last the tears clear and I see the garden again, and watch Augustus as he darts out from under a bush. He glances up and seems to meet my gaze for an accusing second before he slips across the grass to the veranda. The house closes smoothly behind him like water.

A Time of Hard

For years now I had been a student of life. All experiences were instructive, and all had to be taken to myself and embraced, and added to the store of things that had happened to me, that in the end would be my history. I had, until now, embraced them all, much as these two young policemen, flushed with exertion in public with a miscreant of a female nature, were embracing me, and preventing me continuing to make appealing dents in the door of this car, that had so nearly made of me nothing more than a statistic in the week's road fatalities. I, Lil, a woman who filled any room she entered, and drew all eyes to her on the streets that were her kingdom: I would not be reduced by any bit of metal to nothing more than a number in a list.

I loved the policemen's embrace, and felt myself writhing against them, as I had never writhed in passion against any man. But when they brought up a grey van, and thrust me into it, their hands unsympathetic on my large bottom as they shoved me up the metal steps, I did not enjoy it any more, and the glee drained out of me like water from a sock. There was a metal bench in this van, that I crouched on, and a shutter that let only enough light in to see how dark it was, and how small. I could not move my bulk in this space. My arms were trapped by my coat, caught up under me, my legs were cramped by the metal bench opposite, my head was crushed by the metal roof, and I could hear frightened gasping, the breathing of someone close to panic, and knew it was myself locked in the kind of space that was as suffocating as a nasty death.

But I did not let myself be suffocated, and I would not let the poisonous air of panic engulf me. *It is all right, I will be all right*, I repeated to myself, but the van jerked and roared, the air hummed in my ears, my stomach heaved, and when we stopped with a jolt and I was flung sideways and scrabbled against smooth metal, I grew hot and frenzied.

The door opened, though, before fear seized me, and when I saw sky, and sunlight on a corner of building, I was calmed and remembered who I was, and that I was someone enjoying life and its experiences, not someone who could succumb to the first sweat of fear. *Who do you think you are?* I asked the policeman, no longer warm embracers, as they came towards me. *Young men, who do you think I am, some lifeless criminal or other?* But their young faces were closed now under their caps and they did not speak, did not look at my face, only at my fat wrists as they seized them and hurried me into the building and jammed me against a counter like a counter in a shop, but there was nothing to buy here except a fat policeman with a greasy yellow face like a pocked cheese, and I did not wish to buy him. *There is nothing I want here*, I said in my grandest manner. *There has been an error made, and I will leave now.* But the policemen beside me gripped my arms above the elbow, in the flesh that hurt, they knew how to hurt as well as hug, these men safe in their serge, and I could not move, only feel my book bag slip out of my hand. I felt crooked and twisted in my coat, felt the hair slipping into my eyes, felt chaos might not be far away. The man like a cheese pushed his cap back on his head and scratched his scalp so that dandruff floated down and thrust his big yellow face at me. *There is nothing you want here, eh*, he said, mimicking the way I spoke, and mincing in a way I never did. *Nothing you want, eh, well, we want something, dearie, we want a few of your particulars.* He leered at me across the counter and I drew back at the contempt and lechery in his face, and my instinct was to clutch at my particulars and not let him have them.

But we all grew weary of standing at this counter, and I was sick of the way the policemen's thumbs were pressing into my arms, and the way the counter was hurting the flesh of my chest. I gave them my particulars and held my head up, and tried not to feel belittled, crammed against this counter with the policeman breathing hard over each laboured letter, licking his pencil so that his tongue became purple. They wanted to know when I was born, and I let the words ring out proudly across the counter, and the cheese policeman thought, and leered some more, and used his fingers to count, and finally said, *Well, Lil, I would not have said you was in your first youth, but here you are a woman in your forties, you are old enough to know better.* His finger ran down the form again and he said: *Height*, but I had had enough of answering and being sneered at, and did not answer. I nearly fell as the policemen ran me backwards against the wall and straightened me forcibly against it. I stood proudly then, thinking of the executions of brave men against such walls, but when they had measured me they bundled me forward to the counter again and stood holding me crookedly. The cheese policeman, more pocked-looking than ever now his tongue was purple, made a great show then of leaning over the counter to look me up and down and said, *Well, Harry, what kind of build is it would you say, I would say build stout, eh.* They all laughed, and I wanted to shrink in shame, and I was beginning to loathe these men, who were not just doing their job now, but taunting me and loving it, full of hatred for me, and what had I done to deserve all this?

Come on, dearie, the purple tongue said, *come and we'll take your picture, something for us to remember your lovely face by, and will you autograph it for us?* The policemen on my arms sniggered, for this man had stripes on his sleeves, and his jokes had to be sniggered at, and they pushed me against another piece of wall and took my picture. How cross and fearful I must have looked, how despairing, how loathing of these men! I wanted to cover my face with my hands, but the policemen stood beyond the reach of the lens, holding my arms out stiffly like pieces of wood, so my naked face laid bare to the black eye of the lens and a little of my soul was stolen from me.

When the camera had clicked and my fear was caught for ever in it, the policemen let me go for a moment, as if we had all gathered here just for the moment in which the camera had caught its truth. It was only a moment, but it was long enough for me to recapture a morsel of myself and my dignity in being who I was, a substantial woman of character. This woman, who they had tried to mock, still had life in her. I turned my back on the camera and the men, bent over, and pulled up my old black skirt, and there was silence behind me as these men confronted the fact of my large bottom in its large cotton underwear. *If you care to leer and mock, let me give you something to leer and mock at*, I shouted, but when I was forcibly straightened up, and my skirt pulled back over my bottom, there was no leering and no mockery on their faces any more. They had a serious look. I had wiped the laughter off their faces, and taken back the centre of the stage of my own life.

I went quietly with them to the cell where they locked me in with a blanket and a smelly dunny, but I was serene now, having silenced them and proved my power. There was a window in the cell, high up, and I calmed myself watching the blue until it faded into mauve and pink, and finally it was black and my neck was sore from staring up for so long, remembering heaven.

In the morning they took me to the court, and I was scornful of the way everyone whispered in the corridors, and the way they bobbed their heads as if under the axe when they entered. Up above us all, the magistrate was a tiny man dwarfed by his huge bench, another counter, but there was even less I wanted to buy here. The air was full of the murmurings of the damned, outside and at the back of the court where we all waited. We were crims pressed together on a hard bench, in a murmuring that was all round us, although no one could be seen talking.

Names were called out in nasty flat voices and people went sheepishly or swaggeringly to the front to confess that they were that person. I watched and grew anxious, for those flat voices, and the flat grey light, and the hunched figures standing in the dock, were making it hard for me to remember that I was Lilian Una Singer: no one cared, here no one knew my name, and the machinery of this court would roll on over any event or person, I felt, and I began to feel myself disappearing.

I hung on, though, repeating my name to myself, and reminding myself that out there in the real world there were people who knew me, even one or two who might be thought to care for me a little. I hung on, thinking of Frank and Zara, and the man from whom I bought my oysters, with an accent like a foreign language. I hung on, numb from the bench, and at last I heard my name called out in that flat nasty voice: *Lilian Una Singer*. I stood up so quickly, and so awkwardly after sitting for so long, that people began to stare, and I called out in a voice I refused to allow to be reedy: *I am she, I am Lilian Una Singer, and proud of it.* Everyone stared and even the tiny magistrate peered down from beyond his counter: everyone stared, and acknowledged my large existence, and I was restored. Some policewoman of an age to match my own, and with large plain cheeks like mine, bustled me down into the dock, with no gentleness in her hard hands as she pushed at me.

Words began to bounce around in front of me, and I clung to the edge of the dock and tried not to be confused. I awaited my moment, for I had decided that I owed myself a moment in all this gabbled ritual. *Stands accused of offensive behaviour to wit the opening and closing and slamming of car doors on the 15th day of June 1946 apprehended and arrested by Inspector Lush and Constable Sparkman and brought before this court.* All this was gabbled like a spell being cast, but I was a bigger witch than any of them and would not be outshone by their puny magic. I felt my magic threatened, though, felt myself ignored and made tiny again by uncaring men who did not know or care that I was Lilian, and had a soul. There seemed no point at which I could interrupt this spell, so I gathered my courage, which was leaking out of me into this grey room, and cut across it all: *I will not be spoken of like this*, I called out in a dignified way, and was gratified by the silence that fell around me, although I did not know what to do with it. *You are all travesties*, I called, rather wildly now, the words coming at random, *and offensive behaviour is wind in company, and I have never been guilty of wind in company*. There was a tittering around me then, and a mumbling of more animation than before, and I took heart, and felt myself expanding, and held the dock strongly, staring up at the pin-head of the magistrate behind his bench.

I was preparing more words, enjoying this feeling of having an audience, and turning all this theatre onto myself, but the policewoman with meaty cheeks was opening the gate of the dock and pulling me out, and piping words were coming from the tiny head up there, and a gavel banged on the bench, and all at once I was out of the court, deprived of my audience, being hustled with no gentleness back down the hallway of the murmuring souls, and back into the world where faces were made of wood, and did not hear no matter what you said to them.

He has given you hard, a policeman said to me as he propelled me into a van. *Your big fat mouth has got you two weeks of hard*. I thought I must be losing my grip because his words made no sense to me, although I understood each one, and they were not the strange words of the smiling man who sold me oysters, but there was no time to ask him what he meant, or to ask anyone anything, because they were pushing at my bottom again, and I was sprawling again on the metal bench of the dark van, familiar now, and smelling of the piss of someone else's fear, greater even than mine.

I found out what *hard* was in the laundry of the jail, among steam that made me melt, and the hissing and churning of great vats. When I first entered, pushed by a warder with hard hands, I was bewildered by this huge echoing space full of cream-painted machinery and gleaming stainless steel. Above the din of the machines, the voices of the women were as shrill as seabirds, and their cackles, when one of them shouted something they found amusing, frightened me. I was confused by the chaos of such volumes of water, such a roaring and hissing of gas under the vats, such powerful blasts of soap and the smell of starch.

The warder shouted something at me and I shouted back, *What, I beg your pardon?* but she turned and left behind a clanking of locked doors, and I stood alone among the steam until a muscular woman in the coarse green prison clothing poked me in the stomach with a hard forefinger and pushed a broom into my limp hand. I saw her mouth move, and heard a vague roar of words, but could not understand. *What*, I shouted again. *I beg your pardon? What?* The muscular woman stared at me with contempt, as if I was an imbecile given into her care, and she grabbed the broom in my hand and shook it, so hard my teeth rattled together. She shouted again, and I could not understand, but she had vanished now behind something that spurted and bubbled dangerously, and I stood with the broom, confused, until I caught a glimpse of her among cream pipes, and she made violent gestures at me, so I tried to oblige and began to sweep.

It was hard here, I was beginning to see, and I had to learn very quickly how to do things I had never done. All the other women I could see seemed to know how to do everything: how to fold sheets in pairs, walking gravely into each other and exchanging their corners, how to sweep, and how to scrub floors. I could see women doing all these things. I could resist feeling foolish in most situations, but was reduced to feeling contemptible when I realised my life had been privileged.

Here, Miss Fancy-Pants, the muscular woman said, suddenly at my side again, snatching the broom from me as I was fumbling with it and making the mess on the floor worse. *Here, see what kind of a botch you can make of a bit of scrubbing.* She pushed me down on my knees like a cow and thrust a scrubbing-brush into my hand, and I began blindly to scrub, baffled by so much shouting and hostility. The women in green all knew each other and shouted familiarly, slapped each other, touched each other's faces, pushed back the hair on each other's cheeks gone lank with steam. They called and laughed and I could not follow what they said, as if I had suddenly become foreign, or truly mad at last.

I was dizzy from being on hands and knees for so long, and was becoming anxious about the amount of water I had spread on the floor around me, when a siren pealed out suddenly. The muscular woman was nudging me with the toe of her shoe, and, red in the face and wrinkled with rage, she pointed at the wet and soapy floor I was kneeling on with my knees and skirt sodden. She mouthed in fury at me and all I could do was stare open-mouthed back at her, close to tears at all this rage, and at my own confusion and incompetence. With a great hiss and clank, the machinery around us suddenly closed down and in the blessed silence the muscular woman, cords standing out on her neck with the force of her shouting, roared at me, *You, Miss High-and-Mighty, how dare you, how bloody dare you, you will clean up this disgusting mess or get no bloody dinner, Miss bloody Smart Aleck.* I tried to say *But how? How?* but she had turned away and my voice was lost in my throat, came out nothing more than a croak. I was left kneeling in my puddle of dirty water, and had not felt such despair for years, and such an emptiness, having someone shout so harshly at me for no sin I could see. I knelt like a sick cow, my head bowed in my bewilderment, and heard all the laughing women clatter out of the room towards their dinners, and when I heard the laughter fading down the hallway I recovered myself enough to feel angry, and stand up, a person again, Lilian Una Singer, not an animal.

I found my way to the dining room by following the smell along the gloomy corridor and all my anger and bewilderment evaporated in the gigantic hunger I suddenly suffered. But at the door of the huge barn full of long tables, the muscular woman stopped me with a strong palm in my chest. *Well, Miss Prissy, have you cleaned up that mess you made?* and another woman in green yelled with a mouthful of cabbage: *Course she fucken hasn't, she's a fucken bludger, Lois.* Lois span me around then and pushed me out of the warm room where everyone was filling themselves with warmth and chat, and pushed me back along the corridor to the laundry. There Lois saw my sad suds, and pushed me so hard I fell against a machine with a cry of pain that was not all physical. *Scum!* Lois shouted. *Wipe up that bloody slops or there'll be no bloody dinner, and I bloody mean it.*

I was numb now with the outrage and hurt of it, and used my ingenuity. There were no rags, no sponges, none of the things I had ever seen women wiping up floors with, so I took off my coarse green shirt and used that, kneeling in my singlet wiping up the suds, wringing them out clumsily back into the bucket, until the floor was damp but no longer awash. I was trembling now with hunger and unhappiness, and could not wring enough moisture out of the shirt in the end, but put it back on, seeing no alternative, and trusted to body heat to do its job in time, and dry me.

Back in the dining room, I was allowed in now and went to where the food was. There was no meat left, and only stalks of cabbage, and the carrots no one wanted, and sodden potatoes from the bottom of the pot. But I ate without caring, cramming it in, and the women left me alone until I had eaten. Then Lois came over and fingered my wet shirt, and made loud sounds of disgust.

She used her bloody shirt, she is a filthy little miss, eh? The women glanced over at me, sitting hunched up wet and dirty at the table, but they did not care, and looked away again and took up their conversations. Lois hissed at me with the muscles moving in her jaw: *You will learn, Miss Smarty-Pants, and we will see who will have the last bloody laugh, my lady.* My cabbage rose in my throat to choke me, such dislike was in this woman's face, and I was without resource.

Later, four of us were locked together into a cell with bunks, and on that first night, confused and tired after that day of hard labour, I hoped I could restore myself by entering into conversation with these women. *I am Lilian*, I said by way of introduction, for I could not tell if these three women had been scrubbing or folding with me, I found they all looked too much alike in their green garments. *I am Lilian*, I said, and smiled, and tried not to succumb to the soul-stealing effects of the walls of an institution, and indifferent faces. The three women looked towards me as I stood under the bare bulb: we all looked ugly under that light, and when they turned and looked at me without smiling or speaking I wondered if it was my ugliness they found loathsome. *Yes*, one of them nodded at last, and then they went back to talking among themselves in a way I was not invited to join, and I stood in the glare of the bulb and wondered if I existed at all, or if I were invisible.

I tried to remind myself that newcomers are never made welcome in small societies. It was hard to ache in every joint and to long for a bit of a laugh or to share a bit of a story, and to have women beside me who were as unreceptive as any wall. I lay on my tiny bunk, which sagged dangerously under me, and which was so narrow I could not turn over. I lay with the light raining down on me and felt tears sting under my lids and run warm down my cheeks. How many years it was since I had cried, I did not know, but it was years since I had been reduced, as I had been on this day, to being invisible.

There was not a soul here, had not been a soul since I had been thrust into the van, who knew or cared who I was. I was invisible, and how much difference could there be between being invisible and being dead?

I wept silently, and heard the brutal women in green laughing, not at me, I hoped, and whispered urgently. All I could hear from my bunk was *pss pss pss*, like a small dangerous fire.

I could not seem to please the women here. There were women in tight uniforms that made their busts look like small edifices, and there were others in shapeless green garments, but I could not make an impression on any of them.

But I was not an imbecile, and learned quickly. I learned where the sponges were kept, and how to sweep the lint and dirt neatly into a pile and get it into the dustpan. But even when, after a day or two, I had mastered these puny skills, the women still treated me as if I was reprehensible. My voice began to shrink and disappear. I heard it sometimes in the dining room, I heard myself piping to the hard-faced women who doled out the food: *Hello*, I heard myself, *How are you?* I heard myself speak to the woman next in line, with her smeared tin tray: *Looks good*, I would say, *I am hungry, too.* But they never answered, except with a look of contempt, and after Lois yelled at me one day, *Stop your bloody sucking-up, Singer, it will not work here, none of your rich bitch tricks will wash here,* I stopped trying to raise a smile or a word from anyone. The woman next to me in line, perhaps seeing that I was on the point of tears, took the trouble to say, *You lot, you are the fly-by-nights, see, and us regulars cannot be bothered with you.* Then she moved away, just another woman in green, but I thought about what she had said, and saw how bitter it must feel for women who were condemned to fold sheets for years, to have someone like myself, prissy of accent and incompetent with a broom, coming in and leaving again in two weeks. I tried to tell myself that I, too, might be guilty of the same unkindness if I could see freedom being flaunted at me, as they could when they looked at me. And freedom was a relative thing, I saw: I was as free as a bird in their eyes, for what was two weeks, even two weeks of hard, in a sentence of years?

I understood, but it did not reduce the pain or the frightening emptiness, the feeling that my grasp was loosening with each lonely day that passed. I was slipping away from myself, and in the morning when the siren woke us up, I lay for a moment and reminded myself: I am Lilian Una Singer, student of life, and this is an experience. But the hours of being invisible and unheard wore away my certainty as the day passed, and by bedtime I was fearful, exhausted, fighting the panic of being no one at all.

It reminded me, of course, of that other place where I had lost myself. But I did my best not to remember that, because I felt myself close to slipping back into the grey canvas room where no being could prosper. Each morning I reminded myself of my name, and sometimes brought a little William to bear on the situation, my most faithful companion, always waiting in my memory for the hours of greatest need. To the warder with her stick hanging from her belt, who counted us into the dining room at breakfast, I said each morning, *What day is it today?* and when she told me, I comforted myself for the first hard hours with the thought that another day had passed, and that eventually all fourteen of them would have worn away, and I would be allowed to leave.

By the time the day of my release arrived I was wearied into lethargy by so much ignoring. I stood at another counter while they ticked my belongings off on a list and returned them to me, and when I stood again in my own clothes, some of my being and voice returned, although my voice sounded scratchy and strange to me now, the voice of someone who had been declared missing, and was not sure if she could find her way back.

Ah! What a greeting the street was, with Frank waving his bottle at me from beyond a tram, and the din and richness, the clamour and bustle, the colour and exuberance, all the life! How I loved it, coming out of a hell of silence! I almost knelt on the pavement and kissed it, for I saw now that this was my home, I belonged here. I was recognised, I had a part to play here, in the life of the streets. I swore I would never allow myself to be withdrawn again, but live always among these people, and be seen and heard, noticed and remembered. *Frank, Frank,* I blubbered, and hugged him so tightly I heard him grunt. *Frank, I almost died in there, oh, Frank, tell me who I am.* And Frank, that true friend, hugged me back and cried in my ear, *Why, Lil, what did they do to you, you are Lil Singer, of course, larger than life, and the person who matters to us all.*

Daughters of Albion

Extracts from Interview by Gerry Turcotte

I'd like to begin this interview in a circuitous way and ask who you read. You've told me about your admiration for Thea Astley, for example. You've also talked of Virginia Woolf as an idol of sorts. Who are the writers Kate Grenville reads?

The ones I keep going back to are nineteenth-century ones. *Moby Dick* is a book that I keep rereading because the way Melville breaks all the rules of being a novelist is something which intrigues me. I'm also intrigued with digressions in fiction, and also with the connection between fact and fiction and Melville certainly does work with these ideas (although I have to say with shame that *Moby Dick* is the only book of his I've read). To have a novel with long digressions about the shape of harpoons for instance seems to me exciting. I always feel excited about the possibility of fiction when I read *Moby Dick*; it makes me realise that I can go much further and be much more outrageous than I usually dare to be. *Tristram Shandy* I've reread for the same reason.

Both works have very curious structural peculiarities.

That's right. I get very bored and very impatient with a thing that isn't structurally challenging — after all, *life* is. It presents you with an array of things that you have to put together. I am very interested in that sort of structural oddity. Patrick White is another person I read a lot, not for his structural oddity, but for his quirky style. I read a lot of contemporary Australians, mainly out of interest to see what people are doing, and many of them I like. Helen Garner, for example, I like very much. But they're not quite as astonishing as I find some of those nineteenth-century novelists. I'm just rereading Dickens' *Bleak House* — I thought it was "just okay" when I first read it because I only saw the nineteenth-century sentiment and I didn't see that *amazing* capacity he has to draw from the enormous picture down to the tiny detail. Again, it's a structural, almost a pictorial thing, a way of understanding the gigantic shapelessness of life.

In a recent article you wrote "Places aren't very important . . . But the idea of a place is very important indeed. People's idea of a place is why they go to war and why they think it might be worth reducing all places to radioactive dust. So it becomes important to ask where we get our idea of a place." What's your idea of place, and why did you have to leave Australia to get a sense of it?

It seems to me that "place" operates on two levels. There's the place you actually know from your own experience, and then there's the place that you know as a cultural artefact — that's been built up from what you've read and which you know from art. So there are those two separate "places", and one of the problems, of course, with being Australian, is that there's a big dislocation between those two senses of place. The actual Australia that I grew up in wasn't reflected back to me in any art form, and that is one of the reasons I found being overseas activated my imagination. Going to England and seeing things which were culturally totally familiar . . . to have the sense of the first cuckoo in spring; to visit the Lake District and think about Wordsworth. In a funny paradoxical way, living in the cultural artefact of Europe freed me to write about Australia. At a distance it could also become a cultural artefact for me, rather than an immediate, actual place that I was in. If you're too close to it, it *is* just beaches and the washing up and going up the street and buying a loaf of bread. At a distance, I could see that it could become something else, that it could work as a metaphor for ideas as well as being a physical reality.

*   *   *

You've discussed here and elsewhere the fear you had that perhaps you should take another look at your homeland in case one of you had changed. Had you?

Yes, though obviously I would have changed if I'd stayed too, although in different ways, and, yes, the place had changed too. In fact, I was struck by the changes when I got back. For a start, those seven years were the seven years when Australian fiction suddenly took off. They were also the seven years when the society became a bit less narrow and provincial — immigration was more diverse and so on. I'd changed in that I'd begun to see that being a professional foreigner was a bit of a soft option and in the end it could be a shallow way of relating to the society you lived in. That aloof stance of living in a society where you had no responsibility for it — you didn't vote — became unsatisfying.

*   *   *

Did you find that your anger with formulaic writing, and your need to break out of it, conjoined with a growing feminist thought? — in a story like "Blast Off", for example, where the form is so innovative and complements the message.

Yes. That was *exactly* the motivation. When I left Australia and started writing seriously, I felt that there were huge gaps in human experience — female experience — that had never been written about, and that there was no way you could write about them in conventional terms. It somehow just wasn't adequate to talk about them in terms of the conventional, and in nice neat language. The forces operating — anger, frustration, pain, loneliness — couldn't be written about truthfully in neatly ordered fiction. That would trivialise them. It would also blunt the shock that I wanted readers to feel — the shock of recognising truths that had been hidden. I was obsessed with photographing the way things really were, in fiction. Necessarily that brought in the way people's minds really worked and the way they really used words. I loathed — I still loathe — that kind of tidy "dialogue" that's nothing like the way people talk, so it was a kind of anger, and a kind of frustration with the conventions that forced me to look for new ways . . . not that what I was doing was all that new, of course.

*   *   *

What resulted in your providing an extra chapter for the American edition of Lilian's Story?

The editor in New York suggested that Lil got too old and too mad too suddenly. At a purely structural or aesthetic level, she was saying that a transition was missing, and when I reread the section I decided I agreed. My editor here was excellent, one of the best, but I think fiction editors in Australia don't see their role as looking at the large shape of a book. Also, there's no training in that in this country: as for example, a university Creative Writing degree is excellent (and widespread) training for editors in the US. Perhaps, too, writers here don't want or expect that from editors: again, there's not much of a tradition of that here. There were other suggestions the US editor made that I disagreed with and held out for my version, and she was happy with that. But I think the added chapter is an improvement.

I remember reading an interview you gave in 1984 in which you called Lilian's Story *and* Bearded Ladies *comedies. The comic is undoubtedly a strong part of your writing, but its effectiveness, it seems, emerges from its juxtaposition with a darker vision. In* Lilian's Story, *for example, you continually play the nightmarish off against the humorous. How consciously do you use this chiaroscuro effect?*

It's conscious only in the sense that if I write something that looks flat to me, I feel it will be more interesting if I can juxtapose it with something contrasting. I get bored with it if it's only one thing. It's not conscious in that I plan it in advance. I just try to keep it surprising.

Dreamhouse *has a distinctly Gothic feel about it. You use so many conventions of the Gothic genre — the haunted or decrepit house, the landscape imagery which is almost Radcliffean, the hints of incest certainly. How much of the Gothic genre which appears in your writing is deliberately aimed at?*

It's deliberate in retrospect, if you can put it that way. I suppose I could say that for the first draft, nothing is conscious, nothing is deliberate, and after that it probably does become more conscious. When I saw, in the first drafts of *Dreamhouse*, that I had all those elements, then it was easy to think, "Well, here is a convention I can play off." And I had always liked the Gothic fiction that I'd read; I had always found it very interesting. So at that point, I followed it more consciously. It's a funny kind of groping process, and it's very hard to say just where thought takes over from instinct.

In Lilian's Story, *too, as in* Dreamhouse, *the Gothic tends to surface. The old, many-roomed house, the incestual rape, the looming, almost maniacal father figure. But the type of Gothic you seem to use is more reminiscent of Flannery O'Connor, or Patrick White, than any eighteenth-century type of Gothic. Do you agree?*

Yes. I probably don't know enough about any Gothic to really talk about that. But I do remember that the course I did here [Sydney University] on the Gothic novel, although I didn't admire any of those books, they made some kind of impact on me. The idea of good and evil is one that writers keep coming back to, and the Gothic is an interesting vehicle for exploring that in a fairly stylised way, so it doesn't get bogged down in the accidents of human psychology. It embeds itself in a deeper, less personal vision of the world, as dark and light. I should also mention that Flannery O'Connor is one of the writers who influenced me most in America. I'd never read her before, and she expanded my idea of how far you could go with that kind of grotesquerie, and how you might use it to illuminate the contemporary world.

*Do you think the Gothic genre as contemporary writers use it is
gratuitous, or is there a social reason for it? Is it a sensationalistic
thing, or does it get at something in our society which is there —
again, the whole good and evil prospect?*

The good and evil notion is part of every society and there's the
problem of dramatising it. If that's what you are interested in as a
writer. Gothic is a ready-made convention for making the moral
battle interesting and vivid. As Flannery O'Connor said, you
have to write very big for the blind and shout for the deaf. It's also
a bit of camouflage. It's grotesque and unreal, not naturalistic. By
making it look like something that you don't see in real life you
can get under people's guards and get them to accept it in a way
they might argue with if it were presented with the kind of literal
details of, say, a psychological novel about the same kind of
thing. They might argue, "Oh, but that character would never
have done that", and the whole force of the book would be lost.
You could never say that of characters in Gothic fiction; you
wouldn't bother. Nowadays, when morality is hard to talk about
— because we don't have a religious context — a playful convention like the Gothic makes all that solemnity and moralising
approachable.

*Despite the lack of obvious quoting, there is a lot of Shakespeare
in* Lilian's Story. *Particularly* The Tempest. *How did you use
Shakespeare? It seems almost to be a structural usage? How did it
surface?*

It surfaced, like most things I do, by accident. I had written a
fair bit of *Lilian's Story*, and I'd run out of steam a bit. I
remembered that one of the ways that I had started *Lilian's Story*
was by stealing bits of other writers. For example, the very first
thing I ever wrote of *Lilian's Story* was a direct steal of a letter
from Jane Austen to somebody or other in which she says
something about "we sat around at night inventing a few hard
names for the stars". I thought this was such a beautiful phrase
and a lovely idea that I wrote it at the top of a sheet of that funny

yellow paper that you buy in America, and started to write a whole scene from it, which is now in the book. And that gave me the idea that when you're a bit stuck you can go to fairly unlikely sources, and if you can just find the right one, you can pinch a bit, and then work off it, so when I ran out of steam with *Lilian's Story*, when I was back in Australia, I thought about the real Bee Miles. You know, her life had been Shakespeare, so I flipped through his work. Now, *The Tempest* happens to be the first play in my collection of Shakespeare, and I'd never read it, but I did then (because it was the first one in the book), and I realised that, among other things, it was about fathers and daughters, and also about the magic of storytelling. And I was starting to see those ideas as central to *Lilian's Story*. It was also full of these great phrases that I could pinch, so I didn't really bother to look any further than *The Tempest*; it was the one.

Increasingly, The Tempest *is being read in regard to its colonial/imperial concerns, with Caliban and Ariel representing indigenous colonial figures, and Prospero an imperial power. I notice a similar preoccupation with this colonial/imperial dialect in your work. In* Lilian's Story, *for example, the section* "Long to Reign Over Us" *criticises the imposition of decontextualised and useless imperial values on Australian children, and in a recent article you also discuss British attitudes toward Australians as being condescending and so forth. Do you see this as a major focus of your work?*

At the literal, political level it's one factor, though not a major focus. One of the big things for me about living overseas was the realisation of what a handicap we labour under in this country, of being a colony, and specifically of being an English — a British — colony, in the sense that even now publishing agreements limit our access to American writing, for example. But at a less literal level the idea of colonialism as a metaphor is very central.

Do you see the idea of colonialism — or of cultural imperialism —

as a corollary of male imperialism? That is, were you making a deliberate parallel between cultural oppression and individual, sexual oppression — between, say, Lilian and her father?

A book that I read in England which had a big effect on me was *Damned Whores and God's Police* by Anne Summers about women in Australia. Among other things, she draws a parallel between the position of a colonised country like Australia and the "colonised" position of women. That got me thinking about the colonial relationship as a metaphor for many kinds of relationships, of which, of course, the parent-child one is the most obvious. The father in *Lilian's Story* is called Albion, naturally, because he is in that oppressive imperial/colonial relationship with his daughter. So yes, I did see it as a parallel.

The feminist perspective is much stronger in Lilian's Story *than in* Bearded Ladies *or* Dreamhouse. *Was this intentional or inevitable?*

A lot of people actually find it the other way around, because *Bearded Ladies* is more obviously angry, and it's more obviously and pointedly anti-men . . . they actually find *Bearded Ladies* far more feminist. In fact, some of them accuse me of softening on my feminist stance, because they see *Lilian's Story* as "less feminist".

How do you feel about that? Do you agree?

No. I think it's an evolution. I'm as much a feminist now as when I wrote *Bearded Ladies*. But feminism, like any other process of thought, is going to change if you go on thinking. So *Bearded Ladies* is the sort of angry place where feminism actually begins, when you suddenly *see* how the world is really working, which is why I was obsessed with that sort of photographic clarity — people *must know* this is what's really happening underneath the nice rhetoric of romance. By the time I wrote *Dreamhouse*, which came next chronologically, I was beginning to see that women were very much accomplices in that you couldn't just blame the men, as I had earlier. So, the character Louise is a pretty nasty piece of work, and she is much at fault. It takes two, in that relationship, to make it such a disaster. By *Lilian's Story*, I was even able to see that everybody is simply a part of the process, part of the system. Men and women are all trapped, though the cages look different, and women are often in a whole series of cages, not just one.

It seems to me your focus has shifted to societal rather than gender-related victims, which is a nicely tempered and important movement.

I think as long as you're focusing on one part of the system, no matter how true that might be, the possibilities for changing the system are very limited, because you're not seeing *why* the cogs are intermeshing the way they are. Having done the photograph, I'd like to be able to draw the circuit-diagram now.

*   *   *

One of the most effective stories in Bearded Ladies *surfaces again in* Lilian's Story. *Miss Spear in "The Test Is, If They Drown", reappears as Miss Gash. What makes the accounts powerful, I think, is the betrayal which takes place, but more than this, the betrayal of allies in a world which has provided too few. In your eyes, were these characters always similar? And was the betrayal difficult to portray?*

They certainly were similar. I was very conscious that I was reworking that story. I'm niggardly. I believe in recycling. That must be fairly obvious, actually. And it seemed to me that that was a successful story, one that needed a weightier context. It's tossed off as a fairly funny story in *Bearded Ladies*, but for me the idea of betrayal is very central, and deserved a more substantial treatment.

Lilian's Story is really about the suppression of personal language isn't it? Lilian's, John's, the mother's. Even Duncan, Joan and F.J. Stroud are outcasts and so voiceless. Is that a preoccupation of yours?

Yes, very much. The book I'm writing now is about a person telling a hitherto untold story. As well as people telling those untold stories, I'm interested in the storytelling process in general, the way that a story becomes a substitute for what really happened, and the fact that if you have control over the story, then you have control over the truth. That's really the thing that Lilian's interested in, and it is very much what Joan is doing in the book I've just finished. The person who tells the tale has a sort of immortality. The story is going to live forever, where the person who tells it isn't going to. So, whoever tells the story wins in the long run. It's the ultimate revenge of those who've been rendered voiceless.

Can you say something about Joan's History of Australia? *Joan, obviously, is a carry-over from* Lilian's Story. *How important is a knowledge of the earlier character to an understanding of Joan's history?*

I've tried to make it so that it's quite independent. Lilian only appears in one scene in *Joan*, and she has a few cameo roles. So it's not that important. But it would be nice if people read them together. Faulkner is another person I could add to my collection of writers I admire, and I'm very drawn to the idea of building up a whole enormous canvas of books that are quite independent, but if you read them all, they enrich each other.

So you toyed with the idea of creating a fictional community, like Faulkner's Yoknapatawpha, or Margaret Laurence's Manawaka?

In a way, that's what I'm starting to do, in a small way — I wouldn't put myself in the same bus as Faulkner! — because Lilian and Joan are connected. And the book that I plan next is Father's book, so that's also going to be connected. But they're not quite as focused as a unit as Faulkner's novels were.

Lilian's Story and Joan's History of Australia are both pseudo-historical treatments. What is your concept of history?

I'm having a great trouble with that at the moment — with *Joan*. Writing a book is the way I learn things. It seems the only way I can *think* is to doodle with words. I used to have a fairly simplistic view that history was a sanitised version of things that happened, and that you were asked to accept them as the truth, whereas, really, it was just one historian's version of things. In other words, the knowledge that the story is never going to be transparent . . . there is no such thing as a true history; there is always only a perception of history, a story. As a result, I had contempt for the real facts of history, but now that I've actually read a bit of history in the course of doing Joan's history, I think that as well as having to be very sceptical about what you read, you do actually have to read it. In the same way, for years I never read newspapers because I said, it's all a pack of lies, or at least it's just their point of view. Well, now I do, because somehow you have a social responsibility, to learn to read the lines — the lies — or around them *[laughs]*. Or to read enough different lies that you can build up a vision of something that might be closer to the truth.

That's interesting, because what you're really identifying by describing an historian's interpretations is the storyteller's art.

Yes, historians are the greatest storytellers, and they're given this wonderful raw material, some of the best stories. The thing about history is that it ought not to be taught as fact, as it was taught to me. It ought to be taught as a series of fictions, in a way, a series of ideas and possibilities. That's why the historians I appreciate — like Manning Clark or Humphrey McQueen — are the ones who have no truck with dates and facts. Well, they get those right, naturally, but that's not the important thing; the important thing is an attitude to what they're describing. They make their attitude or judgment very clear, unlike some of those others (who embed an attitude just as deeply but pretend not to), so in reading them you can trust them. You can have the same kind of freedom that you do reading fiction. You can use history as a way of thinking about what it means to be human, as you can use the reading of fiction.

In the article "The World is Round Like an Orange" you talk about the "first Australians" and "we invaders", obviously distinguishing between Aborigines and white settlers. I'm curious to know if Joan's history of Australia — despite beginning at the time of Cook's voyage — deals with Aboriginal peoples and issues.

Yes it does. It's been a source of great discomfort to me, great unease, the Aboriginal element. I felt very strongly writing this history that I wanted to put in at least some of the groups that had been left out — mainly the women, but also the Aborigines — and there are a lot of other groups that I haven't put in; you can't put in everything. There are two sections in the book where Joan actually is an Aboriginal woman. She projects herself into that persona. And there are various other times where there are Aboriginal characters, and I feel uneasy about that, because I think . . . I imagine Aborigines reading it and getting very angry, and saying, "Look, here is yet another invader not only taking our country but telling our story as well."

Perhaps the critique you'll get for writing from a male perspective?

Exactly, yes, and on the one level you can argue, as I did about the male perspective, that every character that you write about is fictional. You read fiction with a kind of contract between the reader and the writer, that this is the writer's view of what something might be, it doesn't claim to be "fact". And in a way, any kind of person in the world is raw material for a fiction writer. You shouldn't have to censor yourself, that's true, but at the same time you can't ignore the context — all the outrages we still inflict on the Aborigines. I hope that what I've done with *Joan* is not misunderstood.

*   *   *

You mentioned once that you had written close to a hundred pages of Lilian's father's story. You're obviously planning to return to it — what kind of problems do you see coming up with that new perspective?

One problem will be to resist the obvious, which is always the problem in writing anyway: to overcome my own set of stereotypes about how men in general, or a particular kind of man, might think. But in another way you have to make that leap for any fictional character, so the fact that he's a man is just one more different thing. I was never fat, so I had to imagine that for Lilian — imagine a whole world view for her that I don't really have. Actually, the biggest problem with it, to be truthful, is trying to ignore the voices in my head of the critics and the reviewers, who'll say, you know, "Look at this woman, thinking she can write about a man", and the most difficult thing is to try not to even think about that, and to just write what I feel to be the truth . . . what should be written.

Barbara Hanrahan

EDITOR'S NOTE

Barbara Hanrahan is an artist, printmaker and novelist as well as short story writer. Her first novel, *The Scent of Eucalyptus* (Chatto & Windus, 1973), was written after a number of solo exhibitions in Australia and London had established her reputation as a printmaker. *Sea-green* (Chatto & Windus, 1974), was followed by a series of what are usually referred to as "fantastic fictions": *The Albatross Muff* (Chatto & Windus, 1977); *Where the Queens All Strayed* (UQP, 1978); *The Peach Groves* (UQP, 1979); *The Frangipani Gardens* (UQP, 1980); and *Dove* (UQP, 1982). After *Kewpie Doll* (Chatto & Windus, 1984), a sequel to *The Scent of Eucalyptus*, came *Annie Magdalene* (Chatto & Windus, 1985), which is a decisive break from the style of the earlier books. *Dream People* (Grafton Books, 1987) is her first book of short stories, and her most recent novels are *A Chelsea Girl* (Grafton Books, 1988) and *Flawless Jade* (UQP, 1989).

"Annie M." and "Dream People" were published in *Dream People* (Grafton Books, 1987), pp.37–50, 165–75; "Weird Adelaide" was published in the *Adelaide Review*, 49 (March 1988): 6–7; "Beginnings" was given as a talk by Barbara Hanrahan at Warana in Brisbane, 1987; and "Childhood" is an extract from an interview published in the *Bulletin*, 21–28 December 1982, pp.203–6.

Annie M.

I like chicken legs, I don't like the top part of a chicken — I just don't, I like the legs. Sometimes I make a custard or a jelly. I sit down at the table — I sit down to do everything, even to have my wash. I've got no strength to grip things. I hold the spoon with my best hand and sort of steady it with the other hand while I stir the jelly crystals. Sometimes I do it with the left hand, sometimes I do it with the right, it all depends which hand is sorest. I can't straighten my fingers. My right thumb gets the wobbles and I hold him up straight so he doesn't wobble, my knuckles have come up like eggs. I dropped some wool pieces from my crochet and I had to scoop them up with the fly-swatter.

I have bread and margarine and honey, or bread and margarine and jam for breakfast. I have a hot meal for lunch — I manage somehow with my hands. I get the carrot and saw the ends off, then I stand it up and scrape it, and do the same with the potato, and then I put them in the saucepan with the chicken leg. I have bread and margarine and honey, or bread and margarine and jam for tea, or when I feel like bananas I have a banana sandwich.

But they said at the hospital I passed out in the supermarket because I didn't eat enough. The cashier went and got a bag of beans for a pillow, it was quite comfortable. The ambulance man was an Aborigine and he talked so nice, but the nurses were a rough lot, they hurt me every time they touched me. They brought a bedpan and shoved it right against my tailbone — oh boy, did it hurt. When I told the male nurse he got rid of them and fixed me up. He had a way with him and though I'm deaf (but not stone deaf) I could hear what he said. I told him I was cold and every hour he took the quilt out of the hot room and wrapped it round me and put another quilt on to keep the warmth in. He said, "You can't be worried about modesty," and washed me all over. He washed everything and it didn't worry me (I thought it would but it didn't — once you don't feel well you don't seem to care any more). With my bone trouble I couldn't lift myself up, so he put his arms round me and I put my arms round his neck — just to be out of the road — and he lifted me straight up and I never felt a thing. I told him to call me Annie because I don't like to be called by my surname, it's a Scots name and people don't pronounce it right.

They tried to make me go into a nursing home but I wouldn't, so they sent me back to Pearl Street with a walking-frame and a seat-raiser for the lavatory. I was high up in the ambulance and could see out. They made me have Meals on Wheels and the first two dinners were all right, but then the two old girls spilt the soup. I didn't want soup and I'm not fond of lettuce (I never eat any green stuff) and you have to pay, you don't get them for nothing, so I told them I didn't want Meals on Wheels.

Elly, the small Greek woman, lives up the top end of the street next to Ritsa, the big Greek woman who's all swollen up with something under the skin. They were friends, but Ritsa's creeper keeps going over into Elly's yard so now they don't speak. I can't walk to the supermarket any more so Ritsa gets my chicken legs, Elly gets my bread and margarine, and I've got to work it so they don't meet when they come to see me. I leave the front door open for Elly and she comes in the morning; I leave the back door open for Ritsa and she comes in the afternoon.

Elly can't read and once when I asked her to get extra things she got different things, so now I don't ask her to get anything fancy. Ritsa will get anything I want but I don't like too much fruit and that's the trouble with Ritsa. If I ask her to get me two small bananas or one big one she comes back with half a dozen. I don't want bananas, bananas, bananas — I'm not that fond of them and they go funny in the fridge. But I owe Ritsa a lot. She cashes my pension cheque and pays my bills and puts the rubbish out and washes my sheets and cuts my toe-nails — she sits on the bed with my foot on her lap and trims them down, both feet. I gave her the money to buy the wheelchair in the front room and she'll take me for a walk when I'm ready. I've put a neck rest at the back so when I sit in it I can support my neck. She'll take me round to the supermarket — I've never been further than the front gate with my walking-frame for fifteen months. When you see the food there you start fancying a bit of this or a bit of that. Perhaps a little bit of ham or a little bit of fish, and I'd like a few new magazines and some lollies.

But you don't get much fish now, not nice fish. The fish at the supermarket's not what I want. I want some fish from Port Noarlunga. I waded in the water. We went there for a holiday, and my girlfriend wouldn't go in. I waded in the water and caught a fish with my hands. We took it back to the house where we were staying and the landlady let us use her kitchen and I cut the fish in half — it was a big one and we couldn't eat it all. I gave her the bit with the head on and Gwen and I had the tail.

It's rheumatoid arthritis, not just arthritis. No one knows what it's like except those that've got it, but I suppose it's better it's me than somebody that can't put up with it. I can't think of any part of my body I haven't got the pains in except my eyes. And my private parts, they don't ache (I'm still a virgin, I never had it — poor old pussy). My tailbone is the worst because I lie on it in bed, but I've got a soft pillow I put up under my bottom so it sort of hangs over and then it doesn't hurt. Bed is the best place. I don't get bored. Long as I'm comfortable I'm all right. If I feel lonely I have the wireless going and I do some crochet-work. Ritsa's got six doilies I made, she reckons she can't get enough of them; she'd put a doily under anything. I can crochet for five minutes, and then it takes me an hour before I can pick it up again. The magazines are light and I can hold them to read but they're always about the Prince, the Duchess and Princess Diana. I had a book once — it wasn't a new book but it was heavy and I couldn't read it, my hands just dropped, so I sawed it up in pieces at every chapter with the bread-knife. Then I read it and threw it out.

I'm thinking things in my head all the time. Sometimes I write down words. Anything that'll rhyme with the other words: *masquerade marmalade lemonade promenade parade esplanade persuade* (they just come into my head, I'm smart) *barricade balustrade serenade renegade cascade cavalcade* (you'd never dream there'd be so many) *colonnade accolade cannonade crusade* and: *edge wedge ledge sledge hedge bridge ridge fridge forge fudge smudge nudge trudge budge badge cadge dredge pledge*.

Sometimes I write down songs. I sing some of the old songs I used to know: "Moonlight on the Silv'ry Rio Grande", "Beautiful Isle of Somewhere", "By the Watermelon Vine, Lindy Lou".

I have my tea at six o'clock so I can get back into bed for the seven o'clock News. I never listened to the wireless once, but since I've been in bed I don't want to miss anything. Times are bad now, very bad, things are not right. People killing one another and doing awful things. One woman, they stabbed her in the stomach a couple of times and cut all her fingers off; she's in hospital and doing all right but she's lost her fingers. It was here, in Adelaide, I think, but it might have been Melbourne. There are more murders over in the other states, mostly up in Queensland — they have a lot of murders up there, they don't seem to be able to look after themselves and yet it's hot there, you wouldn't think they'd be worrying about being violent. But it was terrible here at the Zoo. Boys got in and killed the baby animals they were keeping for the children to see. They put those boys away and they're still away and there was some talk of doing away with them.

I have 5DN, turned up loud, and K.G. comes on at four o'clock and has his say about the football and when he doesn't know he says so, but he knows just about everything. He's not rude, not if you get the real K.G. Now and then you don't get the real one — somebody else takes over while he's gone home to have a sleep. He's got a car but he goes home on his motorbike, it's quicker, he can slip in and out of the traffic.

At nine o'clock the one comes on who has the phone-ins. I've listened so long I know his tricks. Any of them that are abusive (they never say hello, they just start jawing), he shuts them up pretty quick. Some people cry and I said, "Oh, shut up, you big boob," to the man crying about his wife. Father Bob, the Catholic priest, comes on round midnight. But I go to sleep when he's talking because I know my religion and they don't use the Bible I use — they've got a different Bible, and they talk their own talk. And I don't believe in this Our Lady business because Jesus' mother, she was his mother, and that was all.

I've got my wireless on the cupboard by the bed, and my emery board and my glasses and my scissors. In the drawer are my handkerchiefs, my purse, my pencil and pad, the peroxide I dab on if I scratch myself, the Vaseline I rub on my neck and face, my barley sugar lollies (I don't suck them, I leave them at the side of my mouth and let them melt). I never shut the drawer. If I leave it just open it's no pressure on my hands to pull it out, but if I shut it right tight — wow!

You've got to have everything handy. I have the walking-frame next to the bed and my wool for crocheting goes in the box in the middle and on one handle is a plastic bag for lolly papers, on the other a bag for dirty handkerchiefs. I don't ask other people to wash my hankies or any soiled garments, I put them in to soak in a dish of water with a spoonful of Morning Fresh. I tried paper hankies in the hospital but I didn't like them. There was a big bag to put the dirty sheets in and I threw the used paper hankies right in and the male nurse looked and said, "You're a good shot." I said, "I always have been." I have, too. I've got a straight eye. Dad would come in and say, "Will you give me a straight eye?" There was a tennis court across the road, before the offices were built, and Mr Williams asked me to play. I said I didn't belong to the tennis club but he said, "I'm asking you, it's my tennis club and I'll have who I like there." So I went, but I won every game because of my straight eye and I knew the other girls were jealous.

Mum's photo is up on the mantelpiece. I put it over to the side first but the light wasn't right, I couldn't see her face, so I shifted it over to the centre. She had brown eyes but Dad had blue eyes and I've got hazel eyes. My brother, Tom, had brown eyes and my sister, Dorrie, had green eyes. I call her my sister but really she wasn't, but Mum brought her up and she was like our family in every way and she had Dad's dark hair and those green eyes — everybody remarked about them. They were always wide-awake eyes, as if they were going to miss something.

Even before I went to school I had a good memory. I'd go up the street to Mrs Fry's place and get all the news and come back and tell Mum. I went on the first electric tram down North Terrace with the nurse, but I don't remember, I was only a few weeks old (perhaps I was the first baby to ride on the first tram). I'm not bragging, but I think I was cleverer than the other children at school, though I talk-talk-talked and Miss Vaux stood me behind the door. When it was the First World War, Sammy Lunn was dancing on the steps of the Grand picture theatre with his walking-stick but the mothers and wives never threw him a penny, and it was their sons and husbands that got any money Sammy collected. So I took the end of his stick and watched his feet and did the same steps as he did and sang the songs he sang, and when I did that they started throwing the money.

A lot of people don't think I'm the age I am. I'm seventy-seven, but even with my bone trouble I still feel young. The skin of my face is smooth — smile lines don't count because everybody wrinkles up their eyes a bit, same with your forehead. I've got wrinkles elsewhere, though; my bust is a bag of wrinkles. I don't know why I've got so thin, unless it's lying in bed. My whole body is thin. My chest is all knobs, there are knobs all over the place, they even try to poke out of my skull. But I've never had a cold since I was a child. I had the influenza then, when everybody else was dying with it. But I lived through it and I've never had a cold since. I must have an angel looking after me, or a good constitution.

My bust went, it just flopped. I don't wear a bra, I haven't got anything to put in it. Once I wore size 34 and I wore it over my singlet to keep me warm in the wintertime. Now I wear a jumper and my pyjama pants to keep warm. Even in the hot weather I still wear jumpers and I don't go out to sit in the sun — I couldn't sit on the seat with my bones, and even when it's a heatwave it doesn't make any difference, I still feel cold. The cold goes right down to my knees, but when I get back into bed it disappears. And I wear a black nylon turban to keep my head warm and a pillow round my neck done up with a safety-pin to keep my neck warm. I made my jumpers before I got bad hands; they're fairly big in the neck and I can get them off over my head, even with it done up in a turban. When I take them off I work each sleeve down till the elbow pokes out at the armhole, then it pulls off as easy as anything. I don't like hair hanging round my face and often wear a few rollers. But it's awkward for my hands, putting in rollers. It takes me nearly two hours to do five. I do one and then I have to have a rest. My hair has grown down to my shoulders and I'd like to go to Feres Trabilsie's in town to have it cut. I thought I might go in a taxi with Ritsa one day. I'd pay for it and take my walking-frame (they could unscrew it and fold it up and put it in the back). I'd let Ritsa go to the shops and buy something while I went into the hairdresser's.

I haven't got a bath and I'm glad; I couldn't lift my legs to get in (even if I could and had one, I might slip and fall and break my ribs). When I wash myself, I get things ready in the kitchen the night before, my towel and my wash-cloth and everything. The kettle's full and after breakfast I put it on. I can't lift the kettle, it's too heavy, so I fill it up with a small saucepan. When the water's hot enough, I put the saucepan on the stove and tip the kettle on its side — it can't slip off because of the things poking up round the gas jet — and the hot water pours in and I add a drop of cold, then pour it over my hair and rub in the shampoo. Then I rinse it and roll a towel round my head to soak up the water and sit down and wash my body with another dish of water, and the last thing I do is my feet. I put them in the water and let them wash themselves and then I take them out and stand them on a towel to dry and then I put my feet in my slippers.

Once I went out dancing. I danced all night and I was fussy, I never danced with anybody that couldn't dance. I liked waltzing and if they put their cheek on mine I left it there, it didn't worry me, because that was as far as they got. Though some kissed me when they took me home and I didn't mind that, but I never kissed back. Some girls were larrikins, they went out with anything, they weren't my type. I went out with Edmund and Skeeter and Eric and did the Moonlight Waltz, the Hyacinth Waltz and my dance dresses were every colour you could think of: red, blue, lavender, pink. I had three pinks because I was a pink bridesmaid three times — a pink lace, a pink French crêpe, a pink taffeta.

I was a sewer. I had sewing on the brain. When I was fourteen I started at the Perfection Shirt Factory, then I went to the sewing-room at Moore's, the big department store in Victoria Square. Then I started sewing at home and I made Mum's clothes and my sister's clothes and my clothes and Mum always dressed very smart, she preferred navy and black, she didn't go in for colours. I made her a black chiffon and a navy crêpe satin and I made her dresses for knocking round, she didn't like getting round any old how. And I made anybody's clothes that came along and wanted clothes. I sewed silk skirts and alpaca coats, bridal dresses and evening dresses. But the girls with too short a neck always wanted high necks to their dresses when they should have had more open necks — not necessarily low necks, but not high.

As well as my dressmaking, I looked after the garden and there was never a weed out of place. A rose tree grew in a diamond-shaped bed; it had bright pink buds and then as they came open I didn't care for them (I only like roses when they're half open). There was a rockery, a fern house and a coprosma hedge I trimmed — it kept me busy, that garden. I had a fig tree but it wasn't a long fig or red; inside, it was a very pale pink. I loved those figs and I had a lemon tree, an apple tree, a Satsuma plum. A grapevine trellis went down the side: muscatels, lady's-fingers, sweet-waters, and then there was a little tiny one like currants.

Now it's terrible, that yard. I've never had a yard like that in my life. There are so many weeds, and the blue flowers have gone wild. They're not hard to pull up, you can pull them up easy, but I've got no pull or I'd have a try.

I don't want the Domiciliary Care from the Council, but I could get a pop-in maid. They advertise in the newspaper and she'd only have to do that room and this room and the kitchen. She'd charge according to what she did, and could come once a fortnight. But I do my best, I try to keep things tidy. I sit on the bed and sweep any wool pieces down into one place, and then I dab them with the broom and they stick to it and I turn the broom up and take them off, and then I put them in the rubbish bag on my walking-frame.

I only have four cups of tea a day but some nights I have to get up every two hours. But of late I've been going every four hours, so it's been very good, it saves this business of getting up. It must be the weather. In the cold weather you make more water, but now it's getting warmer. It's painful to get out and it's painful to get in. Sometimes I think I'll wet the bed and I make an effort to get out, but it takes me so long and I'm wishing and praying I can hold it. I get inside the walking-frame and sometimes I think I might drop my water on the way. I no sooner sit down on the lavatory seat-raiser than away she flies.

The old girl next door, she's no lady, she wets the bed and sleeps in it. She stinks. She sleeps in it and wets it and sleeps in it and wets it. You can smell the stink coming from her window — I've got a good smeller. I don't want her here. I only talked to her once, I couldn't understand her. She had her teeth in but they don't fit, they wobble round and she has to hold them in with her finger. She talked about a husband but she has hallucinations, I don't think she ever had one. She's not right in her head. She should be put away.

I never wanted to get married, I never wanted it, that's just me. When Audrey's husband came round wanting it I didn't feel upset. It doesn't matter what they think they're going to get, they don't get it from me, my mind's made up. Scots people are more that way and I took after Dad. We weren't a sexy family, not a bit. I don't know how Mum had my brother and me, but she did. After that, Dad didn't want it any more. But he loved Mum — he'd put his arms round her and kiss her, but that's as far as it went. There are a lot of people like that.

You hear of girls now, they're not married but they live with their man, they're happy, that's enough. After all, saying a few words doesn't make you any different. But I never wanted to get into bed with a man and I wouldn't like to marry an old man — he'd be too used to it, he'd wear you out. Though I liked talking to men and dancing with them and having a bit of fun, and I liked Hazel's brother, Eric: we danced the snake dance. After he lost his leg in his accident he never worried about women. I might have married him if things had been that way. But he might have got tired of me — and yet again, I don't know, he might have been something like myself. Could have been.

My girlfriend, Mabel, was like that for a while, but then she got married and had children. If Harold wanted something from Mabel at night he'd go on so silly. Sometimes when I was there to tea, I couldn't hear what he said, but the way he was going on, I could have clouted him. It made me shudder to think of getting into bed with Harold and Mabel wasn't very sexy and I suppose he didn't think he was getting enough because he started bringing home flagons of wine. She tried to look as if she hadn't been drinking, but I could always tell. Her words didn't slur and she didn't walk crooked, but it was the effort she put into trying to look as if she wasn't and I knew she was. Then one day when Mabel was under the influence, she got abusive with me and I said if that was all she had to say, I was going. I grabbed my bag and walked out and I never went back. When I finish, I finish.

When it was the Second World War, I worked at Holdens and had full authority over a hundred and twenty girls and five blind men and five deaf and dumb women. Then I worked in the butter room at the Co-op. Then I did sewing and looked after the children for Mrs de Dear. The de Dears were millionaires and after five girls they had Alasdair, and after that Mrs de Dear didn't want any more kids so a nurse came the the next time she was pregnant and put it down the toilet — I don't blame her. The de Dears had a party in their ballroom with oyster patties, crabmeat puffs and stuffed eggs and when the children were put to bed I mingled with the ladies. But not one of them was really smartly dressed. I supposed they thought they'd just wear ordinary and have a few drinks and one thing and another, like they did, those types. I'd put on my party dress of black taffeta and silk velvet (real soft silk velvet, you can't buy it now). Mrs de Dear looked and then realised she was staring. I was too well-dressed to be with them, so I disappeared into my sewing-room and took the dress off and folded it away in my case. Then I put on a pair of slacks and a jumper and a jacket because it was cold weather and went home on my scooter.

Mum died and then Dad died and then my brother died and then my sister died. I'd had such a good time when I was young that when I lost all my people I just went flop. Mrs Warne up the street took me to see a spiritualist, though I said I didn't believe in them. The woman was meant to go into a trance and I thought, You're not going to get any information today, I'm going to control you. I did, too. I broke her concentration. She was getting everybody under her control, but she couldn't get me.

Once I took pills for the arthritis, but they didn't do me any good. I don't believe in pills. I had a laboratory test and they charged me eighteen dollars to check a sample of my water. I won't have injections: over the wireless they said that anybody that's taking any injections must stop immediately — there's something wrong with the injections. The doctor came to see me once; I kept my hands under the sheets so he couldn't see the knobs. I knew he couldn't do anything, so we had a good yap and I'm silly as a wheel at times and he went out the front door still laughing.

I read in a magazine that eating Fairy margarine would help you in a lot of ways with your troubles. I'd been eating it for a while when I suddenly felt my toes move. I thought I must have dreamt it so I swung the bedclothes back and had a look and sure enough my toes were opening out, and then my fingers started to straighten out, too. I'm still eating Fairy margarine and I keep a supply in the fridge. I eat two tubs a week and might get better and live to be over a hundred.

When I go to sleep I have food dreams, but every time I dream I'm going to have a nice dinner I wake up before I get a chance to eat it.

I used to have fowls. I had a big black Orpington rooster, a Rhode Island Red, white fowls and two burnt-orangey bantams called Darby and Joan. After the old black Orpington did the dirty, Joan sat on four eggs; but she was too small to sit on them properly, so Darby helped her and they brought out four chickens: a black, a buff, a cream, a speckly. And I had pigeons and ducks, and Mickey was my last cat. I brought him home from the Co-op as a kitten and he sucked his milk off my little finger (my fingers weren't like they are now) till he lapped from the saucer. He was grey with white paws and a biscuit-coloured front. In the end he went thin and rubbed himself on my legs and, months after, I found him in the bottle-oh's paddock. He was trodden flat, but it was poor old Mick.

All the things I had. I used to love having them. I think about them sometimes. I think, Oh well, they're gone now, but still . . . I still think about them.

Dream People

She was always dreaming when it was a lesson she didn't like at school. She hated sport and when it was basketball practice she'd hide with the girls who smoked behind the shed, but she got caught and they made her the scorer — she was sitting there, supposed to be scoring, but she went into a dream and didn't put anything down. She'd rock herself backwards and forwards and dream about being beautiful, like Constance Bennett in her first talkie film, *Rich People*, and Miss White would creep up behind her and give her a whack over the head and make her stand in the corner. Once she went into her dream when it was geography — she was rocking and dreaming and when Miss White said to point to the place on the map, she just pointed anywhere and it was the exact right place, some place in Africa.

The Black Nun was a dreadful book about the wicked things Catholics did, but it was popular among the Protestants. She read it inside the cover of another book when they thought she was doing her homework, and she read her mother's Marie Stopes book that way, too. Her mother must have done it with her father and it had taken two days for her mother to have her and now her father was dead.

Two nurses up the street did abortions; one had cross-eyes and big thick lips and a daughter who went to the Methodist Ladies' College, and they had girls going in and out the gate all day; Granma said they put some soapy stuff in a syringe and syringed it up. Old Hoppity-go-kick lived one side next door; he was lame and an old devil, and Granma said he'd grab his wife by the hair and drag her inside to do it with her in the daytime. Sucklings' girl lived on the other side; she had all the blokes coming at night, but she said when she got enough money to buy her new false teeth she wouldn't have them come any more.

Sometimes at the tram stop she worried she'd be late for school, so she'd count up to fifty with her eyes shut and hope that when she opened them the tram would have come. Her girlfriends were silly as wheels and once on the tram they kept saying, "French letter" and giggling; the conductor was the young one who flirted and when he asked what they were laughing at they giggled worse. The boys at school were in different classes to the girls, but one room was divided into two by a curtain and the boys kept nudging the girls through it all the time. Some girls went behind the bushes with boys.

Once in drawing lesson she drew a pansy and Miss White said it was the worst pansy that was ever drawn and made her hold it up and everyone laughed. When she left school, she got a job as a commercial artist at a big shop in Rundle Street. She drew cups and saucers, bedroom suites and kitchen suites, but she always wanted to draw fashions. One of the other artists got a lump on his head that grew bigger, and then he had funny turns where he fell down unconscious, and he wore a bracelet to say who he was; he went into hospital to have an operation, and then he had a white bandage round his head that he'd undo to show you what was underneath; then he left work and died. She saw an ad in the paper for someone to demonstrate hosiery but Granma said she had lolly legs so she didn't apply.

The brother of the girl round the corner took her to the pictures, and people complained when he kept his sombrero hat on through the film — he was a boundary rider from the country and was dressed like a cowboy. At the interval he didn't stop talking about how he'd driven a team of nineteen donkeys and eaten snakes and sleepy lizards cooked in ashes, and how goanna meat tasted something like butterfish, only sweeter. Then her shoes started to smell, because they were white satin court shoes she'd bought cheap and dyed black with Raven oil. But the oil wasn't dry and the smell got stronger and stronger and she felt like going home barefoot.

Ray Shegog took her to a dance at the King's Ballroom. One of his friends looked like Tyrone Power and he just sat there reading the racing pages of the *News*; he didn't seem to take any notice of anyone. But after a while he asked her to dance and they both lived at Thebarton, so they went home together on the tram. She started going out with him to the pictures and for walks down the Beach Road where they'd have a lemon squash spider in the shop opposite the billiard hall for a treat. Her favourite tune was "The Last Waltz" and they danced it on Saturday nights when they went to the King's with Ray Shegog and the Ryan girls and a girl who married one of the Junckens. When she won the Belle of the Ball she got a box of chocolates, and she wore a blue crêpe dress her mother made that had blue crêpe flowers round the neck and a fish-tail at the back. But when he took her home he wanted to do it round the side of the house — he said it was a proposition, not a proposal.

She didn't meet his father for ages and then one day he stopped in a taxi, and they got in, and she thought what a big fat man he was. His mother lived with his Aunty Agnes and the night he took her out to meet them they weren't home, but his sister was in the sleepout having a passion scene with her boyfriend. His grandfather said her forehead was the only decent thing she had.

Her mother went with her to buy the woollen crêpe material for her wedding ensemble. You couldn't buy the blue she had in mind, so they bought as near as they could at Miller Anderson's and had it dyed the colour she wanted — a soft darkish greyish blue. She made the dress with a flared skirt and sewed silver bugle beads in a leaf pattern on its waist-band; the coat had a grey rabbit collar made to look like squirrel. She sewed lace flowers on to her scanties and Granma threw off and said, "The best thing you can do is to elope, and go off without all this stupid fuss."

On her wedding day she sat down the yard and painted her nails with pale pink polish and Granma said, "You won't be doing that long — that'll be washed away doing the washing." They were married in the Registry Office, and she thought it was terrible when he went and played football in the parklands afterwards. He wouldn't have his photo taken, and he didn't tell his mother or his Aunty Agnes or his sister because they were Catholics.

They bought a bedroom suite and a kitchen dresser on hire-purchase and lived with his father, who shut his door on a piece of paper so he'd know if they went into his room. If a letter came for her she couldn't get it, because his father locked the letter-box. And his father cooked a stew, left it in a saucepan on top of the stove, and kept adding to it all week; and she'd never seen anybody eat a whole leg of lamb for lunch before.

But he ate his father's stew and he liked curry and gambling on horses — he'd gamble on whether a fly was going to crawl up a wall. He went out with the boys, he was a terrible torment, he'd sulk if he didn't get his own way. He'd won a scholarship to the Christian Brothers' College in Wakefield Street, and when he'd left school he'd gone for a white-collar job in the Railways, because it was big deal to get into the Government in the Depression. He had the qualifications, but they reckoned his eyesight was bad and wouldn't let him in, though he didn't even need glasses to read. He was so disappointed he took a job at Holdens in the machine shop and wouldn't look for a better one.

There were ads in the *Truth* for women's complaints that everyone knew were ads for abortions, and she was scared stiff every month because she didn't want to be pregnant. But then she was, and told her mother, and felt cheeky as she sat on the kitchen table, swinging her legs. When her mother said she didn't have to have it if she didn't want it, she said she was going to — for the first time in her life she'd do what she wanted, she was sick and tired of being told what to do.

She sat out under the fig tree day after day and knitted a shawl — she had to sit on her own, she couldn't let anyone near her when she was knitting, because it had fifty-eight rows to the pattern and she'd make a mistake if they talked. She sewed dresses with pintucks and lace, and wound pink thread round a needle, then pulled it through to make snail rosebuds. She knitted dresses and bootees and decorated a cot up with spot muslin. Her mother knitted a pink cot cover in moss-stitch and plain-stitch squares; and she made bonnets, all very flash, with lace on them and ruching.

He used to drive her nearly insane with his tormenting. One day he chased her with a dead mouse, and she was terrified of mice. He only stopped when his father said it'd do some damage to her, in her condition.

When she took drawings into the Co-op, she wore a navy-blue

suit with the coat left undone and a fox fur round her neck, hanging down over her bulge. Though she wore her wedding-ring, the Advertising Manager always patted her hand and seemed to think she was an unmarried mother. She didn't tell him she wasn't, because she thought he might stop giving her the work.

One day she was cooking a roast dinner but when she took it out of the oven to turn the potatoes, the pan tipped up and fat went all over her feet. It hurt so much that at first she couldn't feel it; she was alone in the house and just stood there and started crying. Then she remembered reading that you put flour on burns, so when he came home from work she was sitting with her feet in the flour tin. The whole of her feet were great big blisters and the doctor had to bandage them up. She had to cut the tops off the blisters with scissors, and put disinfectant on them, and she was worried the baby would have something wrong with its feet. She met someone she knew when she was wobbling across Victoria Square on her bandaged feet to pick up some artwork from Moore's, and she thought, I bet they think I've gone off.

Someone hung a wedding-ring on a string over her and it swung this way, not that way, and predicted a girl. She kept eating oranges — once she ate eight straight off. Towards the end, she felt dreadfully uncomfortable and could only lie on her back to sleep; she didn't like lying on her side, and if she lay on her stomach it was like being up in the air.

Chamberlain had gone off with his umbrella to see Hitler, and people in Adelaide didn't think the War would happen, it all seemed so far away. But it started, and three days later the baby was born.

It was a Wednesday — a hot, awful, windy morning in September when her pains started, so he took her in a taxi to the small hospital called St Ives on the Beach Road. When they examined her the pains had stopped and they said she'd be about a week or so yet, she shouldn't have come. She said she couldn't go home, there was no one there, and they said she could sit outside on the veranda till he came home from work. But it got so hot she couldn't stand it and felt sick, so they said she could go into one of the delivery rooms — there was nowhere else for her to go. They took her into a room with great big lights and put her on a skinny little table; they weren't very sympathetic, and said she was a naughty girl, and went away to look after a lady who was having a baby. She was lying there all on her own when the pains started again and then she felt something go queer — it was the waters breaking, she could feel water all round her; she'd read books about it and knew what was going to happen, but she was still dressed ready to go home. She sang out, "Oh, for goodness sake, something's happened, the baby's coming, I know it's happening." But no one came, till one of them popped in to get something and then the doctor was there and said, "Good God, the head's out." And it was the worst pain in the world, it felt like her whole body was being split open, she thought she was going to die; it didn't seem worth it, nobody could be worth such pain, and she'd just about had it on her own. They said, "Why don't you scream, make a noise?" and she said "What's the good of doing that?" and they put a pad over her nose. Then the doctor held the baby up and said it was a girl and she saw them smacking it to make it cry. They were pushing on her stomach to get the afterbirth out, and she was half daft, and threw the pillow at the doctor and said, "It's not a girl, it's a boy, and they're going to send it to the War."

The first thing she looked at was the baby's feet and it had eyes that were sort of shut, not properly opened, and black hair all over its head in curls and two bright pink cheeks, and it looked like a little Chinese doll on a stick. The nurses carried it round the hospital to show it off.

But when she was on the pot, a horrible thing came out — a thick snaky thing — and the nurse wouldn't tell her what it was. She had dreadful ideas of cancers and all sorts of things; she found out later it was part of the cord that should have come away before, but didn't.

The baby's gums were like razors, they used to hang on, and she thought her nipples would be bitten off. It really hurt, it felt funny. She worried her breasts were too small — some people had big brown nipples, but hers were only very small and a pinky colour. But the doctor said size wasn't important.

She stayed in hospital ten days and then they went to live in a hotel in Light Square in the city, where one of his boyfriends worked in the bar. She hated it there, it was awful. The cook was a huge woman, as fat as she was tall; one day she said she didn't feel well and went to hospital and had a black baby. There were boxers and wrestlers and prostitutes and bad language and an old lady wandering round, drunk, with a candle in her hand, and she thought she'd burn the place down. Nearly every day she walked home to her mother in Rose Street, with the baby in its white wicker pusher lined with pink leatherette. If it was windy the baby loved it; its feet were kicking and it was screaming.

The first time she bathed the baby, she felt almost too frightened to do it — it felt just like a little rabbit; it was so small she thought it was going to slip out of her hands under the water. She washed the nappies with Velvet soap to keep them soft so they wouldn't scratch its bottom. The first thing it ever picked up was a piece of bright red chocolate paper.

She drew farm machinery from photos and when she took the artwork in, she'd put the baby in its cot in front of a mirror so it could look at itself, and give it a whole lot of toys to play with. The girl who did the rooms was supposed to be looking after it, but she worried all the time she was away as it was always crying when she came back. One day he had the baby in the bar with her best handbag round his neck, making out he was a bookmaker, and all the prostitutes were there. She said she wouldn't stay at the hotel any longer, so they went to live with his father in Dew Street again.

She drew gas-masks and people doing first-aid to one another for a book of hints on what to do if the War came to Australia, but she never thought he'd have to join up — a lot of men who worked at Holdens didn't because they were making things for the War.

Then he got wet riding his bike to work for the nightshift. He had an annoying little cough, but wouldn't do anything about it; his cheeks were flushed and, though he still ate curries and stews, he kept getting thinner. At last he went to the doctor on the Beach Road, who sent him to be X-rayed, and when he went for the results it was galloping consumption; both his lungs were affected and there wasn't much that could be done. He didn't want to go to hospital, so she looked after him at home, and had to disinfect everything and wash his dishes separately. Sometimes he spat up blood, and when his ankles swelled the doctor said it was a bad sign, and he had to go into the Adelaide Hospital where they gave him oxygen.

One night when she was there, he told her to take the tubes out of his nose and shift the cylinder — he kept at her till she did it, and then water shot everywhere and the nurses came running. One day they called her in because he wasn't expected to live, but when she got there he was sitting up reading the racing page. He was very thin, his nose and eyes stuck out, he looked like a parrot. He said he was too young to die, but he died the day after the baby's first birthday. For ages after she couldn't bear to look at a parrot and she couldn't be in a room with anyone coughing, it made her feel like screaming.

The night before the funeral, there was a wake at his father's house. His mother and father's Catholic friends sang songs and talked nearly all night. The coffin was in the front room with the lid off, and everyone filed past and said a prayer. His mother made her go in and touch his face — it was like a stone face and cold like ice and she felt she was going mad. When she was in the funeral car with his mother and father, they passed the lane at the back of Rose Street and she saw Granma with the baby in its pusher and started to cry. They stood round the grave while a priest gave a talk, then everyone threw a flower on the coffin when it was lowered into the ground. Trim's, the second-hand clothes people, read his death notice in the *Advertiser* and sent a card to see if she had anything to sell.

After the funeral, his mother shut herself in a room for a week and wouldn't talk to anyone. His father said he'd finish paying the kitchen dresser off and have it for himself. She went back to the house in Rose Street with the bedroom suite, and they put it in the top room for Granma and Granpa. She slept in the next room with her mother and her mongol aunty; and the baby slept there, too, in its cot.

Granma got up one day and suddenly grabbed her by the throat, and she thought she was going to be choked; she cried out to her mother and had to fight to get away. Granpa wasn't very well, he just sat round in a chair. There was a fire down the shed, and he got hit on the head when he went to open the gate for the firemen; it caused a blood clot and he went sort of funny and died, and then Granma died in the hospital by the railway line.

Her mother made a fuss of the baby and said, "Poor little thing, who knows what's ahead of it?" and made it dresses and shawls and took it to the pictures, where it'd cry and she'd have to take it out.

Her mongol aunty touched its face and hands with little pats, and nursed it on her lap — she couldn't walk round nursing the baby, her feet were small and she was a bit unsteady on them; she'd tuck it in its pusher very tight, though it hated that and kicked everything off; and all the old ladies watched over their front fences as she took it for a walk in its pusher up the street.

Weird Adelaide

In Adelaide, anybody can jump out at you and cut you up and put you in a glad bag . . . A kid goes to the loo and disappears — in such a quiet little place, so many folk disappear . . . They say there are more topless waitresses in Adelaide for its size than any other city in the world . . . Adelaide is a lovely place to bring up a family . . . It's full of pickled Old Girls who still put on their best clothes for going to town . . . The open inspection syndrome at weekends . . . Adelaide water is so bad it's like snake piss . . . If you're not one of the Old Adelaide Families you're not an OAF . . . Adelaide is Asthma City — if anybody has a bright idea people clutch their throats and gasp in anguish . . . Adelaide's going — they're knocking the guts out of the place and putting up a new city . . .

Everyone has their own feelings about Adelaide, and they tend to be extreme. It's either Garden City of the South (where flourish the arts and sciences, and all those things which spell the culture of twentieth-century civilisation), or that ideal setting for a horror movie of Salman Rushdie's infamous *Tatler* piece (exorcisms, omens, shinings, poltergeists, things that go bump in the night). The Paradise version features the stock ingredients of well-watered plain, enchanted Hills, girdle of green, white-sand beaches, wattle-bird says goodnight, sun draws his curtains. There are countless bit-players in Amityville-Adelaide. The most prominent seem to be an elegant maiden aunt, all sex-kicks-violence beneath her prim Edwardian exterior; and an innocent in Harrison school shoes, his little-boy image lynched by a tight collar, masochistically running marathons for pleasure. Weird Adelaide. The clichés and contradictions were there at its beginnings: Edward Gibbon Wakefield dreaming up his new England beyond the seas, free of the taint of convictism, as he languished in Newgate Prison to expiate an abduction and Gretna Green marriage with a schoolgirl heiress.

William IV had a pineapple-shaped head and a German consort whose Honiton lace robe was wreathed round the hem with Amaranth, Daphne, Eglantine, Lilac, Auricula, Ivy, Dahlia, and Eglantine again — the initial letters forming her name, Adelaide. She was a noble, sincere, Christian lady, generous and forgiving, who did nothing after dinner but embroider flowers. She introduced Christmas trees to England, and wouldn't let the ladies come *decolletées* to her parties, and carried a statue of her dead baby, little Princess Bess, wherever she went. It was the King's desire that the new colony's capital should be named after her.

And so they came in the *Diadem*, the *Dauntless*, the *Royal Admiral* . . . Abbott, Adams, Adamson, Addison . . . Little Britain across the world, their Pioneer faces stare out from Duryea's photos. Daunting in their respectability. Moderation the keynote. Idlers and drunkards unwanted. The Church, Established and Dissenting. Anglicanism the faith of the social elite; a conforming Nonconformism for the majority. Teetotal, God for Sunday, hanky up your sleeve. *Sinners, whither would you wander? Whither would you stray? Oh, remember, life is slender. 'Tis but a short day*. Steady and sober and utterly extraordinary. How is it that such ordinariness took a leap in the dark to *terra incognita*?

Yet it was pretty to see the trees covered with bunches of yellow blossom, and when the wind blew off the land, the air was so filled with wattle perfume they smelt it on board the ship. Black cockatoos; white cockatoos, yellow- and orange- and pink-crested; parrots and parakeets and black swans flying. They looked at the new place with their Old Country eyes and saw it as a gentleman's park, a nobleman's park, an English park. Once Adelaide had been Tarndakanya. Now there was a Native Location, and an official Native should worship Jehovah rather than a red kangaroo; and for Governor Gawler's Native Reception be decorously clad in blue dungarees or a red flannel dress. A Native was a plaything, a curio, a grown-up child who begged for bicketty and bappy and was regaled with roast beef, sugar, tea, rice and biscuits for the Queen's birthday feast.

It was only 1838, and the workmen were still on the roof of Trinity church, but for Baby Fisher's christening the ladies wore maroon silk, fawn silk, lemon silk, violet silk, pale green silk, stiff corded black silk; and there were lace pelerines, pearl necklaces, crêpe scarves, cherry ribbons, sable boas. The year before, pickled Hottentot fig leaves and samphire gathered at Glenelg had been a delicacy. After the ceremony they walked to Mr Fisher's and partook of an elegant cold collation: giblet and gravy soup, roast sucking pig, fowls — roast and boiled, tongue, chicken pies, plum pudding, gooseberry pie, scalded codlings, damson pie, preserved ginger, tipsy cake, custard and pear tart, preserved orange, plum cake, port, sherry, ale and cheese. Then the ladies walked in the garden and came inside again to dance the Co-quette.

There were giant white gum trees, then, along the banks of the Torrens, and up the slopes of Montefiore Hill. Robert Gouger, the first Colonial Secretary, cut some of them down when he built his house on Strangways Terrace to get a glimpse from his balcony of Government House. Osmond Gilles' residence in the foothills, where Beaumont now stands, was staffed with coolie servants from India. Brides were married in Chinese silk with orange-blossom bonnets. Mrs Gawler wrote home for gauze cap ribbons and silk mitts.

But the climate was not to be depended on. When the hot winds blew, it was like putting your face to the mouth of a baker's oven. In summer, the country round about appeared nothing but a sandhill. Adelaide swarmed with fleas and flies; the Hills had a dried-up appearance. The place was quite civilised, with nothing rough or outlandish, and all its right-angled streets and squares named after leading founders, promoters and settlers. Yet the light was so strange. Everything looked small, and the colours oddly bright; you could hardly believe things to be real. It was like looking at a toy town, set about with figures from a Noah's ark. You were not accustomed to see things so distinctly, at such a distance.

There was a time when South Australia was a land ruled by women. In the gold-rush days it could seem that only they and

children were in existence. All at once it was an old world sentiment that men must work and women weep. They escaped the
parlour to gather the entire vintage of a year and make its wine;
they ploughed and sowed and scattered corn from a seed-slip
slung across their shoulders. And as those heady days receded,
the women of Hahndorf kept tramping down, year after year, to
market in Adelaide.

South Australian women were the first in Australia to gain the
right to vote, but in the centenary year of 1936, E.H. McEllister of
Dulwich could argue, confident of support, in a letter to the
Editor of *The Advertiser*: "The sexes were ordained in such a way
that the man is the bread-winner, and the woman the builder of
the home. Any frustration of this principle and we would merely
become a race of neuters! The only way to accomplish equality
among humans is to abolish the sexes — and very soon equality
and the humans would be abolished, too. Great minds, per-
sonified in Hitler and Mussolini, are leading the world back to
sanity in regard to the correct position and employment of the
sexes. In Spain today 'equality' has reached such a state that
women are fighting in the war alongside the men! What a disgrace
to true womanhood and motherhood! Let women look to the
Mother of our Lord for an example . . ."

Would you, too, like to mould your skinny body, bony arms
and legs into alluring, pleasing shapeliness? Or do you belong to
that group of women whose figures are of the Abdomen Type? It's
either Madame Irene shell-pink corsets or art silk scanties, and all
the time your smile should be a pleasant memory (say Kolynos).
You marry in moderation, have children in moderation, die in
moderation. Scone trays, cake dishes, pillow-shams, doilies, tea-
cosies, blue-beaded milk-jug covers, English china tea-sets with
artistic pink rose sprays. The weirdness of suburbia becomes
weirder when it's set in an exotic landscape. Bearded bottlebrush,
woolly tea-tree, spider orchid, bidgee-widgee. The gum trees rising up, tier upon tier; freaked-out blue of the sky. But at night,
five stars in the form of the Saviour's cross.

After the War there were space dogs and sputniks in that sky,
and an American moon circled the earth. But Adelaide kept being
the cleanest and neatest capital city in Australia, the nicest place

in the world. Though it was populate or perish. The Migration Minister, Mr Calwell, had said an average of seven children a family and Australia's future would never be in doubt, but they kept bringing in New Australians. It was unnatural. Adelaide, with its harbour many miles away, very seldom saw foreign ships, like its sister States. Adelaideans were not accustomed to seeing foreign people in their midst. Suddenly, from nowhere, thousands had come, and a mixture of races was alarming, and lots of them were not a suitable type. They talked to each other in their own tongues instead of English; they shared a taste for Continental foods; they preferred wine to beer; they thought a fine leg was just something that looked nice in nylon. And life was no bed of roses in England now, but even the Pommy migrants were complaining. Could you go into your back garden in Britain and pick a peach, apricot or orange from a tree? They came here expecting the world to be dropped in their laps, and the milk and stout to flow down their throats. And the streets were unsafe for young girls. The big problem was what was to become of South Australia's twenty-four thousand surplus bachelors. It should be arranged for every girl to have two husbands.

And so on to the sixties and seventies and Adelaide starts seeming like somewhere else. The Dunstan Decade, and the State is setting a pattern for Australia. Aboriginal land rights, equal opportunities legislation, the easing of licensing laws and dress codes, homosexual and abortion reforms. Trendy South Australia is the first place in Australia where you can swim nude and still be perfectly legal. For some who see Adelaide sinister, this is where it begins . . . If God saw it was necessary to put clothes on Adam and Eve after they had sinned against His command, why do people think they are doing no wrong by exposing their naked bodies in public?

Rushdie's Adelaide in 1984 was a city of arson and vanishing children and awful murder. "Oh, that someone could be so stupid," said the then Lord Mayor, Mrs Chapman. "That such a person should have been in the depths of depression when visiting our beautiful city is probably a reason why he should not come back." The Premier, Mr Bannon, said that statistics showed

Adelaide did not have a higher rate of "horrible crimes" than other Australian States.

Yet when the baby animals were slaughtered at the Zoo it seemed a particularly Adelaide crime. The city is so clean, so pretty, and so much — despite the cranes on its skyline — the big country town it takes pride in being, that it seems, paradoxically, to suit the more kinky varieties of evil. Even in the daytime the streets of classy North Adelaide and Unley Park can be tunnels, enclosed by green leaves. And so quiet, so secretive; all the people shut away behind their high walls. And the Torrens, with its levelled and lawn-planted banks and picture-postcard University Bridge has had a sinister flavour for years. For so many lost girls of the past in a certain state (which meant an indisposition of several months' standing), those river banks were the place to jump from. And if you did it in a properly weird Adelaide way, you left a confused medley of Scripture texts behind you.

At night, Adelaide turns *film noir*, becomes a miniature Cornell Woolrich city, its empty side streets black and creepy, with a feel of the back lot at Paramount or Universal. The twin towers of the Town Hall and Post Office loom up; the old Queen and her stay-at-home explorers are out in Victoria Square. It's just the setting for midnight chimes heralding in some Dawn of the Living Dead. The neon glitter of Hindley Street takes on a curious excitement, edged by so much gloom. To be there on a Saturday night is like walking some fifties boardwalk. There's a tacky fairground atmosphere. The on-off lights blink their acid-drop colours. The Saturday night pick-ups keep parading. Sandra Dee and Natalie Wood on wobbly high heels; Jimmy Dean and Sal Mineo cruising in their customised Valiants and Holdens. The Monkey Man rolls his shoulders outside the Flash; the kids play the machines in Downtown and Timezone.

Weird Adelaide. The Spooner girls in their silver-spoon private-school uniforms, just the right degree of wrinkle in their socks, outside Sportsgirl in Rundle Mall. The frog cakes on their paper doilies in Balfours; the naughty R rated moulds under the counter (ASK ASSISTANT) in the cake shop in Adelaide Arcade. K.G. on his 5DN sports show throwing the lines open on Martina and Judy; and it might still be the thirties as the unchanging

Adelaide voices come ringing in: *Disgusting . . . Filthy . . . It makes me want to vomit . . . They ought to be gassed . . .*

But weirdness can have a distinctive beauty.

You climb the stairs in the Museum, past the Daughter of Rameses, to the Egyptian Room. Khafra, the Lord of Crowns, guards the door on his lion throne; the mummy man lies shrouded in rusty-red, marked with mysterious stains. And there's the mummified cat, the mummified fish, the mummified hawk, the awful black mummified hand and head. Art Deco lino on the floor; glass cases edged in glossy bottle-green — it's a fantasy Egypt, a perfect place.

The D'Auvergne Boxall Room at the Art Gallery is ranged with heroines: Daphne, Susanna, Queen Esther, the Finder of Moses, the Song-of-the-Shirt Seamstress — all done in marble. And, in glistening High Romance oil-paint, there are more of them: Forgiven, in her poppy-flower dress; Juliet, feigning death; Circe, 1890s vamp; Destiny, A Nymph, The Foam Sprite. And Holman Hunt's risen Christ flings off his bandages in a rainbow haze; while across the gallery He poses dewy-fresh, as Bouguereau's adorable Child.

Glimmers of blue glass are mixed up with the tidy jungle of the Botanic Garden's Tropical House. A midget Crystal Palace, it crowns a moon garden of aloe and agave and cactuses like giant penises and tea-cosies and bunny ears. The sacred lotus-leaf forest rises up about the bronze boy riding his swan; the wisteria arbour vaults you in green-glass shade. In the Rose Garden, bordered by Words of Love irises, ladies under sunshades make a slow, sniffing promenade. Sweet Repose, Angel Wings, Pink Chiffon, Hawaiian Sunset — the names of the Hybrid Teas sound like a roll-call of Elvis' greatest hits.

And there's the Beehive Corner with its beehive, West's Coffee Palace in Hindley Street, the East End Market, the West Terrace Cemetery, the Grand Postal Hall of the GPO and the Mortlock Library, both meticulously restored; the hotels: Botanic, Stag, Brecknock, Austral, Colonel Light . . . and so much more.

In the Maritime Museum at Port Adelaide, one of the most fascinating exhibits is the small treasure trove of objects retrieved from the sea beneath the Glenelg Jetty. Sovereigns and half-crowns; crescent moon and wishbone brooches; lockets and bracelets; opal and ruby and lucky-horseshoe rings, and LUCY spelt out on a gold ring. Suddenly the Victorian and Edwardian photo figures take on reality. She was a girl who wore LUCY on her finger, and walked the streets of the city that's ours today.

Lost Adelaide. In his marvellous, heartbreaking book of that name, Michael Burden catalogues so much of our heritage that's been destroyed. It's still happening in Adelaide proper, and in its suburbs. In 1973 I walked about the streets of Thebarton and Mile End, photographing those bits of the past I thought were beautiful: the Rosella Sauce parakeet on a grocery wall, Hardy's grand house with its lacework trim on the corner of Dew Street and the lane, tiny houses the Pioneers might have come out of in George Street, the old gasometer on the corner of Maria Street; Moran's Corner and Hook the bootmaker's and the Daisy Dell milkbar on the Beach Road . . . The Thebarton Primary School was being pulled down even then, and now everything on that list, and so many other buildings have gone, too. It's happening everywhere; particularly if the suburb is still working-class and untrendy.

Weird Adelaide. Generations and generations of working-class people, quite disappeared. No official bronze plaques on pavements for them. You only find them in the commonplace objects they left behind; and in sepia photographs and yellowing newspapers and old people's reminiscences. Folk heroes who are *Adelaide*, not some slick imitation of Anywhere. Not official worthies or the soufflé and shoulder-pads set, but people like Sticky Davis, friend of countless schoolchildren, who sold big round toffees flecked with flaked coconut, and the milk rock that was *Hindmarsh* rock from his shop on the Port Road. Or Sammy Lunn, popular patriotic worker, who regularly sang and danced on cinema steps to collect money for First War soldiers.

What we want now in Adelaide are writers and artists who work from the heart of those commonplace suburban streets, who recognise the weirdness of the ordinary, who record it before the version of it we have now is swept away. We want passion and intensity, an art that comes from places like Port Adelaide and Thebarton and Holden Hill; that stays unofficially weird.

Beginnings

I didn't plan to become a writer; writing took me by surprise. I was in London — Adelaide, where I'd grown up, was part of another world. I used to dream about it sometimes. Thebarton, the old working-class suburb of my childhood: galvanised iron fences with their trademark of a royal crown; backyards full of fruit trees oozing amber gum; lavatories covered in creeper, and in summer the pods of the lavatory creeper made a sharp cracking sound as seeds like miniature bullets flew out; Rose Street — my street, with the school on the corner and in winter in the schoolyard you could tread on the pepper tree's fallen pink berries and make rainbows in puddles. And the trams rattled past on the Beach Road; the stink of the gas-works was so near.

My father had died when I was a year old. I grew up with the mystery of his disappearance. By his absence, my father could never become ordinary, I couldn't take him for granted. Because he'd died I'd grown up in a household of women.

My mother wore her hair in a Victory roll and went away each day to be a commercial artist. My grandmother and her mongol sister, Reece, were left behind in the pebbledash house with the slippery red veranda, the fig tree, the quince tree, the lavatory creeper and the corrugated iron fence. My grandmother cut my lunch and I took it with me to school, but sometimes I'd come home at lunchtime; creep up on them, surprise them at the oval table by the window: Reece, with her leg tucked under her on the chair, stopping the blood; my grandmother, eating one-handed as she licked a finger and turned over a page of the *Advertiser*. Dipping cold meat in tomato sauce, they didn't know I was there. My grandmother's name was Iris Pearl, and Iris was the goddess of the rainbow; Reece was my great-aunt, older than my mother, yet she couldn't read or write, she stayed a child for ever. They were mine as I watched them like a voyeur. I stood so still by the door, and yet I'd run home from school. Under the pepper tree in the asphalt playground, it had suddenly seemed real that a day might come when they wouldn't be there.

I went to London in 1963 because I wanted to be an artist, and because it was the easiest way to escape Adelaide and a world where they always asked you what school you'd gone to and the proper people's names were down on the social page and the doctors' wives wore electric blue Thai silk and on Flower Day there was either a floral carpet or a floral map of South Australia in front of the War Memorial.

In London I was safe because I was no one. Letters from Adelaide were stamped with pictures of explorers, franked with mottoes like FIGHT BUSHFIRES or SERVE PART-TIME WITH THE CITIZEN MILITARY FORCE. They were messages from a place I'd left. Now I went to an art school in black stockings and a duffel coat (at the Teachers' College in Adelaide, duffel coats had been banned). Mods and Rockers and Buddy Holly got into my etchings. England kept feeling strange. My strongest sense of belonging came from the books I read. Writers, as much as artists, were heroes and friends, and now the places in my mind were different.

I went to Lawrence's Eastwood. And to his Zennor, where the gorse still "blazed in sheets of yellow fire" and the blackthorn was "like white smoke". Lawrence's cottage was still there; and Katherine's cottage, Katherine's tower. And over at St Ives was the far away, midget lighthouse.

Marianne Faithfull sang "Yesterday"; my grandmother died in January 1968. I was in London and she was in Adelaide. Her death didn't creep up on me as something inevitable I'd learnt to accept. It became reality in a swoop — it didn't stop hurting. Somehow, I'd thought she'd go on living for ever.

I started keeping a diary again. I wrote each day in an exercise book. The past was mixed up with the present; sometimes it seemed I was writing a letter to my grandmother, and I didn't want to remember, but I couldn't stop. I made lists of the old streets, of girls I'd been to school with. I was logical and remembered the kindergarten days first:

> Stealing a girl's net milk jug cover trimmed round the edge with glass beads . . .
>
> A girl had a Mickey Mouse book and I crept down to the cloakroom and hid behind the coats to read it, and was found out . . .
>
> Hating rusks and dropping them under other children's chairs so they'd get into trouble, not me. Hating Betty Brown pudding and waiting till last and putting my bowl under someone else's chair. . . .

I wasn't a writer, but the diaries piled up. If I lost one it was like losing a friend. The old life kept getting into them: the blundering furry moths and frail green flying insects round the veranda light; the billowing sleepout curtains . . . Reece, gathering up the tablecloth, shaking the crumbs away — standing tiptoe, showing her garters . . . my grandmother and Reece watching television and Reece stroking her sister's hands, leaning towards her in the room with its china baskets of flowers and china flamingoes, its carpet patterned with fern fronds. London, the great city, was all about me but, paradoxically, I was alone. That aloneness had got me free of other people's expectations. There weren't any restrictions in my mind; in a neutral country I didn't have to play out someone else's role for me.

Books had always been important. In the old days some of my favourites had been in a box in the shed at the bottom of the yard, mixed up with out-of-date *Women's Weekly*s and my mother's discarded clothes: row upon row of crisp Swiss guipure rosette lace frosting the dainty bodice; keyhole neckline, corseted waist, draped flared skirt and a flurry of cloud-white flowers and graceful fronds . . . There were my grandmother's and my great-grandfather's books: *The Girl's Own Annual* of 1911, *Trilby*, *Home Words for Heart and Hearth*. And Grandfather Goodridge's autograph album was there, as well, and he'd died when my mother was a baby. Death and the objects that represented people whose lives were like legends were mixed up with corrugated iron and bridesmaids fern and the rain drumming on the roof of the shed in winter.

That past was shut away inside me, and now in London I read Anaïs Nin and visited Eastwood and Haworth, and I couldn't stop reading Sylvia Plath and then I couldn't stop thinking about her suicide and took the book back to the shop. And I remembered in my diary how Reece's fingers were covered with chilblains in winter and the way her belly rattled. I was a child again, snapping off the Lorraine Lee rosebuds, pretending they were lipsticks . . . and Great-grandfather Collins rubbed his lizard-skin hands together and asked me what I had on under my dress, and the chocolate he gave me was sticky and melted.

The old world was gone from me physically, yet it was inside my body, hurting so much it had to get out. In June 1971, two days before an exhibition of my prints opened at a gallery in the Kings Road, I wrote:

> Decided to buy a typewriter last night. Would like to seriously put some of my writings together and see what comes out. I seem lately to be almost hurting with all the past things that want to be recorded in a truthful way.

In *Exchange & Mart* I found a secondhand red Olivetti Valentine typewriter advertised and bought it. I'd always been fascinated by material things as symbols, and now I had one. I'd just stopped teaching at an art school, and for the next six months I sat down every day and wrote about my childhood in Adelaide. I didn't worry about definitions (were the words making a novel?); I was just writing what I had to; I had a sense of my own responsibility to myself. I didn't know any writers who were alive in the flesh; I stopped telling people what I was doing when most of them were cynical and said I should stick to making my prints. My isolation gave me strength — it made the dream of what I was trying to do more valid.

Dead, my grandmother set me free to write, and I planted her in her garden amongst the fuchsias and Easter daisies and the pink lilies you call naked ladies. I saw her silvery hair snagged with rose thorns, her legs marbled with varicose veins, her big belly that was always wet on wash-day; she was there tending Reece, her eternal child — cutting her toenails, poking at the wax in her ears with a bobbypin. I wrote on and on. Sometimes I felt I was smothering in layers of silence, and it seemed impossible it would ever be finished, and though I wrote of heatwaves the days were always grey and outside the window the blurred cars went past, and I wondered if anyone would ever read what I was writing. The words were always in my head, they started talking to me as I slept. I was scared it'd be rejected and my typewriter broke down.

I did finish it and someone told me of an agent, and when she asked me which writers I admired I mentioned Virginia Woolf, so she sent it to Chatto & Windus because they were linked with the Hogarth Press. It was published in 1973 as *The Scent of Eucalyptus*.

Thinking consciously now, about what I did so unconsciously then, I think the book succeeds, reaches out to so many people whose backgrounds are different to my own, because of its sense of place. I believe that if you can be particular enough — get close enough to your setting and characters and write about them with enough care and honesty and love or hate, the writing jumps free of you, and becomes universal. The fake barriers fall down. Your people become other people's, your place becomes someone else's. You write about Thebarton, but you could also be writing about a place in a Greek myth.

I went on to write a group of novels that are a blend of fantasy and realism, set in a more distant past than my own. Because of this distancing, I might have been writing science fiction; I could create my own worlds. Yet nostalgia for Australia fuels all these books; their grotesques owe as much to Reece as to Flannery O'Connor; many of the female characters reflect my own obsessions. Though *The Albatross Muff* has as its setting a Dickensian London of the 1860s, its heroine shares my own sense of being an outsider and my own interior search for a dead father. *Where the Queens All Strayed* is set in the Adelaide Hills in 1907 and was written after a visit to South Australia when I discovered relatives of my own in those same Hills. *The Peach Groves* is set in an exotic New Zealand of the 1880s — a dream place that owes as much to my admiration for the work of Katherine Mansfield as to any real country. *The Frangipani Gardens* and *Dove* were both written after I returned to live in Adelaide. It was my writing that drew me back to the city I thought I'd left for good twelve years before. I felt with Janet Frame that: "If a writer lives in exile and writes for ever of his native land, his work may fail to develop and mature, or it may be restricted to a narrow period of memory."

I'd been away so long that I wasn't familiar with a great chunk of Australian women's writing. I discovered Mary Gilmore, writing in the thirties of a scented land remembered by her own grandmother — a time when the hills and shores of Sydney Cove were sheets of flowers; Eve Langley, that extraordinary original, dreaming among the gum trees of Oscar Wilde in silk knee breeches; Barbara Baynton, whose dark landscapes cut through the sepia sentimentalities of the traditional bush values of mateship.

In Adelaide I returned to Thebarton. The old suburb was still the same: down at heel, working-class — though the gas-works had gone, and a Greek church stood beside our old house in Rose Street, and there were Vietnamese families in Dew Street where my grandfathers had lived. Without meaning to, I wrote — once again, because I *had* to — *Kewpie Doll*, an autobiographical novel that continued on from *The Scent of Eucalyptus*.

My life had turned full circle; I was back to my beginnings. And out of that returning grew a sense of solidarity with the generations of working-class women who'd gone before me. Their counterparts were still there in the narrow streets off the Port Road — women whose imagination hadn't been educated out of them, whose everyday language was an off-hand poetry.

I didn't feel the enormous themes were the big things of history; on the contrary, an aunty could be a hero. I felt nothing could be bigger than getting down very small and recording the life of one obscure woman, who would stand for all those other women whose lives had vanished. I wanted to write out of the language of women like my grandmother, to set down a culture that would soon be gone for ever. Out of many long conversations grew the novel, *Annie Magdalene*.

I wanted to get behind the silences kept in place by social shame — in Adelaide, Thebarton is still the other side of the tracks. I didn't want to look at Annie sideways; to send her up, examine her from the point of view of someone who'd got away. I wanted to stare at her straight on, to merge with her, to *be* Annie. And so my "I" became Annie's, I was writing *her* language through *her* imagination.

It was the hardest book I'd written. I had to keep my own sensibilities out of it — to think not as myself but as my character. Annie's great strength was her certainty, her lack of questioning — I couldn't write as I usually did and hedge along in a web of nuances, I had to cut out the subtleties; I was continually paring down, as I tried to fashion a written style that would mirror the freshness of memory. For writing is different to speech; once spoken words are written down they often lose their potency. I felt like a translator as I laboured away ordering the random patchwork of memory — innocent and coarse, figured and unfinished — into some sort of chronology.

I wanted to record the life of an unknown woman to whom none of what others regarded as important had happened (Annie had never married, she wasn't over-sexed, she'd never had IT). I wanted to do what the black women writers of the United States were doing: write against stereotypes and record the particularities of a working-class woman: Annie Magdalene — button-sewer at the Perfection Shirt Factory, self-employed dressmaker, aircraft worker at Holdens, butter-packer at the Co-op — singing to her fowls, laying out her dead mother, off with her girlfriend to Kangaroo Island, talking to the bees on her daisy bush.

Childhood

"People like to label my writing Gothic, but it's not at all because there's an earthiness . . . it's real; reality is there all the time." So the mystical, the "freakish", the antiquarian aspects of her novels are rooted in Hanrahan's real world. Experiences from her childhood are startlingly vivid still, like the excursions to her grandmother's family in the Hills: "the smells and everything. And you could always see the Hills anywhere you were in Adelaide, so you could always see this other world . . . the house I lived in (at Mile End) was magical too. I look at it now and it's ordinary but it was the most beautiful house . . . the sharp gravel path and the lilies at the side where everything was damp and never grew properly."

This recall of her own child-perspective of the world is central to Hanrahan's writing: "You find with people the only real part of them is the part that stayed a child, and that part is always there though it may be hidden. If you really know someone it's the child that you know and you've got to be a child as you write; that's the only way. When I write freshly is when I write as a child looking at things. It's another-worldly view . . . someone who stays fresh and isn't labelled. Though you could find children who were like old people when they were ten."

On the other hand, some elderly people are a constant source of information and insight for Barbara Hanrahan. "I visit very often a cousin of my grandmother's who's eighty-seven and lives in the Adelaide Hills. His mind is like a boy's. He's a boy of fifteen, all the time he talks . . . you could use the words that he says straight because they make poetry.

"For *Dove* I put an advertisement in the paper saying I would like to hear from people who could remember Adelaide, Thebarton and Hindmarsh, from 1893 to 1932, because out of talking to them I might get one tiny detail like someone remembering their mother taking them to the seaside and scalding milk and using the cream to rub on so that they wouldn't get sunburnt."

And if the mass of detail of old world gardens, medicines and cures, dress and food are real for Hanrahan so, too, is the seemingly surreal vision of the world experienced by some of her characters. She refutes the term "supernatural" for these people and says they are "the real people" of her books, like Tom (in *The Frangipani Gardens*) ". . . I think of him as a mystic whereas people labelled him as an epileptic . . . I just thought of him as someone who pretended that his mysticism was a fit." She acknowledges a similarity here with some of Janet Frame's work and with some of Patrick White's characters. "My people are nicer . . . cleaner sort of people" than White's.

She continued: "It's the rational thing that makes my fantasy world. I find that something like a Margaret Drabble novel worries me because it seems fantastic, it makes me feel uneasy and I start to worry that I can't fit into that world . . . it's a traumatic experience for me."

So is the business of reading Australian reviews of her novels, usually. "I get reviews that call me 'Barbara' or 'our Barbara' and that's patronising; they make me sound twee, and then people annoy me . . . they take a dreadful bland view that this is just a book about erotic things happening to people; they might not understand that although the background settings are often quite realistic the characters set against them are not meant to be three-dimensional people. I want them to be like strange cut-outs striding along, almost like giants . . . that's something people are too lazy to think about . . . that's when I start to think that Australia's soft mentally; I lose my own Australia, I just see this soft thing like a soft-boiled egg and it's so pathetic. It makes me feel ill physically . . . It doesn't hurt the writer part of me but it hurts the human part."

Beverley Farmer

EDITOR'S NOTE

Beverley Farmer's first novel *Alone* (McPhee Gribble/Penguin) was published in 1980; her first and award-winning collection of stories, *Milk* (McPhee Gribble/Penguin), was published in 1983. *Home Time* (McPhee Gribble/Penguin, 1985) is her second collection of short stories.

"A Woman with Black Hair", "Home Time" and "Place of Birth" were originally published in *Home Time* (McPhee Gribble/Penguin, 1985), pp.53-60, 71-80, 1-25; "Letter to Judith Brett" was published in *Meanjin* 43, i (1986): 142, when Beverley Farmer wrote to the editor of *Meanjin* in response to an article in the preceding issue by Kerryn Goldsworthy, "Feminist Writings, Feminist Readings: Recent Australian Writing by Women", *Meanjin* 44, iv (1985): 506-15; and "Literature Is What Is Taught" is an extract from an interview with Jennifer Ellison in *Rooms of Their Own*, ed. Ellison (Penguin, 1986), pp.115-29.

Place of Birth

On the last day Bell will remember before the snow, on a blue-grey morning of high cloud, the old woman brings out a *tapsi* rolling with walnuts that she has cracked for the Christmas *baklava*. "We'll be shut in soon enough," she sighs, perching on a plaited stool under the grapevine with the *tapsi* on her lap. Bell, her son Grigori's wife, pulls up stools for herself and Chloe, the other daughter-in-law, the Greek one who has come to the village for Christmas; her husband's ship is at sea. The women huddle over the *tapsi* picking out and dropping curled walnuts here, shells there. Chloe's little girl, Sophoula, leans on her mother.

"Me too?" she murmurs.

"Go ahead."

Sophoula, biting her lips, scowls over her slow fingers. With a trill of laughter Chloe pops a walnut into the child's mouth. "My darling! Eat," she says.

"Don't tell me she has nuts at her age?" the old woman says. "You'll choke the child."

"Mama, she's three." Chloe's face and neck turn red.

"Just the same —"

"Oh, I don't like it!" Sophoula spits and dribbles specks of walnut. The shelling goes on; under their bent heads Chloe and the old woman put on a fierce burst of speed. Suddenly all of them flare bright with sunlight and are printed over with black branches and coils of the grapevine as a gap opens in the cloud. Bell leaps to her feet and lumbers inside.

"What's wrong with you?" Chloe frowns.

"Nothing. I'm getting my camera."

"*Aman*. Always photographs," her mother-in-law sighs.

"It's too cold to sit out here," Chloe says.

"Oh, please," Bell wails from the window. "All stay where you are!"

But the gap in the cloud has closed over by the time she gets back, so that what she will always have is a photograph all cold blues, whites, greys and browns: brittle twigs and branches against walls and clouds, the washing hung along the wire, a white hen pricking holes in mud that mirrors her, and the three heads, black, brown and bone-white, suspended over the *tapsi* of walnuts.

Because she takes all the photographs, she won't find herself in any of them.

Six weeks ago, as soon as she knew for certain, Bell wrote to her parents that they would be grandparents some time in May. "You're the first to know," she added, though by the time the letter got to Australia the whole village probably knew. There's no hope now of an answer until after Christmas. But at noon the postman's motorcycle roars past, a fountain of mud in his wake, and stops at the village office, so she wanders down just in case and is handed an Australian aerogram. It has taken a month to get here and is one she will mark with a cross and keep as long as she lives.

Grandma and Grand Pop, eh, scrawls her father. *And about time too. Tell Greg to take that grin off his face.*

"Are they pleased, Bella?" The old woman is kneading the pastry for the *baklava*. Her arms are floured to the shoulders.

"Of course. Dad says, 'And about time too.' "

"No wonder! Considering that you're thirty-one —"

"Thirty —"

"— or will be when it's born."

"Hasten slowly." Bell reads her mother's exclamatory, incoherent half-page, laboriously copied, then goes back to her father's.

It's been three years. You could leave it too late, you know, Bell. With a bub and all that you could find yourselves tied down before you know it. It's hard to think we mightn't live to see our only grandchild. Mum's been having dizzy turns again lately.

*She's had one stroke, as you know. If money's the problem, I can
help you there. Also book you into the Queen Vic or wherever
you like.*

"What else, Bella?"

"Oh, questions. Money, hospitals. All that."

"Surely you're booked into the Kliniki?" Chloe stares.

"No, not yet."

"Well, you'd better do it soon! You don't want to have it in the
Public Hospital! *They* have women in labour two to a bed in the
corridors, it's so crowded."

"I think I want to have it at home," Bell hears herself say.

"At home!" Kyria Sophia is delighted. "Why not? I had all mine
here. Grigori was born in the room you sleep in!"

"It wouldn't be safe." Chloe raises her eyebrows. "Not with a
first child. Anything can go wrong."

"Thank you, Chloe."

"It's the truth. Look what happened to the *papas's* daughter!"

"The *papas's* daughter? You know why that happened? She got
a craving for fried bananas in the middle of the night and her husband wouldn't go and try to find her any. And sure enough —"

"Mama, the cord got round her baby's neck and strangled it."

"Mama, not because of the bananas!"

"You're both fools! Of course it was because of the bananas!"
The old woman rams a grey branch into the firebox of the *somba*.
"*Aman!* How come I'm the only one who ever stokes the fire?"
She brushes a wisp of hair out of her eyes and flours her face.
White like her hair and arms, it sags into its net of wrinkles.

Lunch, Bell's chore today, isn't ready when the old man comes in
from the *kafeneion* and finds her alone in the kitchen. Kyria
Sophia has taken Sophoula with her to the baker to leave the
baklava, Chloe is at a neighbour's place with the baby. He sits by
the *somba*, small and grey and muddy, rolling and smoking one
fat cigarette after another. The *makaronia* have to be boiled to a
mush, Bell knows, before she can toss them in oil and butter and
crumble *feta* cheese over them. Kyria Sophia comes back

exhausted hand-in-hand with Sophoula and as if the day's work wasn't enough, now she has her to spoonfeed.

They eat the *makaronia* in silence. At every mouthful a twinge, a jab of pain drills through Bell's jaw. Not a toothache, please, she prays. Not now, not here.

Sophoula pushes the spoon and her grandmother's hand away. "Yiayia! You have to tell a story!"

"What story?" sighs the old woman.

"A story about princesses."

"Eat up and then I will."

"Now!" Sophoula bats the spoon on to the floor. The old woman gets another one and shovels cold lumps into the child's mouth, chanting a story by heart. Whenever she falters, the child clamps her mouth shut. Bell, stacking the dishes, isn't really listening, but when the bowl is almost empty she exclaims aloud in English, "Snow White! No, Snow White and Rose Red!"

The old woman giggles. "Zno Quaeet," she mocks. "No Zno Quaeet End —"

"Yiayia, *pes!*"

"*Aman*, Sophoula!"

"*Pes.*" She spits into the bowl.

After lunch these days Bell sleeps until it's dark. Now that she is into her fifth month she is sleepy most of the time. From under the white *flokati* she can hear Grigori's voice (so he is back from Thessaloniki with the shopping) and then Kyria Sophia's shrill one. When she wakes properly, ready for another long yellow evening by the *somba*, he is still there in the kitchen finishing a coffee. So is Chloe, red from her sleep, with the baby at her breast. "Hullo," Bell says, kissing Grigori's woolly crown. She fumbles with the *briki*.

"Coffee again?" Chloe mutters.

"Just one to wake me up."

"It's so bad for the baby."

"One won't hurt."

"Oh well, you'd know."

Bell turns her back to light the gas. "Where are the old people?" She touches Grigori's shoulder.

"Milking." His father's grey head grins in at the window; he leaves the milk saucepans on the sill. "You got a letter, Mama said. Are Mum and Dad all right?"

"Yes, they send their love and congratulations." Bell rubs her jaw. There's a hollow ache in her back teeth. She empties the sizzling *briki* into a little cup and takes a furry sip of her hot coffee. The *baklava* is on the table, baked and brought home already, its pastry glossy with the syrup it's soaking in. Grigori's shopping is all around it: oranges in net bags, chestnuts, a blue can of olive oil, lemons and mandarines and — she can hardly believe it — six yellow-green crescent bananas blue-stamped *Chiquita*. "Oh, bananas! Oh, darling, thank you!" she cries out. "We were just talking about bananas!"

"I'm so extravagant," Chloe simpers, "but Sophoula simply loves them. So I gave Grigori the money to buy her some." Her eyes dare Bell to ask for one. A pregnant woman can ask even strangers in the street for food. Bell grins at Chloe, remembering her frying mussels one day in Thessaloniki when a pregnant neighbour squealed from a balcony, "Ach, Kyria Chloe! Mussels! I can smell them!" and Chloe had to let her have a couple. "She never smells anything cheap," Chloe grumbled to Bell.

"Is that so, Kyria Chloe?" Bell contents herself with saying. "Ah, so much lovely food. We'll never eat it."

"*You* won't." The old woman comes in and lifts the milk saucepans inside. "*Aman*, the cold!" She slams the window. "*You* won't eat. You're fading, look at you. White as snow."

"I *will*. That was when I had morning sickness."

"We don't want a kitten, you know, we want a big strong baby."

"Believe you me," Chloe mutters, "the bigger it is, the harder it comes out."

"Ah, *bravo*, Chloe, *bravo*!" The old woman clatters the saucepans, straining the warm milk. "Don't you crave anything, Bella? You must crave something."

"Why must she?"

"Well, to tell the truth, I'd love a banana," says Bell. "It seems like years! Can I buy one from you, Chloe?"

"I'm sorry. There aren't enough."

"We share in this house, Chloe! If you want a banana, Bella, you have one! Don't even ask!"

"No, no, it's all right."

Grigori stands up. "See you later," he says. He grabs a mandarine and saunters outside.

"Not to the *kafeneion* already?" his mother pleads. "You just got here." She stares bleakly after him. "And what would you expect?" She rounds on her daughters-in-law. "Doesn't a man have a right to peace and quiet?"

"Auntie?" Chloe has taught Sophoula this English word. "Auntie Bella? Do they have Christmas where you come from?"

"Yes, of course."

"Did you go to church?"

"No."

"You stayed home at Christmas!"

"We went to the beach," Bell says.

"At Christmas! You're funny, Auntie!"

"Funny, am I?" Bell crosses her eyes. With a giggle, Sophoula sits in her lap.

"Where's your baby?"

"You're sitting on it. Oh, poor baby."

"What's its name going to be?"

"I don't know. What's your baby's name going to be?"

"We won't know till he's been christened."

"Oh, no, I forgot."

"If it's a girl, they'll call it after Yiayia," Chloe interposes. "The same as we did with you."

"Good idea. I'll call my baby Yiayia."

"Auntie, you can't!"

"Why can't I? Not if it's a boy, you mean?" Bell winks. "Then I'll call it Pappou," and she is rewarded with a peal of laughter so loud that it wakes the old woman.

"Let's eat, Mama," Chloe says.

"Is it late?" She blinks, squinting in the light. "The men'll be home any minute."

"No, they won't." Bell lifts Sophoula down. "Can we eat the *baklava* now? I crave *baklava*."

"Oh. All right." Smiling in spite of herself, Kyria Sophia cuts her a dripping slice. As Bell bites into it, the ache that has been lying in wait all day drills through her tooth and she shrieks aloud, letting syrup and specks of walnut dribble down her chin. She swills water round her mouth. The women cluck and fluster. Sophoula clings to her mother in tears of fright. The old woman mixes Bell an aspirin and she gulps it. She is helped to bed, where she curls up moaning in the darkness under the *flokati*. The light flashes on once, twice. She lies still until the door quietly closes.

Grigori is undressing with the light on. Bell rubs her watery eyes. The ache is duller now.

"Were you asleep? How's the tooth?"

"Bad." She probes with her tongue.

He turns off the light and lies on his back with one cold arm against her. "What's all this about having the baby here at home?"

"No! I'd be terrified."

"Mama said you said you wanted to."

"No. She misunderstood. I meant — I just feel — I want to go home and have it." She holds her breath. "Home to Australia."

"How come?"

"Oh. Mum and Dad. You know. Mostly, I suppose. Yes."

"We can't afford the fares."

"One way, we can. Dad said they'd help."

"Ah. One way? I see."

The moon must have risen. In the hollow glow through the shutters the *flokati* looks like a fall of snow on rough ground. "I wonder if it'll snow for Christmas?" she says. "It didn't the other times."

He snorts. "You spring a thing like this on me. What I might feel — you couldn't care less, could you! I wanted to stay in Australia three years ago, but no, you uprooted us, you — *felt* —

you had to go and live in Greece. And now what? Come along, doggy, I want to go home. To Australia!"

She takes a shaky breath. "I feel guilty, I suppose. They're old, they're not well. 'You could leave it too late,' Dad said."

"You know what a pessimist he is. You used to joke about it."

"Can we bank on it, though?" She ploughs on. "It's not as if it would be for ever."

"It might."

"We can always come back."

"Always, can we? Backwards and forwards." He turns his back to her. "I'll need to think it over. I'm tired."

"There's not much time. We've got till the end of February. That's when my smallpox vaccination expires. I can't have another one while I'm pregnant and I can't enter Australia without it."

Lying along his back, she feels him tightening against her. The nape of his neck is damp and has his hot smell. Once he pelted her down a sand dune and was out of sight in the white waves when the hot smell from him buffeted her face. That was at Christmas.

We went to the beach at Christmas when I was little, she remembers. On Phillip Island we had dinner at the guesthouse and then Dad and I followed a track called Lovers' Walk — there was a board nailed up, Lovers' Walk — to look for koalas as they awoke in the trees. First we walked down the wooden pier where men and their sons were fishing. Red water winding and hollowing. Crickets fell silent when I walked in the tea-tree. After sunset the waves were grey and clear rolling and unrolling shadows on the sand. The trees, black now, still had their hot smell.

Some time in the early hours the toothache jerks her out of sleep. Grigori breathes on deeply. Tossing, feverish, close to tears, she stumbles to the kitchen for an aspirin and Chloe, passing through to the lavatory annexe, sees and scolds her. "You shouldn't take any medicines now," she says.

"One little aspirin!" Bell's smile is a snarl.

"Any medicine at all."

"I have a toothache!"

"Still, for the baby's sake."

Bell turns and gulps it down. Back in bed the pain is relentless, it drills into her brain. After an hour, two, of whimpering in her sweat she creeps back to the kitchen and in a flash of bilious light swallows down three more aspirins. No one catches her. In the passage she trips over Sophoula's potty, which they leave outside their door until morning. Splashing away over cold urine, she lets it lie where it fell. Grigori is snoring. "Turn over," she hisses in Greek, and he turns.

A rooster calls, the same one as every morning, then hens, then a crow, so loud that it must be in the yard. How long since she last heard a gull? It must be only a couple of weeks. When was the last time she was in Thessaloniki? Gulls are as common as pigeons in the city. It seems like years.

What does tea-tree smell like in summer?

Their bedroom is white and takes up one corner of the house and of the street, 21st of April Street these days, in honour of the Colonels' coup. The two-roomed school that Grigori went to is opposite. They are on one of the busiest crossroads in the village. All through Christmas Day, Boxing Day and the next day Bell sleeps and wakes to the uproar of tractors, donkeys, carol-singers, carts, trucks with loud-speakers bellowing in her windows. Snow falls. She sits sipping milk at the family table in her pyjamas, staggers to the lavatory annexe and back to her cooling hollow under the *flokati*. She coughs. Her head pulsates. She loses count of how many aspirins. The toothache goes through her in waves. Sweat soaks her pyjamas and sheets and Kyria Sophia dries them again by the *somba*. Grigori takes refuge for two nights at his cousin Angelo's place behind the bakery. Children throwing snowballs yell and swear. The baby wails. From time to time Sophoula opens Bell's door, but slams it in panic when Bell stirs to see who it is. Chloe keeps away in case she and the children catch something. Kyria Sophia comes and sits at the end of the bed crocheting with a pan of hot coals at her feet.

Penicillin, somebody suggests, a shot of penicillin, there's a woman down the street who's qualified. Bell says yes, oh yes, please. Chloe is appalled. But no one ever comes to give the injection. Time has broken down. Sand slides shifting under the scorched soles of her feet. The scream of a gull makes her slip and clutch at the stringy trunk of a tea-tree, but it must be the grapevine. No, she is flat on her back, she is clutching the *flokati* when her eyes open. It looks like snow on rough ground. That scream comes again and it's the baby screaming, Chloe's baby though, not her own, that she can hear, then all the sounds of hushing and commotion as he sobs, then whimpering and quiet.

One morning she wakes and is well, clear-headed, free of toothache and of fever. She opens the windows but the shutters won't move. She is weak, look, trembling. But it's not that: snow is heaped on the sill. She patters to the door and stares down the white street. The sun is rising behind white roofs and trees, turning the snow sand-yellow, shading in the printed feet of birds and a stray dog. The stringy grapevine has grown spindles of ice.

Stooped panting over buckets and *tapsia* of water, she spends the day washing her stiff, sour clothes and her hair, stuck in yellow strings to her head by now; and sitting with hair and clothes spread out to dry by the *somba*. She would love a bath, but not in the dank ice-chamber that the lavatory annexe has become. For one thing, other people are always wanting to get in. And in any case, it's not as if they'll notice whether she does or not, not even Grigori: for fear of a miscarriage, now that she has finally conceived they don't make love. She's well again, she won't risk catching cold. She wraps a scarf over her mouth whenever she goes outside. Now and then a twinge through her tooth alarms her, but the rivetting ache is gone.

Every day there is washing and cooking of which she does her share. When the sun is out she walks around the village photographing crystals and shadows, tufty snow and smooth. The narrowed river is crinkled, slow, with white domes on its rocks. Ovens in the deserted yards have a cap of snow over two sooty airvents and stare back at the camera like ancient helmets. White hens are invisible except for their jerking legs and combs. The storks' nest is piled high; it could be a linen basket up on top of the church tower. In the schoolyard a snowman has appeared — no, a snow woman two metres tall in a widow's scarf and a cloak of sacking under which her great round breasts and belly glisten naked.

She takes photographs of the snow woman and of children hiding to throw snowballs and of the *papas* as he flaps by, his hair and beard like a stuffing of straw that has burst out of his black robes. The family and the neighbours line up for portraits under the grey grapevine. The old man leads the cows out of the barn and poses for her standing between them on the soiled snow while they shift and blink in the light, mother and daughter.

"You can show them to your parents," he says. So all the family knows that she is going home. No one talks about it.

She takes time exposures in the blue of evening as the windows in the houses light up and throw their long shapes on the snow outside. As often as not, Kyria Sophia, Chloe, Grigori, even the old man, can be found in one or other of the rooms, the little golden theatres, that Bell used to love being in. Now she knows the sets, the characters, the parts too well. She would rather stay home alone; she is quite happy babysitting. Having read her own few books too often, she reads Sophoula's story books about princesses. If Sophoula wakes, Bell reads aloud with the warm child in her lap. When the old man comes in they roast chestnuts on top of the *somba* until the others come. They listen in to the clandestine broadcasts on Deutsche Welle, which he calls Dolce Vita: these are banned by the Junta and the penalty for listening could be imprisonment, could be torture. He has enemies who would report him if they knew. "The walls have ears," he growls, the radio pressed to his grey head; he is hard of hearing himself. His wrinkles are so deep that they pull his hooded eyes into a slant and his lips into a perpetual smile around his cigarette.

On New Year's Eve Kyria Sophia announces that she is too tired even to dream of making the family *vassilopita*. "Thank goodness my nephew's the baker," she says. "Angelo says he'll bring us one."

Chloe fluffs up her hair. "My mother always makes ours."

"It's a lot of bother for nothing, if you ask me!" snaps the old woman. "Who appreciates it? Look at all my *baklava* that none of you will eat!"

"Mama, it's a wonderful *baklava*!" Bell hugs her.

"You say that. Eat some then."

"And what about my tooth?"

"*Aman*, that woman!" Bell hears her whisper to Grigori. "I could wring her neck," meaning Chloe, or so Bell hopes.

Then to her further exasperation the old woman looks everywhere and can't find the *flouri*, the lucky coin that she hides in each year's *vassilopita*. Bell gives her the lucky sixpence that she brought from home, the one her mother used to put in the plum pudding.

After dinner, while Grigori and his father are still at the *kafeneion*, Angelo and his mother, Aunt Magdalini, arrive with the *vassilopita*. An elderly doll in long skirts, she falls asleep by the *somba*, steam rising from her woollen socks. Bell wakes her to eat a floury *kourabie*, and again to drink coffee. Angelo has ouzo. It blurs his sharp brown features, so like Grigori's, and makes him jocular.

"What can you see out there, Bella?" She turns from the window. "Your man coming home?"

"The moon rising."

"*Fengaraki mou lambro*," recites Sophoula proudly.

"Good! What comes next?"

"*Fexe mou na perpato!*"

"I'll give you twenty drachmas," Angelo drawls, "if you can tell me what the moon's made of."

"Rock?"

"You lost. It's a snowball, silly. It was thrown so high it can't ever come back to earth."

Sophoula's jaw drops. "Who threw it?"

"Guess." He scratches the black wool on his head.

"A giant?"

"*I* think a bear. There's one up the mountain. There were tracks up there the other day. The hunters are out after her."

"The poor bear!"

He peers out the window. "That's not her in the schoolyard, is it? A huge white bear?"

"Silly." She giggles. "That's only the snow woman."

"The snow woman, is it?" hisses Angelo. "So that's who threw the moon up there!" and Sophoula screams in terror.

Kyria Sophia glares up over her glasses. "God put the moon there."

"Supposing she comes alive at night time? Supposing she comes and stares in all the windows while we're asleep?"

"No, no!" Sophoula clamps herself to Bell. "Auntie, make him stop it!"

"Angelo, please?"

"Of course she doesn't!" cries Kyria Sophia. "Aren't you ashamed to put an idea like that in the child's head?"

The door bursts open on Chloe red-faced and turbulent. "You'll wake the baby! Can't I leave you alone here for one minute?" She drags the child by the arm into their room. There they both stay until Angelo and Aunt Magdalini have gone and Grigori and his father are home for the midnight ceremony of cutting the *vassilopita*. Then Chloe sidles sullenly in with her black hair stuck to cheeks still red with sleep or crying. "Sophoula will have to miss it. She's asleep," she mutters.

The old man, as head of the household, carefully divides the loaf. He sets aside a piece for the church and then for every member of the family, present and absent. The lucky sixpence turns up in Chloe's baby's piece, as it was bound to, and they all pretend surprise. Bell stuffs the sweet bread into the safe side of her mouth. Next New Year, she knows, wherever they all are by then, the *flouri* or the sixpence will turn up in her child's piece.

The New Year card games at the *kafeneion* will go on all night. Grigori walking back is a shadow among other shadows that the moon makes in the snow.

On New Year's Day no bus comes to the village. The road in has been declared dangerous because the two narrow wooden bridges that it crosses are thick with frozen snow. No buses until further notice, bellows the village loudspeaker. People grumble. This happens every winter and every winter the government promises a new road. The mountain villages are worse off, of course;

they'll be snowed in for weeks, not just a few days. Still, since no one has a car, everyone is trapped here while it lasts, except Angelo with his bread van.

Angelo goes on delivering his bread around the villages using chains, risking unmade tracks on hills and across fields to bypass the bridges. Grigori has been joining him lately for the sake of the ride and the company; now he goes on every trip in case Angelo strikes trouble and needs a hand. But Angelo won't take anyone else. "It's not legal," he tells everyone, "and it's not safe." He broke his rule twice last year, he says, and look what happened. The old man that he took to the district hospital in the back of the van survived; but the woman in labour? She lost her baby when the van hit a buried rock miles from anywhere and broke an axle. "Never again, not for a million drachmas," he says. "Don't ask me."

So that evening Bell and Chloe, sitting by the small *somba* in Chloe's room with the work done and the children asleep, are thunderstruck when Kyria Sophia — who has made herself scarce all day — puts her head round the door to announce that by the way she and Grigori are off first thing in the morning to Thessaloniki to see her other grandchildren. Angelo is giving them a lift.

"She can't do that!" Chloe cries out, and follows her into the kitchen. "You can't do that!" Bell hears.

"What? What can't I do?"

"What about *me*?"

"What about you?"

"I brought the children all this way to visit you and it wasn't easy on the bus and now you take it into your head to go off to Thessaloniki just like that and —"

"Look, when I need you to tell *me* what —"

"— And leave us stranded here!"

"What would you do there, anyway?" Kyria Sophia shouts. "Your husband's away at sea for two more weeks!"

"I happen to live there. *Your* husband's here, remember? How will he feel if you go? This is your house, it's not mine. I could have gone to my own village for Christmas and New Year when they begged me to. *My* mother —"

"You're a married woman. It's your duty to come to us."

"Duty? Oh, duty? What about your duty, then? Aren't *you* a married woman?"

"You dare to talk to me like —"

"Mama, you have *no right* —"

"Get out of my kitchen, Chloe. You say one more word and I swear I'll hit you. I'll hit you!"

Chloe strides into the room where Bell and now Sophoula too are listening in horror; she slams the door behind her. Thuds and crashes of glass hit the wall between them.

"*Oriste mas! Oriste mas!*" come her shrieks. "Now *she'll* tell *me* if I can go or not, will she? Twenty-five years old! *She'll* tell *me* what I can and can't do?"

"Mama, what's Yiayia saying?" Sophoula whimpers.

"Never you mind. She's wicked. She doesn't love you or any of us." Chloe bites her lips. "Let the old bitch howl," she mutters. "She would have slapped my face in there! She knows she's in the wrong."

The outside door slams and they jump. Footsteps splash past the shuttered window. The three of them creep to their beds. Bell is still wide awake when at last Grigori comes in and starts undressing in the dark.

"Grigori?"

"You're awake, are you? What happened here? Mama's in a frenzy. She's beside herself."

"She had a fight with Chloe."

"And you?"

"Me? No! I stayed out of it."

"You didn't try to stop her."

"As soon try stopping a train! If Chloe wants a fight, I suppose that's her business, isn't it?"

"If she fights with her own mother it's her business. If she fights with mine it's my business and yours and all the family's."

"So I should have stopped her."

"You were there." He has slid into bed without touching her. "And your place in the family gives you the right."

"Because I'm older than Chloe?"

"No. Because I'm the older brother and you're my wife."

"Oh. I think Chloe was right to be upset. Is it fair of Mama to go off and leave us like this?"

"One more day of Chloe, she says, and she'll go mad."

"Chloe's hard to take. It's the children. They tire her out, you see."

"Mama does everything."

"No, she doesn't. Chloe pulls her weight. I'm here all day and I know."

"*You* know! You live in a world of your own! Chloe pulls her weight, does she? And what about you?"

"Tell me, what do the men do here while the women are pulling their weight? Play cards in the *kafeneion*? Stroll around Thessaloniki? If it comes to that, I'm the one who really needs to go. If I don't get to a dentist, I might lose this tooth."

"Nice timing."

"For every child a tooth, they say. It's to do with lack of calcium."

She feels him shrug. "Drink more milk."

"I'm awash with milk already. Milk won't fill a rotten tooth, though, will it?"

"Well, bad luck," he says wearily. "It's stopped aching, hasn't it? There'll be a bus soon anyway, go on that. The fact is Angelo only has room for two and he needs me."

"Well, let *me* come, then! Explain to Mama!"

"*You* explain to Mama." He waits for her to think that over. "Why all this fuss, I wonder?"

"You're going and leaving me here."

"It's not as if it's for ever, is it?"

"Oh, that's it. I see. You want revenge."

"You're happy to go off to Australia and leave me here."

"Happy? I'm hoping you'll come."

"It's more than hoping, I think. It's closer to force."

They are lying rigidly side by side on their backs and neither moves. "You'd be taking my child with you."

She snorts. "Not much choice at this stage!"

"No. There's not. So I want you to wait."

"I can't, I told you. My smallpox vaccination."

"I know that! I mean wait till after it's born."

She opens her eyes wide in the darkness, so suddenly alarmed that she thinks he will hear the blood thumping through her. "No, I'd be trapped here then," she dares to say.

"Trapped!"

"Besides, the whole point is to be home with Mum and Dad before the birth. And then come back. If you want."

"*Why*? Why does it matter *where* you are for the birth?"

"It just does," she mutters. "I'll feel safer there."

"You're a stubborn, selfish, cold-blooded woman, Bell. You always have been and you always will be."

"Always?"

"You want your own way in everything. Well, you're not getting it."

Calming herself, she strokes the long arch of her belly, fingering the navel which has turned inside out and then the new feathery line of dark hair down to her groin. Once or twice a flutter inside her has made her think the baby has quickened, but it might have been only wind. Soon there'll be no mistaking it, her whole belly will hop, quake and ripple. She runs a finger along the lips that the head will burst through. "What the fuck are you doing?" he mutters.

"Nothing."

"You're breathing hard."

"No, I'm not." She forces herself to count as she breathes slowly in one two three, out one two three.

"I can hear you."

"No." She moves to the cold edge and listens motionless, breathing very slowly. He is silent. He has had his say.

She wakes at cockcrow when he gets dressed. She hears the van come, then go. She has stayed in bed through all the flurry of their departure, and so has Chloe. They open the kitchen door to find the *somba* burning with a bright flame, the milk boiled, the baby's napkins dried and folded, the day's eggs brought in from the bar and the table laid with bread and cheese and honey under a cloth.

"Oh, lovely!" cries Bell.

"You see?" Chloe snorts. "She's sorry."

"She must have been up all night!" Bell could hug the old woman.

"She was. I heard her."

"She didn't have to do all this for us!"

Chloe stares and shrugs. "Why shouldn't she?"

Chloe spends the morning washing and rinsing clothes, Bell taking Sophoula for a walk with the camera. The piles of soft snow were frozen overnight; so were the puddles and the clothes hung out on wires and bare brambles. There are no clouds this morning to block the sun or the faded half-moon, and everywhere they go water trickles and drips and glitters. As they come near the schoolyard Sophoula cringes, pulling at Bell.

"Carry me, Auntie Bella."

"Why, for heaven's sake?"

"The snow woman's there."

"It's only snow! It's only a big doll made of snow."

"It's the wicked witch." She huddles against Bell. "She comes alive at night and stares in the window."

"She does not! Look, she's melted. The poor old thing, she's vanished away." A heap of pitted snow sits under the pines.

"The moon's melting too, Auntie Bella!"

Sophoula keeps Bell company while she boils the potatoes and fries eggs for the four of them for lunch; Chloe is with the baby in the bedroom. But the child is grizzly and cross now and says she isn't hungry: she doesn't want potato or egg or bread or anything. "Have a bit of banana?" Bell pleads. One banana is left. Chloe has made them last, feeding them to Sophoula inch by inch and folding the black soft skin over the stump. But no, Sophoula won't. "I know!" On impulse Bell peels the last banana, flours it and fries it in the pan with the eggs for Sophoula. "My darling, eat," she says. The old man trudges in. Lunch is late again. "Try it? For Auntie? Have some milk with it?"

"Tell a story."

"Once upon a time," she slips a spoonful of banana in, "in a little cottage in the woods —"

Sophoula gags and splutters. The old man stares. "Eat," he growls. "It's good for you."

"No! Auntie, I don't like it!"

"All right, you don't have to eat it." Blushing with shame, Bell gobbles the banana herself before Chloe comes.

"There was a banana," Chloe says when they are peeling fruit into their empty plates later, and Bell tries to explain. Sophoula announces smugly that Auntie ate it all up. So as not to let it go to waste. Bell says, red-faced. "You know she has them raw," Chloe accuses. "No more bananas!" Chloe kisses the child's hair. "Wicked Auntie! Where will I get my darling some more?"

The old man, groping in his pockets, finds a bag of peanuts in their shells and presses it into Sophoula's hand.

"Is it *safe* to give her nuts?" Bell wonders aloud. "They'll choke the child."

In silence she rinses the dishes while Chloe shells peanuts by the *somba*. Abruptly Sophoula hoots and stiffens. Her back arches. Chloe bangs her, shakes her, shoves her head forward, and at last a great gush of sour curds and speckles pours out of her mouth all over her mother.

"Thank God!" Chloe hauls her jumper over her head. "*Aman*, my poor darling!" she moans, dabbing Sophoula's white face. "They're bad, don't ever eat them! Wicked Pappou!" She pushes the whole bag into the firebox and slams the iron door. The old man plods to his room. "There," she says, "let them burn. He won't tell Her," she mutters at Bell, who has brought a glass of water. "Thanks. Don't you tell either, or we'll never hear the end of it."

It is dark these days before the old man wakes to do the afternoon milking. The torch he takes into the barn lights up the ridge of snow at the door. His approach to the house is a clank and slop of saucepans past the window and a red point and trail of smoke, his cigarette. This time he dumps the saucepans caked with dung and hay inside on the kitchen floor and covers them. "Who'll strain the milk?" he says loudly to no one. "Will you boil it or use it for cheese?"

Sullen with sleep in their doorways, the women exchange looks. He is waiting. Chloe tweaks a curl off her baby's damp cheek and kisses it.

"Two daughters-in-law!" barks the old man and they all jump. The baby whines.

"Sssh." Chloe frowns.

"Two daughters-in-law and I do it, do I? I strain the milk! I make the cheese! It's not enough to look after the cows and milk them. I can do the lot!"

The kitchen door slams. Chloe pulls Bell into her room, where they stand listening behind the door as he unlatches the window and clatters the saucepans. Then the front door clangs shut and his boots crunch away.

"He's thrown it out!" Bell mutters.

"Two daughters-in-law and I do it, do I?"

"Sssh. He'll hear!"

"Him, hear?"

"Sssh."

They creep to the kitchen and turn the light on. In the square of yellow it throws outside, Bell can just make out the saucepans on end against the barn wall. The sun never comes there and the snow is still thick, with a pale puddle in it, a cat crouched at the edge, and all around a wide shawl of creamier snow. "Oh! What a waste," Bell sighs.

"Who cares?" Chloe looks in a jug. "Look, there's all this left from this morning."

"He's right, though."

"It's Mama's job!"

"But since she's not here."

"I have two small children I have to everything for."

"Yes, I should have done it."

"You're pregnant!"

"Only five months." She sits down. "I need a coffee."

"No, come on, let's get out of this place before we go mad! We'll take the children to Aunt Magdalini's. Come on."

At Aunt Magdalini's, the village secretary's wife tells them that the bridges have been declared safe for the time being and that a bus to Thessaloniki will run in the morning. Rowdy in her elation and relief and scorn of Kyria Sophia, who might just as well have waited, Chloe hauls Bell and Aunt Magdalini's three daughters-in-law along the crusted, muddy street to celebrate her release at the *kafeneion*.

Inside its misted windows men are smoking at small tables, watching the soccer on the grey television screen (the only one in the village) or looking on while Grigori's father plays the champion at *tavli*. The men all sit with their elbows on the chair-back and their hands flat on their chests, glancing sidelong from time to time at the table of women drinking orangeade. When Grigori's father wins the game he sends the *kafedji* over with another round, and the women raise the bottles smiling in a salute to him.

Chloe tells joke after joke uproariously and the other three are soon helpless with laughter. "What are the men staring at?" she asks, gazing round. "Oh, Bella, it's you!" She swoops and whispers. "Bella, look how you're sitting." Startled, Bell looks. "Bella, your hands!" She has them open over each breast exactly as the men's are, but women never sit like that. She moves them to the slopes of her belly and Chloe giggles and nudges but Bell is too torpid in the smoky heat to be bothered. When the others are ready to go they wake her. The sky is all white stars, frost crackles as they tread. They link arms with Bell in the middle to keep her from a fall. Scarves of mist trail behind them. They drop her at home on the way to Aunt Magdalini's.

Alone in the cold bed, Bell is awake for the first unmistakable tremor of the quickening.

Before daybreak Bell is up to strain the milk — twice carefully through the gauze — and boil it in time for breakfast. Chloe's noisy desperation surges all around her. At last the kisses crushing or missing cheeks and she is away with the children, the old man carrying their bags to the bus, and Bell has the house to herself.

She scrubs the saucepans and puts clean water on to boil. The table is littered with crusts, plates and cups under the yellow bulb that only now she remembers to switch off; she tidies up. She has packing to do as well, letters and lists to write, but that had better wait until Grigori decides whether or not to go with her.

When her saucepans boil she carries them and another of cold water into the lavatory annexe that the old man spent all autumn building and is proud of. In case he tries to come in and wash, she pushes the heavy can of olive oil against the door. There is no light bulb in here yet, only an air vent and a candle stuck on a plate. She leans over to put a match to it and its flame lights her breasts: they are as she has never seen them, white and full, clasped with dark veins like tree roots. Shuddering in the cold, she stands in the *tapsi*, wets and soaps herself urgently, rinses the soap off. Flames go down her in runnels. She is rough all over with goosepimples except for her belly, domed in her hands, warm and smooth like some great egg.

All the water is swilling round her legs in the *tapsi* before she has got all the soap off but she rubs herself dry anyway, pulls on her clean clothes and with a grunt hoists up the *tapsi* and pours all the water into the lavatory bowl. It brims, then sinks gurgling down in froth and a gust of sweet cold rottenness from the sewer belches up in her face.

Still shuddering, she hugs herself close to the *somba*, propping the iron door open while she crams pine cones in. She sits with her clothes open. Perhaps the baby can see and hear the fire, she thinks: did he see my hands in there, by the light of the candle? They must have made shadows on his red wall.

Here we are in a cold white house with icicles under the eaves and winter has hardly begun, but inside its walls are warm to the touch, full of firelight.

She has a couple of hours before she needs to start cooking lunch, and one full roll of fast film left: she will use them to take her last photographs. Bare interiors of sun and shade and firelight, in which as always she appears absent.

Home Time

By late afternoon the sky is a deep funnel of wind, damp and white. She remarks as she passes through the lamplight around his desk on her way to the bathroom: "Doesn't it look like snow!"

"Do you think?" He squints out the window.

"That hollowness of the light."

"It's early for snow."

"*Casablanca's* going to be on TV tonight at eight," she says before he can look down again. "Why don't we go to that bar and see it and then have dinner somewhere after?"

"Mmm."

The room is grey; only the light around him is warm and moving with shadows. The steam pipes are silent. Whenever will they start clanking and hissing and defrost the apartment? "*Isn't* it cold, though!" she says brightly.

"Mmm."

"Maybe I should go for a walk downtown, take some photos of the lights coming on," she says.

"It's a lot colder outside."

"Walking would warm me up."

"Okay."

"Oh, maybe not," she says. "I might write letters home instead." Home is Australia. It's summer there. "Until it's time for *Casablanca*."

He sighs and waits for silence.

She has an electric radiator on in her room — the sitting-room really, but she works in here. She has twin lamps of frilly glass at twin tall windows inside which wasps sizzle and cling and trap themselves in shreds of cobweb. The table she writes at faces the windows. Three times a day she pushes books to one side and turns papers face down, since this is also the table they eat at. The kitchen is next to it, bare and icy, smelling of gas. She pulls her radiator over by the couch and lies curled up in the red glow with her head on a velvet cushion.

Later she half-wakes: he has walked past into the kitchen. When he switches her lamps on and hands her a mug of coffee she is stiffly sitting up to make room. "Did you get much written?" She yawns, stretching an arm warm with sleep along his shoulders.

"Fair bit." He grins. "Did you?"

She is glad she stayed in. "No. What's the time?"

"Hell, yes." He looks. "Ten past eight."

"Oh, we've missed it!"

"No, we haven't. Only the start."

They gulp their coffee and help each other drag coats and boots on. "You must have seen it, haven't you?" he says.

"Oh, yes. Hasn't everyone?"

"Then what's the —?"

She shuts his mouth with a kiss. "I want to see it with *you*. In America."

He smiles at that. They fling open the door and stop short. Snow is falling, must have been falling for hours, heavy and slow, whirling round the white streetlamps. "Oh, *snow*!" She dashes back inside for her camera and takes photo after photo from the stoop, of fir branches shouldering slabs of snow, drooping in gardens, and elms still with gold leaves and a fine white skin all over, and lawns and cars and rooftops thickly fleeced. Passing cars have drawn zips on the white road.

"Now, we're really late," he says. Hand in hand they tramp and slither the few blocks to the bar they like, bright as a fire with the lamps on. Outside it two young men are throwing snowballs. She gasps as one leaps on the other and they flounder giggling at her feet.

"Pussy cat!" one jeers. "That's *all* you is!"

Her man is holding the blurred glass door open. Heads along the bar turn away from *Casablanca* to stare at them. He leads her to a stool, orders a red wine and an Irish coffee and stands at her back. Ingrid Bergman's face fills the screen.

The door opens on a white flurry and the young men stamping

in, shaking the snow off. The heads turn and stare. "Celebrate the first *snow!*" one young man announces. "Have a *drink*, every-buddy!" A cheer goes up. The barman brings her another red wine and him another Irish coffee. The young men have flopped crosslegged on the carpet and are gazing at the screen.

"Oh, they're *so* young," a voice murmurs in her ear; the grey-haired woman beside her is smiling. She smiles in answer and gives herself over to *Casablanca*. He is at her back with his arms round her. When it ends he goes to the men's room.

The old woman is dabbing her eyes. "Oh dear!" She makes a face. "Do you come here a lot? I do. We live just down the road."

Do you come here a lot? I do. We just live down the road. You can see this bar from our stoop and I tell you it's a real tempta-tion, glowing away down here. With that lantern at the door with snowflakes spinning round it and the way the elm leaves flap against it like yellow butterflies — it's like some place in a fairy tale. And here inside it's as bright and warm as inside a Halloween pumpkin. Those lamps everywhere, and the bottles burning in the mirror. And whenever the door opens, a breath of snow blows in and the lights all shift under and over the shadows. Even if *Casablanca* wasn't on the TV I'd have come tonight.

What'll you have, honey, another one of those? What is that, red wine? Jimmy, another one of those red wines and I'll have a Jack Daniels. Yes, rocks. And wipe that silly grin off your face, have you no soul, what kind of a man laughs at *Casablanca*? Thanks, Jimmy. Keep it.

Look through that archway, the couples at their little tables, all so solemn and proper with their vintage wine and their candles — look, their heads are hollow, like the candles burnt their eyes out. They might all have stories just as sad as *Casablanca*, but who cares? It's *Casablanca* breaks our hearts, over and over. You cried at the end, I saw you. So did that nice man of yours. Oh, a bar's the place to watch it, a bar's the perfect place. I cry every single time, I can't help myself, it's so noble and sad and innocent and — hell, you know. I couldn't watch it home, anyway. Bill, he's my husband, gets mad when I cry. He walks out. "Why, am I supposed to stay and watch you slobber over this shit?" he said last time it was on. "Most people got all they need to slobber about in real life."

"You're what *I* got," I said right back.

That's him there, over at the pool table. That your man he's talking to? I thought so. They're lighting up cigarettes and getting acquainted. Isn't that a coincidence? He looks a nice easy-going kind of a guy. But then so does Bill. I love Bill, I love him a lot. I've known that man thirteen years, I could tell you things . . . I'm not blind to anything about Bill, I love him anyway. He loves *me*, though it doesn't feel like being loved much of the time. He needs me. He has to punish me for that. There he is, an older man than he acts. His hair has a grey sheen and his skin hangs loose all over, see the crazed skin on his neck. He's affable and a bit loud with the drink, everybody's pal. Well, when we get home there won't be a word out of him. Under the skin and the smile he's a bitter, fearful man and nobody gets close to him.

He's a second comer, for one thing. He can't forget that. He's my second husband. Yours is a second comer too, is he, honey? Don't mind me sticking my nose in. It's just I can tell. You two are a mite too considerate, too careful with one another, know what I mean? It shows, that's all, if you can read the signs. So what if you are Australians. Oh no. Look, I don't mean you haven't got a nice relationship. But it's only the first time you give your whole self. After that, like it or not, you hold back. You've gotten wise — and you can't pretend *other*wise!

We've been married ten years this Thursday — Thanksgiving Day. You got to laugh. Cheers. Isn't that something, though. My first marriage never got to double figures. I had twenty years alone in between.

Do you remember the first time you saw *Casablanca*? Mine was in 1943, when it first came out, on my honeymoon with Andy. That's reason enough to cry. Bill knows. It's something he can't stand to be reminded of. He pretends it's only Rick and Ilsa making me *slobber*. Men — you tell a man the truth about your life, you end up paying for *ever*. Remember that.

1943! Andy was nineteen, I was seventeen, his ship was sailing for Europe in a week. Our parents said no, you're too young, but we said we'd only run away, so they gave in. We had one weekend for a honeymoon in New York City. The hotel was an awful old ruin — it still is — full of cockroaches and noisy plumbing. We were so embarrassed, you could hear every drop, every trickle. Our room was on the top floor. Through the fire escape we could see the river, and the moon in the mist like a brass knob behind a curtain, and the lights of Manhattan. So it's not a bed of roses, Andy said: it's a bed of lights instead. We saw *Casablanca* and we cried. We were such babies. He was going to be a hero and I was going to wait . . . We danced round the room like Rick and Ilsa did. We sure didn't sleep much. We didn't even know how to *do* it, you know. We were scared. Oh, we soon got the hang of it. And then his ship sailed.

He came back, oh, he came back. He'd won medals in Italy, he was a hero. But he wouldn't ever talk about it. Whatever happened over there, it finished Andy. He started drinking, then he lost his job, and soon he couldn't hold down any job, he just drank and gambled and played the black market. He'd come home once, twice a week, then sleep for days . . .

One night he started hitting me. Everything was my fault, he said. Then he cried. He promised he never would again. I was fool enough to believe it. If they've hit you once and gotten away with it, honey, you're in trouble. It can only get worse.

So, one night I woke up on the kitchen floor. The table lamp was still on, the beer that he spilt looked like butter melting under it. I remember I saw the pattern of brown triangles on the linoleum every time my eyes came open, they looked wet and red, but I couldn't see sharp enough to be sure. The window was black — so it was still night time — and had silver edges like knives where he smashed it. The curtain was half torn down, sopping up the beer on the table and moving in the wind, a white curtain like a wedding veil. *Help me!* I called out. My head felt crushed. The wind must have blown my hair on my face, hair was stuck to it. A long way away something was — snuffling. My nose was flat on my cheek, red bubbles blew out. Andy *wasn't there*. I held my head still and pulled myself up by the table leg: broken glass, slabs of the window pane, and the wet curtain, but no note. No nothing. The room was going all watery and dim as if the floor was hot as fire and yet it was so icy when I lay down, I pulled the curtain down over me to keep warm.

It wasn't till morning that I saw he'd taken all his stuff. God knows there wasn't much, poor Andy. Then I got started all over again: *Don't leave me! Don't leave me alone now! I love you!* Even now I dream — I wake up and for a moment I'm on that floor again knowing I've lost Andy, he's gone for *ever*. Oh, I've never gotten over it.

I'm sorry. Don't be embarrassed. I'll be all right in a moment. Thank you, yes, another Jack Daniels would be nice. Yes, thank you.

Funny thing was, when I got up off the floor next day and my nose was smashed and my eyes looked like two squashed plums and I was shaking so hard I thought my teeth would crack — I ran out into the street in case I could see him and maybe catch him up and all the time I was whimpering, *After all you've done to me, you just get up and go*? I looked in the kitchen window. It was empty, all shadowy gold behind the edges of glass.

Another funny thing — I had a vision in the night, a ballerina came in. (I wanted to be a dancer, I was good, but first the War started, then I got married . . .) Anyway, this must have been the curtain that I saw. She bent down to lift me then she lay beside me, sobbing, I remember that.

Look at us there in the mirror, like two ghosts among the whisky bottles. Okay, Jimmy, laugh. He thinks I'm admiring myself. I'm not that far gone, though I'm getting there. Cheers. Is that really me, that scrawny thing with the spiky grey hair? You'd never think I was a ballet dancer. Bill hates ballet. He says that because the pain and exertion and ugliness aren't allowed to show, it's one big lie. Tinsel and sweat, he says. Dancers smell like horses, someone says, so Bill has to read it to me out of the newspaper. Horse aren't any less beautiful for the way they smell, I say. Horses are dancers too and dancers love them. Anyway, I say, I like the way they smell. You would, he says, you're not what you'd call fussy, are you. Now wasn't that asking for it? *No, well, I married you!* I let it pass, though, and he gives me points for not saying it: just a flicker of the eyelids, but enough.

Most of our quarrels end like that. They're harmless. Nothing

Bill says or does can get to the quick of me like it did with Andy whether he meant it or not. Bill can make me ache with misery when he wants, but somewhere deep down inside me now there's this little tough muscle braces itself so the barbs can't go too far. Bill knows. He's the same. Maybe by now it would have been like that with Andy, who knows? I don't even know if he's alive or dead. My parents came and made me get a divorce. They told him I said he couldn't see me or the kids ever again.

Let me tell you the *worst* thing — let's have another drink? — the worst thing — oh, God, I've never told a living soul this. Jimmy, more of these and have one on me, okay? The worst thing is, when he had me on the floor that night — just pushed me down — and started smashing things and yelled that he wanted *out*, I rolled over and hung on to his trouser leg for dear life and begged him not to leave me. I just wouldn't let go. I — slobbered, and howled and — and I kissed his muddy shoe. So he slammed his other shoe in my face. That's when my nose got broken. I mean, that's why.

I thank God the kids weren't home, they didn't see that. They saw him hit me other times, but not that. They were only little. Rick was about five, Ilsa was just a baby. Something like that, though — if they saw it happen, it'd leave a scar on them. "I won't let Daddy hurt you," Ricky used to say to me. They were at my parents' place in New Jersey because I had to get a job so I couldn't look after them. We called them Rick and Ilsa — well, *you* know why! Ilsa's married, she's in Alaska now, she's a nurse. Rick's dead. He got killed in Vietnam. Got a medal doing it, too. If his Daddy ever heard about it, I suppose he must have felt proud. Or maybe not.

Don't get me wrong, I believe in sacrifice, and love and honour and loyalty, even if it turns out they were wasted — else why would I love *Casablanca*? Rick and Ilsa, they had something or someone they'd give up everything for. I only wish I still did. Real people have their moments of glory. Time goes on for them though, they can't live up to it. But the glory lives on in memory. Bill won't see that. Face facts, he says. You and your glory and your wallowing in the past. It's shit, that's all it is, shit preserved in syrup. That's better than shit preserved in vinegar, the way your's is, I say. Oh, that's good, he says. Make with the witty repartee, babe, you know I dig that. (Bill can never let go of anything. All his past is still there inside of him, pickled). Why better, honey? Shit's still shit, he says then. Who knows the truth? I say. You refuse to, *he* says, and round and round we go.

What you never really get over, I suppose, is finding out love's not enough. Loving someone's no *use*. And you only find out the hard way. No one can tell you. You believe in love when you're young, you believe it's forever, it's the only thing that matters, it'll save you both, if you just hang in there and give more and more. I wonder if Ilsa would have gone with Rick — given up everything and gone with him — would it have ended up with her on the floor with her nose smashed? You never know.

Here they come. Look, they're wondering what we're saying. Look at those suspicious eyes and butter-wouldn't-melt smiles of theirs! Your man's been watching you all this time. Here's looking at you, kid! Easy to see you're new. It's great while it lasts, make the most. The couples have had their wine and candlelight and now they're leaving. Don't you just love a black and white night like this after snow, when it echoes? And you slide and fall down on top of each other all the way and rub each other's feet dry and warm once you're inside. Okay, fellers, home time? I've lost my coat. Thanks, honey. I feel so lit up it's a wonder you can't see me shining through it! I'm sure I don't know why I've been telling you the story of my life. You cried at the end of *Casablanca*. I suppose that's why.

"Can I read that?"

"Read what?"

Her hands have instinctively spread across the pages of blue scrawl. He raises his eyebrows: "What you've been writing half the night."

She passes them over her shoulder. The couch creaks and the pages rustle until at last he tosses them back on the table and goes to make coffee. She stares at them, sweat prickling her. The heating is on full.

"Thank you," she says when he brings her mug.

"Is this finished?"

"Oh, for now, anyway. I was just coming to bed — I'm sorry. Haven't you been asleep?"

"I used to respect writers rather a lot," he murmurs. "Now I'm not sure."

"You're writing your thesis on one."

"Mmm. There's writing and writing. To my mind this —" he points — "is more like scavenging." He waits while she swallows hot coffee. "Perhaps if you wore a badge, a brand on your forehead that meant: *Beware of the scavenger*? Then people would know they were fair game."

"You think *that's* being *fair*?"

"She trusted you, it seems, with the story of her life."

"I hope I can do it justice."

"Justice." He sighs.

She has nothing to say. He finishes his coffee sip by sip, takes his mug and rinses it, then comes back to stand behind her chair. Her mug is clenched in both hands; the light of the two lamps blurs in her coffee.

"I am not to figure in anything you write," comes the smooth voice again. "Never. I hope you understand that."

Hardly breathing, she cranes her neck forward to have a sip of coffee, but he grabs the mug from her and slams it down on the table, where it breaks. Coffee spurts up and splashes brown and blue drops over her pages. This time she knows better than to move until his footsteps creak away across the boards. His chair scrapes. She hears a match strike in the room beyond, and a sigh as he breathes smoke in.

A Woman with Black Hair

Her front door locks, but not her back door. Like the doors on many houses in her suburb, they are panelled and stained old pine ones, doors solid enough for a fortress: but the back one opens with a push straight into her wooden kitchen. Moonlight coats in icy shapes and shadows the floor and walls which I know to be golden pine, knotted and scuffed, having seen them in sunlight and cloudlight as often as I have needed to; having seen them lamplit too, cut into small gold pictures by the wooden frames of the window, thirty small panes, while I stood unseen on the back veranda. (The lampshades are lacy baskets and sway in draughts, rocking the room as if it were a ship's cabin and the light off waves at sunset or sunrise washed lacily inside it. Trails like smoke wavering their shadows over the ceiling are not smoke, but cobwebs blowing loose.) These autumn nights she has a log fire burning, and another in her front room just beyond. With the lights all off, the embers shine like glass. They fill the house all night with a warm breath of fire.

An old clock over the kitchen fire chimes the hours. One. Two.

Off the passage from her front room is a wooden staircase. Her two small daughters sleep upstairs, soundly all night. Beyond the staircase a thick door is left half-open: this is her room. In its white walls the three thin windows are slits of green light by day, their curtains of red velvet drawn apart like lips. There is a fireplace, never used; hardly any furniture. A worn rug, one cane armchair, a desk with a lamp stooped over books and papers (children's essays and poems drawn over in coloured pencil, marked in red ink); old books on dark shelves; a bed with a puffed red quilt where she sleeps. Alone, her hair lying in black ripples on the pillow.

For me a woman has to have black hair.

This one's hair is long and she is richly fleshed, the colour of warm milk with honey. Her eyes are thick-lidded: I have never been sure what colour they are. (She is mostly reading when I can watch her.) They seem now pale, now dark, as if they changed like water. On fine mornings she lies and reads the paper on the cane sofa under her shaggy green grapevine. She is out a lot during the day. She and the children eat dinner by the kitchen fire — her glass of wine glitters and throws red reflections — and then watch television for an hour or two in the front room. After the children go up to bed, she sits on and reads until long past midnight, the lamplight shifting over her. Some evenings visitors come — couples, the children's father — but no one stays the night. And she has a dog: an aged blond labrador, half-blind, that grins and dribbles when it hears me coming and nuzzles for the steak I bring. It has lolloped after me in and around the house, its tail sweeping and its nails clicking on the boards. It spends the night on the back veranda, snoring and farting in its sleep.

The little girls — I think the smaller is five or six, the other not more than two years older — have blond hair tied high in a sheaf, like pampas grass. (The father is also blond.)

Tonight, though the moon is nearly full, it is misted over. I may not even really need the black silk balaclava, stitched in red, that I bought for these visits, though I am wearing it anyway, since it has become part of the ritual. I am stripped to a slit black tracksuit — slit, because it had no fly — from which I unpicked all the labels. I have the knife safe in its sheath, and my regular tracksuit folded in my haversack ready for my morning jog when I leave the house.

Tonight when the clock chimed one she turned all the lights out. When it chimed two I came in, sat by the breathing fire, and waited. There is no hurry. I nibble one by one the small brown grapes I picked, throwing the skins and the wet pips into its flames of glass, making them hiss. Nothing moves in the house.

When the clock chimes three I creep into her room — one curtain is half-open, as it always has been — to stand watching the puddle of dimness that is her pillow; the dark hair over it.

I saw her once out in the sun untangling her wet hair with her fingers. It flowed over her face and over her naked shoulders like heavy dark water over sandstone. The grass around her was all shafts of green light, each leaf of clover held light. There were clambering bees.

There is a creek a couple of streets down the hill from here. I wish I could take her there. It reminds me of a creek I used to fish in when I was a boy. There were round speckled rocks swathed with green-yellow silky weed, like so many wet blond heads combed by the fingers of the water. (My hair was — is still — blond). I used to wish I could live a water life and leave my human one: I would live in the creek and be speckled, weedy-haired, never coming out except in rain. I lay on the bank in spools and flutters of water light. A maternal ant dragged a seed over my foot; a dragon-fly hung in the blurred air; a small dusty lizard propped, tilted its head to take me in, and hid in the grass under my shadow.

Over the weeks since I found this woman I have given her hints, clues, signs that she has been chosen. First I took her white nightgown — old ivory satin, not white, but paler than her skin — and pulled it on and lay in her bed one day. It smelled of hair and roses. I left it torn at the seams on the sofa under the grapevine that shades her back veranda. I suppose she found it that night and was puzzled, perhaps alarmed, but thought the dog had done it; anyone might think so. Another day I left an ivory rose, edged with red, in a bowl on her kitchen table. She picked it up, surprised, and put it in a glass of water. She accused her daughters of picking it, I could tell from where I was standing by the kitchen window (though of course what she was saying was inaudible), and they shook their heads. Their denials made her angry; the older girl burst into loud sobs. Another frilled rose was waiting on the pillow in the room with the three red-lipped windows. I wonder what she made of that. They looked as if they were crumpled up then dipped in blood.

I drop a hint now: I sit down in the cane armchair, which creaks, and utter a soft sigh. Her breathing stops. She is transfixed. When it starts again, it is almost as slow as it was when she was asleep, but deeper: in spite of her efforts, harsher. Her heart shudders. For long minutes I take care not to let my breathing overlap hers; I keep to her rhythm. She does not dare to stop breathing for a moment to listen, warning whoever is there, if anyone is, that she is awake. And at last — the kitchen clock chimes four — she starts to fall asleep again, having made herself believe what she must believe. There is no one there, the noise was outside, it was a dream, she is only being silly.

I make the chair creak again.

She breathes sharply, softly now, and with a moan as if in her sleep — this is how she hopes to deceive whoever is there, because someone is, someone *is* — she turns slowly over to lie and face the chair. Her eyes are all shadow. Certainly she opens them now, staring until they water, those eyes the colours of water. But I am too deep in the dark for her to see me: too far from the grey glow at the only tall window with its curtains left apart.

This time it takes longer for her to convince herself that there is nothing here to be afraid of. I wait until I hear her breathing slow down. Then, as lightly as the drizzle that is just starting to hiss in the tree by her window, I let her hear me breathing faster.

"Who is it?" she whispers. They all whisper.

"Quiet." I kneel by her head with the grey knife out.

"Please."

"Quiet."

The clock chimes. We both jump like rabbits. One. Two. Three. Four. Five. I hold the knife to her throat and watch her eyes sink and her mouth gape open. Terror makes her face a skull. "Going to keep quiet?" I whisper, and she makes a clicking in her throat and nods a little, as much as she dares to move. "Yes or no?"

She clicks.

"It's sharp. Watch this. "I slice off a lock of her black hair and stuff it in my pocket. "Well?"

Click.

"*Well?*"

"Yesss."

When I hold her head clear of the quilt by her hair and stroke the knife down the side of her throat, black drops swell along the line it makes, like buds on a twig.

"Good. We wouldn't want to wake the girls up, would we?" I say. I let that sink in, let her imagine those two little girls running in moonlit gowns to snap on the light in the doorway. Then I say their names. That really makes her pulse thump in her throat. "They *won't* wake up, will they?"

"No," she whispers.

"*Good.*"

I press my lips on hers. My mouth tastes of the grapes I ate by her still fire, both our mouths slither and taste of the brown sweet grapes. I keep my tight grip of my knife and her hair. She has to stay humble. I am still the master.

"I love you," I say. Her tongue touches mine. "I want you." Terror stiffens and swells in her at that. "Say it," I say.

"I — love you," she whispers. I wait. "I — want you."

Now there is not another minute to wait. I throw the quilt off and lift her nightgown. She moves her heavy thighs and the slit nest above them of curled black hair. There is a hot smell of roses and summer grasses. I lie on top of her. "Put it in," I say, and she slips me in as a child's mouth takes the nipple. "Move," I say. She makes a jerky thrust. "No, no. Make it nice." Her eyes twitch; panting, she rocks and sways under me.

I have to close her labouring mouth with my hand now; in case the knife at her throat slips, I put it by her head on the pillow (its steel not cold, as hot as we are), and it makes a smear where the frilled rose was. Her nightgown tears over her breasts, black strands of her hair scrawl in red over the smooth mounds of them, warm wet breasts that I drink. Is this the nightgown? Yes. Yes. Then we are throbbing and convulsing and our blood beats like waves crashing on waves.

None of these women ever says to me, How is your little grub enjoying itself? Is it in yet? Are you sure? Can it feel anything? Oh, well, that's all right. Mind if I go back to sleep now? No, move, I say, and they move. Move nicely. Now keep still. And they do.

"Now keep still," I say, picking up the knife again. She lies rigid. The clatter of the first train tells me it is time. Day is breaking. Already the grey light in the window is too strong to be still moonlight and the dark tree has started to shrink, though not yet to be green and brown. "I have to go. I'll come again," I say as I get up. She nods. "You want me to. Don't you." She nods, her eyes on the hand with the knife.

I never will. I never do. Once is all I want. At night she will lie awake thinking I will come to her again. Just as she thinks I might cut her throat and not just slit the skin; and so I might. But their death is not part of the ritual. The knife is like a lion-tamer's whip: the threat is enough. Of course if the threat fails, I will have to kill her. She, for that matter, would turn the knife on me if she could. Chance would then make her a killer. Chance, which has made me the man I am, might yet make me a killer: I squat stroking the knife.

"Well, say it," I say.

"Yes."

"You won't call the police." She shakes her head. "Or will you? Of course you will." My smile cracks a glaze of blood and spittle around my mouth. In the grey mass on the pillow I watch her eyes roll, bloodshot, bruised, still colourless. "I want you to wait, though. I know: wait till the bird hits the window." A bird flies at her window every morning. I see her realise that I even know that; I see her thinking, Oh God, what doesn't he know? "That's if you love your little girls." Her eyes writhe. "You do, don't you. Anyone would." Girls with hair like pampas grass. "So you will wait, won't you." She nods. "Well?"

"Yes."

Her coils of dark hair are ropy with her sweat and her red slobber, and so is her torn gown, the torn ivory gown that I put on once, that she never even bothered to mend. A puddle of yellow haloes her on the sheet. She is nothing but a cringing sack of stained skin, this black-haired woman who for weeks has been an idol that I worshipped, my life's centre. The knowledge that I have got of her just sickens me now. Let them get a good look at what their mother really is — what women all are — today when they come running down to breakfast, her little girls in their sunlit gowns. "You slut," I say, and rip her rags off her. "You foul slut." Just having to gag her, turn her and tie her wrists behind her and then tie her ankles together makes me want to retch aloud. Having to touch her. But I stop myself. Turning her over to face the wall, I pull the quilt up over the nakedness and the stink of her. I wipe my face and hands, drop the knife and the balaclava into my haversack, and get dressed quickly.

The dark rooms smell of ash. Light glows in their panes, red glass in their fireplaces. The heavy door closes with a jolt. I break off a bunch of brown grapes with the gloss of the rain still on them. The dog snuffles. Blinking one eye, it bats its sleepy tail once or twice on the veranda.

I have made a study of how to lose myself in these hushed suburban mornings. (The drizzle stopped long ago. Now a loose mist is rising in tufts, and the rolled clouds are bright-rimmed). I am as much at home in her suburb as I am in her house, or in my own for that matter, though I will never go near the house or the suburb, or the woman, again. (I will find other women in other houses and suburbs when the time comes. Move, I will say, and they will move. Move nicely. They will. Keep still. Then they will keep still.) And when the sirens whoop out, as of course they will soon, I will be out of the way. I will wash myself clean.

I am a solitary jogger over yellow leaves on the echoing footpaths. No one sees me. I cram the grapes in my haversack for later.

I know that soon after sunrise every morning a small brown bird dashes itself like brown bunched grapes, like clodded earth, at the bare window of her room, the one with its red curtains agape. Again and again it launches itself from a twig that is still shaking when the bird has fallen into the long dry grass and is panting there unseen, gathering its strength for another dash. (The garden slopes away under her room: no one can stand and look in at her window.) It thuds in a brown flurry on to its own image shaken in the glass. It startled me, in the garden the first morning. I think of her half-waking, those other mornings, thinking, It's the bird, as the brown mass thudded and fell and fluttered up to clutch at the twig again: thinking, Only the bird, and turning over slowly into her safe sleep.

But she is awake this morning. She is awake thinking, Oh God, the bird, when will the bird? Twisting to free her hands and turn over: Please, the bird. Her shoulders and her breasts and throat are all ravelled with red lace. Her hair falling over them is like dark water.

Letter to Judith Brett

Dear Judith Brett,

I need hardly say how interested I was to read Kerryn Goldsworthy's article, "Feminist Writings, Feminist Readings: Recent Australian Writing by Women", in *Meanjin* 4/1985. There were statements about my stories that I disagreed with, but every reader reads a different book, I thought, and why not. But a sentence summing them up jolted me out of such complacency: "Given their historical context, her stories in *Milk* (1983) and *Home Time* (1985), written and published out of and into a public awareness of feminist issues, values and strategies, can only be read as reactionary to it." *Can only be read* . . . What we are getting is not "a" feminist reading: this is the only possible reading of my stories?

Paranoia, I muttered, and read on. My stories are reactionary to it, it said, because these days feminism is "a visible ideological position against which to react". Oh. My stories have revealed no "ideologically sound heroines", no women who are "rescuers, supporters and survivors". Readers are "implicitly invited to identify and sympathise" with a writer's heroines, and if under examination they're found wanting . . . well, it goes without saying, that means they're reactionary.

What if I'm neutral, though? I pipe up. *Ideologically* neutral? My stories, I mean? No, it seems there is no middle ground: "ideological 'innocence' is no longer a possibility". And furthermore: ". . . it has become literally impossible for any writer, irrespective of his or her own ideological position, not to engage on one side or the other with the issues that it raises — short of avoiding altogether the representation in his or her writing of the social and sexual relations of men and women".

So from now on, writing (if it deals, as most fiction does, with the relations of men and women) must take into account "the historical and sociological context of post-seventies feminism". Well now, feminism may be "a powerful political force", but it's not a dictatorship. Writers of fiction, in Australia at least, can still keep ideology — *any* ideology — at bay if it so happens that they see human experience in other terms. Fiction is at once more and less than history and sociology; its sources are beyond their reach. There are many ways of writing; and of reading.

Beverley Farmer
Carlton, Victoria

Literature Is What Is Taught

Extracts from Interview by Jennifer Ellison

How did you come to get Alone *published?*

When Sisters Publishing was set up (I think it was 1977), I read about it in a newspaper or magazine and naturally thought there were possibilities there and sent it off. Hilary McPhee read it and liked it but there was a whole board of directors who had to read it and like it, so there were some months of nail biting before it was accepted in 1980.

*   *   *

Was it important to you that Alone *be published by a group like Sisters?*

I wanted it published. I didn't mind whether it was a feminist publisher or an ordinary publisher.

Do you have any feminist sympathies or do you define yourself as a feminist?

Oh sympathies, yes, but I'm not an activist. I'm in sympathy with equal rights and women's emancipation and all that, but the trouble is that women's liberation is such a flexible term. It means something different to everybody.

What does it mean to you?

I don't really want to give a definition of feminism but I expect people to consider women as equal to men and I'm astounded when they don't. But I'm not actually out there in the field battling against prejudice.

How did living in Greece, which is obviously a very male-dominated society, influence your views on the role of women and your views on "feminism", for want of a better word?

I was only twenty-one when I met Chris, my ex-husband. We'd been together for seven years by the time we went to Greece and we'd adapted to each other in Australia. He had accepted that women are freer over here than he was used to. It was only when we went to Greece that we found that the compromise we'd worked out in Australia wasn't going to work in Greece because of family pressures and the scorn of other men, who thought he was hen-pecked if I was allowed to get away with what I took for granted in Australia. It was a very difficult time for us. I thought I was letting him down if I behaved with the freedom that I took for granted. Not sexual freedom, I should point out. And of course it's a generational thing too. His parents' generation were very shocked that I wore trousers, for example, as this was regarded as a radical act, but his brothers and sisters accepted me without question. His sisters were both working. They had had a good education. Now of course, with the socialist government, women's liberation is taking giant steps.

Do you still take an active interest in Greece?

Oh yes, yes. I only lived there for three years but we'd been married four years before then and we only went out with other Greeks. I lived in a totally Greek environment except for school. I had that split between my teaching life and coming home to a Greek household, Greek parties, Greek friends, Greek weddings,

Greek books to read (even in Australia, in Melbourne); and then of course Greece itself, and then coming back here again into a Greek family. I suppose about twenty years of my life were spent in a Greek environment and I'm still loosely a part of the extended family because I'm still my son's mother. And I'm accepted. I went back there in 1983 after seven years away after the divorce, not knowing how I'd be received, but I was very lovingly received.

What sort of difficulties did you have as an Australian operating in a Greek culture? Did it make you more conscious of your "Austalianness", for example?

Yes, in a way it did. I realised that I had a fierce patriotism that I'd never suspected before. I got bitterly homesick for tea-tree and things like that. I think one of the strongest impressions when I came back was walking on a beach and it smelled right for the first time in three years. But that is more subconscious, I think, and it's only in encounters with individual people or incidents that offend you that you realise you're up against a cultural barrier. But you don't see it like that; you see it as Vassily being difficult or Stavros being difficult. It isn't the Greek male against the Australian female but person-to-person problems, just as they are here. That's how it is in the stories too — the conflict is from one person to another, because I'm more interested in the interaction between particular people. The cultural is subtextual I think.

So when did you start to write more short stories and get them published?

I hadn't really thought of the short story again for a long time until 1979. I wrote one — "Gerontissa" — and sent it to *Tabloid Story*. Also I enrolled in a Creative Writing course at the Council for Adult Education. I did one of their short courses and I was interested enough to go on and do a semester at Prahran College of Advanced Education. We had to do short stories as assignments and I began fanatically to read every short story I could get hold of. I really fell in love with the form just as I had with Australian poetry before.

The first strong influence on me of Australian literature as literature — prose, I mean — apart from Mary Grant Bruce and Ethel Turner and all that in childhood, was a Patrick White short story in *Meanjin*, a Greek one too. It made me realise what could be done in Australia, that there were no rules. Coming out of university, I thought that writing anything and sending it out to an editor was more or less like sitting for an exam. Seeing this sort of work made me realise that a writer has to impose himself more or less, just by sheer force. By an "inner force of conviction": I can't remember who said that, but it means that the writer who has the strength to impose her own view will be accepted — you don't write to please anyone; you just write what you have to.

There had been rules at university, categories and criteria, and this author was "in" and this author was "out", and I felt that I had allowed myself to be conned in a sense. I felt that university stifled any impulses to write. I felt we were being trained to be critics or lecturers, academics, and that this training was not only not going to help us write but possibly going to inhibit us and I ought to forget it and overcome it.

*   *   *

Your stories strike me as being particularly well crafted. Is it a fairly meticulous process you go through before you feel you have a finished work?

Yes, it is. I do a lot of rewriting. At first I used to read each story on to tape to make sure that it sounded right, but I don't do that so often now. I think I can hear the inner voice without reading it aloud.

*   *   *

Have there been any significant influences on your writing so far — people? Other writers?

Yes, but they come and go. It's a bit like people that you come close to and then you move away and then perhaps you come close again. It's the same with writers. Patrick White for a long time was immensely important to me because he was doing what nobody else had ever done in Australian writing. He was opening up new freedoms, I thought. Even if you didn't want to write like Patrick White, the fact that he had done this and been abused for it — "verbal sludge" and all that — and had gone on doing it, that's what was brave.

What particularly are you referring to about Patrick White's work?

I think it's imagery and the satire and the mixture of techniques and innovations in syntax, everything. It's a bit like abstract art, a bit like cubism. He was breaking up shapes, and he was abrupt and awkward and not smooth and not what you'd call a well-made writer at all. This was what was so wonderful about it. It was a bit like a Cézanne painting, doing the same thing with writing. And I've always felt, too, with my stories that I like the abruptness and the occasional awkwardness. I'm like that myself. I'm not smooth, I'm not easy. I'm impulsive, I'm jerky and awkward sometimes, and I feel it fits me that the stories are written in that way, that they're not smooth. On a rejection slip once the person said that my writing wasn't smooth and that it was awkward and jerky but the story gets told somehow.

*   *   *

Some of your stories are written in the male voice. Is that something you find difficult to do?

No. I'm glad you asked that, because it isn't something that I feel is a great hurdle to be overcome. In fact, I never thought twice about it. For example, in "Maria's Girl" I was thinking of telling the story from the point of view of the girl, and then of course I realised she knew too little, and the material of it just began to develop. It's a bit like Nadine Gordimer being tackled about how dare she write about black people. As she says, blacks and whites have lived side by side for so many generations that they know each other. It's like any two people who know each other, whether they're male or female, or of different generations. They *do* know and they empathise. It doesn't bother me if men write books from a female point of view or about women. Using a male voice doesn't frighten me in the least because, for one thing, I'm not necessarily aiming for psychological realism. It's not a naturalistic portrait, for example; it's a dramatic action in a sense.

What part, then, does imagination play in your writing?

Oh, it's hard to say. I think I'm almost deliberately not analytical about my writing. It's like the centipede wondering how it walks. I don't really want to analyse the process by which I get a story together. Carlos Fuentes said somewhere, "I am not interested in a slice of life, what I want is a slice of the imagination", and I like that. I love that. But I don't think, ah now I'm leaving naturalism and realism and entering the realms of the imagination. I don't think there's a dividing line.

So you don't think it's important to mirror life accurately in your stories?

I think it's almost more important not to mirror it accurately but to exaggerate just that little bit so that people are shocked into see-ing something differently. Like in a painting: you make something slightly the wrong shape or the wrong aspect, like a Picasso pro-file, so that you jolt first yourself then other people into a dif-ferent awareness by falsifying it. It's like metaphor: it has to be just that little bit wrong to make an impression. If it corresponded perfectly, it would just run through your mind without any friction at all. On the other hand, you can get it wrong and then you strike a real false note and people think, oh no, and they stop and you lose their trust. That's where the craft comes in.

*   *   *

What about the narrator in Alone — *that's you, isn't it?*

When I wrote *Alone* I felt I was revealing not myself but Shirley, who was a creation based very largely on me, but I changed a lot about that. And it helped me to change it. The mother was perhaps a bit like my mother but the father wasn't, and I haven't a sister, and I hadn't walked out of my matric exams (it was at university that the affair happened), and various other changes that I made helped to distance her from me. So that I could create her as a separate person. But what did bother me on publication was that everyone would assume that this was an effusion and that I was just spilling my guts out in the confessional. Worse, in public.

But that wasn't enough to stop you wanting it published?

No. I don't think the fear of how people might receive it ever stops you wanting something published. Because I knew it wasn't just a gush of confession. It was a rounded experience. It was one night in a lifetime — very much a ritualised night. She ritualised it herself, and she had it all planned and she acted it out. Part of being on the borderline of schizophrenia is that you feel you're acting a part all the time: living in mirrors.

How important are reviews to you?

To a career, of course, they're important; they make a big difference to your reputation, to your sales. And a good opinion from people whose opinion I respect is wonderful of course. Getting letters from readers is good too. In any other sort of job you have people you can have a coffee break with. You work with other people all the time. But in writing there aren't many chances for contact over the work and it's good to get responses from people and know that they are reading you. You're not just a book in a shop that nobody takes off the shelf. As I said, you write for the reader. If there's no reader, there's no point in writing. In fact, I don't think a story exists until it's published. I feel it's an embryonic form, it's not born, until it's in print. So I'm very anxious between when a story is finished and when it's in print, and this can be for a year or more.

Do you feel happy with your writing career so far?

The path has been fairly smooth since *Alone* came out. This is a good time to be writing in Australia. If you have talent and you are prepared to work I think this is a good time. Australian writing is being supported by the Literature Board, by the publishers, by the readers. It's not the way it was twenty years ago.

Do you have any thoughts on why that might be so?

I suppose it's because of the devoted and dedicated work of a few editors, publishers, writers, behind the scenes. It didn't just happen by chance. But this isn't really my field, the growth of Australian literature over the last twenty years. I've just been an onlooker. I think I'm a beneficiary rather than a participant.

That sounds so modest.

I'm not modest. Not at all. I hate that word. Writers have immense egos, otherwise they could never keep going.

Why do you think that you're a beneficiary then, rather than a participant?

Well, I feel I've been looked after really, by publishers, by editors, I've been accepted. I've been given chances. I got a grant from the Literature Board. What have I done to deserve this? I haven't edited a magazine. I haven't worked for the development of Australian literature. I haven't been an academic pushing Australian literature in the universities, and that's very important — what is being taught, and taken seriously.

Are they the sort of people who create a receptive climate for Australian literature?

Yes. Roland Barthes said, "Literature is what is taught". He might have been being cynical but I think he was just being truthful. That's how it is. If it's not being taught the assumption is, it's not worth much. Australian literature wasn't taught, twenty years ago. "What Australian literature?" people said.

What about the mechanics of writing: the editing, the redrafting, writing from different perspectives, have you virtually taught yourself all that?

Chekhov taught me and Patrick White taught me. Anything wonderful that you have read is a lesson. There are whole passages, for example, in *A Fringe of Leaves* where I could feel myself going green, not with envy, but because the blood was draining out of me. The intensity of what he was doing was so wonderful.

*   *   *

Do you feel it's difficult being a female writer?

This is the big question, isn't it? If I were a man, would you be sitting here and asking, "Do you feel it's difficult being a male writer?"

No, I probably wouldn't, because it seems to have always been expected that if men want to be writers, they can be writers.

It has for centuries for women, too. I mean, Jane Austen, George Eliot, George Sand — oh, it goes a long way back, doesn't it, that women have been accepted as writers. It's almost like actors and actresses, that writers were emancipated long before the average woman was.

Except that, of course, George Eliot wrote under a male name.

And so did Henry Handel Richardson. If it was required of them, then, it certainly didn't stop them writing. Writing under a pseudonym might even have helped them to distance themselves from the material and the female role, to be the omniscient author. A pseudonym is a mask. There have been men who have used pen names too, like Stendhal. Perhaps not female pen names, though.

I think Dorothy Hewett was terrific on the subject of being "women writers" in Adelaide in 1980, when she gave a speech about how ambivalent she felt about this feminist ghetto that we risk walling ourselves up in, and all the defensiveness and hostility and self-justification that follows from that. You build the wall yourself, and you create your own prison. We shouldn't be doing that. The point of fiction is that it leaps over walls; it turns them into panes of glass.

Thea Astley

EDITOR'S NOTE

Thea Astley has published nine novels: *Girl with a Monkey* (Angus & Robertson, 1958; reprinted Penguin, 1987); *A Descant for Gossips* (Angus & Robertson, 1960; reprinted UQP, 1984); *A Boat Load of Home Folk* (Angus & Robertson, 1968; reprinted Penguin, 1983); *A Kindness Cup* (Nelson, 1974); *An Item from the Late News* (UQP, 1982); *Beachmasters* (Penguin, 1985). Three of her novels have won the Miles Franklin Award for Literature: *The Well Dressed Explorer* (Angus & Robertson, 1962; reprinted Penguin, 1988); *The Slow Natives* (Angus & Robertson, 1965) and *The Acolyte* (Angus & Robertson, 1972; reprinted UQP 1985). *Hunting the Wild Pineapple* (Penguin, 1979) was her first collection of short stories. Her second collection, a series of linked stories, *It's Raining in Mango* (Viking, 1987) won the inaugural Steele Rudd Prize in 1988.

"A Northern Belle" was originally published in *Hunting the Wild Pineapple* (Nelson, 1979), pp.79–95; "Heart Is Where the Home Is" was published in *It's Raining in Mango* (Viking, 1987), pp.81–91; the extracts from "Being a Queenslander: A Form of Literary and Geographical Conceit" are taken from the article published in *Southerly* 36, iii (1976): 252–64, the sixth Herbert Blaiklock Memorial Lecture, delivered at the University of Sydney on 23 June 1976; the extract from "The Teeth Father Naked At Last" is from an essay of the same name published in Thea Astley's *Three Australian Writers*, Foundation for Australian Literary Studies, Monograph no. 5, The Townsville Foundation for Australian Literary Studies, James Cooke University of North Queensland 1979; "In the Decade of the Minorities" is taken from an interview with Jennifer Ellison in *Rooms of Their Own*, ed. Ellison (Penguin, 1986), pp.50–69; and "Writing as a Neuter" is taken from an interview with Candida Baker in *Yacker: Australian Writers Talk About Their Work*, ed. Baker (Picador, 1986), pp.42–43.

Heart Is Where the Home Is

The morning the men came, policemen, someone from the government, to take the children away from the black camp up along the river, first there was the wordless terror of heart-jump, then the wailing, the women scattering and trying to run dragging their kids, the men sullen, powerless before this new white law they'd never heard of. Even the coppers felt lousy seeing all those yowling gins. They'd have liked the boongs to show a bit of fight, really, then they could have laid about feeling justified.

But no. The buggers just took it. Took it and took it.

The passivity finally stuck in their guts.

Bidgi Mumbler's daughter-in-law grabbed her little boy and fled through the scrub patch towards the river. Her skinny legs didn't seem to move fast enough across that world of the policeman's eye. She knew what was going to happen. It had happened just the week before at a camp near Tobaccotown. Her cousin Ruthie lost a kid that way.

"We'll bring her up real good," they'd told Ruthie. "Take her away to big school and teach her proper, eh? You like your kid to grow up proper and know about Jesus?"

Ruthie had been slammed into speechlessness.

Who were they?

She didn't understand. She knew only this was her little girl. There was all them words, too many of them, and then the hands.

There had been a fearful tug-o'-war: the mother clinging to the little girl, the little girl clutching her mother's dress, and the welfare officer with the police, all pulling, the kid howling, the other mothers egg-eyed, gripping their own kids, petrified, no men around, the men tricked out of camp.

Ruthie could only whimper, but then, as the policeman started to drag her child away to the buggy, she began a screeching that opened up the sky and pulled it down on her.

She bin chase that buggy two miles till one of the police he ride back on his horse an shout at her an when she wouldn take no notice she bin run run run an he gallop after her an hit her one two, cracka cracka, with his big whip right across the face so the pain get all muddle with the cryin and she run into the trees beside the track where he couldn follow. She kep goin after that buggy, fightin her way through scrub but it wasn't no good. They too fast. An then the train it come down the line from Tobaccotown an that was the last she see her little girl, two black legs an arms, strugglin as the big white man he lift her into carriage from the sidin.

"You'll have other baby," Nelly Mumbler comforted her. "You'll have other baby." But Ruthie kept sittin, wouldn do nothin. Jus sit an rock an cry an none of the other women they couldn help, their kids gone too and the men so angry they jus drank when they could get it an their rage burn like scrub fire.

Everything gone. Land. Hunting grounds. River. Fish. Gone. New god come. Old talk still about killings. The old ones remembering the killings.

"Now they take our kids," Jackie Mumbler said to his father, Bidgi. "We make kids for whites now. Can't they make their own kids, eh? Take everythin. Land. Kids. Don't give nothin, only take."

So Nelly had known the minute she saw them whites comin down the track. The other women got scared, fixed to the spot like they grow there, all shakin and whimperin. Stuck. "You'll be trouble," they warned. "You'll be trouble."

"Don't care," she said. "They not takin my kid."

She wormed her way into the thickest part of the rainforest, following the river, well away from the track up near the packers' road. Her baby held tightly against her chest, she stumbled through vine and over root, slashed by leaves and thorns, her eyes wide with fright, the baby crying in little gulps, nuzzling in at her straining body.

There'd bin other time year before she still hear talk about. All then livin up near Tinwon. The govmin said for them all to come long train. Big surprise, eh, an they all gone thinkin tobacco, tucker, blankets. An the men, they got all the men out early that day help work haulin trees up that loggin camp and the women they all excited waitin long that train, all the kids playin, and then them two policemen they come an start grabbin, grabbin all the kids, every kid, and the kids they screamin an the women they all cryin an tuggin an some, they hittin themselves with little sticks. One of the police, he got real angry and start shovin the women back hard. He push an push an then the train pulls out while they pushin an they can see the kids clutchin at the windows and some big white woman inside that train, she pull them back.

Nelly dodged through wait-a-while, stinging-bush, still hearing the yells of the women back at the camp. Panting and gasping, she came down to the water where a sand strip ran half way across the river. If she crossed she would only leave tracks. There was no time to scrape away telltale footprints. She crept back into the rainforest and stood trembling, squeezing her baby tightly, trying to smother his howls, but the baby wouldn't hush, so she huddled under a bush and comforted him with her nipples for a while, his round eyes staring up at her as he sucked while she regained her breath.

Shouts wound through the forest like vines.

Wailing filtered through the canopy.

Suddenly a dog yelped, too close. She pulled herself to her feet, the baby still suckling, and went staggering along the sandy track by the riverbank, pushing her bony body hard, thrusting between claws of branch and thorn, a half mile, a mile, until she knew that soon the forest cover would finish and she'd be out on the fence-line of George Laffey's place, the farm old Bidgi Mumbler had come up and worked for. She'd been there too, now and then, help washin, cleanin, when young Missus Laffey makin all them pickles an things.

For a moment she stood uncertain by the fence, then on impulse she thrust her baby under the wire and wriggled through after him, smelling the grass, smelling ants, dirt, all those living things, and then she grabbed him up and stumbled through the cow paddock down to the mango trees, down past the hen yard, the vegetable garden, down over a lawn with flower-blaze and the felty shadows of tulip trees, past Mister Laffey spading away, not stopping when he looked up at her, startled, but gasping past him round the side of the house to the back steps and the door that was always open.

Mag Laffey came to the doorway and the two young women watched each other in a racket of insect noise. A baby was crying in a back room and a small girl kept tugging at her mother's skirts.

The missus was talkin, soft and fast. Nelly couldn't hear nothin and then hands, they pull her in, gently, gently, but she too frightened hangin onto Charley, not lettin go till the white missus she put them hands on her shoulders and press her down onto one them kitchen chairs an hold her. "Still, now," her voice keep sayin. "Still."

So she keep real still and the pretty white missus say, "Tell me, Nelly. You tell me what's the matter."

It took a while, the telling, between the sniffles and the coaxing and the gulps and swallowed horrors.

"I see," Mag Laffey said at last. "I see," she said again, her lips tightening. "Oh I see."

She eased the baby from Nelly's arms and put him down on the floor with her own little girl, watching with a smile as the children stared then reached out to touch each other. She went over to the stove and filled the teapot and handed the black girl a cup, saying, "You drink that right up now and then we'll think of something. George will think of something."

It was half an hour before the policemen came.

They rode down the track from the railway line at an aggressive trot, coming to halt beside George as he rested on his spade.

Confronted with their questions he went blank. "Only the housegirl." And added, "And Mag and the kids."

The police kicked their horses on through his words and George slammed his spade hard into the turned soil and followed them down to where they were tethering their horses at the stair rails. He could see them boot-thumping up the steps. The house lay open as a palm.

Mag forestalled them, coming out onto the veranda. Her whole body was a challenge.

"Well," she asked, "what is it?"

The big men fidgeted. They'd had brushes with George Laffey's wife before, so deceptively young and pliable, a woman who never knew her place, always airing an idea of some sort. Not knowing George's delight with her, they felt sorry for that poor bastard of a husband who'd come rollicking home a few years back from a trip down south with a town girl with town notions.

"Government orders, missus," one said. "We have to pick up all the abo kids. All abo kids have got to be taken to special training schools. It's orders."

Mag Laffey inspected their over-earnest faces. She couldn't help smiling.

"Are you asking me, sergeant, if I have any half-caste children, or do I misunderstand?" She could hardly wait for their reaction.

The sergeant bit his lower lip and appeared to chew something before he could answer. "Not you personally, missus." *Disgusting*, he thought, *disgusting piece of goods, making suggestions like that*. "We just want to know if you have any round the place? Any belonging to that lot up at the camp?"

"Why would I do that?"

"I don't know, missus." He went stolid. "You've got a housegirl, haven't you? Your husband said."

"Yes, I do."

"Well then, has she got any kids?"

"Not that I'm aware of," Mag Laffey lied vigorously. Her eyes met theirs with amused candour.

"Maybe so. But we'd like to speak to her. You know it's breaking the law to conceal this."

"Certainly I know." George was standing behind the men at the foot of the steps, his face nodding her on. "You're wasting your time here, let me tell you. You're wasting mine as well. But that's what government's for, isn't it?"

"I don't know what you mean, missus." His persistence moved him forward a step. "Can we see that girl or not?"

Mag called over her shoulder down the hall but stood her

ground at the doorway, listening to Nelly shuffling, unwilling, along the lino. When she came up to the men, she still had a dishcloth in her hands that dripped suds onto the floor. Her eyes would not meet those of the big men blocking the light.

"Where's your kid, Mary?" the sergeant asked, bullying and jocular. "You hiding your kid?"

Nelly dropped her head and shook it dumbly.

"Cat got your tongue?" the other man said. "You not wantem talk, eh? You lying?"

"She has no children," Mag Laffey interrupted coldly. "I told you that. Perhaps the cat has your ears as well. If you shout and nag and humiliate her, you'll never get an answer. Can't you understand something as basic as that? You're frightening her."

She looked past the two of them at her husband who was smiling his support.

"Listen, lady," the sergeant said, his face congested with the suppressed need to punch this cheeky sheilah right down her own hallway, "that's not what they tell me at the camp."

"What's not what they tell you?"

"She's got a kid all right. She's hiding it some place."

George's eyes, she saw, were strained with affection and concern. *Come up*, her own eyes begged him. *Come up.* "Sergeant," she said, "I have known Nelly since she was a young girl. She's helped out here for the last four years. Do you think I wouldn't know if she had a child? Do you? But you're free to search the house, if you want, and the grounds. You're thirsting for it, aren't you, warrant or not?"

The men shoved roughly past her at that, flattening Nelly Mumbler against the wall, and creaked down the hallway, into bedrooms and parlour and out into the kitchen. Cupboard doors crashed open. There was a banging of washhouse door.

George came up the steps and took his wife's arm, steering her and Nelly to the back of the house and putting them behind him as he watched the police come in from the yard.

"Satisfied?"

"No, we're not, mate," the sergeant replied nastily. "Not one bloody bit."

Their powerful bodies crowded the kitchen out. They watched contemptuously as Nelly crept back to the sink, her body tensed with fright.

"We don't believe you, missus," the sergeant said. "Not you or your hubby. There'll be real trouble for both of you when we catch you out."

Mag held herself braced against infant squawls that might expose them at any minute. She made herself busy stoking the stove.

"Righto," George said, pressing her arm and looking sharp and hard at the other men. "You've had your look. Now would you mind leaving. We've all got work to get on with."

The sergeant was sulky. He scraped his boots about and kept glancing around the kitchen and out the door into the back garden. The Laffeys' small girl was getting under his feet and pulling at his trouser legs, driving him crazy.

"All right," he agreed reluctantly. "All right." He gave one last stare at Nelly's back. "Fuckin' boongs," he said, deliberately trying to offend that stuck-up Mrs Laffey. "More trouble than they're worth. And that's bloody nothing."

The two women remained rooted in the kitchen while George went back up the track to his spadework. The sound of the horses died away.

At the sink Nelly kept washing and washing, her eyes never leaving the suds, the dishmop, the plate she endlessly scoured. Even after the thud of hoof faded beyond the ridge, even after that. And even after Mag Laffey took a cloth and began wiping the dishes and stacking them in the cupboard, even after that.

Mag saw her husband come round the side of the house, toss his hat on an outside peg and sit on the top step to ease his earth-stuck clobbers of boots off. Nelly's stiffly curved back asked question upon question. Her long brown fingers asked. Her turned-away face asked. When her baby toddled back into the kitchen, taken down from the bedroom ceiling manhole where George had hidden him with a lolly to suck, Nelly stayed glued to that sink washing that one plate.

"Come on, Nelly," Mag said softly. "What's the matter? We've beaten them, haven't we?"

George had picked up the small black boy and his daughter and was bouncing a child on each knee, waggling his head lovingly between them both while small hands pawed his face.

Infinitely slowly, Nelly turned from the sink, her fingers dripping soap and water. She looked at George Laffey cuddling a white baby and a black but she couldn't smile. "Come nex time," she said, hopeless. "Come nex time."

George and his wife looked at her with terrible pity. They knew this as well. They knew.

"And we'll do the same next time," Mag Laffey stated. "You don't have to worry."

Then George Laffey said, "You come live here, Nelly. You come all time, eh?" His wife nodded at each word. Nodded and smiled and cried a bit. "You and Charley, eh?"

Nelly opened her mouth and wailed. *What is it?* they kept asking. *What's the matter? Wouldn't you like that?* They told her she could have the old store shed down by the river. They'd put a stove in and make it proper. Nelly kept crying, her dark eyes an unending fountain, and at last George became exasperated.

"You've got no choice, Nelly," he said, dropping the baby pidgin he had never liked anyway. "You've got no choice. If you come here we can keep an eye on Charley. If you don't, the government men will take him away. You don't want that, do you? Why don't you want to come?"

"Don't want to leave my family," she sobbed. "Don't want."

"God love us," George cried from the depths of his nonunderstanding, "God love us, they're only a mile up the river." He could feel his wife's fingers warning on his arm. "You can see them whenever you want."

"It's not same," Nelly insisted and sobbed. "Not same."

George thought he understood. He said. "You want Jackie, then. You want your husband to come along too, work in the garden maybe? Is that it?"

He put the baby into her arms and the two of them rocked sombrely before him. He still hadn't understood.

The old men old women uncles aunts cousins brothers sisters tin humpies bottles dogs dirty blankets tobacco handouts fights river trees all the tribe's remnants and wretchedness, destruction and misery.

Her second skin now.

"Not same," she whispered. And she cried them centuries of tribal dream in those two words. "Not same."

A Northern Belle

The night Willy Fourcorners sat with me, awkward in his Christian clothing, he told me between the clubbing blocks of rain, what it was like sometimes to be black in these parts. He's sat with me other nights as well and what he told me of this one or that, this place or that, was like taking a view from the wrong side of the fence. Wrong's not the word. Photographing in shadow, the object that is? No. I'm still hunting the wild simile. It was . . . it was like inspecting the negative, framing and hanging its reversals, standing back to admire, then crying in despair, "But it's all different!"

People I knew, he knew, but he knew them some otherhow — as if he saw Lawyer Galipo and Father Rassini from the lee side of the banks of heaven. I asked him once why he'd ever left his little house on the outskirts of Tobaccotown, and he was silent a long time. I coddled his silence and at last he told me. I put his story onto their stories and still I get one story.

This is Willy's story, my words.

She was born in one of those exhausted, fleetingly timbered places that sprang up round the tin mines of the north. Not in the poverty of a digger's shack, let it be understood, but in the more impressive veranda'd sprawl of one of those cedar houses that loiter in heavy country gardens. How capture the flavour of those years? Horse-rumps, sweat, hard liquor, crippled shanties, all forgotten in the spacious hours after lunch and before tea when baking fragrance settled as gently as the shadows across and into the passion-vined trellis.

A porky child with a fine cap of almost white dead-straight hair, her body gave no indication of the handsome bones that were to emerge in late adolescence. Skip some years. Now we have her at fourteen bounding confidently across the town hard-court, shimmering with sweat, her hair longer now, darkening now, still fine and unmanageable; but it's still no pointer to the strong-minded Clarice of nineteen who, despite a profile of pleasing symmetry, still boyishly racquet-scooped balls, served low and hard, and later dispensed lemon squash in the tin side-line shed where other acceptables of the town gathered each Saturday afternoon.

She had early the confidence of her class. Her father was a mine manager and owner. "AG" they called him, and he knew to a nicety what line of familiarity to draw with the blacks who still hung about the perimeters of town, even instigating a curfew for them, but was less certain when it came to men of his own colour. Which was either bright red or mottled white. In snapshots from the period he, heavily moustached and mutton-chopped beside his wife, dominated rows of sawney after-picnic guests. She always appeared formidably silked and hatted and her bust was frightening. "Breasts" is somehow too pretty, too delicate a word to describe that shelf of righteousness on which many a local upstart had foundered. Along with the bust was a condescending familiarity with the town's priest, two ministers of other religions, and four members of parliament whom she had seen come and helped go. Clarice was an only child, not as much of a son as the father had hoped for and something less of a daughter; but with the years her looks fined and softened; and if she was not in fact a beauty privilege made her just as desirable in a country where a fine bank account is as good for launching a thousand ships as a face: it's even better.

Her mother was determined Clarice would marry well, but no one was ever quite well enough.

Motor cars and Clarice's teens created small tensions. There were various young men; but the town had little to offer beyond bank- and railway-clerks, or the sons of Italian tobacco farmers whose morals the mother suspected to be doubtful. Should too long a time elapse between the drawing-up of a young man's car and Clarice's flushed entry to the house, her mother would tighten her mouth, draw up that juridical bust, and struggle to find words that were at once proper and admonitory. She was rarely able to draw that nice balance and one afternoon, as she worked with her daughter in the kitchen crumbing butter and flour for scones, she said without preamble and quite formally:

"I was once attacked by a sexually maddened blackfellow."

Clarice was startled.

"That is why." Her mother shut her lips tightly and a little line was ruled.

"Why what?"

"Why you must keep men — all men — at a distance."

"All men?" inquired Clarice. "Or just sexually maddened blackfellows?"

"You are too young, Clarice," her mother said sharply, "to use such words. Girls of sixteen should not even know such words."

"But I don't understand," Clarice persisted. "Were you —?" she hesitated. "Harmed" seemed not an exact enough word. "Were you carnally known?"

Her mother fainted.

"I do not know where," she later gabbled to Clarice's father, "where this — this child — could pick up such . . . I have done all . . . appalling knowledge . . . how the good nuns . . . wherever . . . she must be protected from. . . ."

She spoke at length to her daughter on the necessity of virtue, the rigours of beauty, of chastity, the clean mind, and the need to expunge lust. She went so far as to summon Father Rassini to give spiritual advice. She read her daughter an improving poem. Clarice listened to all this with an expression on her face as if she were trying to remember a knitting pattern. Young men were discouraged from calling. Her current bank-clerk went away in the army and Clarice, after dreadful scenes in which she finally proved herself her father's daughter, took the little branch train to the coast, caught the main line south, and burrowed into essential war industry.

The city was only partly strange to her, for she had been educated at a southern convent where her only achievements had been to stagger the nuns by the ferocity with which she played badminton and Mendelssohn's *Rondo Capriccioso*. She revealed no other talents. They taught her a little refined typing and book-keeping, insufficient to addle or misdirect any feminine drives; enough French to cope with a wine list in the better restaurants; and some basic techniques in watercolours. She had a full and vigorous voice that dominated, off-key, the contralto section of the school choir for three years, but even this mellowed into suitable nuances before the onslaught of the mistress in charge of boarders.

"My dear Clarice," she would reprove icily, "you are not a man."

"*Non, ma mère*," Clarice would reply dutifully, giving the little curtsey this particular order required.

"And further, you seem to forget that men do not . . . oh, never mind!" Mother Sulpice rolled her fine brown eyes upwards, a kind of ecstatic St Teresa, and swished off with her beads rattling.

The boarders pondered Mother Sulpice.

"You can see she was quite beautiful," Clarice's best friend, a thumping girl, commented doubtfully. "Quite Renaissance."

"Do you think she was jilted in love?" The students spent much time in these speculations.

"Oh, I heard. I heard."

"What? What did you hear?"

"Oh, come on! What?"

"My mother told me something."

"Told you what?"

"I shouldn't really say."

"Oh, yes you should," Clarice insisted. She kicked quite savagely at the iron railing of the terrace that looked out over Brisbane hills. "By not telling me you are creating an occasion of sin."

Thumper went pink. "I'm not. How could I be?"

"Who knows what I shall think," Clarice said cunningly. "I could think almost anything. In fact, I do think almost anything."

She looked slyly at her friend and observed the moral contortion with interest.

"You've got to promise," Thumper said, "that you won't tell."

"Well?"

"Do you promise?"

"Of course."

"Well," Thumper said with a pretty play of hesitancy, "well, she was engaged. Before she entered."

"And what then?"

"He died. He was killed in France. It wasn't," she said, lowering her voice in horror, "a true vocation."

"Oh, stuff that," Clarice said. "How did it happen?"

"Mummy said it was quite tragic." Clarice saw her friend's eyes grow moist and noticed she was getting a new pimple. "He was running to regain the trenches and he ran the wrong way. He was dreadfully short-sighted."

Clarice wanted to laugh. Instead, she looked at her friend hard and asked, "Do you think they'd had sexual intercourse?"

"Now you *will* have to go to confession!" her friend said.

"Poor Mother Sulpice!" Clarice sighed.

But it was for her, perhaps for the wrong reasons, transfiguration.

She studied the nun's graceful walk, imitated the Isadora-like arabesques of her hands, modulated her voice, and began training her hair into expressive curves across her ears.

"How Clarice has changed!" the nuns observed with relief. "She's growing up at last."

In class, her mind closed to the finer points of the redundant *ne*, she sought for and thought she discovered the delicate prints of tragedy on Mother Sulpice's completely calm face.

"That will be the way I will bear it," she said to herself.

After she left home the first job she obtained was as an office assistant in a factory supplying camouflage tents to the troops. She left the day the senior accountant, who was married, suggested they take in dinner and a show. When she leapt offendedly onto a tram, an American serviceman asked could he help her with her bag. She had no bag but was so confused by the nature of his offer that before she had gone three blocks she found herself in conversation with him. He told her many lies, but those she most vividly remembered were about a cotton plantation in Georgia, an interrupted semester at Yale, and no engagement of the heart, legal or otherwise. As she dressed in her YWCA cubicle for her third outing with him, she kept telling herself it was Mother

Sulpice all over again, and she dropped her firm tanned neck, glanced back into the speckly mirror, and lowered her eyes in unconscious but perfect parody.

On the sixth outing seven days after they had met, he attempted to take her to bed, but she resisted with much charm. On the seventh he told her he had been drafted to the Pacific and then they exchanged deeply emotional letters that she read again and again, all the time thanking God for the good training which had prevented "that" from happening. "That" was happening all about her. Thumper was pregnant to a marine who had crossed the horizon without leaving any other memento of his visit. Men were all like that, Thumper assured Clarice between her sobs. Clarice thought it a pity her nose got so red when she cried.

Clarice managed to repress her feelings of righteousness and exultation that she was the one spared, and after she had seen her friend take a sad train back to her stunned parents up country she slid into Thumper's job in an army canteen. She was totally unprepared for a letter some months later from Roy telling her he had married a nurse in Guam because he had to. "Honey," he wrote, "you will always be very special to me. You will always be my one true love, the purest I have ever known." He was lying again, but she was spared the knowledge of this.

She was not built for pathos. The troubles of others found in her a grotesque response of incomprehension. She kept meeting more and more men, but they all failed to please, were not rich enough or wise enough or poor enough if wise, or were too worldly or unworldly. And through all of this, growing steadily older and handsomer, she bore her singleness like an outrageous pledge of success.

At parties when other girls more nervous than she spilt claret cup or trifle on the hostess's carpet at those endless bring-a-plate kitchen teas she seemed always to be attending, she would say off-handedly, "Don't worry. It's not *her* trifle," and go on flirting tangentially and unconsummatedly with this or that. She was moving up the ranks and knew a lot of colonels now.

When the war was over she settled more or less permanently into a cashier's desk at a large hotel where for half a dozen years she was still courted by desperate interstate commercial travellers who, seeing her framed between the stiff geometry of gladioli, found a *quattrocento* (it was the hairstyle) mystique which they did not recognise as such but longed to explore. She accepted their pre-dinner sherries with every symptom of well-bred pleasure, went to films, dog-races, and car-trials with them, but always bade them firm goodnights outside her own apartment.

Then her hair began to show its first grey.

Her father died suddenly shouting at a foreman; and after Clarice had gone home to help out her mother held onto her for quite a while, determined to see her daughter settled. Rallying from grief, she arranged picnics, dances, barbecues, musical evenings, card suppers; yet even she gave up when Clarice returned home far too early from a picnic race-meeting with a *fin de siècle* languor about the eyes.

"Where's that nice Dick Shepworth?" her mother demanded from a veranda spy-post.

"At the races, I suppose."

"You left him there?"

"Yes. He is suffering from encroaching youth."

"But, my God!" cried her mother. "He's the manager of two cane mills with an interest in a third."

"He holds his knife badly," Clarice said, picking up a malformed piece of knitting.

"You must be mad," her mother said.

"And he chews with his mouth open."

"Oh, my God!"

She was dead by the end of the party season. Clarice got Father Rassini to bury her alongside AG, subdivided the property, sold at a profit and, having invested with comfortable wisdom in an American mining corporation, retired into her parents' house and spent her days in steady gardening. It became a show place. It was as if all her restrained fertility poured into the welter of trees and shrubs; and if the rare and heady perfumes of some of them made occasional sensual onslaughts she refused to acknowledge them.

The day she turned forty she bought herself a dog.

He was a fine labrador who established his rights at once, learnt smartly to keep away from the seedling beds and to share her baked dinner. They ate together on the long veranda which stared down at the mined-out hills beyond the garden, and the tender antithesis of this transferred the deepest of green shadows into her mind, so that she found herself more and more frequently talking to Bixer as if he had just made some comment that deserved her reply. Her dependence on him became engrafted in her days: he killed several snakes for her, barked at the right people, and slept, twitching sympathetically with her insomnia, by the side of her bed. She only had to reach down to pat Roy, a colonel, a traveller, or even Dick Shepworth, and they would respond with a wag of the tail.

Although so many years had passed since her parents' deaths, Clarice still believed she had a position in the town and consequently gave a couple of duty dinner parties each year — but not willingly — to which she invited old school friends, townsfolk who still remembered her father, and occasionally Father Rassini. He dreaded the summons, for she was a bad cook; but attended, always hopeful of some generous donation. Aware of this, she would keep him sweating on her Christmas contribution till it was almost Easter; and when she finally handed him the envelope they both remembered her stoniness as he had talked to her, thirty years ago, about the sins of the flesh. He'd been young, too; and whenever he sat down to an especially lavish meal at some wealthy parishioner's home he recalled her cool look as she had asked, "Are you ever tempted, Father?"

As her muscles shrank the garden acre flexed its own, strengthened and grew more robust than a lover. There were rheumatic twinges that worried her. One day when she went to rise from where she had been weeding a splendid planting of dwarf poinsettia, the pain in her back was so violent she lay on the grass panting. Bixer nosed around, worried and whimpering, and she told him it was nothing at all; but she thought it was time she got a little help.

She was fifty when she took in Willy Fourcorners as gardener. He was an elderly Aborigine, very quiet, very gentle, who had been for a long time a lay preacher with one of the churches. Clarice didn't know which one, but she felt this made him respectable. Willy wore a dark suit on Sundays, even in summer, and a tie. He would trudge back from the station sometimes, lugging a battered suitcase and, passing Clarice's house and seeing her wrenching at an overgrowth of acalypha, would raise his stained grey hat and smile. The gesture convinced Clarice that though he was a lesser species he was worthy, and she would permit herself to smile back, but briefly.

"Willy," she said one day, emerging from the croton hedge, "Willy, I wonder could I ask your help?"

Willy sat down his bag in the dust and rubbed his yellow-palmed hangs together.

"Yeah, Miss Geary. What's the trouble then?"

She came straight to the point.

"I need help with the garden, Willy." She was still used to command and the words came out as less of a request than she intended. She was devastated by the ochreous quality of his skin so close to hers and a kindliness in the old eyes she refused to admit, for she could not believe in a Christian blackskin, preacher or not. "It's all getting too much for me."

Willy's face remained polite, concerned but doubtful. He was getting on himself and still worked as a handyman at the hardware store. On week-ends he preached.

"Only got Saturdays," he said.

"Well, what's wrong with Saturday?"

"I like to keep it for m'self."

Clarice struggled with outrage.

"But wouldn't you like a little extra money, Willy?"

"Not that little, Miss Geary," Willy said.

Clarice's irritation riveted at once upon the simple smiling face, and unexpectedly, contrarily, she was delighted with his show of strength.

"I'm a fair woman," she said. "You'd get regular wages. What I'd give anyone."

Willy nodded. He still smiled through the sweat that was running down his face, down his old brown neck and into the elderly serge of his only suit.

"Please," Clarice heard herself pleading. "Just occasionally. It would be such a help, Willy. You see, I can't handle the mowing these days." And she produced for him what she had managed to conceal from almost everyone, a right hand swollen and knobbed with arthritis, the fingers craned painfully away from the thumb into the beginnings of a claw.

Willy looked at her hand steadily and then put one finger very gently as if he were going to touch it. She tried not to wince.

"That hurts bad, eh?" he said. "Real bad. I'll pray for you, Miss Geary."

"Don't pray for me, Willy," Clarice said impatiently. "Just mow."

He grinned at that and looked past her at the thick mat of grass that was starting a choking drive about the base of the trees.

"Saturday," he said. "Okay."

He came every few weeks after that and she paid him well; and after a year, as her right hand became worse and the left developed symptoms, he began to take over other jobs — pruning, weeding, planting out, slapping a coat of paint, fixing a rotted veranda board. She grew to look forward to the clear Saturday mornings when with Bixer, ancient, dilapidated, sniffing behind her, she directed him down side paths as he trimmed and lopped the flashy outbursts of the shrubs. Although at first she tended to treat him and pay him off as she would imagine AG to have done, gradually she became, through her own solitariness, aware of him as a human; so that after a time, instead of returning to the veranda for her cup of tea after taking him his, she got into the habit of joining him at the small table in the side garden.

"Where is it you get to, Willy," she asked one Saturday morning as they drank their tea, "when you take the train down to the coast?"

"Don't go to the coast, Miss Geary."

"Where do you go then?"

"Jus' down as far as Mango."

"Mango?" Clarice exclaimed. "Why would you want to go to Mango?"

"Visit m'folks there," he said. "Got a sister there. Visit her kids. She got seven."

"Seven," Clarice murmured. "Seven." She thought of Thumper. "That's a large number, I must say."

"They're good kids," Willy said. "My sister, see, she'd like me to go an' live down there now they're gettin' on a bit."

"She's younger than you, then, Willy?"

"Yeah. Fair bit younger."

"And have you any, Willy? Any children, I mean?" She knew he lived alone, had done since she had come back to live.

"Two," he said. "Two boys. Wife died of the second one. But they had been gone a long time now. Real long time."

"Where to?"

"South," he said. "Down south."

"And what do they do? Do they write?"

"Yeah. Come home sometimes an' stay with m'sister. One's a driver for some big factory place. Drives a truck, see? Other feller, he's in the church. He's trainin' to go teachin' one of them mission places."

"Well, he's certainly done well," Clarice said. "You must be very proud of him."

"Pretty proud," old Willy said. "Teachin' up the mission when he's through. Up Bamaga way he'll be. Might get to see him then, eh?"

"Do you get lonely, Willy?" she asked. But he didn't answer.

Bixer developed a growth. When Clarice noticed the swelling in his belly she summoned the vet from Finecut who took one look and said, "I'll give him a shot if you like."

"Get out!" Clarice said.

She cared for him as far as she was able, but he could only shamble from bedroom to veranda where he'd lie listless most of the day in the hot northern sun, not even bothering to snap at the flies. He lost control of his bladder and whimpered the first time he disgraced himself on the bedroom floor. Clarice whimpered herself as she mopped up.

Willy found her crying over the dog one Saturday morning. Bixer could hardly move now, but his eyes looked their recognition as Willy bent over him.

"Best you get him put away, Miss Geary," Willy advised, touching the dog with his gentle fingers. "Pretty old feller now."

"Help me, Willy," she said. "I can't do that."

He brought along an old tin of ointment he'd used for eczema on a dog of his own, and though he knew it wouldn't help he rubbed it in carefully, if only to help her.

"There y'are, Miss Geary," he said looking up from where he knelt by the panting dog. "That might do the trick."

She was still tearful but she managed a smile at him.

"Thank you, Willy. You're a good man."

It didn't do the trick; and when finally on one of the endless bland mornings of that week she found he had dragged away to die under the back garden bushes she could hardly bear it. She sat for a little on the veranda, which became populous with the ghosts of the endless summer parties of her youth. The smack of tennis balls came from a hard-court. The blurred voices of bank-clerks and railway-clerks and service men and travellers, and even the sound of Dick Shepworth eating, hummed and babbled along the empty spaces where her mother still sat in her righteous silks.

She put on her sunhat and walked down town to the hardware store, where she found Willy sweeping out the yard.

"You've got to come, Willy," she said. "He's dead."

"Strewth, Miss Geary. I'm real sorry. Real sorry."

"You'll have to help me bury him, Willy. I can't dig the hole."

"Strewth, Miss Geary," Willy said. "Don't know whether I kin leave."

He propped himself on his broom handle and regarded her awkwardly. She was trying hard not to cry. He felt all his age, too, leaning there in the hot sun thinking about death.

"I'll fix that," she said. She was still AG's daughter.

After it was over she made some tea and took it out to the garden. Willy looked hopelessly at her with his older wisdom.

"Don't you worry none, Miss Geary," he kept saying. "I'll get you a new little pup. A new one. Me sister, she got plenty. Jus' don't worry, eh?

But she was sobbing aloud now, frightful gulping sounds coming from her as she laid her head on her arms along the table.

"Please, Miss Geary," Willy said. "Please."

He touched her hand with his worn one, just a flicker, but she did not notice, did not look up, and he rubbed his hand helplessly across his forehead.

"Look," he said, "I got to be goin' soon. But true, me sister she's got these two dogs an' they jus' had pups. I'll get you one of theirs, eh? You'd like that. There's this little brown feller, see, with a white patch. He's a great little dog. You'd like that, eh?"

"Oh, Willy," she said, "that's so kind of you. It really is. But it won't make any difference."

"But it will," Willy argued, human to human. "Nex' time I come to mow I'll bring him back. You see. You'll love him."

He pushed his chair back, came round the table and stood beside her, wanting to cry himself a bit, she looked that old an' lost. She looked up at him, messy with grief, and Willy put his old arm round her shoulders and gave her a consoling pat.

"There," he said. "Don' you mind none."

He'd never seen a face distort so.

She began to scream and scream.

Being a Queenslander: A Form of Literary and Geographical Conceit

There is a saying in Queensland that the real Australia doesn't begin until you are north of Rockhampton; and as a Queenslander and a passionately arrogant one — but not defensive — I place this statement beside those pejorative remarks that have accumulated over the years — Queensland the home of cockroaches, white-ants, bananas — the slick offences from that part of my childhood spent in Melbourne. My father has gummed to his subeditor's desk in the *Courier-Mail* a verse that greatly amused him. He had cut it out of the Melbourne University magazine:

> The people of Melbourne
> Are frightfully well-born.
> Of much the same kidney
> Is the beau Monde of Sydney.
> But in Queensland the people insult yer
> And don't 'ardly know they've been rude
> They're that ignorant common and crude.
> It's hardly worth
> Mentioning Perth.

Many people have speculated on suffering as being an impetus to the creative instinct. Similar to being a Catholic perhaps, with Catholicism's early emphases on the nature of guilt, damnation, eternal punishment, the beauty of suffering (not involuntarily but voluntarily), being a Queenslander in Australia provides much in the nature of achieving possible apotheosis.

Originally it was the isolation of the place, the monstrous distances, the very genuine suspicions of political neglect and expedience by a federal government located two thousand miles away. And when I say two thousand, I am referring, of course, to those areas where the real Australia begins. When I was a teacher in Townsville, during the Punic Wars as Albee might say, I always remarked silently and amusedly the manner in which the locals referred to southerners — and they didn't mean the people of New South Wales or Victoria — or even Tasmania (where is it?); they meant Brisbane.

Queensland separated from New South Wales in 1859 when it received self-government. What is there that is different? What causes the listener who has been told "I come from Queensland" to repeat the words always with rising inflection and ever so slight italics? — "You come from Queensland?" After all our origins were much the same as Sydney's — convicts, brutality. We killed the local inhabitants with as much brio. This is only a suggestion but I think it goes back to something far more basic than this. The human race places great store on the outward trappings of conventional behaviour — or conformist behaviour. Almost from the first, Queenslanders made no attempt to reduplicate the architecture of their southern neighbours. Houses perched on stilts like teetering swamp birds, held stiff skirts all round, pulled a hat brim low over the eyes; and with the inroads of white-ants not only teetered but eventually flew away. And then, we tend to build houses so that we can live underneath them. Perhaps those stilts made southerners think of us as bayside-dwelling Papuans. Our dress, too, has always been more casual. Our manners indifferent, laconic, in temperatures that can run at over ninety for weeks on end.

Growing up in Brisbane in the thirties and forties meant alignment with a shabby town, a sprawling timber settlement on a lazy river; meant heat and dust and the benefits of the sub-tropics — brighter trees, tougher sunlight, slower-moving people and a delicious tendency to procrastinate. I think it was the weather. These virtues were raised to the nth power north of Rocky. Our school readers, apart from standard classics, promulgated those writers we learnt to associate with Queensland influences, if not Queensland birth. Brunton Stephens, Essex Evans and Ernest Favenc we took jealously as part of our culture; add to this that writers like Zora Cross, Steele Rudd, A.G. Stephens, William Baylebridge and Vance Palmer were actually born there and these names became pennants we waved.

I have an idea that Queenslanders were not early conscious of a kind of federal racism directed at them until late in the war and after. The scandalous implications of the Brisbane Line which still brings a rush of blood to the necks of old-timers were perhaps what first directed the Queenslander's realisation that he was disregarded, a joke, a butt, to the attempt to compete and prove cultural worth. Queensland had already produced two artists who received national recognition — Lahey and Hilder — and after the American rape Brisbane's little cultural parterres blossomed in galleries, theatre and literary magazines. *Meanjin* had its birthpangs on the subeditor's table of the *Courier-Mail* where Clem Christesen was working. A few young students from Brisbane High conceived the idea of a youth magazine called *Barjai* which ran for at least five years and was the nurturing ground of writers like Barrie Reid, Laurence Collinson, Vida Smith, Charles Osborne and myself. Later again the Brisbane Art Gallery received a much needed injection when it was directed by Laurie Thomas. (Memories here of a childhood trailing the brown paintings the directors previously had so loved — my paternal grandfather in those days had a landscape hung — and we could religiously stand before it in those gloomy rooms before taking a breather under the cotton palms of the outside garden and eating stale scones and drinking scalding tea — very brown — at the kiosk.)

I don't think my love affair with Queensland ripened into its mature madness until I came south to live. Maybe it was the resentment I felt when the Education Department appointed me on the status of "first year out", negating at a pencil-stroke the five years in which I had been teaching in the north. Maybe it was the remark of a head teacher here who stated solemnly that Queensland had the lowest educational standards in the world. Those things, together with recollections of the grotesque black comedy of teaching conditions, the un-withheld warmth of people who had become dear to me, and in latter years, the monstrous bathetic quality of him I can only refer to as Our Leader — who is not indeed, a Queenslander, but as one of my colleagues says, "One of nature's Queenslanders".

Since the war there has been interested and active writing growth. When I was eighteen, I met Paul Grano who was on a

Commonwealth Literary Grant and had just published a collection called *Poems Old and New*. Although Grano was born in Victoria, he had lived in Queensland since 1932. Many of Grano's poems in this collection were the direct result of the Queensland environment, and if you will again forgive my *levitas* — I quote in full:

> Patriotism (After visiting the Rest Room at the Queensland Government Tourist Bureau).
>
> All wood here used is Queensland wood,
> the blossoms pictured are of Queensland trees,
> the table, too, is as it should
> be, a product of our factories,
> we must agree are not so good
> the paper flowers with wiry stem
> but let it quite be understood —
> they're Queensland flies that crawl on them.

I ignore totally the irony of Grano at this point and cite the poem only as a positive pronouncement on the aggressive patriotism of the Queenslander which he saw, understood and was amused by.

But his own nationalism was never in doubt. He says in "Quest":

> Should I set out for Seville,
> (O orange-scented air!)
> it'll be in search of Gosford
> and gold-pied orchards there.
>
> In dim Westminster Abbey,
> where memoried great men lie,
> I'll seek the long forgotten
> graves where the teams went by.
>
> On cold starlighted prairies,
> where covered waggons pressed,
> I'll listen for the hooving
> of cattle to our west.
>
> O when I sail from Brisbane,
> I'll search each stranging way
> to find the flaming visions
> that home-blind eyes betray.

It was for me, anyway, quite remarkable to find that someone could draw his poetics from Samford and Cleveland and write in his semi-satiric poem "A New Shirt!" Why? (Grano wore dark green shirts only):

> That day on Coot-tha
> when we saw fall
> from furnaced clouds
> rain sifting down
> like golden ash
> on Brisbane town

— and it was about then that I realised the shabby areas of town and country which I publicly demolished to my southern friends but privately adored could be unashamedly declared as lyric argument. You see the nub of my paper is that literary truth is derived from the parish, and if it is truth it will be universal. A colleague, Manfred Mackenzie, says of me "You may think I'm parochial but I'm really elemental". Further to this point here is a comment from Grano's notes on *Poems Old and New* about a poem called "The Tree Planter":

> Written about 1938. I had in mind the case of a wife of a canefarmer in north Queensland. He specialised in working up farms and then selling, so that the family were frequently on the move. In some thirty years they had twenty-two different homes! At each new place she would plant fruit trees hoping that at last the wanderings were done with and the family finally settled. The trees had not matured before the family shifted to another holding. The final shift was to a suburb of Brisbane.

Here is the poem:

> She so often planted trees,
> tidy orange and cool-leaved custard-apple,
> shrubby mulberry and dark-shadowed mango,
> but ever her sorrow she saw no fruit;
> if there for the blossoming
> she had left ere the ripening
> and others it was who ate of her labour
> or greedy for caneland put axe to the roots
> of the trees she had mind to grow old with.
> And now she is old, with no orchard to walk in;
> and her mouth, should it harshen with longing,
> there is none of her fruit for its comfort
> but only the cart — or the shop-bought!
> Her sorrow it is
> who planted so many trees.

Instantly there comes to mind the Victorian Bruce Dawe's poem "Drifters". (Dawe now lives and works in Queensland.)

One day soon he'll tell her it's time to start packing,
and the kids will yell "Truly?" and get wildly excited for no reason,
and the brown kelpie pup will start dashing about, tripping everyone up,
and she'll go out to the vegetable-patch and pick all the green tomatoes from the vines,
and notice how the oldest girl is close to tears because she was happy here,
and how the youngest girl is beaming because she wasn't.
And the first thing she'll put on the trailer will be the bottling-set she never unpacked from Grovedale,
and when the loaded ute bumps down the drive past the blackberry-canes, with their last shrivelled fruit,
she won't even ask why they're leaving this time, or where they're heading for
— she'll only remember how, when they came here,
she held out her hands bright with berries,
the first of the season, and said:
"Make a wish, Tom, make a wish."

I suppose Dawe's poem is the better written. I think it is. But to support my statement that the parish is the heart of the world, I argue that the idea behind both poems is the same — each deals with the insensitivity and materialism of the male, and the more poetic "nesting" sensibility of the female (not only in practical terms) and so each poem contains its own universality. Whether a writer takes his matter from an isolated hamlet in Patagonia or the lushest cities of Europe, the cliched beauties of the English countryside or the salt-pans west of Isa, it is the manner in which these things are seen and interpreted that creates the truth and the poem — not the thing itself.

*   *   *

Writing too, is a form of emotional cannibalism. Even the critics are our dinner — and nothing, not one jot of an experience in place or person is wasted. I left Brisbane to live in Sydney when I was twenty-three, but the loyalties that persuade my entire being are to the north and funnily enough, the far north, so that when my plane circles the last small white-housed town along the reef and I watch hungrily through the port window for the high green-blue rise of tableland behind that town, I feel always that I am coming home. Home in its very nature that one must be able to laugh at with love as well as weep over. In 1970 and 1971 I was asked to give lecture-tours for the Commonwealth Literary Fund in north and central Queensland. I toted Patrick White and the myth from Mt Isa through Cloncurry (pure Drysdale) and Julia Creek to the coast; back again as far as Clermont and Springsure, through Gladstone, Rockhampton, Townsville and Cairns. In a way they were disappointing trips, and in quite another way they were totally satisfying. When I say they were a disappointment, it was perhaps because the attendance was small — average audience twelve, including babes at the breast — but those who did come had read White and Stow, did want to hear and discuss, hungered for library visits to larger centres and showed me a warmth and hospitality that was quite remarkable. My paper was a simple one, non-academic, but I still remember the woman on whose property I stayed somewhere back of Richmond who said to me after the lecture that night: "I know you're tired. I don't want to keep you up. But I can't tell you what it's like just to be able to say the word 'book' to someone." At that point I felt the taxpayers were well repaid.

Queensland has always suffered from being a cultural joke to southerners. But the early efforts to involve the people culturally in Queensland from the days when Tommy Hudson managed a Shakespearian company in Rockhampton in the sixties of the last century and Shakespeare came to the goldfields by bullock-dray with Mr and Mrs J.L. Byers playing Desdemona and Othello at Gympie Creek to appreciative audiences of settlers and miners and some few astonished Aborigines are not really a matter for laughter; in fact even less so than Harry M. Miller's productions of the vulgarity of rock operas. Round about 1868 French Charley, Charles Bouel, opened a hotel, store and theatre at Nashville (Gympie), with the motto "Live and Let Live" emblazoned across his front doors.

As a piece of *poēsie trouvēe* for the times I offer, extracted from the *Nashville Times*:

French Charley
To the diggers of Nashville
and the One Mile
C. Bouel, T. Fawcett & Co.
Novelties Every Night
at the
Theatre Royal, One Mile.
They will always do their best to please
the public in general.
THE BAR
As all the boys know, is always supplied with
the best of
Liquors and Drinks
Knock-me-downs, Pick-me-ups, Smashes,
Cocktails, Flashes of Lightning, Volcanoes, etc.
Theatre opens at 7 sharp; ring up in half an
hour after.

The prima donna, Miss Gardiner, had doubtless far more expertise than any collective dozen pop stars foisted into our youth culture of the seventies.

For comparison with Charles Bouel's poem of the last century I offer a 1976 version from a Sydney Leagues Club:

Welcome

WHEELER/DEALERS . . . HOUSE HUSTLERS . . . FIGURE FINDERS . . . AND EVERYBODY . . .

Here is what you have lined up

AT APPROX. 8PM *ECLYPSE* WILL START PLAYING DANCE AND DINNER MUSIC.

8.30 A COLD SALAD AND PLATTER WILL BE SERVED.

8.45 HOT Curried Prawns/Stroganoff will be served.

9.00 *FIRST SHOW* Presenting beautiful *HOLLY DAVIS*.

9.30 HOT Curried Prawns/Stroganoff second helpings.

10.00 Apple Struddle and cream will be served.

10.30 SECOND SHOW Last Australian show for LONNIE LEE who returns to Nashville, Tennessee.

AT ANY TIME DURING THE NIGHT YOU MAY DANCE YOUR TINY TOOTSIES OFF TILL IT'S ALL OVER AT 1 A.M. WHEN THEY SWEEP US ALL OUT.

It seems to me that we haven't moved forward from Queensland down here. We've gone back!

Perhaps it is amusing that those people travelled by dray; perhaps the ponderous journalese of the times amuses too; perhaps it amuses that culture struggled to live in canvas tents and was offered to an audience without the middle-class pretensions of first-nighters in Sydney. But what is not amusing, what is magnificent, is the human spirit, the heart of the parish, that made them want to do these things. And what is even more amazing and unmagnificent is that with all our present technological advances, widespread education and apparent sophistication, we can find monstrous crowds struggling to fifth-rate entertainers who wield guitars like phalluses, know four chords and dress like drag queens.

The trouble with Queensland these days is that it's filling up with southerners. Sometimes when I go north I feel I'm the only Queenslander left. I used the term "conceit" in the title of this paper and I mean by that that it is the especial quality of the Queensland oddball — that and the space — that give the state its overblown flavour. Stories filter south of plans to put Brisbane's police squad on pushbikes to facilitate speed in arrival at the scene of a crime. Recently there was a suggestion that the whole of Brisbane be surrounded by nuclear warheads. "But which way would they point?" one of my colleagues asked. Smiling. The state does seem to attract a conceitism of behaviour that maybe is due to the heat and the distance. Once in a bayside village halfway up the Queensland coast, one of the twenty or so permanent residents raced up to me pulsating with excitement. "There are people called Murphy moving in next door," she said. "Now at last I will be able to discuss Teilhard de Chardin!" She was wrong. But what a concept!

Yes. It's all in the antitheses. The contrasts. The contradictions. Queensland means living in townships called Dingo and Banana and Gunpowder. Means country pubs with twelve-foot ceilings and sagging floors, pubs which, while bending gently and sadly sideways, still keep up the starched white table-cloths, the heavy-duty silver, the typed menu. Means folk singers like Thel and Rick whom I once followed through to Clermont on that lecture-tour while they cleaned up culturally ahead of me; but it also meant listening to the now extinct State Queensland String Quartet play-

ing the Nigger Quartet in my fourth-class room among the sticks
of chalk, the tattered textbooks; means pushing your way
through some rainforest drive laced with wait-a-while to hear the
Lark Ascending, or more suitably, the Symphonie Fantastique
crashing through the last of the banana thickets.

And the distance. Since the days when the Petrie brothers
opened up the Darling Downs or the younger Scottish son
planters endeavoured to recapitulate gracious Delta living in
sugar plantations around Mackay, since Atherton opened up
north Queensland and Christy Palmerston rolled triumphantly
back into town (Herberton) after going bush with the Aborigines
for years, Queensland has retained much of its quality as an
abstraction, an idea — a genesis still preserved in the current
publication of the *Wild River Times*. The vast spaces, the smaller
population bring unexpected *rencontres*. You step off the plane in
Cloncurry and the sole passenger stepping on is someone you
haven't seen for twelve years. You borrow a bike and pedal
savagely ten miles north simply to get out of a place, only to run
into a colleague unseen for five years who has been stationed at a
whistle-stop school twenty miles away and has been pedalling
south for the same reason. You drive fifty miles for lunch. It's
nothing. I have friends who'll travel a hundred miles to get to a
concert and another hundred home afterwards. "It's quicker than
crossing Sydney," they say. And that's unanswerable.

Once I thought the special flavour was due to the train: those
other years when, wistfully from mixed-goods paralysed at shunt-
ing points, you would look out train windows blurred by soot
and time at friends travelling in opposite directions. The gulp.
The wave. The shouted précis of a year fading at last as you
pulled apart at ten miles per hour. But it's not only that. It's as if
the vast distance itself had rendered time static; as if the passage
from claypan to coast, from the ugly to the beautiful so essential
and complementary to each other in this place that they become
one and the same, were no passage at all.

Queensland isn't the home of the tall yarn. It's where the tall
yarn happens, acted out on a stage where, despite its vastness, the
oddballs see and recognise each other across the no-miles and
wave their understanding.

So be forgiving if the sight
Of sudden glory in some worn-out thing
Sheds broken words from me, if too much light
Has made me blind and blundering.

Peter Miles wrote those words in the forties and I repeat them now with a final reference to Rodney Hall's poem "Personal Tour":

Here, my hand is warm,
I'll guide you through my province,
off the main road, down a cul de sac,
away from any sign of suburb
into the gully where juicy leaves
tremble by the cliff.
                                        It took me
years to cut these steps in rock.
The bridge across my creek
is narrow, growing shaky, I'll admit.
But everything belongs.

Extracts from
The Teeth Father Naked At Last: The Short Stories of Barbara Baynton

> The Swiss scholar Bachofen suggested for the first time in his book *Mother Right*, published in 1861, the idea, embarrassing to the Swiss, that in every past society known a matriarchy has preceded the present patriarchy. His evidence, drawn from Mediterranean sources, was massive. Just as every adult was once inside the mother, every society was once inside the Great Mother.
>
> The Stone Mother perhaps represents in history the Mother culture during the time it was implacably hostile to masculine consciousness.
>
> In some cultures she is called the Teeth Mother. The intent is the same — to suggest the end of psychic life, the dismembering of the psyche.
>
> *Robert Bly*

In his poem, *The Teeth Mother Naked at Last*, Robert Bly, the American poet, discusses the savagery of war and the aggression principle as mythified in female presence. In a long essay, "I came out of the Mother Naked" he admits to the protective and creative mothers of poetry and living, basing his arguments on anthropological and mystic research. I take my title for this paper as a parodic version of the Bly thesis, for Baynton's stories undoubtedly equate maleness with savagery and brutality.

H.B. Gullett's portrait of Barbara Baynton, given as introduction to the Angus and Robertson edition, offers the appreciative reader an unfortunate otherness to contend with. I would suggest that the stories be read before the biographical sketch, lest the middle-class arrogance which Gullett hints at allows the reader to regard "The Chosen Vessel", "Squeaker's Mate" and "Scrammy 'And" as exercises in Australian Gothic rather than the horrible realism of selector life they are. A.G. Stephens's declaration that conventional Australians of her time were not ready to accept her outspokenness is politically interesting. The stories do tend to tarnish the golden myth of the bronzed bushman, the Galahad of

Grong Grong who, while he regarded women as less important economically or socially than his mate, horse or dog, nevertheless was depicted in the writing of Rowcroft, Kingsley, Boldrewood, Clarke, Lang, Lawson, Praed, Furphy, as treating women with sentimental courtesy, rough or polished, according to his selector or squatter class. Stephens, in his review of *Bush Studies*, published in 1902, wrote:

> Its truthful glimpses of Australian life, graphically expressed, could not (would not) have been printed in any Australian paper, though they rank highly as literature and are circulated widely in book form when issued by an English publisher. We are too mealy-mouthed (in print) and stuff far too much respectable wadding in our ears.

I do not altogether agree with Stephens that they rank highly as literature, but as an expression of revolt, particularly a revolt against the feudal conditions of life for women in the bush, they are valuable; and coming as they do from one who was prepared to form three acknowledged unions with the "enemy", they are fascinating. That two of these unions were socially and economically advantageous makes the reader wonder also whether Baynton were not applying practical solutions to the plight of her gender. It also strengthens the credibility of her stories, for they are not written from a background of deprivation and its consequent rage and bitterness.

*   *   *

There are six stories in *Bush Studies* and perhaps the dominant theme, the lingering acrid taste on the palate, is that of male brutality. Bly might write of the Teeth Mother, but in Australia we have always been conscious of the Teeth Father, whether it be the Teeth Father of the transportation system, overseer or felon, of our origins, or the Teeth Father emancipist settler removing the indigenes from their inheritance. In England the Teeth Father of British Victorianism disguised his force under religious or puritan cant, could sublimate this fearful paternity as factory owner, member of parliament, professional soldier or church god-man. The peasant Teeth Father has been with us always, modelling himself painstakingly on the primitivism of his betters but displaying it unadorned, ungraced by social euphamism. And it was to this country that a peasant Teeth Father was imported, the Father of Ockers, the despiser of sheilas, the Meat Man of David Ireland's *The Glass Canoe*.

The reality is unquestionable. What there is of dream, mystery and the unexplained, comes from detail in the characters' response to landscape; from the landscape itself. Yet the actions within the stories are so austere they create another dimension of horror by the very nonchalance of the acts themselves and the nonchalance of Baynton as narrator. A.A. Phillips talks of her "pouncing feminine accuracy". I dislike the words "pouncing feminine". They make Baynton's own point! They smack of the Teeth Father as critic; are pejorative in their essence. Were Baynton a man, Phillips would probably have used the word "discerning". The peasant element, which Phillips insists Baynton directs her anger at, has not weakened in the seventies of this country. The whole cultural interest of the media is to protect the peasant Teeth Father's social manners while endowing him with the material properties of a Roman Senator. One has only to regard the advertising craft of the Singletons of this country, the vulgarity of national comics like Kennedy, Walsh, Hogan, and the newspaper caution and respect for white-collar crime, to realise that the characteristics of the Teeth Father are respected as virtues.

*   *   *

"Squeaker's Mate" is a monstrous story of a bushwoman married to a loafer. The Squeaker is not monstrous in that his behaviour is macabre, perverted. The monstrousness lies in the man's laconic indifference; his callousness, his lacking even the most primitive refinement of feeling. He is ocker supreme. When his wife is injured by a tree she has been felling while her layabout husband sweats on tucker time, she lies in frightful distress and pain (subsequently we discover she has been paralysed) and unwilling, (perhaps unable at that moment, certainly) to speak. " 'Did yer jam yer tongue?' " he solicitously inquires. After a period of grudging and minimal care, for he hates the extra work his wife's incapacity gives him, Squeaker shifts his paralysed wife to a back shed, introduces another woman to the house, a mate whose laziness matches his own.

*   *   *

All through the story are comments that spell out male indifference, but done so casually, so off-handedly, they seem as natural as the landscape. Horror! They *are* as natural as the landscape.

*   *   *

In a country that has established a hierarchic order of man, mate, horse, dog, wife, other women, black people — then anything is possible. Squeaker is heir to centuries of convinced faith that woman is object only, a kind of domestic machine, preferably self-mending, without feelings. It has been common in this country and other western countries for men to describe women as castrators — it is their final insult; but men have always been what Brian Matthews calls vulvators; they add that extra physical dimension, establishing two apertures in females, an additional one where the cerebellum is.

Baynton does admit a kindness on the part of Squeaker's pals who give some minimal care to the injured woman. But even the pals have a poor opinion of Squeaker: "Him they called 'a nole woman', not because he was hanging round the honey-tins, but after man's fashion to eliminate all virtue." This appraisal of Baynton's is as savage and direct as Christina Stead's but not nearly as skilled. The Baynton voice cries through. With Stead we see the men actively showing their teeth, for her characters almost always expose their own faults and the authorial voice practically never intrudes. Sam Pollit is self-condemning.

One of Baynton's skills in this story is to give the injured wife a minimum of dialogue. Silent, she has even greater force. After the accident she utters the one word "pipe". From that point she does not open her mouth for the reader again. She is described as speaking to her husband but we are never allowed to hear her words; only his. And this is marvellously effective, for the husband's words are so crammed with his smallness of spirit, the reader quails. To his wife's hope she will soon be better, he tells her bluntly: " 'Yer won't. Yer back's broke . . . yer won't never walk no more.' " When she tells him of things he could do on his own around the place, "he whistled while she spoke, often swore, generally went out." His reply is often " 'Go and bite yerself like a snake.' "

Everything about Squeaker is vile. He pretends he has been bitten by a snake as an excuse for drinking the last of the brandy; he threatens his wife he will set her hut afire; he flaunts his new woman before her; he is useless at doing the practical things men traditionally have done. And after the last terrible scene in which he smashes his wife's arms and is attacked by the loyal dog, he is reduced to whining and pleading when he realises his new woman has fled back to town. He suggests his wife sool the dog onto the fleeing woman. " 'It's orl er doin,' " he pleads. (I believe this trait is known nationally as buck-passing.) No. Not one redeeming quality anywhere in this portrait of bush bully: lazy, cowardly, cruel, deceitful. Where, where are the tender Giraffes of Lawson?

*   *   *

"The Chosen Vessel" is an economic story, savage and disturbing, about a woman alone in her hut with her baby. She is attacked, raped and eventually killed by a swagman. What disrupts the story for me is the interposing of a sub-plot that distracts with its introduction of bush-politics and an Irishman's decision to give his vote to a candidate not favoured by the priest. This Irishman sees the fleeing, frantic woman, interprets her night-gowned form as a vision of the Virgin and decides to cast his vote as the priest has suggested. Of course the introduction of this sub-plot serves to underscore the heavy irony of the title; more ironically so, when the priest explains to Hennesey what it is he has actually seen and berates him. The opening of the tale has us once more view a cow and its calf, a natural complement for the woman and her baby. The story ends, too, with a glimpse of the killer and his dog.

Many miles further down the creek a man kept throwing an old cap into a waterhole. The dog would bring it out and lay it in the opposite side to where the man stood, but would not allow the man to catch him, though it was only to wash the blood of the sheep from his mouth and throat, for the sight of blood made the man tremble.

In the opening paragraph Baynton reveals how the woman fears the cow; but her fear should be as nothing to that which she has for the husband who forces her to run and meet the advancing cow, calling her 'cur' for her cowardice: " 'That's the way!' The man said laughing at her white face. In many things he was worse than the cow."

Baynton handles suspense superbly: lonely huts, prowling swagmen and the desolate acres of moonlit bush come tremblingly, quakingly alive under her pen, and the terror mounts in almost geometric progression for not only are the primitive elements loose in nature but females are placed within this environment as the natural prey of the male hunter, placed as the elected and eternal victim. It is a pity in a way that Baynton closes "The Chosen Vessel" with the glimpse of the killer at the creek. His trembling can be due only to superstitious fear like that of Hennessey, for the arrogance of almost every male figure in Baynton's work, the callousness and the brutality do not for one moment line up logically with a sense of remorse. Tears for a dog — yes. A horse — yes. Perhaps a mate, though when we read "The Union Buries Its Dead" by Lawson, we know the grief is only temporary. No man would have written these stories, for other men would have found him traitor and called him liar. But from Baynton's stance the stories ring horribly true, send out peal after peal of rage against belittlement and against that especial male fury that demands a victim.

"The women of the bush have little to share," Baynton says. But it would seem from these stories that though they might have few material things to give or lend each other, they have a vast river of spiritual injustice on which to draw, a river that spills out over their whole lives.

Baynton's attitudes as displayed in her stories were hardly engendered by the bitterness of poverty, failure to get a husband or barrenness. For practically all her life, she was comfortably off,

happy and busy. One can only conclude — and a horrifying conclusion it is — that her stories were the result of a cool observation.

In the Decade of the Minorities

Extracts from Interview by Jennifer Ellison

You once said that a novel lasts only six months, unless it's War and Peace. *Do you still think that?*

Yes, I think novels should probably have a date stamped on them, like milk. "Read by 18 October." Because the publishing world is so big, and because everybody in the world seems to be hitting a typewriter, I think that a tremendous amount is being published that naturally must fall by the wayside. I can't help wondering whether some of the books that have survived from the nineteenth century have survived purely because there wasn't this enormously fecund publishing industry there is now. And maybe books from that period, assuming that they had modern subject matter, wouldn't find a publisher today. I don't know. I just feel so much is being published.

Do you think there's too much being published?

No. I wouldn't say that. I think we live in an age where we're used to disposables. I think people have been geared to regard a lot of the printed word as throw-away. And I think a lot of the stuff *is* disposable. Probably what I write is disposable, probably what a lot of people are writing is.

But isn't it encouraging that A Kindness Cup *is still on the HSC list so many years after it was first published?*

Oh, my dear, I didn't know it was on the list. It seems to be the only book that little royalty cheques keep appearing for, so I suppose I should have guessed, you know, but no one would have told me it was set. I know some of my books are occasionally set at universities . . . But just because *A Kindness Cup* has done the best for me financially doesn't prove it's not disposable, does it?

Well, it proves it's enduring.

I don't know about that. We're in the decade of the minorities. I suppose there are relatively few books written by Australians about Aborigines. There's *Jimmy Blacksmith*, which I think is an absolutely superb book, and there are books by Colin Johnson.

*   *   *

What sort of changes have you noticed in the Australian literary scene since you were first published?

Well, there are a lot more people writing, a lot more people getting published, but the sort of thing they're writing about I think constitutes the greatest change. I think it's become an urban writing. Even if they're writing about country town, or bush, it's an urban, a more sophisticated approach, an approach that doesn't just accept the laws and values of the bush, a more analytical approach to what's going on in the backblocks. I don't know whether this is due to more widespread education since the war. I mean people seem to be more probing, more analytical, not as willing to accept the Australian myths at face value. And I think this is excellent, and I think a lot of it, too, has been induced by the multicultural society we've got here. I mean if it hadn't been for that, we mightn't have got those marvellous stories of Beverley Farmer's in *Milk*. I do think the migration programme has made a difference to our attitudes, and these attitudes obviously come out in the writing. Also, we have access to American writers, and I think they've been very influential. The

New Journalism of Tom Wolfe has been very influential, in my view.

Vance Palmer said, in 1923, that a man wants of novels vivid character, robust humour, a tough philosophy, and tragedy without a superfluity of tears. And that seems to me to describe your work. Do you think that men and women each want different things from novels?

I think they probably do. Women certainly want different things from the ones men offer them on the relationship level, so I would imagine they might want different things from their intellectual pursuits. I used to think we were all humans, men and women (there wasn't all *that* much difference), and I know a lot of pleasant, sensitive blokes who loathe what happened in Vietnam, who are caring about their kids, and so on. But you do get the feeling that overall, men demand more violence, or aggression. I honestly don't know about this. I said to someone in an interview once that I grew up believing that women weren't really people, and didn't matter in the scheme of things. You've got to remember my age. Men didn't listen to women when they expressed an opinion. I always felt that they wouldn't read books written by women, because it would be like listening to a woman for three hours, which would be intolerable. And when I started to write I knew I had thoughts going on in my brain, you know, and I'd have little opinions about things, but I knew they didn't rate, and I didn't know what voice to write as. You see, it wasn't popular in my day to talk about menstruation or periods or the angst of having children. That was just a step above Ethel M. Dell, or Mills & Boon, and I felt I'd been spiritually neutered by society. I get infuriated when they talk about women as castrators. I remember talking to Brian Matthews about this: I said, but men have done something quite different to women, they're removed their brains, you know, and substituted genital organs where the brain should be, and he said, "Yes, let's call them vulvators."

So when I came to write, I thought, well, no one's going to listen to me, or read me, or be interested anyway, but maybe there'll be a chance of being read if I concentrate on the male characters in my book, or write as I did in *The Acolyte*, using a male character's point of view rather than a female's. And I can't say I felt particularly comfortable doing this, but I suddenly realised, at fifty-plus, when I came to write *An Item from the Late News* and I had a female voice talking throughout the whole book, that I didn't know how women thought. Although I had my own ideas, when I tried to write as a woman speaking, I suddenly realised I didn't remember how I thought when I was fourteen, eighteen, twenty-five, because we were not supposed to think. I used to read books by feminist writers and I was filled with envy, and admiration for the way in which they make women's problems and the woman's voice seem not only intelligent and interesting, but totally credible. That was my first reaction to *Monkey Grip*, as a matter of fact. I thought, God, isn't it marvellous the way Helen Garner can deal with female situations of getting meals (I've always avoided meals, you know) and deal with the mundanities of a woman's day, and make it alive and intelligent and believable, without its looking twee. And I thought, I can't do this. How the hell do they do it?

I read an article about your work which said it's possible that you use males as central characters because many women perceive male characters as not marked by gender, but female characters as distinctly female.

Well, it's true. I think it is true. And consequently of little importance. That's the next step in the syllogism.

But you do feel that's changed?

Not for me, but I feel it's changed for a lot of women writers, and I think they've managed to make women and their pursuits intelligent and alive and interesting, which they always have been. I mean, all right, housework was dreary and drudgery, but now they manage to say it's dreary and drudgery, while being amusing about it. They're not whining all the time, you know; they do use it for humour, and also for making a sociological point, whereas I've avoided it like the plague, because it was one of those grey areas of living that men knew went on back there but didn't want to hear about.

In your recent novels, An Item from the Late News *and* Beachmasters, *you have become more overtly political. The nuclear issue in* An Item from the Late News *is an example.*

Well, that's really what the book was about, but you're the only person who's ever mentioned it to me, and thank you very much. I mean that. You're the only person who's mentioned it to me. Yes, that's why I wrote it.

Do you think it's important for writers to tackle social political issues?

Yes, it is. I probably should have done it years ago, but someone like Olga Masters, say, in *The Home Girls*, is very much tackling social issues, while doing a Jane Austen, which is why I admire her work so much. You know, she's dealing with this tiny canvas of living, but she's tackling things that are much wider than that, and that's marvellous.

Do you think writers have a role in helping society to evaluate itself?

Yes, I do. They're always talking about big themes for us. I'm not sure what they are, because, you see, in those stories Olga Masters has touched on one of the big themes of this decade, of women's issues, without for one moment sounding off and sounding like a strident feminist at all. She's merely telling the stories, and their brutality is absolutely entrancing. I mean, you can write wider-issue novels, Rambo-type novels, like *From Here to Eter-*

nity and all these war books that have come out since World War II, and I suppose there are publishers for all the big themes, but also they're subscribing to that Vance Palmer theory of what the male reader wants. I can't imagine a man in a plane being seen dead reading *The Home Girls*, unless he happened to be an academic who's giving a paper on it. And that's not a criticism of Olga Masters; that's a criticism of some constant in our society which no one is ever going to change. I remember once, when I had been lecturing on *The Fortunes of Richard Mahony* at Macquarie, I mentioned that Henry Handel Richardson was a woman. One of the boys in my group came up to me afterwards and said, "Are you telling me that *The Fortunes of Richard Mahony* was written by a woman?" I said, yes. Now this happened in 1970. He said, "Well, I shan't read it." I said, "That's fine, I shall make it a compulsory question in the examination paper." And he didn't read it, and he didn't answer the compulsory question, so he failed. But he'd done so badly on the other questions that he would have failed anyway.

*   *   *

Why haven't you explored the short story form, apart from Hunting the Wild Pineapple?

I do occasionally. I'm doing some now. I'm trying. I think it's a much harder form than a novel, and I think probably a play is the most difficult of all. I couldn't write a play. I think you need wonderful techniques to convey mood and character and movement and emotion just through dialogue. I think one of the best story writers in English of the last two decades is John Cheever. I think he's absolutely marvellous, and I'm re-reading Cheever, trying to stimulate myself.

You know, I'm always surprised when people such as Beverley Farmer, say, or Olga Masters, start off on the short story, because of its difficulty. I've always said, the novel's like charity, it cloaks a multitude of faults. You're so exposed in the short story. It's got to be so good, because of its size, for a start. I've just been reading

Morris Lurie's *Outrageous Behaviour*. I think he's very good. You have to do so much in so little, and if you can't do it, it shows straight away.

*   *   *

Do you think there's a distinctively Australian literature, now?

Look, I don't know. They always ask that at conferences and everywhere. Actually I do honestly think if you were given unknown passages by British writers, American writers and Australian writers, you could spot the British very easily. There's a kind of cold-climate moribundity, isn't there? Even if all place names were eliminated, there's a kind of tone. I think Australian writing now would sound more American. I'd like to think that Australian writing is becoming denationalised and has a more international flavour at the moment. If I'd read Beverley Farmer's *Milk* without knowing where she came from, and all place names were changed, I think I would have said it was American. I don't know why I would have said it. Maybe this is what's Australian now, that people are floating loose, as if they're not attached to the shores here, as they were at the turn of the century.

In a lot of your work you have attacks on the Church and Christianity and Catholicism. What's all that about?

Do I attack them?

I think so.

Oh, I was brought up as a Catholic. I'm not a practising Catholic now. I miss it very much, but I do believe in God. I don't like the trendiness of the Church. I think they've sold out to the twentieth century. I could understand the Church better when it didn't bend sideways, when it was inflexible, and you knew where you stood.

I liked the Mass in Latin. But I do regard most of the Christian churches — I'm not talking about the Catholic Church alone, I'm talking about the Anglican Church as well — as sorts of great PR organisations, like multinationals, and I think if Christ came back, He wouldn't know which door to go in. He certainly wouldn't recognise what He set out to establish. I think the residue of what Christ taught lingers on with priests who are working in places like Guatemala or Nicaragua, among the peasants, but there are so many unsavoury things about the Church's big business. It appals me.

I miss the security it offered. You know, like . . . it sounds like a ticket to Paradise — I miss that, that certainty that if you do this you're right, do that and you're wrong.

I miss the metaphysics of it, because I think everyone needs that. I think it's why so many kids these days are turning to alternative religions, because I do believe there's . . . well, I don't know whether you'd call it a soul, but I believe humans do have something inexplicable — otherwise I don't see how you can explain people like Mozart or Beethoven. And I think that the spiritual yearning in kids is determined to be fed somewhere. I mean they've made a god of pop, they make gods of rock stars, but I think because they're dissatisfied with the expression of Christianity in the twentieth century churches, that is why so many of them have turned to eastern meditative religions. It's got to be fed somewhere, this extra dimension of human make-up, the spirit, whatever you choose to call it, the intellect, or whatever it is that demands it. I think it's very sad, actually, because I think all humanity wants to worship something, even if it's only the races or the footballers, but they seem to me to be such boring gods to substitute.

Writing as a Neuter

Extracts from Interview by Candida Baker

A lot of your books are written from a male point of view, and obviously it doesn't matter to you which point of view you write from. When you're writing as a male do you feel any differently inside to when you're writing as a woman?

I'm glad you brought this up because I've never really talked about it. The thing was that I grew up in an era where I was completely neutered by my upbringing. I'm a normal heterosexual, I think, I hope — but I grew up in an era when women weren't supposed to have any thoughts at all, and if they did express thoughts then either no attention was paid to them or they were considered brash and aggressive. I also grew up in an era where they talked about "women's" literature. "It's a *woman's* book", they'd say, as if there was something wrong with that. So when I was eighteen or nineteen I thought to myself that the only way one could have any sort of validity was to write as a male. It seemed to me that male writers were accepted, and what they said was debated and talked about, whereas women writers were ignored, or whatever women did was ignored. "A woman said that", "a woman did that" . . . it's a wonder they didn't say "woman teacher", or "woman nurse". I sound aggressively feminist, don't I?

No, it sounds quite normal to me.

Well, it's just the way things were. I don't think men read women's books for a start, it would be like listening to a woman talking for a couple of hours, which would be pretty declassē, you know. I'm talking too much . . .

Not at all.

So I thought the only way a book might have validity would be to concentrate on the male characters, even though I couldn't really see things from a male viewpoint. Quite honestly I don't know what the female point of view is either. When the feminist movement of the late sixties started and women were writing about menstruation, and how they felt about being pregnant and having orgasms, I thought "I can't do this. I don't know how to express myself as a woman". I am filled with envy by someone like Helen Garner for instance. I re-read *Monkey Grip* a while ago and it's even better the second time through. I find her domestic dialogue splendid, but I always feel that if *I* put it down in that way it sounds naive and twee but she gives it a real currency of worth. I don't even know how women in general think. I've been neutered by society so I write as a neuter.

Jessica Anderson

EDITOR'S NOTE

Jessica Anderson had written a number of stories and radio plays before her first novel, *An Ordinary Lunacy* (Macmillan, 1963; reprinted Penguin, 1988), was published. Her novels explore a number of genres: *The Last Man's Head* (Macmillan, 1970; reprinted Penguin, 1987) is a psychological suspense novel; *The Commandant* (St Martin's Press, 1975) is an historical novel. Both *Tirra Lirra by the River* (Macmillan, 1978; reprinted Penguin, 1987) and *The Impersonators* (Macmillan, 1980; reprinted Penguin, 1982) won the Miles Franklin Award, in 1978 and 1981 respectively. *The Impersonators* also won the New South Wales Premier's award in 1981. She published her first collection of short stories, *Stories from the Warm Zone and Sydney Stories* (Penguin) in 1987.

"Under the House" and "Against the Wall" were published in *Stories from the Warm Zone and Sydney Stories* (Penguin, 1987), pp.3–16, 45–66; "Mates or Martyrs" is an extract from an interview with Jennifer Ellison in *Rooms of Their Own*, ed. Ellison (Penguin, 1986), pp.33–44.

Under the House

"If you don't wait under the house," said Rhoda to me, "she won't come at all."

Sybil, at Rhoda's side, jumped up and down and said, "She won't come at all if you don't."

"And for all we know," said Rhoda, "another visitor might come with her. So go on, Bea, wait under the house."

"Go on, Bea."

At the foot of the wooden steps, which jutted like a ladder from the veranda of the house, the three of us stood in the solid heat. We all wore dresses of brown and white checked cotton made by our mother. Rhoda, who now took me by the shoulder, was ten, Sybil was six, I was four. I deduce these ages from my knowledge that when I was five we left that house, which, with its land, was known as Mooloolabin, having been called after Mooloolabin Creek, the secreted stream on its northern border, to which our brother Neal, the eldest of us all, was allowed access, and we girls were not.

Rhoda's long greenish eyes, as I pleadingly sought them with my own, did not regard me with her usual love, her almost maternal concern, but were made remote and pale by the projection of herself into her intention, by the heat of her imagination. I had had much delight from my sister Rhoda's imagination, but that day I was resistant. I felt she and Sybil were deserting me. "I want to wait here," I said.

"Not in the sun," said Sybil. When Sybil asserted herself, she sought the backing of our mother. "Mum would be angry if we left you in the sun."

"And you would go to the gate and peep. I know you," said Rhoda, turning me by the shoulder. "You can't peep from under the house."

Rhoda could be coaxing and implacable at the same time. She kept hold of my shoulder as she and Sybil walked me alongside the cool breath of ferns under the steps, and then beneath the floor of the veranda. In the vertical slats encompassing that area which is still called, in Queensland houses, the under-the-house, there were two gaps, back and front, and through the front gap I was now ushered, or pushed.

"And no coming out and looking down the front paddock," warned Rhoda, as she and Sybil hurried away.

I could never go alone into the under-the-house at Mooloolabin without an uneasiness, a dogged little depression. Unless it was raining, no lines of washing hung there, and nor did my father use that space for his workbench, as he would do in the suburban house to which we were soon to move, for at Mooloolabin all such needs were filled by the Old Barn, the first shelter my father's parents had put up on their arrival with their family from Ireland.

So, in the under-the-house at Mooloolabin, there was no extension of the busy house above except the meat safe hanging from a rafter, the boxes of wood cut for the stove, and the tins of kerosene used for the lamps. These objects, dull and grey in themselves, left dominant to my eyes the sterile dust at my feet, the rows of tall sombre posts with blackened bases, and the dark vertical slats splintering the sunlight outside. Broken cobwebby flowerpots were piled in one corner. From a nail in a post hung the studded collar of the dog Sancho, who had had to be shot, and from another hung the leg irons dug up by my grandfather, relic of "some poor fellow" from the days when Brisbane was a penal colony.

Feeling imprisoned, put away, discarded, I stood where Rhoda and Sybil had left me, waiting for them to get too far away to detect me when I ran out and peeped through the garden gate. Above my head, in the big front bedroom where the three of us slept, I heard Thelma crossing the floor, slow as ever in her clumsy boots. Thelma came in from one of the nearby farms to help my mother. By the brief muffling of her footsteps, I knew when she passed over the red rug beside my bed. My discontent with the dust and husks of the under-the-house made the bedroom upstairs seem packed with colour and interest, the lace valances over the mosquito nets, and that particular red rug, so memorable because of that dawn when Rhoda had plucked it from the floor and flung it over my shoulders.

We had both been wakened by the silence, the cessation, after so many days, of the hammers of rain on the iron roof. Warning me to hold the edges of the rug together, Rhoda took me by the other hand. We crept down the front steps, stealthily opened and shut the gate dividing garden from paddock, and ran splashing down the broad rutted track towards the road. It was a quarter of a mile (my brother Neal has since told me), but memory, woven tight though I know it to be with imagination, insists that it was longer, showing me, beyond correction, a flat extended prospect crossed by those two running figures, one backed with red wool, the other with her long tangled brown hair.

I had no goal in mind. My elation in the expanding daylight was enough. But when we reached the road, a goal was provided. Heard before seen, the gutter was running with water, a miniature torrent, over stones a cascade. Instructed by Rhoda, I squatted beside it. Still holding the edges of the rug together, I put the other hand, cupped, in the torrent. I shouted to find myself holding a ball of live water. I was amazed, enraptured by such resilience, freshness, softness, strength. I had never seen a swiftly running stream, had never seen the sea. Rhoda took no part, but stood at my side, satisfied with my delight, with the rewards of the entertainer, until she judged it time for the scene to change.

"Come on. Come back. Quick. Or they'll catch us."

Who would? I didn't ask, but gleefully connived, adding my own hints of danger. The sun was prickling the tops of the uncropped grass as we ran back.

Now I heard my mother enter the bedroom above my head, her footsteps also muffled for a moment by the red rug. I could not distinguish the words she said to Thelma, yet could hear the swishes and soft bumps as they gathered up the mosquito nets and tossed them on top of the valance frames, out of the way before mattresses were turned and beds made.

My mother's presence in the bedroom stopped me from running out and peeping through the gate. The bedroom window overlooked the front garden and the paddock beyond, and if she happened to look out and see me peeping, she would call to me in her pleasant commanding voice and ask why I had been left alone. Rhoda, when delegated to mind me, was gravely warned never to leave me alone, because of the creek.

So I fidgeted and waited while her footsteps crossed and recrossed the floor above my head, brisk and staccato above the indecisive steps of Thelma. She wore neat black or brown shoes (polished by Neal) laced over the instep. Her parents had emigrated from England when she was three. Both she and Thelma wore aprons, Thelma's of opened-out sugar bags, hers of checked cotton.

They went at last, together, but left me in indecision by standing talking in the corridor near Neal's room. I would feel safe once they were in there, working. Neal's room, like the creek, was forbidden to me, though in this case the risk was to him. I had drawn a margin of red crayon round a page in one of his exercise books, in emulation of his own neat margins ruled in red ink. The consequent hullaballoo he raised is my strongest memory of Neal at Mooloolabin. Visually, all that reaches me is the misty outline of a thin figure, not much less than man-sized, standing in profile, with the hump of a school satchel on his back.

Neal and Rhoda went to the local school, where the teaching was deplorable and they were likely to get nits in their hair. "Are we to bring up our children among ignorant cow cockies?" my mother sorrowfully asked my father, by lamplight. They owned half an acre of suburban land, near a "good" school. They could sell here and build there. But my father, though agreeing about the teaching and the nits, was reluctant to leave his father's meagre acres. From an office in Brisbane he instructed others how to farm, how to treat disease in stock and crops, but still hankered to return to farming himself, so that sometimes he would respond to my mother, "Better a cow cocky than an office johnny."

As soon as I heard my mother and Thelma go into Neal's room and begin work, I ran out from under the house and stood at the gate, looking through the palings. But no visitors were approaching, neither by the track across the paddock nor through the long grass from the clump of she-oaks to one side.

But suddenly, under the she-oaks, I caught a movement, a flash of shining blue. I jumped to the bottom bar to get an unimpeded glimpse between the pointed tops of two pickets, eager to see again the exotic high gloss of that blue.

Instead, I saw a boy emerge, in grey and white. For a moment he stood uncertainly in the sun, they ran back into the she-oaks. As he was about the size of Curly Moxon, from the adjacent farm, who was moreover the only child within range, I thought that Rhoda and Sybil had been diverted, the game of visitors abandoned, myself forgotten.

The sun beat on my back and penetrated my green-lined sunhat. I went back under the house and wandered drearily about. In Neal's room work was still going on. I passed beneath our parents' bedroom (which I remember only as white, starchy, insipid, and often locked) and wandered about beneath the other side of the house, longing for solace and company, tempted by the red and blue medallions on the kitchen linoleum, the blue and white crockery on the dresser. In the windowless living room, dimness would make magnetic the forbidden objects — the dark books on the higher shelves, the shining violin in its red velvet nest, the revolving top of the music stand. But the books on the lower shelves were permitted, and beyond the glass doors, on the veranda, stood canvas chairs with sagging mildewed seats wide enough to contain entirely my curled body.

Thelma and my mother crossed the corridor into the kitchen. I saw myself standing at the table (spoken to, tended, receiving something on a plate) and considered wandering out to the foot of the back steps and having a fit of coughing. Yet when I heard Thelma come out of the back door and embark on the stairs, I instantly took off my hat and slipped behind the nearest post, my heart beating in that manner so interesting when Rhoda was with me.

Thelma took a plate of meat from the hanging safe. I was much thinner than the post I stood behind, and I held my hat crushed against my chest, but I must have moved; she must have glimpsed me as I had glimpsed that flash of blue under the she-oaks.

"Hey, who's that?" she called out. "Beatie? Syb?"

Behind my post, I did not move.

"One of you, anyway," concluded Thelma.

She turned and started up the steps. With one eye, I watched her feet rising between the treads. Then I ran over and seized the tennis ball lying among the boxes of wood and, by the time my mother's feet appeared between the treads, I seemed engrossed in bouncing the ball against a rafter, and catching it and bouncing it again.

"Beatie?"

My mother stood in the gap in the dark slats, behind her an expanse of sun-yellowed green and the weathered silvery timber of the Old Barn. The horse Pickwick was moving into the gap with his usual slow intent, cropping grass.

"Beatie, where are Rhoda and Sybil?"

I resumed my game, saying they had just gone off for a while.

She came and took the ball from my hand. "Gone off where?"

"You'll spoil it."

"Spoil what?"

"It's a game."

"What kind of game?"

Did she know about our visitors? She had sometimes stunned Rhoda and me (though not Sybil) with her knowledge of our secrets. "I have to wait here," I said with crafty vagueness, "till they come."

She looked dubious, but gave me back the ball. "You *will* wait here?"

"I promise."

"And not go wandering off to the creek?"

"I promise. God's honour."

"Your promise is quite enough," she said with a tartness I noted but did not yet understand. She twitched straight the hat I had put on in such a hurry. "And that sandal is loose. Here."

As she had crouched, I extended a foot and submitted to this service I could have done for myself. Her hair was already grey, making her olive skin look fresh and polished, and kindling her eyes beneath their dark brows. At that time she must have been in her early forties, about the age at which Rhoda died. She rose to her feet to go. "Mum?" I said.

"Yes, dear?"

"Ro won't get into trouble for leaving me?"

"Rhoda has been told again and again." My mother turned and started back up the stairs, adding, "We will have to see."

"We will have to see" meant that it was important enough to consult my father. I crushed the tennis ball between my palms, hoping that Rhoda would get off with a reprimand, chastisement being the alternative. As soon as my mother's feet disappeared, I dropped the ball and ran towards the front of the house. Warnings must be carried. But when I reached the ferns under the steps I heard the high affected voice of a visitor, and I stepped back under the house and waited.

Rhoda and Sybil came in from the sunlight. Rhoda wore a floppy-brimmed hat of shining blue crinoline and carried a little petit-point bag. Her cheeks and lips were pink with cochineal and her face white with what could only have been talcum, for our house was as unprovided with face powder as it was with lipstick and rouge. She held the bag at a dainty distance and swung her hipless body from side to side, while Sybil, dressed as a boy in grey pants, white shirt, and a tweed cap, tried to trudge.

"You are Beatrice, I believe?" said Rhoda, in a high, bored drawl.

But I could not rise to my part. I was distracted not only because I had betrayed Rhoda's dereliction to our mother, but also by the evidence which Rhoda and Sybil presented of other punishable acts. It did not matter that the clothes Sybil wore were Neal's, made to fit by many pins and tucks, nor that the tweed cap was my father's. Forgivable also were Rhoda's apricot silk dress, court shoes stuffed with paper, and little handbag; all were play property, donated by my mother's youngest sister, who was modern. And Rhoda's hair was not really cut, but looped and pinned to the top of her head, so that beneath the crown of the blue hat it approximated the look of the bobbed hair she longed for, but which was denied to her though granted to Sybil and me.

No, it was the hat itself that alarmed me, the hat, the hat. Not even the modern aunt would have worn it. It was the type called by Rhoda a "see-through" or "actress" hat. It was in fact by these descriptions of hers that I recognised it as utterly foreign, and certain to fall into the category of the forbidden. It looked brand new, too, and attached to its band was a bright pink rose of stiffened cloth. And then, to divert my attention (if anything could) from the scandal and mystery of the hat, were the military medals and regimental colours pinned to Sybil's shirt.

Rhoda's body was moving from side to side in a stationary sashay. "The little girl must be shy," she remarked to Sybil.

"Why don't you answer, little girl?" gruffly demanded Sybil.

I cried out at Rhoda, "Where did you get that hat? It's brand new. And those are Neal's medals."

"Oh, no, no, no," said Rhoda with a laugh. "Those are Johnny's father's medals. But goodness, I quite forgot to introduce us. I am your sister Rhoda's rich friend Maisie Lemon. And this is Johnny Pumper."

Overhead, Thelma clanked a bucket down on the bathroom floor. By my mother's footsteps I could locate her in the kitchen. Under compulsion not to shout, I wailed instead. "It's not Johnny Pumper. It can't be. And where did the hat come from? It's *new*. And those are *Neal's medals*."

On my forbidden forays into Neal's room I had seen how he kept those Anzac decorations in little separate boxes, each laid out on a piece of card, with a border ruled in red ink. I was aghast at Rhoda's sheer nerve in having gone in there and simply grabbed them.

But Rhoda was looking at me with mild adult surprise. "Who is Neal, little girl?" she asked. Sybil frowned and folded her arms.

"You'll get into awful trouble," I said.

"What a silly little girl," remarked Rhoda to Sybil. Sybil shook her head in wonder at my silliness. Rhoda turned again to me.

"Johnny's father was a war hero, killed at Gallipoli."

For a moment I was arrested. At the nitty school there were many fatherless children. But the attraction of the word "hero" could not conquer my distress, my confusion at having been presented with too many problems at once, so that I did not know which to tackle first. I said, trying to be calm, "That is not Johnny Pumper. And how will you know the right boxes to put the medals back into?"

Sybil gave a gasp and turned shocked eyes on Rhoda. For a moment Rhoda's eyes responded in kind, but in the next moment

she had converted her shock into the energy with which she patted her hair and thrust forward her painted face.

"Little girl," she said with clarity, "you are not very polite. I
introduce Johnny and myself, and instead of saying how-do-you-
do, you go on with all that bunkum. I will give you one last
chance." She indicated Sybil, who again folded her arms and set
her feet apart. "This is Johnny Pumper, and I am your sister's
great friend, Maisie Lemon."

Also with my feet apart, I flailed my arms around like a wind-
mill. This reduced my impotence and anxiety, and enabled me to
say, "Those are stupid *stupid* names."

Rhoda did not move nor speak. The hand with which she had
indicated herself remained suspended in graceful limpness near
her chest, a hostage to the game behind which she could withdraw
into brief consultation with herself. For of course I was right. The
names were stupid. Rhoda had reached that point in her creation
where her characters had slipped away from her first flippant
choice of names and now needed rechristening.

"It is true," she said at last, "that I am not Maisie Lemon."

I pointed vehemently. "And that is not Johnny Pumper."

For very near the heart of my offendedness was Sybil's imper-
sonation, which deprived me of the original Johnny Pumper, a
foolish pigeon-toed redhead who resided in the sky and was often
in serious trouble with his father. Whenever it thundered Rhoda
said that Mr Pumper was roaring at Johnny, and demonstrated
the terrified tumbling gait at which Johnny tried to escape his
father.

"No," admitted Rhoda, "it's not Johnny. That's true, too."

"Then why did you say it was?"

Rhoda's eyes were narrowing, her tone becoming threatening.
"I had an important private reason. It is something to do with the
government. And now, dear —"

"And the hat!"

"And now, dear," said Rhoda, in steady and overt threat, "I
have a little present for you."

I was silent at once. After giving me a glare of warning, she
opened the petit-point bag and took out a small parcel. Unwrap-
ped, it disclosed three big lollies, tenderly pink, perfectly

globular. We were seldom allowed sweets, and these looked as desirable as the kind bought in shops. I put my hands behind my back and stared at them. Sybil shuffled closer, licking her lips. I said, through my watering mouth, "Where did you get that hat?"

"You may take one, little girl."

Suddenly Sybil and I both plucked with greedy little hands at Rhoda's palm. Rhoda took the remaining sweet, raised her eyebrows as she examined it, then slowly and fastidiously put it into her mouth. With my own sweet still melting in my mouth, I flung both arms round Rhoda and clutched her tight.

"Ro! Tell me about the hat."

"I shall never tell you about the hat," said Rhoda blithely.

"Ro!"

"I shall carry the secret of the hat to my grave."

One of Rhoda's eyes had a cast. It was extremely elusive. Like that flash of blue under the she-oaks, or the movement Thelma glimpsed of the child behind the post, you saw it, then doubted that you had. Even at her photographs I must look closely to detect it.

She can't have been physically punished — chastised — for leaving me unguarded, or I would have remembered it. At that time illness was taking hold of my father, stiffening and hollowing out his big frame, and sometimes, after he had made the long journey home from Brisbane, his coughing and exhaustion left my mother room for no other concern. In any case, it was certainly not one of those occasions when Rhoda, her face wet with tears, would hug me and whisper that she was going to run away, and would give me as a memento her cinnamon brown handkerchief with the clown embroidered in one corner. How we bawled and clung! The next day she would take the handkerchief back.

As for the medals, I recall only my mother saying, with absent-minded benignity, that no great harm had been done, and Neal could put the medals back himself, though Rhoda must promise not to take them again.

Maisie Lemon evaporated, as characters will when untimely exposed, and so did both Johnny Pumpers, the fake drawing the original with him. Rhoda's attempt to reinstate the original during the next thunderstorm met with my absolute stubborn and insulted resistance. Later, an attempt was made to bring on a Christabel Someone and a Cyril Somebody-else, but before they could take hold, we moved to the suburban house.

As soon as we moved from Mooloolabin it became Old Mooloolabin, by the same process as, when our paternal grandparents moved from their first stout unornamented shelter, it became the Old Barn. At the new house we had less need of outright fables. Relations and our parents' friends could easily visit, other children lived nearby and could be asked home, and we could see, passing in the street or standing behind counters in shops, persons of sufficient familiarity, yet sufficiently strange, for Rhoda and I to graft upon their lives our frequently outrageous speculations.

And in a bush gully at the straggling end of the street ran a creek frequented by children my mother would have called rough or even undesirable. We did not have that child-tracking device, the telephone; I would say I was going to Betty's or Clare's and would go instead to hang around at the creek, keeping a slight distance, shy yet fascinated. I kept the creek secret even from Rhoda, feeling that it would lose value if it were not all my own. Rhoda, now that she had friends of her own age, also had her secrets, but in spite of our different preoccupations a special fidelity to each other remained, and for me, the hat remained a marvellous apparition, ever blue, shining, and brand new. At first I continued to beg Rhoda to tell me where she got it, losing my temper and pummelling her when she wouldn't; but she would only give her former answer, or would smile as if at private knowledge as she fended off my fists. And after a few months, though I continued to ask, my question — Where did you get the hat? — became cabalistic, something to sing into a silence, to murmur for the mystification of cousins, or to whisper for reassurance if we found ourselves isolated in uncongenial company.

Only once did the ground of our tacit deceit shift a little. Now that we lived near shops we managed to get more manufactured sweets than before, but I continued to remember as so excellent those three pink lollies that one Saturday afternoon, when my mother was not visiting, attended by Sybil, and Neal was helping my father in the garden, I persuaded Rhoda to show me how to make them. I watched closely as she mixed icing sugar, milk, coconut and cochineal, and as she rounded the mixture between sugared palms. She covered it briefly — a magician's gesture — before presenting it. And I saw that it was imperfectly round and slightly grey with handling. Yet there was Rhoda's face, as confident and triumphant as at Old Mooloolabin.

I took the lolly, put it in my mouth, and twirled away through the house until I reached the front veranda. Here I rotated quickly and silently, the better to meditate on what I had just learned. Rhoda came out and twirled nearby. The wide verandas and smooth boards of the new house had set us dancing, and a Christmas play had given us our models.

Coming to a stop beside Rhoda, my speculation complete, my decision made, I advanced my right foot, curved my right arm above my head, and gazed upward at my hand. Rhoda, the backs of her hands forward, bowed low to the audience. Beneath our feet, in the under-the-house, the leg irons hanging from one nail, and Sancho's collar from another, were seldom noticed among all the stuff from the Old Barn. Outside in the garden Neal, now clearly defined as a tall youth with dark curls and a meritorious frown, walked in a strenuous slope behind a lawnmower. Gazing upward at my primped hand, I said to Rhoda, "That hat wasn't new."

"It's true," she said, "it wasn't *new*."

Undefeated, she contrived to imply, by that slight inflection, that its lack of newness was a distinction, adding mystery, extending possibilities. Filled with delight, I flung myself twirling away down the length of the veranda. Once again, as when we ran back from the marvellous torrent, I fully connived, this time by silence, so that together, twirling at different parts of the veranda, we put my new-found cleverness in its place.

Against the Wall

F's and S's were the worst, but I was sure I remembered a time when even they came unimpeded from my mouth.

My stammer was one of the many things not mentioned in our family, but I often pondered it in my mind. It baffled me so much that at last I went to Rhoda, who was six years my senior, and asked if it had begun after I had that f-f-fall from the ladder propped against the wire enclosure of the half-built tennis court in the park.

Rhoda said she was pretty sure I used to stammer a bit at Old Mooloolabin, before we moved into the suburbs and became acquainted with such things as tennis courts and parks. I asked Sybil, but she, close to my own age, remembered no more than I did. But when I asked Neal, the eldest of us all, he replied reluctantly that yes, if I must know, I was already stammering a bit before we moved into the new house, and that the best thing to do was just to ignore it.

I went and asked my mother if I had been born with it. "Indeed you were not," she indignantly replied. She always resisted any suggestion that any of her four children had not come perfect into the world. In a Church of England upbringing she must have heard of the sins of the fathers, but perhaps she was required to stifle all such ignorance and superstition when she became active in the Queensland labour movement in which she met my father.

"It's not a stammer at all," she said. "It's only a little hesitation. Ignore it, and it will pass."

I imagine us both standing in the radiation from the wood stove. I often approached her as she worked there, because I did not want her undivided attention. We employed no farm girl now to come in daily to help her, but only Mrs Hanly on Mondays. I fiddled with the row of ladles and spoons and said, "Then why isn't it passing?"

"Did you stammer just then?"

"No," I admitted.

"Well, you see?"

"But I do other times."

"That's because you dwell on it. Stop thinking about it, and it will pass."

But I couldn't stop. It was so mysterious. I was puzzled especially by its long remissions. It would be absent for hours, even for days, and then suddenly, there it would be, in response, I felt, to some emanation, either from inside myself, or issuing from those I was speaking to. *What is it?* I would inwardly cry, while outfacing mimicry or commiseration.

What *is* it? There was no reply. I tried to settle for the family attitude: ignore it and it will pass. At home and with my friends this was fairly easy, but at the ugly school across the park it was considerably less easy, and when a new teacher, Miss Rickard, came into the classroom one day and took charge, it became impossible.

Miss Rickard did not like teaching us.

"Oh, you po-or barbarians. Or, as you yourselves would say, *pore*."

Sometimes she would take the class into her confidence. "I have travelled," she once loudly announced, "in realms of gold." She let her glance move slowly over us, showing incredulity at her own presence before us. She was short and slender, about forty, and wore interesting embroidered blouses and short, dark knife-pleated skirts.

When I mentioned the realms of gold at the table at home, my father remarked that she must have been quoting, Sybil said that Miss Rickard had spent two years in Europe, and Neal said, indistinctly but forcefully, "Much *have* I travelled in *the* realms of gold."

He had not been quite able to finish one of his huge mouthfuls before speaking. "Neal makes me sick," cried Rhoda with equal force.

"That's enough," said our parents together.

"Keats," said Neal contentedly.

The word-blocking emanation issued very strongly from Miss Rickard, or from myself in her presence. When called on to answer a question, I held up the class and diverted everyone's attention, so was excused from answering until, one afternoon, Miss Rickard happened to follow in the footsteps of myself and my friends, Betty and Clare, across the park.

"You," she said the next day. "You can speak perfectly well when it pleases you. Now, stand up."

I stood, the hinged seat clacking against the desk behind mine. I knew I was not innocent of provocation. It was likely that she had heard me asking Betty and Clare just to look at that pooh-ah little bird.

"Now," said Miss Rickard, "you will kindly answer this."

As I struggled and hissed, the class grew restless. Some giggled. "Very well," said Miss Rickard. "Perhaps tomorrow you will change your mind. Now please go and stand against the wall."

Miss Rickard did not give cuts, but used her cane only as a pointer. She told us she would not demean herself by giving cuts.

For a week or so Miss Rickard would challenge me to answer a question, and a few minutes later, there I would be, against the wall, wiping with the sole of one sandal the timber on which the feet of trouble makers had left a row of marks like the shadow of darkened teeth. Then, for days, perhaps for a whole week, she would suspend the challenge, and I would hope that she had understood, or had forgotten me. Now I think it likely that she herself was sick of it, worried by it, and wanted a rest. In any case, she would always return to the attack.

"Come along now. Stand up and give us the answer. We all know that you know it."

I can't imagine why Miss Rickard believed I had devised this torment for myself, nor why she persisted in her belief, and kept us locked in a struggle she was doomed to lose, for as I stood and struggled to speak, the former emanation came to seem like a substance, visualised by me as a tangled mass of some sort, spiny, prickly, or a forward-inclining jagged rock which blocked at last even the contorted sounds I had managed before. I think she did suspect then that speech was truly beyond my control, because she spoke to me, less curtly, of will power, but that exhortation did not help either.

Somewhere in Australia in the twenties there may have been parents' associations, but I have heard of none in Brisbane. On the contrary, parental intervention was considered very eccentric, and was dreaded by the children themselves. At the nitty school Neal and Rhoda had attended when we lived on Old Mooloolabin, our father's intercession in school affairs had resulted in daily taunts from the other children that Rhoda and Neal had a mad father. The nitty school was one of the reasons my mother had advanced for moving from my father's childhood home, and I now often heard her commend the ugly school across the park, saying with the utmost confidence that it was one of the best schools in Queensland, and my father would agree, replying that in that respect at least, the move had been a success. Sybil, two classes above mine, did not complain, and Rhoda had had an uneventful attendance there before going on to high school. So that left me, only me — my troubles must be my own fault, in accord with my transgressions, such as arriving in class late, going to play with the poor kids at the creek, smoking Betty's father's cigarettes, and stealing threepences to buy pies from the pieman who came to the school in his painted cart, ringing his bell, every lunch hour.

I am not sure how my parents came to hear of my trouble, but as it was only a few days after the headmaster came into the classroom and found me against the wall, I think he must have summoned my mother, by letter, to the school. I heard of it only when Betty and Clare, as we set off one day for home, whispered that they had just seen my mother going with Miss Rickard into the headmaster's office. I gasped, and we all three tried to think what I had done. I could think only of the pies, which my mother said were nasty unhygienic things, on no account to be touched.

At home, I said nothing to Sybil (I always thought of Sybil as "on the other side") but waited with anxiety until I heard Rhoda's tread on the side steps.

I trailed after her to her room. "Ro, do you know what? Mum's over at the school."

Rhoda put her panama hat on the bed, upside down, to let the sweat band dry out. "You've been dawdling across the park again, I bet, Bea, and getting there half an hour late."

"I haven't. Not si-si-si"

"Since Miss Rickard?" Rhoda sat on the edge of her bed staring at me while she unlaced her shoes. "Do you do that much there?"

"I told you about it," I said angrily.

"Then that's it. Holding up the class."

"You forgot I told you."

"I have things on my mind."

"What things?"

"It's too hard to explain."

"I wish I could run away."

"Don't worry. If they go after school, hardly anyone sees them. Not like dad that time. When I think of it!"

"It can't be only for holding up the class."

"You could ask mum when she comes home."

"You know she won't tell me. They never tell us anything."

"Well, it will come out in the end."

Rhoda took off her school tie and hung it on the end of the bed to dry out. In spite of daily baths in the cold hard tap water, and an occasional sluice with the precious rain water from the tank, all the older ones must often have smelled of sweat. Rhoda took off her navy blue skirt and held it up to see if the pleats were sharp enough, or if she would have to light the petrol iron and press the sweat back into the serge. I still wore my gingham dresses, which Mrs Hanly washed every Monday, and hung, with Sybil's, in a row on a line across the back yard, or, if it rained, under the house.

When my mother came home from the school, she put a kindly hand on my shoulder, but I saw that she was smouldering and taciturn, and when my father arrived home from work, and I lolled about his chair, she told me to leave the room; she wished to speak to him privately.

I went to pester Rhoda again, but she was cleaning the bath, and was in high declamation.

"It's not my turn, it's Syb's turn. Why does mum always say it's my turn? And anyway, why can't Neal have a turn? He's the biggest and dirtiest. Just because he's a boy. Or man, according to him."

At the table that night it was apparent that my mother's taciturn mood had been dispelled by her talk with my father. Both were noticeably gentle and attentive towards me, and towards each other were rather humorous and conspiratorial. My reading of these signs gave me nothing specific; it was not until I went to the school next day that I got a glimmering of what had happened in the headmaster's office.

Miss Rickard, after asking me a question, told me not to bother to stand. She explained to the class that I was to be excused from standing, but would stay seated, just as I was, and they would see how nicely and promptly I answered. And in the weariness and irony with which she soon passed the question to another child, I heard her addressing my mother.

When I reached home that afternoon, my mother was on the side veranda to greet me.

"How was school today, dear?"

"Good." I ran past her, through the dining room, into the kitchen — her footsteps following — and took the lid from the bread crock.

"I hoped it would be," she said.

My side vision caught a nervous gesture of hers, patting or smoothing the dress over her thighs. "Bread rolls!" I said joyfully.

"I was sure," she said, "that that little hesitation became worse in class because of the psychological effect of having to stand and draw attention to yourself. I explained to your teacher that if you answered sitting down, it would be just like speaking at the table with us."

"Yes," I said. I sliced a bread roll, trying to sound like Sybil. "Oooo, I love these bread rolls. I'm terribly hungry."

My mother could always be distracted by our appreciation of food. It gave her intense satisfaction to feed us well. It expressed both her love for us and her triumph over the shortages of an immigrant childhood. Hovering, wishing to share the ritual, she removed the gauze dome from the butter and cheese, reminded me that there were plenty of tomatoes, and suggested that there might be ripe bananas on the hand hanging under the house.

The next morning, I stole a packet of dates from the pantry, and instead of going to the school, took my satchel and lunch to the forbidden territory of the creek.

A few months before, among the children of vagrants I met at the creek on Sundays, two new ones had appeared, a twin brother and sister, the Kellaways, both very thin and knuckly and narrow, almost albino. Everything about these two interested me. I was fascinated to observe the way their joints moved, their forearms scaled by the sun, the blinking made conspicuous by their whitish lashes, the set of their hand-me-down felt hats, their professional way with the yabbies. And they were so good-tempered with me, almost condescending as they put their heads back and squinted drolly at me down their cheeks. I always felt joyous after seeing them, and would run home waving my arms pointlessly about. When they disappeared, without warning, as such children did, I felt so deprived that I had to convince myself they would soon return; and now, while my expectation was still high, there they were, as if in reward for my first truancy, in their unmistakable grasshopper crouch by the creek.

Shouting their names — Peggy! Des! — I ran recklessly down the slope, vaulting the low scrub, yelling and halloo-ing, my satchel flying and thumping, until I saw that Peggy was running softly towards me, tapping her lips. As I slowed down I heard Des say, "Damn and blast it."

"There," said Peggy. "That's all your noise. It was a big one, too."

"Ar, well," said Des, with the cadence of resignation.

Des and Peggy took their yabbies home for food. If I caught any, they took those too. "Gee," I said, "I'm sorry."

"Ar well," said Peggy.

"I've got a packet of dates."

"Never mind," said Des. "I'll get him yet."

"He didn't take the meat," said Peggy. "That's one thing."

"I've got dates."

"We heard you," said Des. "Now shut up till I get him."

"I'm so sorry," I said again.

"Ar, well, never mind," they said together, with their lilting resignation.

I took off my sandals, lay on the rough ground, and rubbed the soles of my feet luxuriously against the trunk of a she-oak. Holding aloft *The Last of the Mohicans*, first in one hand and then in the other, I read, mechanically waving away the mosquitoes and wiping ants off my legs with my feet. Peggy and Des murmured and fished, the thin foliage shifted against the bright sky, the print blurred, and I lay on my side and slept. At that time I often slept in the day because my nights were disturbed by the dark angel in his various forms. I was wakened by Peggy and Des wiping the ants off me and asking me "What about those dates?" A sustained distant aerial hub-bub told me that school was out for lunch. I could have worried, but would have been ashamed to show concern before the Kellaways. The yabby tin was full, and for a while after lunch we ran around in the heat, flinging ourselves violently to the ground and shooting our enemies with sticks. Practised in being an enemy, I was admired for the loosened knees and head wobble with which I went down. I already knew that their father had shot many people during the war, and today, as we cooled off with our feet in the clayey mud, I also learned that their mother was the most beautiful woman in Queensland, and that they lived in the best camp on Budjerra Heights.

"If anyone moves into the camp while we're away," said Des, "they know they got to get out the minute we get back. No fight, no roaring, they just got to go."

Peggy was nodding, seeming to share a musing pride and happiness in their camp. And I was suddenly begging them to take me to see it. I begged desperately, but they would not promise. I told them about *The Last of the Mohicans*, but they knew all that, because they often went to the pictures. I told them about *Treasure Island*, and they listened intently, and asked for a loan of the book.

"If I can come to your camp," I said.

"Righto," said Des.

"We'll have to ask first," said Peggy.

The word-blocking emanation seldom came between us, and when it did, they were able to dispel it by giving me that droll squint down their cheeks. They went off with their tin of yabbies, and I went on with the Mohicans, until once again the aerial hubbub reached me, and I knew I had to go home.

In the kitchen, Sybil was taking bread from the crock. She excitedly told me her class was going to be allowed to use the school tennis court. She jumped up and down and said, "Isn't it marvellous!" She had not noticed my absence. The next day, afraid to go to school without a note of explanation for Miss Rickard, I took extra sandwiches, and three bananas, and went to the creek again.

The Kellaways were not there, but except when the miniature pandemonium of lunchtime stirred my anxiety, I passed the day contentedly enough, reading, eating, paddling, and in the afternoon becoming absorbed in searching the ground for treasure. I had never looked for treasure at the creek before, and was surprised by what I found. How did all those little pieces of patterned china, those smoothed fragments of bubbly glass, like petrified water, come to be in this little bit of bush between two suburbs? The little rubber bag I found being too small for a balloon, I decided it was a toy titty bottle. I washed all these treasures in the creek, set them out on a log to dry, and at three o'clock wrapped them in my lunch napkin and set off for home.

Hoping for a miracle, but feeling doomed, I dawdled, indulging in a daydream in which Peggy and Des were old enough to adopt me. When I got home, after four, I saw Sybil in the back yard practising serves with Rhoda's racquet. My mother was sitting at the dining room table, writing a letter. She said without looking up, "Come here."

I stood at her side. She did not stop writing. My eyes gathered the words from her page . . . *interested to know if you grow roses there* . . . She was writing to the Indian woman from Penfriends for Peace. "You weren't at school," she said.

. . . *as you are on the cooler highlands* . . . "Who told you?" I asked.

"That's beside the point."

. . . where I have heard that even daffodils . . "What are you going to do, mum?"

"Speak to your father. Where were you?"

. . . and other English . . . "At the creek", I said.

She stopped writing. "Who else was there?"

"Nobody."

"Then what did you do all day?"

"Nothing. I read *Owd Bob*. I made a collection."

Recalling how warmly she commended Neal's various collections, I swooped into my satchel, which smelled, as always, of banana skins, and rose unfolding the napkin. "Look, this glass. And this china with tiny perfect fl-fl-flowers on it. And look, a toy —"

She was on her feet. I had already seen her face set in its lines of frightening disgust. She seized my collection, went into the kitchen, lifted the lid of the stove, and dropped it in. I ran after her, babbling about the beautiful glass. She drew me by the wrists to the sink, scrubbed my hands, then her own, and dried them on the roller towel. She walked away from me, with a firm pressure of her heels, sat down and continued vigorously to write. I ran to her, crying. The shape of the toy titty bottle, as it dropped into the flames, had made in my mind a lightning connection. I believed I had kept my attendance at the creek secret from my family because it was all my own, and because to reveal it would be to end it, but now I admitted as another reason that ritualistic "showing" of the genitals. I put my head against my mother's arm. "Mum," I said.

"Go away."

I wouldn't move. Her hand sped across the page.

. . . surprises many people that in this sub-tropical climate we grow splendid roses. Here I have a clay sub-soil . . . "Go away," she said.

In the back yard, Sybil was just about to serve. I rushed her, twisted the racquet from her grasp, and threw it over the orange tree. "Pimp," I said.

"I had to. Miss Rickard told me to."

"You could have warned me. You saw me come in. Pimp, pimp, pimp."

"You see," said Sybil, "you can talk if you want to. It's true — you do just put it on. Dad will thrash you, and it serves you right."

Girls at the school had told me I would be hanged if I killed anyone, and of all the deaths that occupied me, hanging was the one I currently feared most. I took my fury away, running up the side steps three at a time. Through the door to the dining room I saw that my mother still sat, one foot advanced as when she played the violin, engrossed in her letter. I went to the front of the house and took the Gladstone bag from the hall cupboard. I was in the room I shared with Sybil, stuffing the bag with books and clothes, when Rhoda came in, carrying her heavy school case and her panama hat.

"Mum says you played the wag."

"Excuse me. I am running away."

Rhoda at fifteen had only recently stopped packing the Gladstone bag herself. "Where will you go?" she asked calmly.

"I know places. There are little camps, where anyone can live."

"Camps? Humpies. You mean humpies. Who would live in a humpy?"

"People."

"Yes, the sort of people who go to the creek. That's what made mum really wild. You went to the creek. She says you put yourself in danger."

"Nobody in this house knows anything."

"Why did you *tell* her you went there?"

"She asked straight-out. You know how hard it is when they ask straight-out."

Rhoda stuck her hat on top of her head, set down her school case, and sat astride it. "If all this is because of that trouble at school, you should listen to yourself now, Beatie. You *can* talk."

I burst into tears. When tears came into her eyes, and she reached out to hug me, I punched her away. I shut the Gladstone bag and picked it up. She tried to wrench it from me. Screams of rage would have brought my mother. Instead, I kicked her school case, then seized her panama hat and threw it into the furthest corner of the room. "The *expense* of those panamas!" my mother often said. I knew it would draw Rhoda after it.

All the same, she wasn't far behind me as I lurched and staggered along the veranda and down the front steps. It was my first experience of the weight of books. On the front lawn Rhoda caught me, and we stood and fought. Mr Mead and Mr Greenlees passed, on their way home from work, but were too discreet to look. Young Mrs Cookson ran past on her high heels, carrying her little white parcel of chops, and called out a careless admonishment. "Now then, girls!" "It's all right, Mrs Cookson," called Rhoda in reply. "It *is not*," I furiously gasped. I was beginning to be appeased, but did not want to show it yet. I knew that no matter what I pretended, I could trust Rhoda not to let me go, and in the end I allowed myself to be led back, exaggerating my exhaustion, feeling less debased than before. Rhoda carried the Gladstone bag. "Golly, what have you got *in* it?"

Sitting on the edge of the bath while Rhoda washed my face, I told her about the china and glass I had found at the creek.

"How did it come to be there? It's a real mystery. And I f-f-found a rubber thing too, with a teat on it, like a toy titty bottle."

"I know those things," said Rhoda.

"What are they?"

"Men put them on their dongs."

"Yes, but why?"

"Gwen and I think so that if they leak a bit, they won't wet themselves."

"Boys don't put them on."

"No," said Rhoda dubiously.

"Are they expensive?"

"How would I know? I'll comb your hair. Bea. You look awful."

But now I recalled my mother's face as she seized my treasure, and as Rhoda combed my hair I said calmly, "I think they're for something worse than wetting."

"That's what two girls in our form say. These two say they know, but they won't tell Gwen and me. But don't worry, we'll get it out of them."

"Will you tell me when you do?"

She stood back and looked at my hair. "You're hair's hopeless," she said absently, and added in the same tone, "I can't tell you everything, Bea. There isn't time, or something."

On the edge of the bath, I let my shoulders droop and my hands dangle between my legs. "Ar, well," I said, like Peggy and Des. "Ar, well, never mind."

"I've got to go," said Rhoda, unwilling at the door. "I've got to go and do my bloody homework."

She was trying to divert me, but her curse failed to make me give my usual joyous shout. "Wait," I said. "Ro, Syb says dad will thrash me."

"Bea, if it were only playing the wag, you might get out of it. But the creek. Nothing will get you out of that. I would only make it worse. 'Is it a matter of indifference to you'," asked Rhoda in our mother's voice " 'that the child puts herself in danger?' No, Bea, your only hope is if dad comes home sick."

"I hope he does," I said.

"Don't say that," said Rhoda, worried.

"I hope he comes home terribly sick. I hope —"

Rhoda sprang from the door and put a hand across my mouth. "Don't say that. You can't hope that. It's terribly unlucky."

But the flood of guilt was a relief. I needed it, it seemed, to match my rising anger. When Rhoda ran away with her hands over her ears, I shouted after her, "I can hope it. I do! I do!"

From under the frangipani tree, I watched my father come down the street from the tram stop with Neal. Two thin men in dark suits, both over six foot, they walked into the red light from the setting sun. I stood on the bottom rail of the fence, holding two palings. My father's fixed spine made him seem to walk slightly backwards. Beside him Neal moved fluidly. I could hear Neal unloose his laughter when they were still a long way off, and when they drew closer I heard my father's fainter laugh in response.

It must have been one of those times when the western sky was red every evening, when the park was parched, our lawn only prickled with green, and most of the rungs of the tank resonant under the sounding stick. My father was always better then; the droughty weather eased his tortured lungs. When Neal and he were close enough to see me, and to expect me to respond to a wave, I jumped down from the rail and went indoors.

Rhoda was doing her homework in her room. Sybil was cleaning the bath and sobbing because it gave her a stomach-ache. Restless and defiant, I waited to be summoned. I knew that in the dining room most of the usual rituals would be suspended, and dinner delayed, until the matter of my truancy had been dealt with. Waiting, I dared to say aloud, "Just let him try. I will kill him. They don't hang children."

Neal came to fetch me. I knocked his hand from my shoulder but walked at his side with seeming meekness. At these hearings, only the culprit and the parents were allowed, but Neal, since wearing a suit and working in the city, had become rather officious, and after bringing me in, he took a chair at the table. But he had not yet developed a shell over his natural tenderness, and when my father turned on him with a glare, he got up and went away blushing like a child.

My father was sitting, my mother standing beside his chair, as if for a photograph. I saw them with an exaggerated clarity, noticed my father's look of being thinly wrapped in his skin, his veins and bones apparent, and the contrast of my mother's smooth swaddling. Both were looking solemn and perturbed, and were giving me their undivided attention.

I knew there was some ideal of justice at work here, and that I was supposed to respect it, but I was too angry; my inner voice was still saying with furious concentration, *Just you try!* I was ready to jump at my father's face and to strike his wan cheeks.

But as his first question — "Why didn't you go to school?" — my rage drained out of me. Nobody else had thought to ask it. My taut shoulders settled, and I was left with only my guilt. I had said those words; I had spoken my intention to murder. It was from inside myself, this time, that the word-blocking emanation came. I tried to speak, but could not get one word across that barrier. I blushed with shame at the sound I was making. My shoulders tensed again. My parents watched with wonder.

"Is it like this at school?" suddenly asked my father.

I violently shook my head, then gulped and nodded.

"Still?" asked my mother.

I nodded.

"Child," she cried, in ringing perplexity, "why didn't you tell us?"

I managed to say I didn't know why. "Well, run along now," said my father curtly. "Charlie," said my mother in distress, "there is still the matter of the creek." "*Run along*," repeated my father with force. And when my mother asked, then, if I would like my dinner on a tray in bed (as when I was sick) I knew I was not to be chastised. Exhausted, I shook my head.

Neal was the only talkative one at the table that night. Feeling the pensive weight of my parents' glances, I bent my head to my plate. When Rhoda reached out gently to put my hanging hair behind my ears, I winced away like a nervous horse. When Neal asked my father a question about the great flood of '93, and I realised how my treasure came to be on the ground at the creek, I almost sat up and cried out my discovery, but the reminders, the allusions, my treasure bore, made me sink back again.

At that time the front or dormitory part of the house was left unlocked at night, the doors wide open and hooked back against a wall. The lavatory was under the house, and if I wanted to go there at night, I would slip out of bed and waft in my pale pyjamas through the house, through the open door, across the side veranda and down the steps.

I was the one, through restlessness or need, who made this journey most often. Sometimes, when I passed the door, always shut, of my parents' room, hearing in full force one of my father's attacks of coughing, I would leap and run out of its range, and would rush my passage back. At other times, from behind that door, I heard the low chatter of simple conversation, often interrupted by laughter, and then I would not change my pace and would raise my arms high on the steps as if I were a bird about to rise in flight. But when those voices sounded intense and sibilant, I would walk quickly past their door and be glad to reach the stone path at the foot of the steps, not because such conversation made me fearful, as did the coughing, but because I did not wish to seem to be spying on them in a state of disagreement. As discreet and respectable as Mr Mead and Mr Greenlees, I would glide swiftly past their door and neatly down the steps.

It was this kind of low intense conversation I heard on my way to the lavatory on the night after the truancy hearing. Sybil was on the lavatory seat. I had not noticed her absence from her bed under its mosquito netting. "Wait for me, Bea," she said. "Leave it open and keep guard."

The guard was against the nightman. We never knew what time the new man would come. I sat on the step and looked up at the stars. In permitting the lavatory to be put under the house, the council had anticipated their own sewerage plan. The perfumes of the garden contending with the power of phenol made acceptable, or perhaps only familiar, the smell of our excrement. Sybil got up from the seat and said, "Now I'll keep guard for you."

She sat on the step. "Mum and dad are talking about you," she said.

"They are not."

"They are so. I heard them."

"I heard them too. They were talking about money."

"I thought it was you."

"No, money. I heard them distinctly."

I don't know why I told this lie; it was quite spontaneous. After I had finished, Sybil and I wandered about the grass, putting our heads back to look at the stars. We put our arms round each other's shoulders and pretended to be falling over backwards. Our animosity was always in abeyance out of doors at night, perhaps impossible to maintain under that rich hypnotic sky. Sybil went to the laundry, also under the house, to wash her hands, while I, who thought this practice silly when I had touched nothing but my pyjama pants, continued to stagger about beneath the stars.

All was silent as we glided past our parents' door.

"They must have decided," whispered Sybil as we reached our beds.

"About the money, I mean," she added in quick appeasement, as we slipped under the white nets.

*   *   *

For the next two days I was kept home from school while my mother went out on conferences.

"We will do all we can," she assured me before she left on the first day, so that when, a little later, I saw her from the kitchen window, crossing the park towards the school, walking down Honour Avenue and twitching her arm in that familiar way, I did not feel my usual apprehension, but calmly continued to iron all the household handkerchiefs and table napkins. I loved this task, which I had only recently learned to do. I felt deeply complacent as I watched the flawless white swathes appear across the damp linen and pressed the squares exactly. "Aren't you afraid she'll blow herself up with that petrol iron?" one of my father's cousins had asked. "Indeed I am not," replied my mother.

"Well done, dear," she said when she came home from the school. She picked up one of the handkerchiefs. "Miss Rickard had a handkerchief arranged in her top pocket in such a novel way."

But she had a trace of her brooding look. "All my girls are good with their hands," she then said sharply. And at that moment an image settled into my mind (and has remained with me) of her and Miss Rickard, two small affronted women, standing face to face on Miss Rickard's dais. Miss Rickard puts one hand flat on the table and leans forward from the waist to address my mother with her insulting clarity. My mother stands upright, listening, her eyes flashing and her right upper-arm twitching once before she replies.

On the second day my mother dressed to go to the city.

"I am meeting your father, Bea. We have an appointment with someone we know in the department."

I was given no tasks, and was free to revel in the rare sensation of being alone in the house. In this treasured privacy I did nothing forbidden, but did even the most usual things with a rapturous deliberation. When I sat in my father's big chair, I listened to the leather cushion hiss slowly beneath me. When I pulled a carrot from the garden and gave it to the horse, I watched intently his top lip retract from his long teeth, and heard his chomping, and his breath on my hands as he nuzzled for more, as if I had not heard both a hundred times before. When heat collected in the house, and I took my book and searched for cool spots, I found, among the currents of air at floor level, some I had not discovered before. (Later, when we had a dog, he would lie in those same spots.) I did not give a thought to my trouble at the school. My faith in my parents' ability to do, to act, to make changes, which had wavered lately, had been fully restored by their present energy and determination, and by their appeal to someone they knew in the department.

"Someone we know in the department." I reconstruct the scene in the city. Though there was bitterness in their retreat from Labor politics, many of the friends with whom they had shared opinions (radical in that time and place) were now in government. I see them entering one of the big polished hollow-sounding offices, the secretary shutting the door behind her, the man rising from his chair. The handshakes. The naming. "Charlie." "Iris." The arm extended for a moment across my father's shoulders. The swivelling chair, the leisurely talk. Some laughter. Always some laughter. Then the cocked head, the raised brow. "What can I do for you?"

My father, who had taken time off from work, did not go back, but came home with my mother into my silence. Again I was summoned before them, but this time they were both sitting, my mother, looking tired, with an elbow on the table and one hand, still gloved, under her chin.

"This is the best we can do," said my father. "You are to stay home from school for a year. You will have correspondence lessons sent each week from the department."

"As country children do," interposed my mother.

"Your mother will supervise your lessons, and you will go once a week to a teacher of speech in the city, to correct that hesitation."

I wanted to ask if at last I was to be allowed to travel to the city alone, but felt again the speech-blocking emanation rising between us. My malign passion of the day before, when I had wished to fly at his face, had laid down a most regrettable pattern, which he and I were never to be free of until his death. But as neither of us knew this yet, I patiently struggled, and he and my mother watched with equal patience, until my mother told me to stop and take a deep breath, and by doing that, and then addressing her instead of him, I was able to speak. When I learned that I was to be allowed to go to the city alone, I gave a whoop and a twirl of joy, watched with relief and indulgence by them both.

"Sometimes you will have to stay home alone, too," declared my mother. "I can't take you everywhere."

I knew she could not, for example, take me when she visited her own mother, to whose house my father's children were not admitted. I foresaw a repetition of the hours just past, the long long stretches of luxurious privacy. When Rhoda came home I ran to her room.

"No school! No school! No school! And I'm allowed to go to the city alone. And learn speech."

"As if you need to," said Rhoda. "Did they make you promise not to go to the creek?"

"No."

"They will."

"They mightn't. They might forget."

"You've no chance."

I knew I hadn't. I knew I would be made ceremoniously to promise, and that kind of promise I had never broken. I now perceived, however, that there may be ways of dodging around it, and already, before I had been required to take the vow, I was devising ways of doing this. At the edge of my calculations I could see my father's blue glare turned on my dishonesty, but the lure was too strong, and even through this discomfort, I went on. To see Peggy and Des at the creek would be to break the promise, but to see them at their camp at Budjerra Heights would not. Would there be time, when I was left home alone, to make my way to Budjerra Heights? And where, exactly, was Budjerra Heights? I could point in the right direction. I could say, "Over there." But that was not enough.

Sybil was delighted by my news. She saw it as distinguishing me, setting me apart. She had a talent for transforming facts, the Irish ability that had missed my father, or had been conscientiously repressed in him, but which had burst out in different ways in his three daughters. When I went down the street to tell Clare, Sybil insisted on coming with me, hugging my arm, giggling, and calling out to anyone we met, "My sister is to have private lessons."

In Sybil's hugging, and in the mild responses of our amiable neighbours, I felt myself imprisoned in a region from which I would never again escape to the sharper air of insubordination. With an inventiveness sharpened by this sudden desperate suffocation, I realised that I would only have to say Neal, "Budjerra Heights is near the river," to make him indignantly refute it. I would persist, and so would he. Of all Neal's collections, he took most pride in his collection of facts. Neal was eager in dispensing his facts, and could not bear the contradiction of the ignorant. As I submitted to Sybil's hugging, and listened to her talking to Mrs Mead, I could see Neal angrily drawing me a map.

Mates or Martyrs

Extracts from Interview by Jennifer Ellison

I think it was on the cover of The Last Man's Head *that you were quoted as saying you feel out of place in Australian literature because you feel work has a dramatic, rather than a documentary, focus.*

Yes, I do too.

Do you feel, then, that most Australian writing has a documentary focus?

It's changing slightly now, I believe. There's more dramatic writing, now. But I think for quite a long time it had a strong documentary bias.

Perhaps the documentary style really only started to emerge more recently, say, from around the sixties, because before that there was the great tradition of English literature, which was very much based on telling a story.

I feel that I belong to the English and American traditions, but particularly to the English tradition. I started out in the world reading English novels and American novels. I did read Australian novels, but they didn't supply much for me. They were mostly blokey and outback. They don't supply much for a girl or a woman. Women were either mates, or martyrs in the kitchen, or chopping the wood, or killing snakes.

In Aspects of the Novel, *Forster asks three different men what they think a novel should do, and the last one shakes his head solemnly and says something like, "It should tell a story. Oh, indeed, yes, a story." Do you agree?*

Yes, I believe that, too, and of course radio work does support that tendency. But it isn't absolutely imperative. There are writers who can just weave a spell and you don't care, you just read them for pleasure. But it's rare. Even when you can't easily find that plot, it is there. Even in novels like *To the Lighthouse*, you care if that child gets to the lighthouse, you want to know if he does.

Do you still feel out of place in Australian literature?

If I do feel out of place I no longer care enough to make the statement. Perhaps I should put it like that.

*   *   *

Were there any writers that made a particular impact on you when you were younger?

I think dozens of them. Everything I read, apart from "Twinkle, Twinkle, Little Star," perhaps. Dickens must have been a tremendous influence on me. I read him so often when I was a girl. Jane Austen, perhaps. You know, all the old books that were in the house. Henry James I read very thoroughly in my twenties. The Elizabethan poets and prose writers were a tremendous admiration of mine. I don't think I've been influenced by some people I particularly admire. They are out of my range, like Cervantes, you know — *Don Quixote*, I love that book, but I am not influenced by it. It's too different from my concerns. *Moby Dick*, Saul Bellow, *Catch 22*. Patrick White I admire tremendously, but I can admire him without being influenced by him. Christina Stead — I could never write like her, she's so voluminous and so copious, but I admire her greatly and I think she had an effect on me just by writing about Sydney. She gave me courage. She did. But her style never affected mine. I don't know who did. Probably so many people that I can't enumerate them. The English writers, Waugh and Henry Green and Muriel Spark, I like those, too. I love Henry Green's novels, I really love them. I think they're . . . beautiful novels. If I could choose which novels I'd like to have written I would choose his, all of them. They're lovely, aren't they?

*   *   *

Tirra Lirra's heroine, Nora Porteous, seems to be something of a victim. Do you think she was typical of that period, or were you more concerned with Nora as an individual?

I think I was writing about a woman who was born at the turn of the century who, for a start, had those three great events — the First World War, the Depression, and the Second World War — fracturing her life, and also a woman (and this is more important) who was actually a born artist, but was in a place where artists, although they were known to exist, were supposed to exist elsewhere. She was born among that kind of people, and she herself doesn't know that she's an artist. She struggles through, trying to arrive at her art and never succeeding.

So is that what you feel to be the backbone of the novel, the plight of the unrecognised artist?

Not an unrecognised artist, but a person who *is* an artist but doesn't succeed even in being *conscious* of being an artist. She had a kind of buried talent, buried in herself. The sewing, the tapestries, had to be something acceptable to her society. She wasn't a strongly original person. Not many of us are.

Novels written in the first person inevitably seem to suggest a stronger autobiographical basis than others. Is Tirra Lirra *perhaps more autobiographical than your other novels?*

No. But you don't make any character that hasn't something of yourself in it. She was within my range, as all of my characters are.

*   *   *

A lot of your female characters are very strong, independent-minded people, but there's never any strident feminism apparent. Does this mean you see the women's movement almost as a non-issue?

Oh no, I don't think it's a non-issue. I think it's an important issue. I think it's a marvellous movement, and it's a movement that has occurred again and again over the centuries, and at last I think it has a chance of succeeding. Biology has defeated it before, always, but with contraception as it is today, it has a chance. Mind you, as all of us know, there are gains and losses, but there have been great gains.

I'm sorry for all the hurtfulness of it: the men who've been hurt, and the women who have been hurt — to say nothing of the children, and the extreme stances that have been taken. But again, extremes have to be stated, and I believe that generally speaking it's been a very good movement. When did you last hear a joke about a woman driver? When I get on buses and see women driving I'm always so pleased. And I see some marvellous things. Men in supermarkets carrying their babies, and they look so good, they look so natural. And it's very nice, isn't it? It's encouraging. It truly makes me believe that we can't go back now. And men often believe that too. But there's a very angry backlash against it. I don't know what will happen. But I hope it goes along.

You don't seem to have any qualms about writing quite intimately about male characters.

No. I don't feel quite so much at ease with them, but I do my best. I mean, I've known a large number of men, and I suppose I know what men are like, you know. I don't feel they're my most successful characters, though.

* * *

Do you have much contact with other writers?

No. I know people here and there. I should think I know a number of writers, but I don't know them well. A few I do, but our type of writing is so different that we don't affect each other's writing or talk of each other's work much.

Do you think there have been any personal costs in choosing to be a writer?

Oh yes. But there are personal costs in choosing to be a doctor, or a nurse, or a housewife, or a bus driver.

You don't think the costs of being a writer are particularly great?

I think it must be hard to be married to a writer. They do get very much engrossed in their work. It's understandable that wives and husbands of writers sometimes feel a bit left out of it. People try to understand, but there's this . . . shadow that comes across their face when they come home and you're still working. It's understandable, isn't it? But there are many successful marriages among them too. I think it's slightly more of a hazard, I should say, but there aren't any gross difficulties there, I don't believe. If you reverse the position, and look at women who work, with husbands at home who are writers, they are equally susceptible to this feeling of being excluded or put down a little bit, or taking second place. I have heard women say so. So it isn't a masculine thing only. Although I think men are more prone to it, because they're more accustomed to exclusive attention. Perhaps today it's changed, now and then men and women so often both work from the start. When I was married, and writing at home (writing was my second job; my first job was the house), I never longed to go out and work in an office or a supermarket. I thought I was terribly lucky to have three hours a day or five hours a day I could sneak in for writing. I never craved to be out in the workplace, as it was being called at the time, never. Of course, when you are home, writing, you're earning too, but your earnings are spasmodic. The earnings that are keeping the house going are your husband's, and so he has the primary position in the house and he feels — most husbands feel, I'm not talking personally — the prime earner has rights over the secondary earner, and perhaps they have a case. Money comes into everything, as a character in one of my books remarked.

Olga Masters

EDITOR'S NOTE

Olga Masters had a number of short stories and journalistic articles in the *Sydney Morning Herald* before the publication of her first collection of stories, *The Home Girls* (UQP, 1982), which won the National Book Council Award. This was followed by a novel *Loving Daughters* (UQP, 1984) and a collection of linked stories, *A Long Time Dying* (UQP, 1985). Her last novel, *Amy's Children* (UQP) was published in 1987, and her most recent collection of stories, *The Rose Fancier* (UQP) was published posthumously in 1988.

"The Lang Women" and "Leaving Home" were published in *The Home Girls* (St Lucia: UQP, 1982), pp.93-100, 2-36; "The Christmas Parcel" was published in *A Long Time Dying* (St Lucia: UQP, 1987), pp.44-63; Masters's comments on Monet's *The Meadow* were published in *Sydney Morning Herald*, 15 June 1985; and "War Gave Women a First Taste of Liberation" was published in *Sydney Morning Herald*, 13 August 1985.

The Lang Women

Lucy was a thin, wistful wispy child who lived with her mother and grandmother and had few moments in her life except a bedtime ritual which she started to think about straggling home from school at four o'clock.

Sometimes she would start to feel cheerful even with her hands still burning from contact with Miss Kelly's ruler, and puzzle over this sudden lifting of her spirits then remember there was only a short while left to bedtime.

She was like a human alarm clock which had been set to go off when she reached the gate leading to the farm and purr away until she fell asleep lying against her grandmother's back with her thighs tucked under her grandmother's rump and her face not minding at all being squashed against the ridge of little knobs at the back of her grandmother's neck.

Her grandmother and her mother would talk for hours after they were all in bed. Sometimes it would seem they had all drowsed off and the mother or the grandmother would say "Hey, listen!" and Lucy would shoot her head up too to hear. Her grandmother would dig her with an elbow and say: "Get back down there and go to sleep!" Lucy was not really part of the talk just close to the edges of it.

It was as if the grandmother and the mother were frolicking together in the sea, but Lucy unable to swim had to stand at the edge and be satisfied with the wash from their bodies.

Lucy made sure she was in bed before her mother and grandmother in order to watch.

It was as if she were seeing two separate plays on the one stage. Carrie the mother performed the longest. She was twenty-six and it was the only time in the day when she could enjoy her body. Not more than cleansing and admiring it since Lucy's father had died five years earlier. Carrie was like a ripe cherry with thick black hair cut level with her ears and in a fringe across her forehead. She was squarish in shape not dumpy or overweight and with rounded limbs brown from exposure to the sun because she and her grandmother Jess also a widow and the mother of Carrie's dead husband worked almost constantly in the open on their small farm which returned them a meagre living.

Carrie was nicknamed Boxy since she was once described in the village as good looking but a bit on the boxy side in reference to her shape. When this got back to Carrie she worried about it although it was early in the days of her widowhood and her mind was not totally on her face and figure.

Some time later at night with all her clothes off and before the mirror in the bedroom she would frown on herself turning from side to side trying to decide if she fitted the description. She thought her forehead and ears were two of her good points and she would lift her fringe and study her face without it and lift her hair from her ears and look long at her naked jawline then take her hands away and swing her head to allow her hair to fall back into place. She would place a hand on her hip, dent a knee forward, throw her shoulders back and think what a shame people could not see her like this.

"Not boxy at all," she would say inside her throat which was long for a shortish person and in which could be seen a little blue throbbing pulse.

She shook her head so that her thick hair swung wildly about then settled down as if had never been disturbed.

"See that?" she would say to her mother-in-law.

Jess would be performing in her corner of the room and it was usually with a knee up under her nightdress and a pair of scissors gouging away at an ingrown toenail. She never bothered to fasten the neck of her nightdress and it was an old thing worn for many seasons and her feet were not all that clean as she did not wash religiously every night as Carrie did. She spent hardly any time tearing off her clothes and throwing them down, turned so that the singlet was on the outside and when she got into them in the morning she had only to turn the thickness of the singlet, petticoat and dress and pull the lot over her head.

Carrie did not seem to notice although she sometimes reprimanded Jess for failing to clean her teeth. When this happen- ed Jess would run her tongue around her gums top and bottom while she ducked beneath the covers and Lucy would be glad there was no more delay.

It was only the operations like digging at a toenail or picking at a bunion that kept Jess up. Sometimes she pushed her nightdress made into a tent with her raised knee down to cover her crotch but mostly she left it up so that Lucy hooped up in bed saw her front passage glistening and winking like an eye.

The lamp on the dressing table stood between Carrie and Jess so that Lucy could see Carrie's naked body as well either still or full of movement and rhythm as she rubbed moistened oatmeal around her eyes and warmed olive oil on her neck and shoulders.

The rest of the little town knew about the bedtime ritual since Walter Grant the postmaster rode out one evening and saw them through the window. It had been two days of wild storms and heavy rain and the creek was in danger of breaking its banks. Any stock of Carrie's and Jess's low down would be safer moved. Walter on his mission to warn them saw Jess with her knee raised and nightgown around her waist and Carrie's body blooming golden in the lamplight for they were enjoying the storm and had left the curtains open. Walter saw more when Carrie rushed to fling them together and rode home swiftly with his buttocks squeezed together on the saddle holding onto a vision of Carrie's rose tipped breasts, the creamy channel between them, her navel small and perfect as a shell and her thighs moving angrily and her little belly shaking.

After that the town referred to the incident as that "cock show".

Many forecast a dark future for Lucy witnessing it night after night.

Some frowned upon Lucy when she joined groups containing their children at the show or sports' day.

The Lang women's house had only one bedroom, one of two front rooms on either side of a small hall. The hall ran into a kitchen and living room combined which was the entire back por- tion of the house.

It would have been reasonable to expect them to make a second bedroom by moving the things from what was called the "front room". But neither Jess nor Carrie ever attempted or suggested this. The room was kept as it was from the early days of Jess's marriage. It was crowded with a round oak table and chairs and a chiffonier crowded with ornaments, photographs and glassware and there were two or three deceptively frail tables loaded with more stuff. On the walls were heavily framed pictures mostly in pairs of swans on calm water, raging seas and English cottages sitting in snow or surrounded by unbelievable gardens.

Even when the only child Patrick was living at home and up until he left at fifteen he slept in the single bed in his parents' room where Carrie slept now. He was fifty miles up the coast working in a timber mill when he met Carrie a housemaid at the town's only hotel. They married when he was twenty and she was nineteen and pregnant with Lucy who was an infant of a few months when Patrick was loaned a new-fangled motor bike and rounding a bend in the road the bike smacked up against the rear of a loaded timber lorry like a ball thrown hard against a wall. Patrick died with a surprised look on his face and his fair hair only lightly streaked with dust and blood.

Jess was already widowed more than a year and managing the farm single handed so Carrie and Lucy without a choice came to live there.

Lucy could not remember sleeping anywhere but against her grandmother's back.

Sometimes when the grandmother turned in the night she fitted neatly onto the grandmother's lap her head on the two small pillows of her grandmother's breasts.

She was never actually held in her grandmother's arms that she knew about. When she woke the grandmother's place was empty because it was Jess who was up first to start milking the cows which was up to twenty in the spring and summer and half that in the winter. Carrie got up when the cows were stumbling into the yard seen in the half light from the window and Lucy waited about until eight o'clock when they both came in to get breakfast. Lucy was expected to keep the fire in the stove going and have her school clothes on. She usually had one or another garment on inside-out and the laces trailing from her shoes and very often she lied when asked by Carrie or Jess if she had washed. Carrie did little or not housework and Jess had to squeeze the necessary jobs in between the farmwork. Carrie was content to eat a meal with the remains of the one before still on the table, cleaning a little space for her plate by lifting the tablecloth and shaking it clear of crumbs, sending them into the middle of the table with the pickles and sugar and butter if they could afford to have a pound delivered with their empty cream cans from the butter factory.

Carrie trailed off to bed after their late tea not caring if she took most of the hot water for her wash leaving too little for the washing up.

Jess grumbled about this but not to Carrie's face.

Once after Jess had managed on the hot water left and the washing up was done and the room tidied she said in Lucy's hearing that she hoped Carrie never took to bathing in milk.

Lucy had a vision of Carrie's black hair swirling above a tubful of foamy milk. Her own skin prickled and stiffened as if milk were drying on it. She left the floor where she was playing and put her chin on the edge of the table Jess was wiping down waiting to hear more. But Jess flung the dishcloth on its nail and turned her face to busy herself with shedding her hessian apron as the first step towards getting into bed.

This was the life of the Lang women when Arthur Mann rode into it.

Jess and Carrie inside following their midday meal saw him through the kitchen window with the head of his horse over the fence midway between the lemon tree and a wild rose entangled with convolvulus. The blue bell-like flowers and the lemons made a frame for horse and rider that Jess remembered for a long time.

"It's a Mann!" Jess said to Carrie who did not realise at once that Jess was using the family name.

The Manns were property owners on the outer edge of the district and they were well enough off to keep aloof from the village people. Their children went to boarding schools and they did not shop locally nor show their cattle and produce at the local show but took it to the large city shows.

But Jess easily recognised a Mann when she saw one. When she was growing up the Manns were beginning to grow in wealth and had not yet divorced themselves from the village. They not only came to dances and tennis matches but helped organise them and there were Manns who sang and played the piano in end-of-year concerts and Manns won foot races and steer riding at the annual sports.

They nearly all had straight dark sandy hair and skin tightly drawn over jutting jawbones.

Jess going towards the fence got a good view of the hair and bones when Arthur swept his hat off and held it over his hands on the saddle.

"You're one of the Manns," said Jess her fine grey eyes meeting his that were a little less grey, a bit larger and with something of a sleepy depth in them.

Arthur keeping his hat off told her why he had come. He had leased land adjoining the Langs' to the south where he was running some steers and he would need to repair the fence neglected by the owners and the Langs neither of whom could afford the luxury of well fenced land.

He or one of his brothers or one of their share farmers would be working on the fence during the next few weeks.

"We don't use the bit of land past the creek," said Jess before the subject of money came up. "The creek's our boundary so a fence is no use to us."

Arthur Mann's eyes smiled before his mouth. He pulled the reins of his horse to turn it around before he said there would be no costs to the Langs involved. He put his hat on and raised it again and Jess saw the split of his coat that showed his buttocks well shaped like the buttocks of his horse which charged off as if happy to have the errand done.

Jess came inside to the waiting Carrie.

Lucy home from school was playing with some acorns she found on the way. Jess saw her schoolcase open on the floor with some crusts in it and the serviette that wrapped her sandwiches stained with jam. Flies with wings winking in the sun crawled about the crusts and Lucy's legs.

"She's a disgrace!" Jess cried trying to put out of her mind the sight of Arthur Mann's polished boots and the well ironed peaks of his blue shirt resting on the lapels of his coat.

With her foot Carrie swept the acorns into a heap and went to the mirror dangling from the corner of a shelf to put her hat on. Jess took hers too from the peg with her hessian apron. She turned it around in her hands before putting it on. It was an old felt of her husband's once a rich grey but the colour beaten out now with the weather. It bore stains and blotches where it rubbed constantly against the cows' sides as Jess milked. Jess plucked at a loose thread on the band and ripped it away taking it to the fire to throw it in. The flames snatched it greedily swallowing the grease with a little pop of joy.

Lucy lifted her face and opened her mouth to gape with disappointment. She would have added it to her playthings.

"Into the fire it went!" said Jess. "Something else you'd leave lyin' around!"

She looked for a moment as if she would discard the hat too but put it on and went out.

It was Carrie who encountered Arthur Mann first working on the fence when she was in the corn paddock breaking and flattening the dead stalks for the reploughing. Almost without thinking she walked towards the creek bank and stood still observing Arthur who had his back to her. He is a man, she thought remembering Jess's words with a different inference. His buttocks under old, very clean well-cut breeches quivered with the weight of a fence post he was dropping into a hole. He had his hat off lying on a canvas bag that might have held some food. Jess might have wondered about the food and thought of a large clean flyproof Mann kitchen but Carrie chose to look at Arthur's hair moving in a little breeze like stiff bleached grass and his waistline where a leather belt shiny with age and quality anchored his shirt inside his pants.

He turned and saw her.

As he did not have a hat to lift he seemed to want to do something with his hands so he took some hair between two fingers and smoothed it towards an ear. Carrie saw his fine teeth when he smiled.

"Hullo . . . Shorty," he said.

"No . . . Boxy," she said.

She was annoyed with herself for saying it.

He probably knew the nickname through his share farmers who were part of the village life and would have filled the waiting ears of the Manns with village gossip. Carrie did not know but he had heard too about the nightly cock show.

Arthur thought now of Carrie's naked body although it was well covered with an old print dress once her best, cut high at the neck and trimmed there and on the sleeves with narrow lace. Carrie was aware that it was unsuitable for farm work and took off her hat and held it hiding the neckline. She shook her hair the way she did getting ready for bed at night and it swung about then settled into two deep peaks against her cheeks gone quite pink.

"Come across," said Arthur. "I'm stopping for smoko."

Carrie nearly moved then became aware of her feet in old elastic-side rubber boots and buried them deeper in the grass.

She inclined her head towards the corn paddock as if this was where her duty lay. Still holding her hat at her neck and still smiling she turned and Arthur did not go back to the fence until she had disappeared into the corn.

Carrie spent the time before milking at the kitchen table in her petticoat pulling the lace from the dress. Lucy home from school with her case and her mouth open watched from the floor. When Carrie was done she stood and pulled the dress over her head brushing the neck and sleeves free of cotton ends. She swept the lace scrapes into a heap and moved towards the stove.

"Don't burn it!" Jess cried sharply. "Give it to her for her doll!"

Lucy seized the lace and proceeded to wind it around the naked body of a doll that had only the stump of a right arm, its nose squashed in and most of its hair worn off.

A few days later Arthur rode up to the fence with a bag of quinces.

Lucy saw him when she looked up from under the plum tree that grew against the wall of the house. She was on some grass browning in the early winter and her doll sat between her legs stuck stiffly out. Arthur raised the quinces as a signal to collect them but Lucy turned her face towards the house and Arthur saw her fair straight hair that was nothing like Carrie's luxuriant crop.

In a moment Carrie came from one side of the house and Jess

from the other. They went up to the fence and Lucy got up and trailed behind.

Arthur handed the quinces between Carrie and Jess and Jess took them taking one out and turning it around.

She did not speak but the eyes shone no less than the sheen from the yellow skin of the fruit.

"The three Lang women," Arthur said smiling. "Or are there four?"

Lucy had her doll held by its one and a half arms to cover her face. Ashamed she flung it behind her back.

Arthur arched the neck of his horse and turned it around.

"I'll buy her a new one," he said and cantered off.

Neither Jess nor Carrie looked at Lucy's face when they went inside. Jess tipped the quinces onto the table where they bowled among the cups and plates and she picked one up and rubbed her thumb thoughtfully on the skin and then set it down and gathered them all together with her arms.

Then she went into the front room and returned with a glass dish and with the hem of her skirt wiped it out and put the fruit in and carried it back to set it on one of the little tables. Carrie's eyes clung to her back until she disappeared then looked dully on Lucy sitting stiff and entranced on the edge of a chair. She opened her mouth to tell Lucy to pick up her doll from the floor but decided Jess would do it on her return. But Jess stepped over the doll and put on her hessian apron and reached for her hat. She turned it round in her hands then put it back on the peg. Carrie saw the back of her neck unlined and her brown hair without any grey and her shoulders without a hump and her arms coming from the torn-out sleeves of a man's old shirt pale brown like a smooth new sugar bag. Then when Jess reached for an enamel jug for the house milk Carrie saw her hooded eyelids dropping a curtain on what was in her eyes. Carrie put her hat on without looking in the mirror and followed Jess out. She looked down her back over her firm rump to her ankles for something that said she was old but there was nothing.

In bed that night Lucy dreamed of her doll.

It had long legs in white stockings with black patent leather shoes fastened with the smallest black buttons in the world.

The dress was pink silk with ruffles at the throat and a binding of black velvet ribbon which trailed to the hemline of the dress. The face was pink and white and unsmiling and the hair thick and black like Carrie's hair.

Lucy lay wedged under the cliff of her grandmother's back wondering what was different about tonight. She heard a little wind breathing around the edges of the curtain and a creak from a floorboard in the kitchen and a small snuffling whine from their old dog Sadie settling into sleep under the house.

Lucy marvelled at the silence.

No one is talking she thought.

Every afternoon Lucy looked for the doll when she came in from school. On the way home she pictured it on the table propped against a milk jug, its long legs stretched among the sugar bowl and breadcrumbs.

But it was never there and when she looked into the face of Jess and Carrie there was no message there and no hope.

The following Saturday Lucy could wait no longer and sneaked past the cowyard where Jess and Carrie were milking and well clear of it ran like a small pale terrier through the abandoned orchard and bottom corn paddock to the edge of the creek. Across it, a few panels of fence beyond where Carrie had first encountered him. Arthur was at work.

Under her breath Lucy practised her words: "Have you brought my doll?"

She was saying them for the tenth time when Arthur turned.

She closed her mouth before they slipped out.

Arthur pushed his hat back and beckoned.

"Come over," he said.

Lucy hesitated and looked at her feet buried in the long wild grass. I won't go, she said to herself. But the doll could be inside Arthur's bag hung on the fence post.

She plunged down the creek bank and came up the other side her spikey head breaking through the spikey tussocks dying with the birth of winter.

Arthur sat down on some fence timber strewn on the ground and reached for his bag. Lucy watched, her heart coming up into her neck for him to pull the doll from it. But he took out a paper bag smeared with grease which turned out to hold two slices of yellow cake oozing red jam. When he looked up and saw the hunger in Lucy's eyes he thought it was for the cake and held it towards her.

"We'll have a piece each," he said.

But Lucy sank down into the grass and crossed her feet with her knees out. Then she thought if she didn't take the cake Arthur might not produce the doll so she reached out a hand.

"Good girl," he said when she began nibbling it.

The cake was not all that good in spite of coming from the rich Mann's kitchen. It had been made with liberal quantities of slightly rancid butter.

Lucy thought of bringing him a cake made by Jess and imagined him snapping his big teeth on it then wiping his fingers and bringing out the doll.

"I should visit you, eh?" Arthur said.

Oh, yes! He would be sure to bring the doll.

"When is the best time?" Arthur said folding the paper bag into a square and putting it back in his bag.

"At night after tea? Or do you all go to bed early?"

Lucy thought of Carrie naked and Jess with her legs apart and shook her head.

Why not at night?" Arthur said. "There's no milking at night, is there?"

Lucy had to agree there wasn't with another small head shake.

"What do you all do after tea?" said Arthur.

Lucy looked away from him across the paddocks to the thin drift of smoking coming from the fire under the copper boiling for the clean up after the milk was separated. She felt a sudden urge to protect Jess and Carrie from Arthur threatening to come upon them in their nakedness.

She got to her feet and ran down the bank, her speed carrying her up the other side and by this time Arthur had found his voice.

"Tell them I'll come!" he called to her running back.

Carrie was in bed that night with much less preparation than usual and even without the last minute ritual of lifting her hair from her nightgown neck and smoothing down the little collar, then easing herself carefully down between the sheets reluctant to disturb her appearance even preparing for sleep.

To Lucy's surprise her nightgown hung slightly over one shoulder and she was further surprised to see that Jess had fastened hers at the brown stain where her neck met the top of her breasts. Carrie had not cavorted in her nakedness and Jess had not plucked at her feet with her knees raised. Lucy looked at the chair where Jess usually sat and pictured Arthur there. She saw his hands on his knees while he talked to them and curved her arms imagining the doll in them. An elbow stuck into Jess's back and Jess shook it off.

"Arthur Mann never married," said Carrie abruptly from her bed.

Jess lifted her head and pulled the pillow leaving only a corner for Lucy who didn't need it anyway for she had raised her head to hear.

"Old Sarah sees to that," said Jess.

Before putting her head down again Lucy saw that Carrie was not settling down for sleep but had her eyes on the ceiling and her elbows up like the drawing of a ship's sail and her hands linked under her head.

Jess's one open eye saw too.

Lucy had to wait through Sunday but on Monday when she was home from school for the May holidays she slipped past the dairy again while Jess and Carrie were milking and from the bank of the creek saw not only Arthur but a woman on a horse very straight in the back with some grey hair showing neatly at the edge of a riding hat and the skin on her face stretched on the bones like Arthur's. The horse was a grey with a skin like washing water scattered over with little pebbles of suds and it moved about briskly under the rider who sat wonderfully still despite the fidgeting.

Lucy sank down into the tussocks on the bank and the woman saw.

"What is that?" she said to Arthur. Then she raised her chin like a handsome fox alerted to something in the distance and fixed her gaze on the smoke away behind Lucy rising thin and blue from the Lang women's fire.

Lucy had seen Arthur's face before the woman spoke but he

now lowered his head and she saw only the top of his hat nearly touched the wire he was twisting and clipping with pliers.

The horse danced some more and Lucy was still with her spikey head nearly between her knees staring at the ground. The woman wanted her to go. But Lucy had seen people shooting rabbits not firing when the rabbits were humped still but pulling the trigger when they leapt forward stretching their bodies as they ran. Perhaps the woman had a gun somewhere in her riding coat and breeches or underneath her round little hat. Lucy sat on with the sun and wind prickling the back of her neck.

"Good heavens!" the woman cried suddenly and wheeling her horse around galloped off.

Lucy let a minute pass then got up and ran down and up the opposite bank to Arthur.

He went on working snip, snip with the pliers until Lucy spoke.

"You can come of a night and visit," she said.

Arthur looked up and down the fence and only briefly at the Lang corn paddock and the rising smoke beyond it.

"I've finished the fence," he said.

Lucy saw the neat heap of timber not needed and the spade and other tools ready for moving. She saw the canvas bag on top, flat as a dead and gutted rabbit.

"I know why you didn't bring the doll," she said.

"Your mother won't let you."

Leaving Home

There was a practice at Berrigo to gather at the Post Office in the afternoon to wait for the mail.

The doors closed while it was sorted and by the time they were ready to open a crowd swelled by children from both the public and Catholic school had filled the porch.

Weeks before Sylvia McMahon was to leave for Sydney to find a job she was singled out for attention when she arrived with the others to wait for the mail.

"Won't be long now," said Mrs Percy Parnell (there was also Mrs Henry and Mrs Horace) who as the youngest of the trio felt she had a licence to use current slang terms of which this was one.

Sylvia smiled, pleased all the attention focused on her.

"Three weeks," she said, feeling the old familiar tingle.

"And three and a half days," said her small sister Esme who blushed and hid her face in her sister's skirt when everyone laughed.

Esme aged ten amid the flock of schoolchildren could have collected the mail but Sylvia sixteen and waiting for departure day dressed herself like the adult women of Berrigo and went daily to the Post Office, probably to collect no more than a *Farmer and Settler* and a doctor's bill which Mrs McMahon would throw in the fire since she had not paid for the confinement resulting in Sylvia much less Frank, Lennie, Esme, Rose, Yvonne and Jackie.

It was true that Sylvie could have been employed helping her mother but the income from the farm was stretched to the limits, and it took a good season during which the cows gave liberally of their milk to atone for the bleak winter when grocery bills mounted month after month and unlike the doctor's bill could not be thrown into the stove and forgotten.

Mrs McMahon now past forty hoped for no more children and

avoiding old Doctor Hadgett was relatively easy as he spent most of his time behind the high garden wall of his house and surgery within arm's reach of his liquor cupboard.

These days he was of little use in confinements anyway handing over to the district nurse when a birth was imminent and charging for the lavatory.

But it was a different matter in relation to the town's only grocery.

L.F. Parrington was a prominent local figure running the agricultural show and sports' day or running the committee running the events. L.F. as the townspeople called him was churchman, sportsman, businessman and with one of the district's best farms. He was in everything and everywhere. You would have to be a recluse to dodge him. Mrs McMahon gave him the child endowment cheque each month in the winter and was grateful for the brief lift of his hat when their paths crossed.

Since no jobs were offering in Berrigo or larger towns within a radius of one hundred miles it was proposed that Sylvia go to Sydney before the winter set in and with luck get work. With a little more luck the pay might allow her to send some money home.

"Parcels too," said Sylvia at home after the post office jaunt and wiping up for her mother with a threadbare tea towel. The subject as invariably the going away.

She glanced at her mother seeing side-on the drooped eyelids and corresponding droop to the mouth still soft and pretty in spite of all the children and hard work.

Mrs McMahon had been silent while Sylvia rattled on. Now Sylvia saw something set and unyielding in her mother's profile.

"Things are so cheap in Sydney," Sylvia said.

Mrs McMahon spoke at last.

"You're not there yet," she said.

Sylvia laid down a plate in fear. Would it be possible her mother would change her mind and not let her go? She must know at once if there was a hint of this!

She stared hard at a handful of forks.

"Can we write and say the date I'll be there?" she said.

Oh, God don't let her say I can't go!

Mrs McMahon took the washing up dish and moved up a step onto the verandah tipping the contents onto flowers that grew below the rails.

Sylvia watched her back, heard the rush of water.

When she turns and shows her face I'll know, Sylvia thought entertaining the idea of rushing on her and begging her not to say no.

But the McMahons did not demonstrate affection and they kissed begrudgingly the children fearful of hearing the words "Don't slobber like a calf!"

Mrs McMahon kept her eyes down when she stepped back into the kitchen the dish under her arm.

"That's done," she said hanging it in its place above the fountain in the stove recess.

The recess and a door leading outside took up one end of the kitchen. Built of corrugated iron smoked grey-black the recess was big enough for both the stove and an iron grate for an open fire in the winter.

Sylvia saw herself sitting by it with the others on cold nights, her father taking most of the lamplight reading the *Farmer and Settler*, her mother in the shadows making what she called a "start for tomorrow" which was slicing bread for school sandwiches and soaking oatmeal for porridge.

A chill as cold as the coldest night ran through Sylvia. Would she be here this winter and the winters to come, all her life in Berrigo with no one decent to marry? Oh my God to end up a Gough, a Motbey, a Wright, a Henry or a Turner! To die would be better!

All her youth spent with no money of her own, no job but helping her mother around the house, nothing to go to but the Berrigo Show and the Berrigo Sports and the Agricultural Ball where Berrigo's idea of decoration was to pile the stage with potatoes, pumpkins and marrows and cross stalks of corn around the walls! You felt you were dancing in the farm sheds.

She sank onto a chair pushing her feet out before her and raising her eyes to see a piece of sky visible where the galvanized iron did not quite meet.

Oh to be free as the sky, to escape forever the closeting of the kitchen!

"Can't we write to Aunt Bess and say when I'll be coming?" she said staring at her skirt stretched tight across her knees.

Her mother was dragging the sewing machine to catch the late afternoon light from the one window and didn't hear or chose not to hear.

She sat at the machine and began to sort through a little pile of cut-out garments still with the paper pattern against each piece.

My dress! thought Sylvia. She has been reminded to sew my dress! But Mrs McMahon bypassed Sylvia's dark grey flannel with a white pique intended for wearing to job interviews and selected a skirt for Esme cut from a tweed suit sent in a parcel of good worn things by Bess, a sister of Mr McMahon who had promised temporary shelter for Sylvia in Sydney.

"I am sorry she cannot stay permanently," wrote Bess in reply to her brother's suggestion.

"But George and I have reached an agreement owing to all the relatives coming to stay with us since we came to Sydney." (George was a policeman.)

"I get no extra money from him when they are here and it is a struggle to keep the meals up.

"So we decided none of his come and none of mine.

"But Sylvia can stay until she gets a job and we will help her find a boarding place.

"Our Margaret is doing very well and got a raise last week. They are not putting any more girls on there."

Mrs McMahon got up from the machine now and laid Esme's skirt on the table to remove the pattern and put the pieces together for machining.

Sylvia stood too. Her mother did not appear to notice as she sat again and slipped the tweed under the machine needle. When the wheel began to whir Sylvia got up and let herself out of the kitchen.

The sky was right above her now with clouds idling across it in unconcerned fashion.

Her father and Frank and Lennie were finishing the day's farm jobs and Esme, Rose, Yvonne and Jackie were on the rails of the fence around the dairy watching. Esme was on the top rail her long thin legs dangling and Jackie who was three had his neck between the two lowest like one of the young calves.

"Sylly, Syllvy!" cried Esme seeing her.

Sylvia turned and made for the fence surrounding the house. She heard Jackie's wail and his cry "Take, me, take me!" and turned once as she scaled the fence to see his woeful moonlike face and the others sober too in the afternoon light.

She took a track that led to the well, a slab covered hole of water of a milky substance that supplemented the tanks of rainwater during a dry spell and was used mostly for washing clothes and scrubbing the dairy.

Behind the well on a small rise there was a clump of wattles with roots raised above the ground forming a kind of armchair. The spring that fed the well kept the grass there soft and green.

It was a place for Sylvia and the others to rest when they took the slide and cans to draw water.

If I am here in the winter I'll be carrying that blasted water again, she said to herself rocking her body and letting the roots hurt her.

The hills were folded in front of her to meet the sky and there was nothing much to gaze upon but tracks running through the grass even now threatening to turn a pale early winter brown.

Sylvia stood and grasped a branch of the wattle and shook it.

"I hate them! I hate them!" she cried.

Then she shut her eyes and laid her head on the branch until her anger was partly spent.

When she opened her eyes there was a horse and rider crossing the hill on one of the tracks.

"Arnold Wright!" she whispered, sinking down onto the grass. "I can see his buck teeth from here!"

Arnold was riding in the direction of the Wright farm one of the poorest in Berrigo. If she sat still and pulled a branch over her head he might not see her when he crossed the gully a little higher up riding by the straggling fence that divided the McMahons from their neighbour.

Seeing him with one eye a new thought struck Sylvia.

Berrigo would know she wasn't going to Sydney after all! She would have to face the Post Office crowd! She would drown herself first! She looked towards the well where the water winked between the slabs.

She saw herself look terrible with her hair plastered on her head and her clothes stuck to her body, perhaps her shoes missing. No she would not die that way.

She would walk to Sydney! Forgetting the proximity of Arnold Wright she pulled the branch aside to see where the road showed patches of beige coloured gravel through the trees. She could walk and walk and walk with the signposts telling her the way. She would leave at night when they were all asleep and would be too far away when they found her missing. She would arrive at Aunt Bess's and then it would be too late to be dragged home. The idea was so appealing she leapt to her feet and Arnold quite close now saw the flash of her old pink spotted dress. He jerked his surprised horse to a halt and after sitting a moment climbed down and tied the reins to a post. Sylvia was trapped. She could not run home and she could not escape Arnold striding towards her. She sank down onto the grass again.

"I thought it was you," Arnold said.

Who else would it be? Sylvia thought with scorn and snapped a twig off the wattle branch.

In the silence following she traced a pattern with it on the tree root.

"Gettin' in some practice for writin' home?" Arnold said squatting beside her.

Oh, what a clot! she thought, lifting her head.

But Arnold thought he had something smart and stretched his lips farther over his teeth.

You think he's grinning all the time but he's not, Sylvia thought.

Arnold sobering drew his lips as far as they would reach to cover his teeth and glanced towards the road.

"I'd like to be goin'," he said.

"What would you do there?" said Sylvia half scornful although she had resolved not to speak to him just remain mute.

"Work. Get money," said Arnold.

Sylvia realised she had been pressing the twig deeply into the root when she heard it snap.

"See all that life," said Arnold. "Jeez, you're lucky."

Sylvia lifted her chin, shook back her hair and let the breath out of her body.

She was going! She was going!

She felt an overwhelming pity for Arnold. He was stuck on that terrible farm with a simpleton brother, hillbilly parents and grandmother and his young sister Nellie.

She looked into his face amazed that in spite of this fate he seemed normal, as normal as Arnold could be.

Does he think of drowning himself, she wondered.

Arnold looked at her leaning back wriggling her toes inside her old sandals.

"You'll miss the well chair," he said.

"How do you know we call it that?" she said.

"Esme told Nellie," he said.

He looked away and swallowed.

"I ask her," he said.

He gripped both his knees.

"About you," he said.

Sylvia felt her face warming.

The horse by the fence snorted and shook its head.

It startled them both.

"You should be going," Sylvia said.

He didn't move and she felt a small gladness that he didn't.

She stole a glance at his profile. Except for his teeth he wasn't bad looking. Arnold Wright good looking! She must be mad! She snorted not so loud as the horse and Arnold turned her way. He has nice eyes, she thought. Oh hell and damn! Those were the words she was going to use freely when she got to Sydney. She was going to paint her face and curl her hair, things she wasn't allowed at home. Oh God, if she didn't go! She moved her toes again curling them inside her sandals. Arnold saw. He looked as if he might lay a hand on her feet.

"Got chilblains?" he said.

Chilblains! Of all the impossible people. Arnold was the most impossible! Daggy. That was the word for him. A word that was probably well aired in Sydney but not in Berrigo because it was too close to the bone.

Daggy sorts. Arnold was a daggy sort. She must get away! She had to go! She got to her feet as if she would take off then. Arnold was leaning on one elbow staring up at her.

She sat down again swiftly at the sound of steps. They were Esme's running along the track to the well.

Esme pulled up sharp when she saw them and stood legs apart several yards off as if reluctant to trespass upon their privacy.

"Come home, Mum says," she called.

Sylvia leaned back on an elbow slightly towards Arnold.

The spectacle caused Esme to stiffen like a small statue among the waving grass.

She plucked a piece and chewed it.

"Hullo Esme," called Arnold with something close to music in his voice.

It struck Sylvia that way too.

His voice should sound daggy, she said to herself glancing at him and deciding his teeth weren't so bad when he smiled a face splitting smile as he was doing now and showed them all.

"Mum's making gingerbread for our supper," Esme called.

Sylvia swallowed away the trickle of treacly syrup that invaded her saliva.

"She's making your blasted skirt!"

Arnold looked as if he liked her spirit.

Esme was astounded at the swear word.

"Oooooh, aaaah," she said both loud and hushed.

"Go home!" said Sylvia.

"She'll send me back!" said Esme.

"I won't be here," said Sylvia.

No one including Sylvia could work this out in that moment.

"I'm going for a ride on Arnold's horse!" Sylvia called out suddenly.

"You're not allowed," said Esme breaking a small silence involving them all even the horse who flung his ears back and his nose up.

"Can I?" said Sylvia turning to Arnold who would have gladly given her the horse along with himself.

She stood and he did a moment later.

"You ride behind," she said making for the fence.

Esme watched as Sylvia climbed the fence and slipped a leg across the saddle. The horse inquired with a shake of its neck. Arnold patted its rump soothingly then jumped on.

Sylvia took up the reins.

"Go home, pimp!" she called to Esme who after a moment started running hard towards the house.

Arnold wished there was no saddle to separate his body from Sylvia's. There was this hard raised rim under which he forced his crotch and Sylvia's beautifully rounded bottom at the end of her straight back seemed yards from him. He laid a hand just above her thigh. She didn't object so he laid the other hand near the other thigh.

Sylvia swished her head around and Arnold got a mouthful of her dark hair.

"Hang onto the saddle," Sylvia said.

Arnold obeyed. They moved off, the horse staying close by the fence and its rump broadening as they went up the incline.

When the fence turned a corner so did Sylvia and she kicked the horse into a canter down by the line of oaks on the western side of the McMahon's farm. Esme now on the woodheap by the house saw the flash of Sylvia's pink dress and raced inside to tell the others. When Sylvia and Arnold were clear of the oaks the McMahons like a small defending army were at the woodheap. The children not as tall as their parents stood on pieces of wood so they appeared a uniform group.

Sylvia pulled the horse up sharply and swung around to face them.

"Just what do you think you're up to, miss?" called Mrs McMahon across the couple of hundred yards separating them.

"Put your arms around me," said Sylvia to Arnold.

Arnold placed his hands lightly at her waistline.

"Where they were before!" said Sylvia.

Arnold lowered them an inch.

Esme jumped from her block of wood to the ground and Mr McMahon took a few strides forward.

"Lovely goings on!" called Mrs McMahon.

"Them hands should be round cows' tits where they belong!" called Mr McMahon.

Arnold withdrew his hands and clung to the saddle.

"Put them back," said Sylvia low to Arnold.

Before he had time to Mrs McMahon called out again.

"There's no Sydney trip for you, miss!"

Esme gasped loud at this news and hopped in her agitation like a spider back onto the woodheap.

Arnold in deep shock looked for a change in Sylvia's expression.

She merely tilted her chin and lowered her lashes.

Under other circumstances Arnold might have crushed her small waist between his hands.

All he could do now was cling wretchedly to the saddle.

"Mum made the gingerbread!" called Esme.

"Shut up about the gingerbread!" said Mrs McMahon.

All of them heard the tears in her voice.

"Get down and come home!" said Mr McMahon somewhat feebly.

"I haven't finished my ride!" said Sylvia, pulling the horse's head back as if preparing to canter off.

"Getting around with Berrigo riff raff!" said Mrs McMahon.

"He's not riff raff!" cried out Sylvia.

Arnold bowed his head longing to lay his forehead on Sylvia's neck.

Esme agitated at the thought of losing the friendship of Nellie when her mother's remark reached the Wright household gasped and hopped off the woodheap.

Mr McMahon took a couple more steps forward and picked up a stick lying in the grass, a piece from a quince tree abandoned by one of the children at play.

Who would he hit? thought Arnold. Please, not her!

Sylvia with her head up pulled the reins and the horse danced two or three little steps turning as it did, so that Sylvia and her father were almost face to face. Mr McMahon saw how her body flowed into the horse's body. They moved as one shape. She can ride, he thought, how well she can ride! Her hair swept past her cheek onto her neck. Her cheeks were pink from the ride and there was the rise of her bosom under the old spotted dress with the collar fastened loosely just above her breasts. If Arnold looked over her shoulder he could see between her breasts through the opening. Mr McMahon felt anger towards his wife. She had no right to sew clothes with openings in them like that!

Arnold sat in misery with his hands hanging on the horse's sides. Mr McMahon watched to see if his gaze fell over Sylvia's shoulders.

If he looks I'll kill him, Mr McMahon thought.

The buck toothed bastard, he's not getting her!

"Come home," he said hoping no one detected the pleading in his voice.

"There's nothing to go home for," Sylvia almost curled her lip towards the shabby old farmhouse with the smoking chimney.

Mr McMahon knew his wife would move a few steps towards him.

He saw her face creased and suddenly old.

"We've had enough of this, miss!" she called.

"Me too," said Sylvia.

"Listen to that cheek! It didn't take her long!" Mrs McMahon looked briefly and with hate at Arnold.

"Go on up inside," said Mr McMahon throwing a brief look at his wife.

"Huh!" she said ugly and angry. "Much good you've done! Haul her off that horse and send that riff raff packing!"

Arnold waited for Sylvia to say he wasn't riff raff.

But Sylvia's cool eyes held her father's eyes unwavering while the horse arched and swung its neck and took two more dancing steps.

"Use the stick on her!" shouted Mrs McMahon.

Mr McMahon looked at the stick as if he'd forgotten he held it.

Sylvia looked at it too and stretched her mouth in a little smile.

"Look at the cheeky grin!" cried Mrs McMahon.

It's not a cheeky grin, said the heart of Mr McMahon.

It's my daughter leaving me.

He threw the stick from him and turned and walked towards the house.

"Leaving me to do the dirty work!" shouted Mrs McMahon.

"Go to hell!" Mr McMahon shouted back.

She raced after him and caught him by his old blue shirt.

He pulled free and walked faster.

Mrs McMahon stood with her legs apart looking from him back to Sylvia and Arnold.

The wind whipped her apron like a white flag and Sylvia as if seeing it as a symbol of surrender climbed from the horse. She stood a moment with her face almost against the slippery leather of the saddle.

"I'll say goodbye," she whispered.

Arnold sat still with tears in his eyes. His mouth nearly covered his teeth as he hitched himself onto the saddle and when Sylvia turned away he slipped his feet into the stirrups and wheeled the horse around.

It allowed itself a shake of the head as if to say it knew all along things would finish this way.

Arnold did not turn his head when he cantered off.

Sylvia climbed the fence and Rose, Yvonne and Jackie ran to her and held her by the waist and legs. Esme and Lennie and Frank watched soberly from the woodheap.

Sylvia put Jackie on her back and made her way towards the house.

Mrs McMahon did too and near the woodheap stopped to pick up an armful of wood.

Sylvia stopped with Jackie still on her back and scraped up large chips dumping them in her skirt and gathering it up with one free hand.

"Lady Muck might soil her lily white hands!" cried Mrs McMahon.

"We'll do it!" said Esme.

They all went into the house.

Mr McMahon was sitting by the kitchen window with his hands on his knees.

He was looking out at the sky grey now.

Sylvia dropped the chips into the stove fire and put the kettle over the ring.

She sat and Jackie climbed on her knee and she linked her arms about him.

When the fire began to glow they showed smooth and white and round like the work of a sculptor.

Rose set the table and Esme sliced the gingerbread.

Mrs McMahon sat at the machine and let her face fall on her hand while she stared at the little pile of sewing.

Mr McMahon saw the white of the collar of Sylvia's dress now on the top of the pile.

He wanted to take it and tear it savagely between his hands.

But he sat with them still on his knees and said nothing.

The Christmas Parcel

Christmas in 1935 would have been a dreary affair for the Churchers but for a parcel, more like a small crate, sent from the eldest, Maxine, in Sydney.

Maxine was eighteen, and had been away two years. The first Christmas she sent a card, and the Churchers were delighted with this and stood it against the milk jug on the table for Christmas dinner, which was baked stuffed rabbit, for they were plentiful, but money was not.

The next Christmas Eve the driver of the mail car gave several long blasts on the horn passing the paddocks where the Churcher children were standing, spindly legged among the saplings and tussocks, trying to invent a game to ward off disappointment that there would be no presents.

Their mother had warned them. Sometimes she cried softly as she told them, sometimes she was angry and blamed their father for his inability to find work, sometimes she was optimistic, indulging in a spasm of house cleaning, washing curtains and bed clothes, whitewashing the fireplace ready to fill with gum tips, and scrubbing the floorboards until they came up a grey white, like sand on some untouched beach.

Who knows, something might turn up, she would say as she worked. Her better off sisters in distant towns might send a ten shilling note in their Christmas cards, which would buy lollies, cordial, oranges, bananas, and raisins for a pudding, and be damned to Fred Rossmore who would expect it paid off the account, owing now for half a year.

The clean house gave her spirits a lift, as if they were cleansed too, and she would finish off the day by bathing all the children in a tub in front of the stove, adding a kettle of hot water with each one, washing their heads as well, and sending them out to sit on the edge of the veranda and share a towel, very threadbare, to dry.

Their old skimpy shirts and dresses were usually not fastened properly; it didn't matter, it would be bedtime soon.

The young Churchers would feel lighter in spirit too, sniffing at the soap lingering on them, although it was the same Mrs Churcher used to wash the clothes. They would look forward to fried scones for tea, and some stewed peaches, a small greenish variety, sour near the stone, eaten bravely while trying to avoid thinking of the sugar and cream that would make them so much more palatable.

Mr and Mrs Churcher were sitting on the woodheap when the mail car driver blew the horn through a cloud of dust.

"And a Merry Christmas to you too!" Mrs Churcher shouted. She was in a black mood, and Mr Churcher feared it and feared for the children, soon to trail home, not giving in readily to the futility of hanging stockings. While she angrily shuffled a foot among the chips, he looked at the children like stringy saplings themselves, some like small scarecrows, for they were playing a game with arms outstretched, their ragged old shapeless clothes flapping in the wind that had sprung up, kindly cooling the air after one of the hottest days of the summer.

Mr Churcher watched as one of them suddenly tore off to the track that led to the road. It was Lionel, racing hard and soon lost to sight where the track disappeared into a patch of myrtle bush. Mr Churcher was surprised at the energy with which Lionel ran. He worried about the children's not getting enough to eat, but perhaps they were doing better than he thought. Anyone who could run like that after tearing about all day must be suitably fuelled. He felt a little happier, and looked at Mrs Churcher, surprised she was not sharing this feeling. She looked over the top of their grey slab house at some puffed up clouds, but not seeing them, he was sure, for the clouds had a milky transparency and he foolishly thought they would have a softening effect upon her. But her face wore a cloud of another kind, dark and thunderous. There was mutiny in her dark eyes, creased narrowly, not wide and soft, not even her body was soft, but gone tight in the old morrocain dress, practically the only one she owned.

"I'll chop the head off the wyandotte," Mr Churcher said. He was proud of his knowledge of poultry, and they had a cross breeding in their meagre fowl run, comprising cast offs from other, fussier, farmers who pitied the impoverished state of the Churchers.

They rented their old place from the Heffernans, who had built it as their first home when they settled on the land fifty years earlier. Heffernan bought an adjoining property as fortunes improved and used the old place to run cattle. Since the house wasn't fenced in it was difficult, due to wandering steers, to grow produce to feed the eight children, or seven, now that Maxine had gone.

Mr Churcher was in constant conflict with Jim Heffernan. He (Mr Churcher) considered the five shillings a week rent unreasonable; he was actually doing the Heffernans a favour living there in a caretaking capacity, stopping the house from falling to ruin. He never tired of pointing out the work he put into the fowl run, although he had actually stolen some wire netting from a bundle delivered to the roadside for the Heffernans to extend their kitchen garden. Mr Churcher saw the heap and sent Lionel for pliers to snip a length from the roll, which he was sure would escape the notice of the Heffernans.

Mrs Churcher was distressed to see the children a witness to theft, but put those feelings to one side when she saw Mr Churcher had made a good job of the pen and more eggs appeared, since the fowls did not continue to lay in obscure places like inside blackberry bushes and up hollow logs.

Mr Churcher was thinking now of making some reference to the fowl pen to expose (once again) a more commendable side of his character and get him into his wife's good graces, although he did not think there was much chance of this. He took up the axe and spat on the blade, rubbing the spittle along the edge.

"I'll chop off its head before they get here," he said, seeing the ragged little army, still several hundred yards off.

"It'll be tough as an old boot," Mrs Churcher said looking at his. Her own feet were bare.

"It'll make good gravy and there's plenty of 'taters," he said, injecting cheer into his voice.

Mrs Churcher was going to say the dripping to roast the fowl in was needed for their bread, for they had not eaten butter in weeks, when a shrill cry made her look towards the myrtle patch on the rise.

Lionel came screaming out of it, like a brown leaf bowling along, aided by a strong wind, his feet beating so hard upon the earth, Mr and Mrs Churcher expected the vibrations to be felt at the woodheap. They stood up.

"He's bitten! A snake's got him!" she cried out. (Her mood would not allow for anything but the worst news.)

But Lionel had stopped yelling to fly towards the woodheap, with the other children breaking into a run and shouting wildly too.

Lionel flung himself upon his father. He was a skinny boy of eight, so red of face now his freckles had disappeared in what looked like a wash of scarlet sweat. His brown straight hair, in need of a cut, was standing upright in spikes or plastered to his wet ears. His chest, no bigger it seemed than a golden syrup can, heaved and thudded and his little stick-like arms were trembling.

"It's a parcel! The biggest I've ever seen! With Dad's name on it! Mr Barney Churcher, it says. And there's a million stamps!"

That was as much as he could say. He breathed and puffed and held his father's waist for support.

"Barney Churcher! That's me!" Mr Churcher said. He stroked down his front and looked up the track. "That's me alright!"

Lionel sat panting on a block of wood. "Oh, it's big, it's so big!"

The other children, all six of them, had reached the woodheap by this time. Ernestine was first. She was thirteen, and fairly fleet of foot too. "The mail car left us a parcel!" she called back to the running knot.

"Big!" Lionel cried now, with enough breath back to stand and throw his arms wide. "Take the slide for it!"

"Hear that boy!" said Mr Churcher looking at Mrs Churcher, watching for the film of ugliness to slide from her face. He's a smart boy and he's ours, was the pleading message in his eyes.

"Go and get whatever it is, and I'll stoke the stove, for God knows what we'll eat," Mrs Churcher said, walking off. Mr

Churcher told himself her body was softening up a little and that was something.

"Come on!" he called, sounding no older than Lionel, and seizing the rope attached to the slide standing on its end by the tankstand. The slide flew wide with the great tug Mr Churcher gave it, and the children laughed as they jumped out of its way.

"Lionel should get a ride!" Ernestine cried. She was brown haired and slender like Maxine, and would be a beauty too.

"He should and will!" Mr Churcher shouted and steadied the slide while Lionel climbed on and made a small heap of himself in the middle. Raymond, who was fifteen, took a part of the rope, and like two eager horses with heads down, father and son raced ahead, the slide flying over the brittle grass, barely easing its pace up the rise.

The parcel was from Maxine. They knew her writing. The contents were enclosed in several sheets of brown paper, then the lot wedged into a frame of well spaced slats. Mr Churcher's name and their address was written on a label nailed to one side. Above the writing was a line of stamps, some heavily smudged with the stamp of the post office through which it was sent.

Mr Churcher and the children crowded around it, sitting by the slip rails, the gate long gone, unhinged by the Heffernans and used on their new property. All of them, even four year old Clifford who had ridden to the road on Ernestine's back, bent over the parcel, stroking the paper, patting the wood, jumping back to keep their eyes on it, as if it might disappear. How different the road, the sliprails, the deeply rutted track leading to the house, looked with it there. Leave it, leave it! cried part of the minds of the Churchers. Take it away and the emptiness will be more than we can bear!

"Come on!" called Mr Churcher, as if he too had to discipline himself to break the spell. He flung the parcel onto the slide and put Clifford beside it.

"Not too fast!" cried six year old Josephine, who was not as sturdy as the others and suffered bronchitis every winter. Ernestine took her on her back for she was no heavier than Clifford. She whispered into Ernestine's neck that the parcel might be opened before everyone was there, for Mr Churcher and Raymond were flying down the track with the wind taking all of Clifford's hair backwards.

"No, no!" cried Ernestine, breaking into an energetic jog. "We'll all be there!"

Mrs Churcher was watching the track. "There's Mum!" Clifford shouted.

"We got it!" screamed Lawrence, who was nine and between Gloria and Lionel in age. (Which accounts for all the Churcher children.)

Mrs Churcher watched, as if mesmerised, the parcel sliding to a stop at the edge of the veranda. Mr Churcher took his eyes off it to fasten them on her face. A crease at each corner of her mouth kept any threatened softness at a distance.

"From Maxine," Mr Churcher said, pleading. He looked down on it beside Clifford, who was still on the slide reluctant to climb off.

"The stamps," Mr Churcher said, touching them with his boot. "Look what it cost even to send it."

"It's a parcel for us for Christmas, Mum!" Ernestine said, brown eyes like her mother's begging with some impatience for her excitement.

"There'll be nothing to eat in it," Mrs Churcher said. "Toys and rubbish, I'll bet." She looked hard at it, perhaps to avoid the eyes of the children, every pair on her she felt.

"I'll knock the old chook's head off," Mr Churcher said.

"Not Wynie!" came in a chorus from most of them.

Gloria, who had wild red hair, sat on the edge of the veranda and held her bare feet. "We can eat anything," she murmured dreamily.

"Anything you'll be eating too!" Mrs Churcher said.

"It's soft," Lionel said. "So I reckon it's clothes. Clothes." The light in his eyes ran like a small and gentle fire setting alight the eyes of the others.

"It's heavy, even for Dad," Ernestine said. "There's something in there for you, Mum, I reckon. New plates, like you want."

"Plates! They'd smash to smithereens. We'll be sticking with the tin ones!" Her eyes rested briefly on Mr Churcher. It's your fault they're only tin, they said.

Mr Churcher looked down on his hands wishing for a cigarette to use them, but he had no tobacco. There might be tobacco in the parcel. Yes! A packet of Log Cabin and papers. Two packets. Maxine used to sit on his knee and watch him roll cigarettes when she was a little thing, no more than two and the only one. They thought there would be no more and life would be fairly easy with the Great War finished and not too many joined up from Cobargo, thank heavens, to show him up. (He had no sense of adventure where war was concerned, no inclination to join in fighting.)

They had rented a little place in the town for six shillings a week (one shilling more than this and a palace in comparison, as he was always threatening to inform Jim Heffernan) and he had work, stripping bark, cutting eucalyptus, navvying on the road now and again. But the Depression came, and so did the children. Sometimes he went away for work, down as far as Moruya, coming home with his clothes in one sugar bag and some produce in another, oysters one time which the children had never tasted and passionfruit, which had been growing wild on the side of a mountain cleared for a new road. Mrs Churcher waited hopefully for him to produce some money, but there was always little of this. Once there was a pound note which the children looked upon as a fortune. It was a terrible disappointment to them when Mrs Churcher gave it to Fred Rossmore to ensure credit for a few more weeks.

Mr Churcher was thinking of past homecomings now, looking at the parcel, still on the slide with Clifford, irrelevant thoughts, for they concerned Maxine, not likely to come home herself, spending all that money on things for them. The children saw. They found other things to look at momentarily, but in a while their glances strayed back.

"Did any of you find any eggs today?" Mrs Churcher said. (For the fowls had found means of escaping the pen and were reverting to former laying habits.) They had not, it seemed. They stared at the parcel, as if the remark had insulted it.

"Then what do we eat?" Mrs Churcher said. She did not look at Mr Churcher, who turned his face towards the paddocks, hard and dry like his throat.

"You'll find something, Mum," Ernestine said. "You always do."

"There comes a time when you don't!" Mrs Churcher said. "It's come at Christmas. A good time to arrive!"

Her voice, hard as the baked, brittle paddocks, gave the words a ringing sound like an iron bar striking earth it couldn't penetrate.

Mr Churcher longed for an early evening, for long striped shadows to bring a softness to the hard, harsh day.

"Will we have nothing for Christmas dinner?" Clifford said, huddled and dreamy on the slide. The others felt their bodies twitch, hungrier suddenly than they were before.

"Remember last year?" Gloria said. "We had baked rabbit and Maxie's card."

"This year is better," Lionel said. "We got the parcel."

"If Mum will let us open it," Gloria said.

Mr Churcher looked at Mrs Churcher's set face.

"It's not addressed to me," she said.

Mr Churcher slapped a top pocket as if tobacco were already there. "It's not Christmas yet," he said. They looked at the setting sun filling the sky with salmon and peach jam and beaten egg white.

"We'll go into town and ask Fred Rossmore for some stuff!" Now he was patting his pockets as if money were there. He put his hands down and his face away. "We can pay after Christmas."

"With the endowment money I want something for the kids to wear back to school!" Mrs Churcher cried.

The children wondered briefly which of them might have got something new.

"There might be things in here we could wear," Lionel said, with a gentle toe on the brown paper.

"Come on!" Mr Churcher said, and began to walk rapidly off. He was taking the short cut through the bush, cutting off a quarter of a mile of road. Lionel ran to him and they both stopped and looked back to see who else was coming. Even with distance Mr Churcher's face showed he wanted Ernestine.

"I'll get my shoes and carry them!" she said, and was in and out of the room where the girls slept before Mr Churcher turned his head towards the track again. She ran to her father, not looking back.

Raymond, after standing with legs apart for a moment, holding his braces with fingers hooked in them, let the braces snap back into place and followed, racing past the little group to sit on a log some hundred yards ahead and wait, picking up bits of dead wood, rabbit dung and anything big enough to throw at nothing.

After a while they were lost to sight of those on the veranda, the gums and wattles and grey white logs, their roots exposed like a mouthful of rotten teeth, swallowing them up.

"I wonder what they'll bring back?" murmured Gloria. Clifford stood up and jumped off the slide, a very small jump he tried to make big. Lawrence moved along from his place on the veranda and put both feet on the slide.

"I'll stay with the parcel and mind it," he said.

Mrs Churcher padded to the kitchen, opening the stove door and shutting it with a clutter of metal so loud Gloria came uneasily inside.

"Did you see that?" Mrs Churcher said, sitting with her knees spread, stretching the morrocain until you saw through it.

Gloria did not know what she should have seen.

"Him!" Mrs Churcher said.

That meant Mr Churcher. That much she did know.

"Do you know why he made Ernestine go?"

No, Gloria didn't. Her chest went tight. Perhaps Ernie was his favourite. She (Gloria) was ugly (she thought). She and Lawrence were the two heavily freckled and with bright red hair. She had only sandshoes and could not have gone to town on Christmas Eve. Not that she would cry about it. There might be shoes in the parcel for her. She sat forward in her chair so that she saw a corner of it, watched by Lawrence, Josephine and Clifford, close together on the veranda edge. She was sorry she had come inside. Her mother strode to the stove now and put in a piece of wood Gloria thought too big and green to burn properly.

When Mrs Churcher went back to sit by the kitchen table she put her head on her arm and began to cry. "Rotten men!" she said, sitting up suddenly and wiping her eyes with her fingers.

A thin smoke began to bathe the log in the stove and some of it ran out of the stove door. "You need some chips," Gloria said, anxious that her father should not be blamed too harshly for the wood he had brought in. Perhaps it was the smoke that sent more tears running down Mrs Churcher's cheeks.

"He took her with him to get stuff easier from Fred Rossmore!" Mrs Churcher said. "I know Fred Rossmore!"

Of course, Gloria thought. Everyone in Cobargo did. Even children knew he was a powerful man in the town.

"He's fond of girls," Mrs Churcher said. That seemed alright in Gloria's view, except for the tone of her mother's voice (like an iron bar on hard dry earth it couldn't penetrate).

"Huh!" Mrs Churcher said, which could be interpreted as meaning that Gloria knew precious little about Fred Rossmore's character. "Not for their good, but for his!" Mrs Churcher said.

Gloria pondered this. It appeared to mean that with Ernestine there, Fred Rossmore would not be handing out goods from his shelves. Her heart was troubled for her father coming in empty handed.

"He touches diddies if you let him," Mrs Churcher said. "And up here." She touched the morrocain stretched across her chest.

Gloria considered this a small price for butter, bacon, tinned peaches and biscuits, but dared not say so.

"And that parcel," Mrs Churcher said. "I wonder about that."

Gloria bent forward again to see it, the most innocent thing in all the world.

"To start with, a man would put it in a frame like that. Not her."

I wish she wouldn't say her, Gloria thought. Maxine had the nicest name of them all. Ernestine was next. After that it seemed Mrs Churcher's selection of names was clouded by her worries at feeding and clothing them all. Gloria had been told an aunt, a sister of her father, had named her after the film star Gloria Swanson. Gloria felt a deep shame that she failed to turn out looking anything like Miss Swanson.

The green wood was filling the kitchen with smoke and Mrs Churcher got up and rubbed it into the hot ashes for it to burn quicker.

"For all we know a man might have bought what's in it. I reckon he did."

"For touching her diddie?" Gloria said.

Mrs Churcher was across the room in a second with a slap across Gloria's face so violent, Gloria lost her balance on the chair, and the noise brought the three from the veranda running to the door. They returned almost at once.

"Only Mum whacking Gloria," Clifford said, sitting down even closer to the parcel.

"There!" Mrs Churcher said, working the legs of the chair into the floor as she sat down. Gloria lay her face on her knee and cried softly. Mrs Churcher also cried. She allowed the tears to run in a great hurry down her cheeks, and when Gloria lifted her head she was surprised to see her mother's eyes quite bright and her face quite soft. She left her chair and went and sat on her knee. The fold of her stomach was soft as a mattress, and her shoulder a pillow, a fragrant fleshy pillow.

Mrs Churcher began to rock Gloria and this appeared to set them both crying without sound. When the others came in, tired of waiting by the parcel, Gloria lowered her face and Mrs Churcher turned hers. But they saw enough to make their eyes water too, so they moved together in a little bunch and stood giving all their attention to the stove fire.

Lawrence went off and returned with his old hat full of peaches. Gloria brought in some spindly wood that helped the green piece burn. Josephine asked if she could set the table, and Gloria, frowning on her, said to bring in some clothes from the line. The peaches were not as small and hard as those usually found, and when they had rolled to a stop on the table and Gloria brought a saucepan and a knife, Mrs Churcher said: "You'd better let me."

The four of them pressed their small chests against the edge of the table as they watched the peeling. It was a miracle of thinness, the furry skin falling from the knife like pale green tissue paper. Look at our Mum, said their eyes to each other. If only there was sugar to shake on some spoonfuls, without spilling a grain.

Mr Churcher brought some. Clifford, going out to check on the parcel, saw them come out of the bush and start their troop across to the house. He yelled as loud as Lionel when he found the parcel.

"They've got something!" he cried, flying inside then out again. The others followed except Mrs Churcher, who went to the stove with the saucepan of peaches and stayed there, making sure the lid was tight and they were on the right part of the stove to cook gently. Gloria allowed herself a brief look at the returning party, then when her mother had hung up the hessian oven rug, she went and hooped both arms around her and lay her face in the hollow of her breasts.

"They're coming," Mrs Churcher said, not actually pushing her off.

"Sugar, Mum!" Lawrence cried, as Mr Churcher put the little brown bag on the table with two tins of herrings in tomato sauce, some cheese, cut into such a beautiful triangle it would be a shame to disturb it, and a half pound packet of tea and some dried peas.

"And look what Ernie's got!" Lionel cried, stepping aside from in front of her to reveal her holding clasped against her waist a paper bag. Everyone knew, by the little squares and rolls and balls making little bulges in the paper, it could be nothing else but sweets.

"Lollies!" screamed Clifford, and Mrs Churcher turned to the stove again and they saw by the neck showing under the thick straggling bun of her grey and black hair that she was crying.

"Stop crying, Mum," Joseph said. "Ernie will give you one."

"They're for all of us to share," Raymond said, in case anyone should begin to think differently. He sat on the doorstep with a glance backwards at the parcel, the afternoon sun making diamonds of the tacks holding the label in place.

"Mum's not well," Mr Churcher said. He was standing in the middle of the room, one hand near his waist, the fingers spread as if a cigarette was there. "She's having another one."

Mrs Churcher sat and found the hem of her petticoat to wipe her nose.

"It'll be the last," Mr Churcher said.

The eyes of the children said this might or might not be so. Ernestine put the bag of sweets at the end of the top shelf of the dresser and snapped the doors shut. She moved to the table and put the other things from Fred Rossmore's inside the food safe. Mrs Churcher's wet eyes followed her. Ernestine's old sleeveless print dress showed her round tanned arms, and her hair heavy as a bird's nest showed bits of her neck, pure white inside dark brown slits. She brought out flour to make fried scones, holding the bag between breasts beginning to pout. Tears ran over Mrs Churcher's cheeks as Ernestine lowered the flour to the table and took a mixing bowl from a crude shelf above her head.

"There's four boys and four girls in this family," Lionel said. "So the next one can be anything it likes."

Mr Churcher was on a chair with his elbows on his knees. "Well said, Lionel. A smart boy that." He longed to be brave enough to look into Mrs Churcher's eyes. "You're all smart, all of you," he said.

Raymond looked at the kitchen floor boards between his feet. He had left school a year ago, and still had no job except for trapping rabbits in the winter and selling the skins, a great pile of them for only five shillings. The tips of his ears were very red.

"Next year things are going to be better," Mr Churcher said. Everyone half believed it, and Mrs Churcher, as if her mind were on something else, took out the sugar, and carrying it to the stove tipped a little onto the peaches. They all watched her fold the top of the bag down letting nothing escape.

"Yes, I reckon next year will be better," Mr Churcher said, putting a hand to a back pocket and moving it around there, as if making room for a packet of tobacco.

"And there's the parcel!" he said, throwing back his head suddenly like a terrier about to bark.

Josephine flung herself on Ernestine, as if the excitement was too much to bear alone. Raymond drew himself into a tight ball with his face crushed between his knees.

Lionel and Lawrence went to the veranda to each put a light foot on the parcel. Clifford climbed onto his father's knee, and Gloria leaned against her mother, with the cheek still red from the slap rubbing gently into her morrocain shoulder.

"And it's Christmas tomorrow!" Mr Churcher said, with his head back again and the words coming out like a terrier's bark. Out of the corner of his eye he saw Mrs Churcher's face start to go soft, then tighten again. She stood, taller than normal, he thought and looked across at him. Her eyes swept the children to one side. She might have sent them from the room, though all were there, faces tipped up at her, eyes begging for harmony.

"That parcel was sent from the place where the bad girls are," she said.

There was a rush for the veranda to look at the parcel again. Even Mr Churcher screwed his head towards it, but turned it back almost at once. His face did not believe it.

Gloria had a vision of a great mass of girls with pinched and sorrowful faces and their skirts dented deeply in the region of their diddies. She looked at Ernestine, who was measuring flour into a bowl with lowered eyes, but there was nothing to be seen past her waist, which was level with the table.

"Make sure you sift that flour properly," Mrs Churcher said. Then she sat on a chair with her head up, not looking at Mr Churcher. "You can see on the stamps where it was sent from."

"She could have given it to anyone to post. It's a great thing to lug herself," Mr Churcher said.

"She never writes," Mrs Churcher said.

"She was saving up for all those stamps," Mr Churcher answered. He got up and went and pulled the label from the parcel, looking at the stamps and postmark.

"You see it? Kings Cross! That's where she is!" Mrs Churcher took the bowl of flour from Ernestine and buried her hands in it. She began to cry again.

Mr Churcher put the label in the dresser next to the lollies from Fred Rossmore.

"Now it doesn't matter where it came from," Lionel said. Mr Churcher's eyes told Lionel this was wisely said.

Josephine went to Ernestine to cry into her waist. "We'll never know what's in the parcel!" she wailed.

"That's right!" Mrs Churcher was mixing dough fast with a knife, her tears temporarily halted. "We'll send it back!"

Josephine wept louder and Ernestine, checking that her mother's hands were covered with dough, and Josephine seemed safe from a blow, held her very tight.

Raymond went pale, and the freckles stood out on Gloria and

Lawrence for their faces had a pallor too. Lionel, sitting suddenly beside Raymond, turned the sole of one foot up and looked long and intently on it.

"You're a cruel woman, Maudie," Mr Churcher said.

The children were not as frightened by his words as they might have been. He called Mrs Churcher Maudie in the soft moments.

Mrs Churcher, her face clear of tears, tossed her head high and banged the frying pan on the stove. It was not a terribly loud bang though.

"I know my Maxie," Mr Churcher said. He was seated with his elbows on his knees. He held two fingers near his face and the children looked hard to be sure he had no cigarette.

"Your Maxie!" Mrs Churcher said.

"Our Maxie!" Mr Churcher said. "A good girl!"

"Yes, yes, yes!" came in different voices, Josephine's the strangest, for she was laughing as well as sobbing. Ernestine wandered outside, still holding Josephine, and Gloria followed.

Under the old apricot tree, from which the fruit had been early and hungrily stripped, they put their backs to the trunk.

"I'm frightened," Gloria said. "If there are gold and jewels in that parcel, what will we do?"

Ernestine tried to shrink the parcel in her vision. Mr Churcher came to the back door and filled the opening. Ernestine, Gloria and Josephine went and sat at his feet on the slabs laid on the earth to make a rough veranda. Ernestine held up a quilt, a snowy white fringed quilt with herself a little while, looking away to the mountains gone black to show the sunset up all the brighter.

She lifted her face, no less lovely, to her father. "You open the parcel, Dad. Like Mum said, it's addressed to you."

"By jove I think I might!" Mr Churcher said, loud enough to swing Mrs Churcher's face from the food safe to which she was returning the flour.

"I'm setting the table here," Mrs Churcher said. "Without any help as usual!"

"Leave the table setting!" Mr Churcher said. "I'm bringing in the parcel!"

He didn't go through the kitchen but strode around the house with Ernestine, Gloria and Josephine clinging to him.

Raymond, Lawrence, Lionel and Clifford were around the slide when they reached it. Mr Churcher lifted the parcel as if it were a pillow.

"Our Dad's so strong!" cried Lawrence. They stepped back like a guard of honour for him to go to the kitchen. He laid it on the table end.

"Don't break the box!" Lionel said. "It'll be handy for something!"

"A doll's cradle!" Gloria said. "If there's a doll in there for Josie!" Her eyes then sent an agonised apology to her mother.

There was no doll in there. But Josephine forgot her disappointment when the paper was pulled away and Ernestine held up a quilt, a snowy white fringed quilt with the honeycomb pattern broken up with a design of roses as big as cabbages, and trailing stems and leaves.

"Look at that!" someone cried.

"For Mum's bed!"

"And Dad's!"

Ernestine put it tenderly on a chair.

"Towels!" shrieked Gloria as four were found inside and four sheets with only a little fraying at the hems.

After that came a tablecloth, heavy and white, a beautiful thing for Christmas dinner, and several tea towels.

Ernestine held them up against the open doorway and there was hardly any wear showing.

"Give them all to Mum!" Gloria cried.

Mrs Churcher was on a chair, hands on her thighs, trying to keep the hardness in her eyes.

Mr Churcher sat on the door step where Raymond had been. He was watching Ernestine, Gloria and Lionel come to the end of the parcel.

Lionel shrieked when he held up a single page with Maxine's writing on it.

"I hope you like these things," she wrote, "I work for these people called Pattens. Mr Patten has a shop. He brought home some new sheets and things, all in colours which is the new fashion now. Mrs Patten decided to give me the old ones, or some of them, to send to you. She is not paying me this week, but says she has a Christmas present for me. They are having roast pork for Christmas dinner here, but I would rather be having what you are."

Lionel read the letter and everyone hearing it was quiet.

Mrs Churcher bent down to look into the stove fire, which was smoking again, so she needed to find her petticoat hem to wipe her eyes and nose.

Mr Churcher stared at his hands as if for the first time he realised they were holding nothing.

War Gave Women a First Taste of Liberation

I remember nothing of VJ Day, absolutely nothing. Not the hour I heard the news, not the kind of day it was, not the task I was engaged in, nothing of that day.

Perhaps one of the children was sick, upsetting the domestic routine, something contributing to a lapse of memory. I strain my ears for the shouting from the wireless, the blast of car horns, train whistles, for all these must have heralded the end of war, the real end and not the other, three months earlier on VE Day when the peace treaty was signed in Europe.

But I can't remember anything about it.

A shameful confession that, particularly with the memory of VE Day remaining so clear after forty years.

One reason might be the tie with the Mother Country, as England was called then, that gave so much significance to Victory in Europe. We were conditioned to revere her. She was more than the Mother Country — she was the Mother under whose skirts we had sheltered for more than 100 years, on whom we depended. We always knew she would put things right in the end.

Perhaps VJ Day came as a sort of anti-climax. The Bomb was dropped and that was an ending of a kind. We had won. Winning has always been of great importance.

We were, of course, deeply frightened when Japan came into the war. The bombing of Pearl Harbour was terrifying news. We listened to the wireless through the fall of Singapore and while the enemy inched its way down New Guinea — not too far away as it happened, living as we were then on the mid North Coast of New South Wales.

But the fears were in bursts, rippling across the surface of our lives, young mothers and children, meals to find from fairly flat purses and well-handled ration books.

A neighbour would come in with a child on her hip to talk about what we would do if the Japs came.

One or another had relatives in a remote part of the continent offering to take her in. Another was thinking of an air-raid shelter in the back yard, but it seemed a shame to tear up the garden after all the hard work.

We were not told of the air raid on Darwin until the event was more than a week old. We were rather like children with the birth of a sibling kept from us until all dangers had passed and father could announce all was well.

Japanese submarines came into Sydney Harbour but we chased them off. They might have been small boys throwing stones at our high, well-barred windows. We might have said, "phew, that was close".

We were a pretty naive lot in those days. Not only did we still believe if God saved the King he would save us too, we did most of the things our mothers did and their mothers before them, and nearly all of them came from the United Kingdom, the very name suggesting power, protection and obedience. Our obedience.

We inherited from our forebears the idea that women were inferior to men and here, by George, it was being proved. They were over there and up there fighting for our land and our lives, regardless of the safety of their own. If flat feet or curvature of the spine kept them out of the forces, they were working in an essential industry.

Our job was to brush the hearth, see that dinner was ready on time, and vote the way they told us to.

Not only were we naive by today's standards, but downright ignorant. Jogging was something we did when the butcher was selling sausages without asking for meat coupons. Heroin would have sounded like the name of a bird. We never knew of a child dying of cancer. The pill was taken for constipation. Gay was the way we felt most of the time, even while 22,000 Australian men and women were prisoners of the Japanese.

We had tennis on Wednesdays, and if the conversation got around to marital relations, the word sex was not used. It was heard only when our children were born and we wanted to know if they were boy or girl.

It is true that war shapes our lives. Perhaps truer to say it reshapes them. Truer perhaps of women than men.

The American servicemen had something to do with the reshaping. They opened car doors, brought flowers, told the women they were beautiful, talked to the married ones with children as the young and single. They sent home to the US for the first silk stockings we had seen in years. Perhaps they listened more attentively than the Australian men. Whatever it was, some time during those years and afterwards a confidence grew, a belief in the person one was.

Not every woman holding down a man's job while he was at the front gave it up when he returned without some forceful speaking (this was considered an attitude of the most unladylike kind). Some time later — it took up to twenty years — came the creeping revolution and there was almost a full-scale entry into what was quaintly called a man's domain and women got a voice in running the country — with and without a war — and made it known they weren't just there to see to the supper.

There was something else we did with equal thoroughness during the war.

We hated. We hated the Japanese — not only the leaders of the war, the instigators of the slaughter, deprivation and suffering, but every one — born and unborn.

When Pearl Harbour was bombed a woman in a Sydney department store smashed down a stand of china stamped "Made in Japan". A shop assistant came up with a dustpan and swept the pieces into the bin. His face was as grim as hers. He could not, at the risk of losing his job, have done such a thing, but he was glad somebody did.

Last month in Western Australia I watched while 9,000 US sailors poured off nuclear warships for rest and recreation leave after months in the Indian Ocean.

The clock might have been turned back 40 years. Outside the port, there was the rush to join the queue for taxis, the flash of shiny black shoes, sailor collars lifted in the wind, duffle bags dumped on the footpath. Heads were lifted to sniff air no longer pungent with salt. New smells. A perfumed shrub, smoke from a wood fire, fumes from cars and buses, a tarred road, the scent from a woman's ears and wrists.

There were little knots of the women, with backs half-turned, as if meeting a sailor was the last thing they had in mind.

Under the white gobs' caps, the clean shaven faces, the short cropped hair, the sailors were no different to the servicemen of the forties.

But some were Japanese.

Monet: The Meadow

Bourgeois and irreverent as it sounds I think of a certain cartoon many times when I am drawn to a famous painting. This cartoon depicts a politician viewing a picture and offering the timeworn quote: "I know nothing about art, but I know what I like." He is looking at a portrait of himself.

Looking at *The Meadow* one sees oneself, the child, the adult, the familiarity of time and place.

The village is French, the dress of Monet's time when he was middle-aged towards the end of the nineteenth century.

But it could be New England in New South Wales with the poplars and the church spires and the light of early afternoon.

The adults are at the edge of the meadow, one with a parasol. She does not trust the elements but the children rushing forward see no danger, no risk of a sudden downpour of rain, no sunstroke, no snake or spiders.

They would throw off their restricting clothing and hampering hats if they dared but this would impede their escape.

"Back here at once!" the mothers would scream, or use a more suitable French term. Then the children would have to turn and deny us the exuberance on their faces, and Monet's brush would have gone still on the canvas, like his trees and houses and churches and sky. They would have to be retied of shoelace and hair ribbon and grass seeds plucked from muslin and ordered to remain close to their peers and wear chastened expressions, while the peers were allowed to look as lofty and disdainful as they liked.

Afterwards at nursery tea of mutton broth and croutons, the mothers are contrite. "We know it was only a little romp in the meadow but we love you and don't want anything to happen to you."

But what they really say is: We don't want adventure for you. We want security. We want you still and safe with us. (And like us.)

Monet put roads in his painting, a network of them. The children want nothing of them. Their backs are turned on them. Man-made, they are only for straight and narrow feet.

Perhaps they see a circus ahead. The edge of a village is just the place to set one up. The colours are brighter than the yellow flowers through which they plunge. Or, if there is no circus, one could come any moment.

Drawn to a painting, impressed by this master Impressionist, a question is raised. Why the attraction to *The Meadow?*

Monet the rebel is there in his painting. He broke away from tradition, cast off restrictions imposed by art circles and went out and painted people, ordinary ones in all the different lights. He kept his ethereal or spiritual influence but he made his people real, liking them better than cathedrals, trains, boats and waterlilies.

He met opposition when he dared make change. But, like his running children, he didn't want only to admire the flowers in the meadow but get among them. And to search for something better, believing it to be there.

His parents opposed his ideals, chastised him, punished him. He is both the running child and (most likely when his turn came) the parent imposing his own set of restrictions on his own children.

We like what is familiar, what we understand. What is us.

The politician looking at his own portrait in approval was not that far out after all.

Elizabeth Jolley

EDITOR'S NOTE

Elizabeth Jolley began her writing career by writing stories for the BBC World Service and she has frequently been broadcast on British and Australian radio. She immigrated to Western Australia from England in 1959. She has published three collections of short stories: *Five Acre Virgin* (Fremantle Arts Centre Press, 1976); *The Travelling Entertainer* (Fremantle Arts Centre Press, 1979) and *Woman in a Lampshade* (Penguin, 1983). Her novels are *Palomino* (Outback Press, 1980; reprinted UQP, 1984); *The Newspaper of Claremont Street* (Fremantle Arts Centre Press, 1981); *Miss Peabody's Inheritance* (UQP, 1983); *Mr Scobie's Riddle* (Penguin, 1983); *Milk and Honey* (Fremantle Arts Centre Press, 1984); *Foxybaby* (UQP, 1985); *The Well* (Viking, 1986); and *The Sugar Mother* (Fremantle Arts Centre Press, 1988). Elizabeth Jolley has been a part-time tutor at Curtin University and at the Fremantle Arts Centre; she has also been awarded a Senior Fellowship from the Literature Board of the Australia Council.

"Hilda's Wedding" was published in *Woman in a Lampshade* (Penguin, 1982), pp.39–46; "The Well-Bred Thief" was published in *South Pacific Stories*, ed. C. & H. Tiffin (SPACLALS, 1980), pp.121–131; "The Fellmonger" anticipates the theme of Jolley's subsequent novel, *The Sugar Mother*, and was published in *Times on Sunday*, 22 February 1987; "Helen Garner: Rescuing Fragments" is extracted from a review published in *Scripsi* 3, ii & iii (1985): 17–20; the review of *Lilian's Story* was published in *Sydney Morning Herald*, 29 June 1985; and "Fringe Dwellers" is an extract from an interview with Jennifer Ellison, in *Rooms of their Own*, ed. Ellison (Penguin, 1986), pp.174–91.

Hilda's Wedding

Everyone said Night Sister Bean was a witch.

"Never let her look at a transfusion," Casualty Porter said to me my first night on duty.

"Why ever not?" I asked him.

"Never let her look directly at a blood transfusion," he said and he refused to say more and I waited for him in the doorway of the night porters' pantry.

"What harm can a kipper do?" Smallhouse was asking Gordonpole. The men were having their meal and took no notice of me. Gordonpole got up from the table and bashed about in the cupboard looking for the chutney.

"It's a shabby world," Smallhouse continued. "You want to look at the prison farms," he said ignoring the noise. "Just you what what stock they put in their paddocks and do the same yourself," he said. "Whatever it is the Government's doing, just you do the same as them because, I'll tell you this, prices will alter to suit what they have to sell. And, if you sell when they sell you'll be a rich man. Take a case in point, take beef now, there's no price at all just now for it, but you go out there and take a look at the beef cattle running and fattening on the pasture of the Crown."

Smallhouse and Gordonpole polished the whole hospital every night. It took them all night. They emptied the bins too and they were allowed to smoke which was fair enough when you saw what was sometimes thrown away from the operating theatres.

"Do they own land?" I asked Casualty Porter later and he laughed at my reverence. He shook his head.

"Not even a window box," he said. "It's all in the mind," he said and then he introduced me to Feegan, an old man dressed in black. He was engaged for ever in an endless dance up and down and across, back and forth all through and over the whole building all night long. With a special clock strapped to him he checked the fire-fighting equipment. He looked like a little black machine.

Everyone said this thing about Sister Bean.

"Always stand between Sister Bean and the drip," they said. They said if she looked directly at it something would be sure to go wrong with it. An air bubble would develop or it would go through too quickly or too slowly or stop altogether causing the patient to deteriorate rapidly perhaps even to death.

It seemed I was always to be on special nursing in some dark screened-off corner of the ward working stealthily beside a doctor busy with an unknown person, someone I'd never seen before and probably would never see again. That's what it was like being a relieving night nurse.

This thing they said about Sister Bean was hard to believe because she'd been so intimately concerned with life and death for over forty years. She had black coffee every night at ten past twelve and I was supposed to take it to her; so on top of all my other worries I had to think of this too.

I thought I would discover the truth about Night Sister and I stood aside on purpose when I heard her coming. She always came accompanied by the little breezes of her own rapid movement. She muttered too, a kind of hoarse whispering of names and diagnoses. It was like a dispensing of spells and curses as she came scurrying through the half-dark ward. All at once she was beside the bed and stood with her head bent while I told her about the patient. She nodded twice, her starched cap seemed top heavy on the small withered bean stick of her body.

I looked sideways in the frail light to the transfusion and waited for her to follow my sidelong look. The life-giving drops, quivering red berries were trembling and falling with promise, dropping steadily one after the other.

It was a faultless transfusion and the patient was warm and asleep. No one knew I was throwing away the ultimate chances of the transfusion and gambling with a man's life. No one at all knew what I was doing. I handed her the special charts.

Night Sister flicked her torch over them and handed them back.

Instead of standing between Sister Bean and the drip I looked sideways at it again silently inviting her to follow my look. It was as if, fully acquainted with her witch-like powers, she either refrained from using them, or at this time, did not choose to do so.

The hospital building glowing with subdued light in the night was like a great ship forever in harbour. Human life in this ship was divided into blocks. One block for hearts and one for chests, a block for bladders and one for bowels, a block for bones, one for women's troubles, one for mental disorders, one for births and all for deaths. I spent the nights in all the different parts of the hospital busy with the post-operative care of patients and worrying about Sister Bean's little white starched tray-cloth.

When I went through the half-lighted basements of the kitchens I met Maggie the hairless cook. Her head was always tied up in a greasy cloth. With her was Hilda, the fat maid who was always pregnant and a Boy. He had no name and no one knew how old he was. He worked all night quietly going about setting steam gauges, cleaning out ovens and bread crocks. He scoured the milk churns and prepared enormous cauldrons of peeled potatoes. He raked and stoked the boilers and he never spoke to anyone. No one had ever heard his voice.

"All nurses must show their little pink forms before entering," Smallhouse said when I went down to the pantry to fetch Casualty Porter.

"What did the gynaecologist say to the actress?" Gordonpole said. He was coiling lengths of cable flex.

"Oh I haven't time for your silly riddles!" I said to him. "Listen!" I said. "I think Hilda should be married. It's time Hilda was married."

"Good idea!" said Smallhouse. "I'd be only too glad to give her away," and he roared his head off. They had to hold each other up they laughed so much.

"Oh! my! Mind my polisher!" Gordonpole clutched his sides.

"No listen!" I said. "I'm serious. I think she needs a nice kind husband, a father for her children." They all looked at me and they all looked at each other.

"Sister Bean's had an operation, she's safely away in the

women's surgical ward," I said. "So now's the right time for the ceremony and, in any case, as you can see for yourselves we haven't much longer."

"But the trouble is, we're all married already," Smallhouse said. And then we all looked at Casualty Porter who seemed to have lost something under the table.

"It's very informal everywhere tonight," I told them. "There's a chocolate cake in Matron's office and someone's fixed a wireless in the broom cupboard, there's to be dancing later."

Smallhouse and Gordonpole were enthusiastic and in a short time we managed to get Casualty Porter to be agreeable. He even went and fetched flowers from the passage outside the private wards. He put a poinsettia in his buttonhole and then we dressed Hilda in one of the gowns they use in X-ray.

"It's a lovely green," I told her. "You should always wear this colour." I made her a veil with three packets of sterile surgical gauze.

"You look a treat!" I told her.

We had to wait until Feegan, bound by the checking clock, could make a brief appearance in the kitchens to perform the ceremony before being forced to set off again on his light prancing up the well of the first staircase.

Smallhouse would give the bride away and Maggie was to stand in as mother of the bride.

"Oh," I said, "you haven't got a hat for the wedding." We all looked in dismay at Maggie's lack of suitable clothes.

"Wait," I said and I rushed up to the linen room by the out-patients' hall and quickly searched the shelves. "There that suits you very well," I said, pinning one of Sister Bean's caps on to the greasy head-cloth.

"It's really you!" I said when she began to protest she wouldn't be seen dead in one of them.

"Well," I told her, "you're not dead yet." I pinned a draw sheet on to Hilda's plump shoulders.

"Gordonpole can be a page," I said and I made him hold the end of the sheet like a train. Hilda was delighted. She stood swaying and her melon-coloured face shone with a big smile.

"I've lost my way in the seasons," Smallhouse muttered while we waited impatiently for Feegan. He consulted his diary. "Hm I see shearing time is nearly with us," he snapped the little book shut.

"That's just like you farmers," Casualty Porter said with his customary good humour. "You look at a date and you shear your sheep no matter what the weather is and you let them starve with cold! I've seen it with my own eyes. It's the same with burning off, that's why the whole country gets burned to a crisp just because a date is set for being able to burn no matter how dry the season."

Smallhouse looked coldly at the bridegroom and turning away he addressed Gordonpole. "How are things up at your place?" he asked.

"Terrible," Gordonpole sighed. "It's the poultry," he said. "They lay one egg between them, it's union rules, you know, the 'State Amalgamated Fur and Feather', one egg only in twenty-four hours, it's a sort of lay to rule they've started. There's nothing I can do."

"Too right!" Smallhouse nodded. "As if there isn't enough far-myard stress already. Mine have gone off their heads too, lost their minds completely. They're eating their own eggs!"

"That's because you're not feeding them right," the bridegroom interrupted again. The father of the bride and the page turned angrily towards the bridegroom.

"Now!" I said quickly, fearing a threat to the domestic harmony. "I think we should move that trolley with the bins." Smallhouse and Gordonpole lit their cigarette ends and tidied the stinking bins into a corner. They had just finished when Feegan came in stepping lightly between the buckets of carnations and roses.

"Did you remember a prayer book?" I asked Casualty Porter. Of course he had forgotten.

"I've got this," Feegan said pulling a small book from his tight black pocket. "It's a Cricketer's Manual," he explained. "It's very old, it's dated 1851, an heirloom, in a sense it's a sort of treasure," he seemed to apologise. We had never heard him say so much before, his voice was very pleasant, it was an agreeable surprise.

"Well then," I said. "Read a bit of it please." We all sang "Here Comes the Bride", and Feegan read from his little book, "The

moral character of any pursuit is best estimated by its conse-
quences to individuals and its effects upon society. If the absence
of evil be not a permissible proof of innocence it ought to imply
assent, when no positive evidence stands in opposition —"

"That was very nice thank you," I said quickly. I was afraid
time would run out.

"Anyone here object to this, er, marriage?" Feegan gave a hurried glance round the assembled company. Somewhere the other
side of the kitchens the Boy dropped something heavy, it sounded
like a hod of coke.

Feegan hurried on. "Dust to dust and ashes to ashes," he gabbled. "I declare you man and wife."

Hilda gave Casualty Porter such a hug he gasped for breath.

The telephone was ringing and ringing in the outpatients' hall
and he had to rush off to answer it. Feegan danced off into the
darkness and we threw rice and bits of torn-up coloured paper
over the radiant Hilda.

While we were hurriedly eating some sausage rolls, Smallhouse
made a speech.

"Unaccustomed as I am," he said, "I would like to make a few
comments on the cauliflower which is perhaps the oldest sex
symbol known to man. We should," he said, "in this shabby
world look to the prison farms. The prison farm," he drew breath,
"and the coins of the realm," he seemed lost in thought and chewed his sausage roll gloomily. "Coins of the Realm," he said.

"That was very nice thank you," I said anxiously looking at the
clock.

"Coins of the Realm," Smallhouse said again and shook his
pockets. He was still searching in his pockets when Hilda clutched
herself and gave several great moans. We all looked at her in
dismay.

"Her waters have been and gone and broke," Maggie said
knowingly. I told Gordonpole to get the trolley and I rushed to
the phone.

"Archbishop here," Casualty Porter answered it in an over-
developed Oxford accent. "On behalf of Royalty and ourselves
we wish the bride all happiness, a message from the Queen herself
reads, 'We are amused,' telegrams are arriving from —"

"Get me maternity quick!" I interrupted him.

"Ward 4 speaking."

"Hilda's in labour," I said.

"How frequent are the pains?" came the competent reply.

"It's all one big pain," I said.

"Where's the head?" said the cool voice.

"What?" I said. "Oh I think, somewhere between the stove and the sink."

"The head," the Charge Nurse on Ward 4 said patiently, "Is it on the perineum?"

"Oh that head! Oh yes I should think so," I said, dreadfully afraid Hilda would be delivered on the kitchen floor.

"Nurses never think. They know," the Charge Nurse said coldly. "Bring the patient straight up." And she rang off.

Hilda's baby was born while we were in the lift.

"Turn the blanket back," she said, "so as I can get a look." Somewhere in between Hilda's big thighs and her coarse underwear a small damp wrinkled creature gave out a great cry and Hilda smiled. "Isn't he lovely," she sighed and her big face was surprisingly sweet and fresh.

We hurried the trolley along as quickly as possible.

"Keep still," I said sharply to Hilda. I was afraid she would crush her own baby.

Hilda and the baby and all the muddle of wedding clothes and flowers were swept off into the antiseptic fragrance of the maternity ward.

On the way down I called in at the women's surgical ward and I peered round the first screen inside the door. Sister Bean looked smaller than ever lying on her pillow without her big white starched cap. She turned her bright little eyes to me. And, as if she knew why I had come to visit her, she gave a withered little smile.

"Since when did varicose veins get a transfusion nurse?" she said. "All the same, thanks for coming to see me."

I went on down into the underworld of the kitchens. I saw the Boy standing alone in the mess of makeshift confetti and scattered rice. Bruised and dying flowers were all over the place and the Boy was just standing in it all, his broom and dustpan on one side as if he'd forgotten them. His face was all puffed up and, from where I was, it looked as if slow heavy tears were crawling down his smeared cheeks.

The fresh milk had come so I stopped and drank a basinful.

The empty milk churns were being taken away from the ramp outside the kitchens and the city beyond was beginning to wake up. A thin trickle of tired sad people left the hospital. They were relatives unknown and unthought about, they had spent an anonymous night in various corners of the hospital waiting to be called to a bedside. They were leaving in search of that life in the shabby world which has to go on in spite of the knowledge that someone who had been there for them was not there any more.

The air was surprisingly sweet and fresh at the edge of the kitchens where the inside of the hospital flowed out to meet the outside world. I stood there, full of fresh milk and I took deep breaths of this cool air which seemed just now to contain nothing of the weariness and the contamination and the madness of suffering.

It seemed too that it was more of a certainty than merely a possibility that at some time Night Sister Bean would be admitted for major surgery and then we would know once and for all the truth about this thing everyone said about her.

The Well-Bred Thief

Roadside Mail one,
Medulla,
Western Australia.
1st January

Dear Barbara,

You'll be surprised to have a letter from me. It's years since we moved up together from Fraser Street Mixed Infants and passed out from St Mary's Big Girls.

I had a mattock head sent from England and there in one of the newspapers used for packing was your picture! I suppose it's your husband with you and your son who has done so well at school.

You've hardly changed, well of course you're older, but you don't look any too old.

I'm sending you the manuscript of a book I've written. Please could you submit it for me? I notice you work for a publisher. I'm living all alone in the country waiting for the jarrah to grow. Donald and Mary have left home and there's no one to talk to except the fowls, that's why I've written this book.

No one at all knows I have written it. I have put in a postal order for expenses and a tea cloth decorated with Kangaroo Paws. They are wild flowers, our National Emblem. They look better with the sun shining through the red and green plush of their stalks.

I suppose Peter will be going to university after getting such high marks. You must be proud of him.

This summer is very dry, all life seems withdrawn in this heat. The honey trees are covered in creamy balls of flower and the noise of the bees is like distant church music. These trees light up the countryside, they remind me of the candles of the horsechestnuts in England, though if I could see them again, I would know they are not at all like our honey trees.

I hope your winter is not too severe with fog and snow.

Very best wishes,

Mabel Morgan

Holly House,
Tarbridge,
Kent, UK
3 March

Dear Neckless,

*I simply can't think of you by any other name than your old nickname. I have read your charming and poetical book. I am sure you can write but the **Question** is **What**! I found myself completely absorbed. I have let my impressions simmer, and have since had it read by one of the **Younger Set** at **Trotter and Trotter**. The Reader said **Perfectly true** things but was absolutely **Not in Tune** with your writing, though you do have a **Taut and Telling** line. Your characters are very real but would people want to read about the very real? You do rather overdo Beethoven. I am sure he is completely **Out** now. Years ago **we** discovered him. I remember my own elephantine gyrations to the grand finale of his Seventh. But do people **really** want Beethoven now? All this **maddens** me. You have a remarkable aptitude for evoking sights and sounds and especially smells. Why is the main character, Edna, so battered in the first half of the book when in the second half she does all the battering? Leila certainly pulls the book into shape as do the bulldozers in the new shopping centre, a clever image! I love your disastrous dinner party and the arrival of the police. You certainly understand the problems of teenage boys. Walter made my heart **bleed**. But why keep his box a secret? and why keep the reader in suspense over the killing of the little girl?*

Peter hopes to spend summer in Athens and will be starting university after the long vac. If he doesn't work for his exams we have threatened him with Australia. How on earth do you manage for **culture** *over there.*

Yours ever,

Barbara

P.S. What is jarrah? and why do you have to wait for it?

Roadside Mail one,
Medulla,
Western Australia.
20th May

Dear Barbara,
I have just received your long letter of 3rd March. You forgot to put any stamps on it so it has come surface mail. I'm very relieved to have it at last. I'm interested in what you have to say about my book. In the writing I'm trying to discover if a person finds peace within himself rather than in the world outside or whether the true meaning of life really comes from external circumstances. Edna changes because she chooses the man with prospects rather than the man she loves. The second half of the book deals with her striving to rebuild her collapsed life. I have tried to show this unpleasant character as an honest one.

Leila and her mother are symbols of suburban comfort and complacency. For them there is no struggle, they don't know unemployment and poverty. For them there are no wars and no famines. In their lives there is no poetry or music either, and no drama of love and hate. Even the word "government" really means nothing to them.

Walter, the product of Edna's unhappiness, does understand but is inarticulate. He breaks away from the conventional education Edna wants for him but later struggles back to the desirable comfort of the suburb. The girl from the greengrocery store is merely his accomplice. Neither of them can expect a wider horizon. The delayed explanations are necessary, if I revealed the contents of Walter's box too soon, there would be no point in the book.

I did not mean to write for a particular audience. I thought there might be many kinds of minds in the reading public. I realise you can't submit a second time to the same publisher especially as you work there. I would be grateful if you would try another publisher please.

I hope you all keep well. I hope Peter studies as you want him to. It's no use for a young man to come out to Australia unless he has qualifications of some kind.

My best wishes to you,
Mabel

P.S. Jarrah is a kind of tree. I sold the farm but am still living here as the new owner agreed to my staying on till my crop matured. I planted a jarrah forest. I'll be here for some time. The children have gone as I told you. I do miss them.

Mabel

Holly House,
Tarbridge,
Kent, England.
30 May

Dear Neckless,

I am appalled my letter went without a stamp. I do hope you didn't have to pay up. From March to May is rather a long time to wait for a letter. Really I am terribly sorry.

Life has been very erratic and hectic ever since Christmas and we all had colds and 'flu. Really our English winters! I will get out your MS again when I've re-read your letter. At present we are trying to decide on fresh colour schemes for the hall and the bathroom. Matching towels are such a problem aren't they!

I wonder if you would do something for me? A friend has just emigrated to Sydney, her name is Mrs Flint, and the address is Avon Park. Do you think you could call on her? Thanks most awfully.

Yours Barbara.

Roadside Mail one,
Medulla,
Western Australia.
14 June

Dear Barbara,

Please don't worry about the unstamped letter. I never see the postman, he leaves the letters in a drum down on the road. It's too far for him to come up to the house.

I hope you are all better now.

I'd like to visit your friend Mrs Flint but I don't think I'm able to go the two thousand miles over to Sydney. You see I only get up to town here twice a year. I hope the lady is settling down, it takes a while to get used to a strange place. There is nothing worse than loneliness.

I'm looking forward to hearing from you soon.

Yours ever,

Mabel

As from Tarbridge
Kent.
UK
28th June

Dear Neckless,
I am being very wicked and stealing an airgraph from the firm.

I did buy one but left it at home. I bring sandwiches to the office and type in the lunch hour as my evenings are filled up with meetings —

I am dreadfully ashamed but I have to confess that for the moment I have mislaid your book. How I can have lost it I can't imagine! I'm quite certain it's the first time in thirty-five years of handling manuscripts. You probably gathered I was in complete chaos when I wrote before. Peter had just collapsed with 'flu, Ernest went down while on a Business Trip and, though I was subclinical, I got the **Full After Effects***. I pushed everything into the spare room. Then, when your letter came I was* **Absolutely Appalled** *that the MS wasn't where I thought it was. I'm quite sure it will turn up. I'm one of those people who find things if they don't look for them.*

I'm not being casual about this. I realise apologies won't help! I'm inclined to advise you to wait a little before submitting the book anywhere else.

Of course it's **"Not Done"** *for me to quote what other Readers have said. But Edna's squalid life alone in the hut certainly impressed and so did the poignant luxury of the white and gold bedroom scenes later. Ah! the sadness of loving too late . . . And, added to all this your apparent knowledge of life inside a prison. However could you give the appearance of being so familiar with this?*

Ah well, I hope you will be forgiving about the loss of Edna and Leila and all of them.

I am not so chaotic as a rule. If you can stand the expense and my **outspokenness** *I'll be only too glad to read anything else you care to send.*

Yours ever,

Barbara

P.S. I feel awful.

*   *   *

Roadside Mail one,
Medulla,
Western Australia.
6th July.

Dear Barbara,

Thank you for your letter. I was so impatient to read it, I opened it right down there on the road. I must admit it is a terrible shock to me that the book is lost. An unbearable loneliness on top of the loneliness I've got already came over me as I read your letter. I felt as if I'd lost a child somewhere and was too far away, too isolated, to do anything about it. I came straight back up to the house. It's intolerable here, there's no one I can talk to about the loss of the book. I keep walking on to the veranda and looking down the long paddock. But there's nothing there except the tufted grass all the way to the edge of the bush. It's so quiet except for the noise of the crows. Their indifference only makes the loneliness worse. I feel quite helpless so far away from the places where I could enquire and search for my book. I have never felt like this before, it's as if I can't really believe what you have written and yet I know I must believe it. I'm sorry to go on like this!

I should not have troubled you with it when you have such a busy life.

Please do write at once when you find it. Perhaps by now you will have found it. I do hope so.

Yours ever,

Mabel

Roadside Mail one,
Medulla,
Western Australia.
20th October.

Dear Barbara,

It's nearly the end of October and I've been waiting since July hoping for a letter from you. Have you by any chance found the manuscript of my book *The Leila Family*? I do hope you have.

I hope you are all well and that Peter will enjoy university.

It's very dry and dusty here. I seemed to spend my days going down to wait for the mail and watching the sky for rain clouds. Please write soon.

Yours ever,

Mabel

Holly House,
Tarbridge,
Kent. UK
10 November.

Dear Neckless,

I am ashamed and quite **appalled** *by your letter. I can't believe all those months have gone by and all the time you have been waiting for your MS to come safely back home. It's unthinkable — you alone in your little wooden hut under the hot sun with your galvanised water tanks running dry — is this a correct picture I have?*

I have been in the throes of an **occasion** *since your correspondence. Please don't argue, I insist on sending you ten pounds towards making up for the loss of the MS. I insist that you accept it. I shall not* **feel** *the sending of it as I am about to receive a Bonus for something I am doing at* **Trotter and Trotter**. *I am afraid the MS did not turn up during our Spring cleaning and it's too late to enquire at the railway now —*

I've had your name at the top of my list. I wish I had got my letter in first. I am sorry.

Yours,

Barbara

P.S. **In August we had ten days motoring in the Pyrenees. Glorious weather.**

Roadside Mail one,
Medulla,
W.A.
18 November

Dear Barbara,

Please don't upset yourself so much and please don't send me the money. As Autolycus says in A Winter's Tale "Simply the thing I am shall make me live."

I can't help hoping the book will be found.

Yes you are right, we have water tanks but not dry yet thank goodness. The home is weatherboard with a veranda all round. We have an iron roof and the tanks are to one side. I have roses and geraniums and of course the jarrah saplings, what's left of them, after Donald and his friend made a dirt track of the place with their old cars.

Donald and Mary are still away somewhere. I do miss them. I keep hoping for them to come. And I do hope the book will be found.

I hope all is well with your family.

Yours Mabel

Holly House,
Tarbridge,
Kent, UK
28th November.

Dear Neckless,

We didn't do Winters Tale at school. How come you know it? I wouldn't have thought Shakespeare had got down under!

*I was glad to get your letter and to know you can take things to philosophically. I am also glad to lower my sights over the MS but I do want to send you **something** and have done so today. I have posted you a dress length. Please don't feel I have been extravagant, it's something I happened to have by me. I hope it* will not be ruined crossing the equator. The psychodelic colours are just not **me**. I hope they will be **you**. I expect you have long evenings to fill up so have enclosed two adult education essays I have written, you may enjoy reading them, also Mrs Cole's notes on Poe.

I would be very interested to know if you are thinking of writing more about Leila and Edna and the others. If you are, perhaps you could write back at once. Quick notes will do, and send me any other ideas you have. Perhaps you could do this soon, as soon as possible please. Could you?

Peter is thrilled with his campus. His digs are rather far off but he seems to have good food.

Yours,

Barbara

P.S. My parcel won't get to you in time for Christmas but it should be there soon after.

P.P.S. You are sure aren't you that no one else knows that you have written the book.

The Fellmonger

Unable to place the man Dixon thinks he is probably a fellmonger. He, the fellmonger, probably works in large sheds open at the sides with names painted in red on the corrugated iron. He might even own the sheds. On either side there would be smaller sheds and, at the far end, a small house. Hungry greyish-white hawks would hover endlessly over the dunes and the surrounding scrub. An unmistakable smell would never be absent. It is possible that this smell would hang forever about this man.

Dixon, aware of the rose-water fragrance of his own hairdressing, watches the man, who is big, moving lightly for his size as he gently, with little possessive circlings and extendings of his thick arms, encourages the girl to move towards a secluded corner. Sitting opposite Rosie in the expensive candle light Dixon is able to see through beyond the ornamental arch to the place described as the cocktail bar. A few noisy young men — it is easy to see that they are farmers — are celebrating together. They ignore the fellmonger. He is not one of them.

The fellmonger and his girl sit in the armchairs recently occupied by Rosie and himself. Perhaps he had, with the same possessive circlings, unknowingly looked like the fellmonger. Naturally they could not really look like each other because of the various differences, significant differences of background, social and cultural and intellectual. It is not possible to make comparisons except that while guiding Rosie to and from the armchairs he had not been aware of what he now observes in this other man.

In the face of this observation, though he does not like to admit this, the differences — the educational and the financial — do not now seem important.

This other man is not young. Like Dixon he is older than his chosen girl, but he is nowhere near Dixon's age.

Rosie, to Dixon's surprise in the armchair part of the evening, had chosen Coca-Cola with a measure of Southern Comfort. It now looks as if the other girl, the fellmonger's girl, has made a similar choice. Dixon keeps to his usual whisky. He notices that the fellmonger has a beer which remains at his elbow untouched. He is taking this girl out for the evening and wants to remain well mannered and chivalrous for the whole time. He is looking after her with a clumsy reverence and is not going to spoil his intention with any crudity.

Dixon smiles glancing, like a conspirator, at Rosie whose eyes shine with a wonderful soft gentleness. That is one of the tricks of the candle light. Dixon knows this. His drink will not in any way inhibit his own performance. A sophistication the fellmonger obviously does not have and so he is cautious. Dixon, still smiling enjoying a secret superiority, thinks for a moment of the double bed in the motel room. Their bed, his and Rosie's. He knows, too, that the kind light of the candles flatters his own complexion and the silver wealth of his hair.

The dining room, designed to be like a part of a ship, is very cold. He is glad he suggested to Rosie to bring her cardigan. He asks the waitress to have the air-conditioning turned off. They are the only people at present in the dining room. Dixon orders soup, a cream of vegetable, and waits for it impatiently. Rosie says she likes soup and that she will have whatever he is going to have after it. He chooses fish, dhufish, pan fried with vegetables though he knows he will not be able to eat the sweet corn. He momentarily wonders why a restaurant would serve corn on the cob when it is such an awkward thing to eat. They have a bottle of white wine from a local vineyard. It is well chilled, and, when the soup arrives, Dixon feels approval creeping through his comforted body.

Rosie, the daughter of an unexpected housekeeper, does not talk much, partly, he supposes, because he is so much older and because he is, as Rosie's mother describes him: highly educated

(Renaissance and some desultory literary wanderings) and because he is married. Rosie sometimes has asked about Delia, what her favourite colours are, that sort of thing, but Dixon does not want, when he is with Rosie, to talk about Delia.

He thinks during the meal that she might be missing her mother though it is not long since they left. She is used to being with her mother all the time, a sort of symbiotic relationship. He has not known them very long. Rosie's mother has become, because of locking herself out of the house next door accidentally, the unexpected housekeeper for Dixon. On the night when they came to him for assistance he felt obliged, because they were unable to break into the house, to invite them to stay overnight. They have, after one or two very short absences, been staying with him ever since as Delia is to be away for several months and Rosie's mother is an excellent cook. Choosing roses to leave with Rosie's mother and for Rosie to hold in her lap on the journey Dixon realises that he has embarked on a plan from which there is no turning back.

The excitement of this, at his age, is remarkable and he is not prepared while standing by the florist's counter and selecting one perfect bloom after another, breathing in the sweet perfume, to consider, to stop and consider his actions in the light of his friends' (his and Delia's) opinions.

Surprisingly Dixon finds it easy to talk to Rosie's mother and has confided that it is a grief to him that he and Delia have no children.

"That is a great shame," Rosie's mother said then. She said that he and Dr Delia must miss the patter of little feet terribly. During one of her nightcap glasses of port she discusses various solutions to the problem of being childless.

"Rosie, if I put it to her, would carry for you," she says holding her glass to the light and squinting into its ruby redness. "I'd have no trouble with Rosie," she says.

"Sorry?" Dixon is perplexed.

"I'm saying that Rosie would oblige with carrying for you and Dr Delia," Rosie's mother explains. "It's being done all over the place nowadays."

"Oh, I see," Dixon feels self-conscious and awkward.

"There's different ways," Rosie's mother says. "I favour

nature's way myself. It's like home baking, you know what's in it."

"Yes, I see." Dixon, contemplating Rosie's body and the idea of its being used in this way, is completely taken by surprise. The surprise is not disagreeable but he is apprehensive.

"Take to it slowly," Rosie's mother says, "and never you worry Dr Dixon, just let nature take her course. There's nothing to pay till conception and then we'll go from there." She accepts another port. "Make sure," she says "make sure she lies on her face."

"I'm sorry?"

"I'm saying make sure afterwards that she lies face down straight after, straight after, you know what, to make sure she falls."

"Falls? I'm sorry."

"Falls pregnant, it never fails."

"Oh, I see. Yes. Yes, of course."

Dixon, impressed with Rosie's mother's suggestion, agrees to the fee mentioned and a situation develops which is pleasantly agreeable to him. The little holiday he is taking with Rosie is meant to show her something of the coast but it is also because he wants to talk with her. When they are with her mother she does all the talking, and Dixon has discovered, during the few nights he and Rosie have had in bed together, that she falls quickly into a sound sleep and so their conversations are restricted. He cherishes the idea of waking up in the night to turn to her, or better still, to have her turn to him to rouse him. He wonders whether an alarm clock would be a good idea.

During Delia's long absence and with Rosie and her mother in his house there is a domestic calm which he has never had before. Life with Delia is governed by clocks and by telephone calls from the Mary Joseph wing of the district hospital. Babies are born at all hours and Delia does not try to regulate her working hours. Mostly it is a matter of emergencies. Certainly an alarm clock now would make the house once more like it is when Delia is at home. Rosie's mother, who keeps discreetly to her own room, would come running clutching her dressing gown about her if the clock went off at 2.30 in the morning. Dixon enjoys smiling at this private image. He is fond of Rosie and his fondness is increasing.

It takes the shape more and more of wanting to teach her, to show her things, to introduce her to books and to music so that she can share the things he loves. They are not sure yet if she has conceived. He does not think about this much, it is something outside his experience. Vaguely he remembers when friends of theirs (his and Delia's) travelled with small children they sent postcards from Naples, Grenoble and Vienna with no message except that one child or the other was sick. He, when he does think about it, is not in a hurry for conception to take place. Delia, who is very recently gone away, is to be away for a year.

The fellmonger is gazing at his girl who is as badly dressed as Rosie is. Dixon, in his mind, dresses Rosie in green and white which he regards with reverence as being the colours of the Elizabethan court, the area of his thesis many years ago and now in the same obscurity as the other aspects of his work. But the freshness of green and white is something he can tell Rosie about some time soon. The fellmonger, in his gaze, seems to admire his girl's dress, it is dark red and clumsy. Obviously, Dixon thinks, all those tucks and pleats have been done by hand by a mother with a great deal of patience and absolutely no taste. This mother, he thinks, must approve of the fellmonger's financial state to encourage her daughter to accompany this man who is certainly not handsome. Perhaps the girl's mother is imagining the proposal being offered at this moment. Visions of an unwieldly kitchen come quickly — homemade ply-wood cupboards and cracked but well-scrubbed tiles behind the too small sink, a wood stove and stretches of worn linoleum, a laminex table with chrome legs and four ugly chairs to match — a back-door straight on to the dirt of the yard. The fellmonger might, in his earnest conversation, be at this moment offering his previously unwifed home to the one person he sees as eminently suitable to be wrapped up in an apron and up to her elbows every day in flour and soap suds. He is possibly at this moment seeing little fellmongers, two or three podgy small versions of himself, crawling on the worn linoleum and hanging on to the uneven hem of her skirt. As he leans forward even more in his conversation it is as if the future wife's airless bedroom is being exposed. From the unopened windows of this room is a narrow view of the tufted grass and a part of the immense sand dune at the side of the shed opposite. Dixon is sure the fellmonger lives where his work is and does not notice the smell. He will expect his wife to get used to the sight of the hairy matted hides and their smell. Rosie's mother, Dixon thinks, approves of his (Dixon's) financial status. He knows that though she does not really know him she knows more about him than he knows about her. Her wonderings at this moment as she sits alone waiting for a telephone call from Rosie are unimaginable. Watching the fellmonger as he leans to speak to his girl and watching the girl sipping her large dark drink (it must be at least a pint of Coke) he feels a curious sense of something undefinable, something he does not want to feel or think about, something disturbing so disturbing that he puts down his heavy knife and fork rather suddenly.

"Is your fish not nice?" Rosie, with her mother's kind of question, asks. His action has obviously surprised her into initiating a question.

"Oh perfectly," he says at once and, dabbing his lips with his napkin, he reaches for the wine. Lifting it from its bed of crushed ice, he tops up their glasses. He smiles at Rosie, and she smiles back with her usual shy look. They sip their wine, looking across the small table at each other.

The food, which is well cooked, together with the quality of the wine, restores Dixon. The small tour of sightseeing in what seemed to be a ramshackle town has depressed him. He realises now that a Saturday evening is not the best time to be cruising in a slow-moving, expensive car through streets of closed-down sandwich bars, cheap clothing shops and shabby Chinese restaurants. The street corner population, these groups of youths, all turned to look as he was obliged to reverse all the way from the end of a street from which, because of some half-finished industrial construction, it was impossible to turn. He felt then all the more conspicuous because of Rosie, who is very young, sitting close up beside him. To have a holiday anywhere he knows he needs his books and his music with him. He likes his own bed, and he is used to the bathroom at home and, because of this, he has always felt it better for him to stay at home. "What if we go to Europe," Delia has often made suggestions, needing a change from her demanding work.

"Why don't we go to Spain, or what about a month in Paris?" Stubbornly, he has refused to travel and, when Delia's work demanded the year away, he said at once that she must go by herself, and that he would be perfectly all right looking after himself at home. After all, he reminded her pleasantly, he did vacuum the house didn't he? And it was he who, at about 4.30 in the afternoons, went to the supermarket to replenish the pantry. He had developed quite a skill in recent years at discovering the bargains, and had learned to look the other way when he saw wives of colleagues advancing with conversations which would hamper him. Rosie coming freshly and unexpected into his life is an unasked-for gift, and this little holiday is something different. Apart from the love-making, the getting Rosie with child, for which there is ample opportunity at home since the idea has been a suggestion from Rosie's own mother, he feels he wants a chance to talk with Rosie, to know and understand her. It is the excitement of offering her his intellect, which he wants and, for this, he needs to have time alone with her. At the beginning, he had been afraid that this was all that he would be able to offer and, on discovering that this was not so, he is now agreeably pleased with himself, and is able to put aside those doubts which grow from gossip and hearsay about advancing years and the ensuing lack of ability.

He watches Rosie eating hungrily and is glad they gave up the idea of trying to find an interesting place in what seemed to be industrial areas and used car saleyards. The motel, though dull, is proving to be quite satisfactory. He had previously no idea that a town could offer so little. His first feeling on arrival, a few hours earlier, had been the wish to drive on to the next place, which must surely have more promise, and would be worth the extra long distance he would have to drive. Rosie, who is plump, likes her food. She eats all the sweet corn and, with an unselfconscious use of the white table napkin, wipes the melted butter off her face. Dixon, still watching, smiles.

The one redeeming thing about the town is the distant sound of the sea. He imagines that this can be heard constantly at regular intervals. It is a faint, deep roar followed by a long-drawn-out sigh, as if the waters of the ocean, swelling with waves, come up dashing against the steep, hard sand of the beach, only to slide back into the dying fall of the wave before the next one comes riding in. He looks forward to hearing this sound during the night when Rosie will be beside him, both of them relaxed and contented in each other's arms. Dear Rosie, he smiles at her again as he feels the welcome desire returning as it so often does now. There is no reason why they should not go to bed early.

The fellmonger is bringing his chosen girl to the table just across from where Dixon and Rosie are sitting. It is clear at this moment that for the fellmonger no-one exists except this girl. She has, Dixon notices now that she is closer, a mauve-coloured plastic hair band, an amusingly simple dressing for her long straight hair which comes straight down on either side of her country red cheeks. Like Rosie she does not have a great deal to say but answers the fellmonger's slow earnest conversation with a few quietly spoken words. When the fellmonger speaks he leans towards her tilting his head and pushing it forward swaying slightly as cattle do when they turn slowly to regard an intruder. Dixon wonders whether the girl is inwardly shrinking from the man, whether beneath the folds of the ugly dress her legs are pinchingly drawn close together. Certainly her feet in her white plastic strap sandals are placed neatly close side by side drawn back a little towards the shelter of her chair. Perhaps the fellmonger too has a motel reservation and will plan to go to bed early. On reflection he is sure they will have a wedding first. Rosie, when they were walking briefly at one stage in the exploration of the town, kept wanting to pause to look at wedding clothes in a rather mean shop window. In their wanderings they came to the shop more than once and Rosie searched the display each time saying which bride's dress she liked best and why. Dixon, when his attention was drawn to it, agreed he had never before realised how attractive a square of heavy lace on the bodice of a simple bride dress could look.

The fellmonger must have ordered champagne. The waiter brings it with a little flourish. The ice bucket is ornamental with silver lilies of the valley and is on a special trolley with tiny competent wheels. Honey-coloured wood has been used for the trolley and carved ribbons and roses have been glued along both sides. A contemporary replica, Dixon knows, of an ancient art in furniture making. He is surprised that the decoration is not plastic. Rosie is eating apple pie and cream.

"You're very quiet," surprisingly Rosie ventures a remark. "You're not talking very much," perhaps she has noticed him watching the fellmonger. Dixon laughs with the pleasure of feeling criticised by her. "It's you, you are quiet," he teases, longing to hold her close.

"Am I?" she asks.

As he looks at her round face and the sweet expression in her eyes, he suddenly thinks of something so awful he wishes he had not the power of thought and reason. His thought is linked to the thought he has earlier in the meal. He knows at once that he is suffering from one of the most powerful of human emotions. Perhaps envy paves the way to jealousy, he winces at his own cliché. He is not envious of the fellmonger's possession, not jealous over that, it is something more complicated and far more difficult to face with reason. It is something which the fellmonger has as he sits there opposite his girl, it is something about his hopes which Dixon, in spite of his experience, his good looks and his position and his money, does not have.

Dixon wakes up with a backache so severe he thinks he will be unable to move. It is some time since he has had a backache like this. Rosie, towards the other edge of the bed, is still asleep. The motel room in the early morning, with the heavy curtain pulled aside slightly, is diffused with a grey light making everything dreary. The dark blue tiles in the bathroom the night before were depressing and the matching blue towels did not seem quite clean. The smell of an air-freshening tablet fastened in a hidden place is nauseating. The cup of tea Rosie made before they went to bed simply tasted of this, pine was it, disinfectant. Trying to ease into a more comfortable position he wonders whether it is the sea he can hear or is it merely the air-conditioning plant for the motel. He thinks once more about the town. Unless a visitor wants boating or fishing or simply a clean stretch of beach it is not possible to visit a place for a holiday. "Mr and Mrs Crabber," he has seen notices, "welcome for bed and breakfast." The only way to take a holiday is to drive on to the next place and then on to the next and in every place to spread temporarily, shrinking from contact with the unwashed counterpanes, one's belongings taken out for one night and then to repack them the next morning in order to be off on the long straight main road once more.

The motel room has in it a double bed and a single bed. Rosie's mother could have come with them. The agony of his back and this ludicrous idea of three adults sharing one bedroom causes him to twist his lips into a smile. A notice pasted firmly on the inside of the door states that, under the Lodging Houses Act, five adults are permitted to occupy the room. The evening before he and Rosie laughed about it.

"Five men or five women."

"Two couples and one mother-in-law."

"Four men and one girl — four women and one old man." The possibilities, they decided, still laughing, were endless.

The fellmonger when he was talking to his girl during dinner, Dixon remembers, had quite a tender expression in his eyes, an expression which could transform even the face of an oaf. For the man was an oaf . . . It is possible, Dixon thinks now, to imagine the girl's mother, in her hopefulness for the girl's future, reminding her repeatedly about table manners and other little ways of being agreeable to her companion. Until her mother tells her the girl will not understand that in the immediate future with the fellmonger she will be expected to rear a hand of boy children. The fellmonger's business will need them.

Rosie, of course, knows now her part in the arrangement they have made. He wonders if she understands how he has come to feel about her in spite of the relationship simply being an arrangement between her mother and himself. Ardently, at times, he

wants her to know. At other times he is not at all sure that he
wants a child after all. He has never been certain that Delia does
and when he looks in the mirror he feels as if he is looking at a
stranger. In this uncertainty and that particular despair picked up
in passing from the despair felt by other travellers, like an infec-
tion picked up in the street or in the bathroom at the motel, Dixon
is surprised to find himself wondering if the fellmonger's future
bride will choose, as her right, the bride dress with the wonderful
breastplate of lace. Mechlin — Honiton — Chantilly — does that
girl know, does Rosie know, he wonders, these diversifications of
embroidery. Perhaps the fellmonger's future mother-in-law will
sew the dress herself and will make the same pleats and tucks with
which she is familiar in white slippery material instead of the
heavy red. Rosie, he thinks, by rights should be having the wedding dress. The fellmonger, a distinctly ugly and commonplace
man, offered affection during that dinner the night before, an
affection with a humble sincerity which would last. He offered
hope and an intense but carefully hidden desire. He offered his
future. Dixon, allowing his realisations of the night before to
spread over him in the bitterness of a terrible remorse, groans
aloud.

"Rosie," he says softly in the end of his groan. "Rosie, are you
awake?" he moves towards the sleeping mound. There is a comforting softness and a warmth. When she wakes and turns
towards him he begins at once to feel better. Taking her in his
arms he begins to stroke and to fondle her young breasts and feels
with pleasure her response matching his own.

Perhaps that oaf, the fellmonger, does have, in his own way,
this knowledge of life beneath the skin. Perhaps he knows more
than many about the life which springs from the bone and the
hide. He, the fellmonger, Dixon is unable to dismiss him from his
thoughts during the mounting rhythm of their movements, probably understands far more. He will know, for instance, that
human life depends so much on animal things, things like bone
and glue, things which smell so terrible that they cause the sides of
the mouth and neck to stiffen in readiness for the power of
vomiting. He will tell Rosie, in a minute about the making of furniture . . . the fellmonger will probably know that animal glue

has to be kept warm . . . Rosie, he will tell her, did you . . . He is as close to Rosie as one human being can be to another and she is as close to him. Rosie, do you know, he will tell her soon, that rose petals and ribbons like the flowers you held in your lap yesterday can be carved in wood and they can be held fast by animal glue which never gives way. The petals and the ribbon, he will tell her . . .

The carved petals and the carved ribbon, which is folded into a bow, he holds her with his legs, are pressed deep into hot sand, he will tell her and she will ask him, and he will tell her — to darken the edges in places to give the rose petals burnished shadows on their crinkled edges and to give the ribbon the reality of the folds of the bow as it is tied in taffeta or silk. There is no reason, he will tell her, that something really felt deeply should not last for ever. If it is felt only once that once should be enough to hold for ever. In a minute he will tell her . . .

"Rosie," Dixon says stopping the car in the main street of the ramshackle town. "What would you like?"

"What d'you mean? Something to eat? I couldn't after all that breakfast. I really love hotel breakfasts."

"No I mean some other thing," he says smiling at the memory of the motel dining room. He puts one arm round her shoulders and gives her a small hug. They are in the main shopping part of town. It is Monday morning and their weekend is over. Rosie without hesitation says: "I'd like the bride dress, the one with the lace — if you are thinking of something big like that."

"Oh?" Dixon tries not to show his surprise. "Are you sure that's what you'd like?" A feeling of tremendous relief which came unexpectedly while he was in the shower is coupled now with the pleasure of being about to leave the utter boredom of the small town and set out for the long drive home. He enjoys driving. Rosie, unprepared, had called out to him in the bathroom that she needed to find a chemist or a supermarket. She wasn't due for another week but she supposed it was the excitement of going off for the weekend. She said she was sorry to be such a nuisance. "I feel a right dill," she said. "I'm flooding all over the place."

Dixon, laughing with a sudden delight, had reached from the shower and pulled her in under the warm water. "Nonsense!" he heard his own voice crack with joy. "You could never be a nuisance. Never!" He had soaped her all over and, hardly able to stop himself, his laughter had become high pitched, uncontrollable — almost, the relief was so tremendous.

"I'll pad myself up somehow with all my pairs of pants," Rosie was suddenly competent, "till I've done my shopping."

"Are you sure about the dress?" Dixon asks again, an uneasy thought crossing his mind. She surely couldn't be hoping for the impossible. He begins to compose a fatherly little speech about himself and Delia and how they hold the bonds of marriage to be sacred but Rosie interrupts him.

"If it's a big thing I can have, I really would like the dress," she nods towards the shop window. The slanting rays of the early morning sun are contriving somehow to make the material of the dress gleam so that, in spite of its mean setting, it looks rich and full of promise.

"Oh, doesn't it look lovely," Rosie exclaims. "You see," she says, "I'd been thinking that as soon as I'd done surrogate I'd look around and get married. And now that I'm not surrogate — and you don't mind — there's nothing to stop me and I'll have my dress all ready and . . ."

Buying the dress, Dixon thinks as he swings the car round the roundabout and on to the long straight road he enjoys so much, is the smallest thing he could have expected to do. After remembering with more than slight annoyance that he has left his corset, for him an almost irreplaceable item, on the back of the motel bathroom door he returns to his good fortune, dwelling on it with enough pleasure to enable him to dismiss the unfortunate loss of the unmentionable garment. He refrains from congratulating himself too much and increases his speed so that the small houses and gardens are soon left behind. It is hard to know what Rosie thinks as she sits holding the silver-wrapped parcel across her lap. She is gazing now at the wide calm waters of the estuary where pelicans glide slowly just beyond the reeds. He wonders vaguely why, during his climaxing, he should have wanted to tell her how certain kinds of furniture is made. He has not told her, but reminds himself to tell Delia. "What a hoot!" she will say. They, both of them, like to have things like that to tell at parties.

Rescuing Fragments

Review of Helen Garner's *The Children's Bach*

A novel is often required to do many things. It may present itself as potted contemporary history or it may espouse a cause as does that work by a writer, two generations sunk in irrecoverable night, which mounts to the climax of "Women doctors. Yes." All this may increase the readership of the novel and yet be far removed from its true object. Perhaps it can be said that the function of the novelist is to increase awareness of human life. Sometimes such increased awareness will suggest judgements to the reader but it is the increased awareness not the judgments which is the novelist's concern.

Helen Garner's earlier novel *Monkey Grip* confronts the reader with "smack habit love habit", "desperate relationships" and "hard drug addiction" but the book is far from resembling a government paper or a recommendation on what ought to be "done about" the existence of people thus caught.

*   *   *

Helen Garner, in her novels, accepts completely her characters' needs and hopes and the society in which they are making their efforts at day to day living. Her writing is heightened by the attention she gives to the small but essential details of this daily living and these assume a sacramental value: her characters cut up or squeeze oranges for each other, they hang dripping sheets and children's track suit pants on clothes lines, they sweep floors and weed paths: "neat piles of weeds all along the path to the lavatory". In the story "Honour" a married couple, now ex, have an animated conversation in the presence of the husband's new lover about people and incidents which belong to a previous time. Nora and Clive in *Monkey Grip* take the children to the baths on bicycles: "the cicadas beat a rhythm that comes in waves, like fainting or your own heartbeat". Dexter and Athena, in *The Children's Bach*, walk at night: "They kept pace easily not touching. They covered miles each night in the dark . . . Dexter wanted to live gloriously, and on the night walks he did."

Joseph Conrad wrote:

> To snatch a moment of courage, from the remorseless rush of time, a passing phase of life, is only the beginning of the task. The task approached in tenderness and faith is to hold up unquestionably, without choice and without fear, the rescued fragment before all eyes in the light of a sincere mood. It is to show its vibration, its colour, its form; and through its movement, its form and its colour reveal the substance of its truth, disclose its inspiring secret.

In writing *The Children's Bach* Helen Garner uses apparently simple methods and material with tenderness and faith to produce a short novel which holds the attention and haunts the memory. The book is written in a series of episodes, vivid pictures often ornamented with unexpected flourishes. One example is when Elizabeth is waiting at the airport for her young sister Vicki. The plane is late and she does not like people to notice that she is being kept waiting: "She strolled into the shop, stole a twenty-five dollar Dior lipstick and a cheap plastic-covered address book and tried again." And there is this revealing sentence about Philip: "Philip fell into strange beds in houses where a boiling saucepan might as easily contain a syringe as an egg." It is followed by some of the superb poetic imagery which Garner uses to weave together the glimpses of life and effort which, in sequence, make the novel:

> He [Philip] came home at that hour when light is not yet anything more than the exaggerated whiteness of a shirt flung against a bookcase, a higher gloss on the back of a kitchen chair.

Then there's a snatch of gossip, no great revelation in itself but in Athena's response to it a great deal is revealed about her:

> "The woman next door", said the friend, "went and had colonic irrigations. And the lady who did them found stuff inside her that she'd eaten ten years ago!"
> "How could she tell?" said Athena.

Vicki, cold round the tops of her thighs, unable to fall asleep in a double bed shared with her older sister Elizabeth, goes to live with the Fox family (Dexter and Athena) and walks, inadvertently, into the bathroom ". . . in which Athena — lanky legs, rounded belly, drooping breasts with pearl-grey radiating stretch marks — was stepping out of the shower reaching for a towel". It is as if Vicki "like a tourist, bored in a gallery, has turned a corner and come face to face with a famous painting".

The dialogue throughout the book is at once natural and pointed. It becomes impossible to quote as each sentence leads inevitably on to the next adding illumination after illumination. A whole character can be shown in a single phrase. Dr Fox, Dexter's father, says to Elizabeth: "At forty you can no longer harm any one, and no one can harm you." A very great deal is crammed into a few lines. Dr Fox's skill is in offering a consolation which cannot really console but which with Elizabeth's complaisance does, though at the same time she is thinking: "That can't possibly be true."

Acceptance is a part of the novel's strength. The characters do accept and, in turn, so does the reader: "The Fox family's kitchen was like a burrow, rounded rather than cubed, as if its corners had been stuffed with dry grass." The detail of a world is built up: Dexter's ungraceful eating and the fact that Athena obviously has not, in private, corrected this. Items of news from the papers: ". . . she absorbed *pollen* through her *skin* . . ."; Dexter standing in a puddle of oil, insisting on cooking the spaghetti; the women hiding in one of the bedrooms. Poppy putting on her school uniform once a day to practise getting used to it. The apparition of an androgynous creature in a raincoat — Athena and Elizabeth in conversation:

> The music stopped.
> "Did you see that girl? Is she all right?"
> "I saw a thing in a raincoat," said Elizabeth, "with no features on its face."
> "She was vomiting. Do you think I ought to do something?"
> "What — clean up? They hire people to do that."
> "But she looked like a child."
> "They all do," said Elizabeth. "They are."

The quote, "Bach is never simple, but that is one reason why we should all try to master him", appears in the book of studies for the piano, *The Children's Bach*. Elizabeth responds to this by saying it is pompous. She quotes a saying remembered from her mother who is now dead: *If only those birds sang that sang the best, how silent the woods would be*.

Perhaps Helen Garner's characters are singing, even those who are not absolutely able. Helen Garner's writing, however straightforward it may appear at times, is never simple. It would be impertinent to speak of mastering such writing but it certainly requires our unremitting attention and amply rewards it.

In her first novel *Monkey Grip* Helen Garner presented with sincerity a world which was largely unknown to a great many readers. The world of *The Children's Bach* seems to be more "everyday". The characters and their progress interest and enlighten. On the whole they will not shock or surprise readers though they might well have startled our grandparents!

Helen Garner is the kind of writer who, like Virginia Woolf, rekindles awareness and makes you want to bring your own life back to life.

Facts, Fat and Frailness

Review of Kate Grenville's *Lilian's Story*

Lilian's Story is Kate Grenville's first novel and with it she won the *Australian/*Vogel Literary Award in 1984. This novel follows her first collection of short stories, *Bearded Ladies*, published in 1984.

Modern writers often develop Tolstoy's text that "all happy families resemble one another, but each unhappy family is unhappy in its own way". Among other things, *Lilian's Story* is an account of an unhappy family.

Like Tess, Lilian is a part of nature's holy plan. She has never been asked if she wished for a life on any terms other than those laid down by a disappointed and obsessed father. The obsession manifests itself for much of the time in the form of facts. Albion Singer, Lilian's father, has a room devoted to newspapers and clippings. *It is a fact that Eskimos never eat ice-cream . . . Here is a fact: the French eat four million and several thousand snails each year . . .* facts pour from him.

Lilian, subjected to his theories and to unwilling visits to his fact-crammed study, draws a picture of him:

> I drew his head as a square brown box on his shoulders, and drew the facts coming out of his mouth. *What are those lines, Lilian?* Miss Vine asked at school. *Has he been speared, Dear?* and I would have to try to explain. *Those are father's facts, Miss Vine.*

Lilian's mother is kind but is too fatigued to respond to her daughter's needs. She has been squashed into a dreamy existence of drawn curtains, important preoccupations, vague smiles and cold compresses.

Alma, the maid, alleviates and silences by slipping Lilian date slices, raisins, pikelets, cold left-over potatoes, bread and dripping and, as a last resort, the heel of an old loaf. Lilian is fat and very quickly fatter and then enormous. "I carried my bulk around with me like someone else's suitcase . . ."

John, the brother, four years younger, collects hands and feet and folds his ear lobes inwards: *One morning I will wake up deaf.* Like Tess's brother, he is a captive passenger. He is firmly under the hatch of Albion Singer's ship. Already purblind without his glasses (which need constant wiping), he intends to become deaf.

This very moving and sometimes funny novel is written in a series of fragments, each with its own heading. The surprises in the story are not the events in themselves, for the horrors of family life and adolescence are not new. The surprises and flourishes are in the evocative and poetic writing of the episodes, every one of which reveals some detail of human frailness, and many include the daily crucifixions in the playground, at the family meal table, at birthday and tennis parties and during those unsparing moments of forced or cruel choice between individuals.

The dialogue is spare, carefully selected as if distilled. The characters leap from the essence of their own words sprinkled as they are throughout the narrative. The unusual use of italics adds power to these snatches of speech. *He was such a skinny boy, and inept. Is he heavy now?* (Aunt Kitty about Albion to Lilian's mother with sinister overtones.) *Kitty is constantly pickled* (Albion about his sister Kitty), *John, do not gnaw like that . . .* (Albion to his son) and perhaps the neatest reference to the onset of menstruation ever written; *Go to Matron at once* (Miss Vine to Lilian).

There are several lives shown in the glimpses as Lilian moves through her life. Kate Grenville presents with sympathy, alongside the clumsy developing Lilian and her peers, the perplexities, the patience and impatience, the acceptance and the horror of those forced to gaze upon the results of their rather one-sided (Albion's) waxed paper intimate meetings.

The fragments are welded by sophisticated spacing and much is made clear to the reader without being actually stated. The "small tinny noises like rats' feet" as Albion drops his cardigan and becomes yet again part of the "desperate machine" of incest is just one example.

It has been said in legends that man creates best from that which is the rejected part of him. In Part Three, titled *A Woman*, Lilian, still dreadfully fat and still acquainted with grief, after a lifetime of being despised and rejected, laughed at and misunderstood knows what she really wants and what other people are missing in their conventional lives. She accepts herself. She finds solace with others whose needs match hers. She becomes what is known as a tolerated, even loved and respected by some, eccentric living in a stormwater drain, wandering in city parks, offering during her many tram rides recitations from Shakespeare for a shilling.

The novel ends with Lilian's final taxi ride. "The story of all our lives is the story forward to death, although each of us might hope to be the exception." After all she has endured Lilian is able to say: "I have seen much, but would not claim to have seen everything. I would not mind another century or two, to see some more."

Fringe Dwellers

Extracts from Interview by Jennifer Ellison

I would describe a lot of your characters as fringe dwellers, people who for one reason or another find themselves on the edge of society. Would you agree with that?

Yes, well, I think people are on the edge of something, and some people who even seem to be in the thick of things are on the edge in another sense. It has been said that I don't have any straight sex in my stories, that everything's bizarre and grotesque. I think that what I really see is the individual, and the particular aspect of loneliness, or fear, that that individual has, which puts him immediately on a fringe of some sort. And I think most people are like that, though they do have a little structure that keeps them going. If the structure is taken away then they really become very much on the fringe. And I don't intend to write about sexual perversion at all. It is just that certain things drive people to certain relationships, or they snatch at certain relationships.

What do you think is the function of that bizarre sexuality?

It seems to me that there's a sort of ridiculous side to life, to living. And I don't quite know what is meant by a straight sexual relationship, because even that has its ridiculous side. I suppose it is indeed to show the ends to which people are driven, though none of my people does anything evil. I mean, it's all harmless, and possibly they fulfil various needs or emptinesses in life.

*　　　*　　　*

Another strong motif throughout your work is the land. Can you trace that association?

Well, in a personal way, I have a great wish to have land. My own father came from a family of farmers in the south of England. They were not very well off. My father became a teacher; so did my aunt, but my father always had a great yearning for land and he had what is called an allotment. I don't know whether you know what that is, but as well as having a garden with the house you could rent a piece of land — just, oh, quarter of an acre or something like that, a strip with a whole lot of other strips. My father would work the allotment and grow vegetables. When I married, my husband and I also had a house and a small garden, but wherever we lived we rented an allotment and grew vegetables and things. Well, in Western Australia there aren't any allotments, but as soon as we felt able to, we purchased five acres of land forty miles out of Perth. Territory matters very much to me. I'm a sort of territorial person, perhaps a bit grasping over land. It matters enormously to me to have my own place, and on the whole I think I'm happier not leaving it. I can get homesick by the time I get to the airport.

* * *

What image did you have of Australia before you arrived?

I had an absolutely blank mind. I knew very little, I regret to say, about the country. I looked up the rainfall, and found that it was much the same as Glasgow, but in Western Australia it all falls at once, instead of the year round. I knew that the population was small, but I don't go in for figures, and I knew it was a long way away. But there was a kind of challenge about it, and I knew that Leonard wanted to come. I think we're very glad that we did.

It's amusing that you refer to Western Australia as a country. Do you feel that it is quite distinct from the rest of Australia?

It is a separate country in a way, and if you live there and write, and you want your writing to get published, you really have got to cross, as though from one end of the world to the other, to get to Sydney, to Melbourne, to get to London, to New York. You could live and write there and never get over, but obviously the writer wants his work seen ultimately, and this is one of the things that you're very much aware of. Your work has to spring from where you are, and it's got to take tremendous leaps. But people in Sydney won't have that feeling. They don't feel they have to get across to Western Australia. And I quite understand that.

*   *   *

What prompted you to start submitting your work to publishers?

I started submitting because around then I wondered if I was mad, and whether my writing was readable by anybody else. You see, you're very alone, and you can't give your writing to your friends, really. I started to submit in a very tentative way, and of course everything came back. But the BBC World Service was a good market, and the ABC did take some short stories, and I gradually began to break into the journals, but very, very slowly. It was a very slow, painful thing. I've had as many as thirty-nine rejections in one year. But everything that was rejected has now been accepted. Some pieces I reworked. Others are just as they were. I think that often the writer is writing things that are not acceptable because perhaps the writer is aware of things in life around him that publishers' editors feel the reader is not ready for. Also, I think, editors really want to know whether you are serious as a writer, and perhaps they want to see a lot of things before anything is taken.

How did you feel during that period when your work was rejected?

Oh, well, I used to get very down. I can be very, very depressed and low. I can get like that even now. It's a fearful thing, and I wonder sometimes why I do write. Once you start to get accepted, of course, you have to follow up with other things. It's no good just selling one story. If you want to be published, you've just got to keep going. I must have a streak of optimism in me, and it was a sort of challenge really. Perhaps it's like gambling — send three stories off and see if one will get accepted. You know, a kind of horrible excitement.

But you must have had a certain belief in your writing, to persist?

Well, I couldn't believe that the writing that was rejected was so much worse than what was being accepted. I took a strong look at it and I read contemporary fiction to try to see and learn. I do read a great deal, anyway, because I'm interested in reading, and because it excites and pleases me, and I read all sorts of writers. I did wonder if there was something hopelessly wrong with my work. You see, you don't know yourself, you aren't always your own best judge.

During that period, were you writing virtually full time? Or how did you manage to write?

Oh no, it's only in the last two years that I've written full time. I was doing eighteen hours' teaching before. Before that I did other jobs. As a housewife and mother you don't have a lot of time for writing. But I would squeeze in the time. I've been used to making time, because that's what I wanted to do, you know. I would often write late at night and early in the morning. I still do that — that habit still hangs on. You have to make time, for anything. If you want to weave, or make pottery, you've simply got to hurry up with the shopping and cooking or whatever.

When did you decide that you wanted to be a writer?

Well, I never decided, and I never called myself a writer, until I was called "writer" from outside. I would never have put it as my occupation. I was a nurse by training. But I'd never called myself a writer. It would have felt as though I was claiming something that I wasn't, and I wouldn't want to do that, you know.

Why do you think you had difficulty claiming that, when you were writing?

Well, I suppose because I wasn't published. And I suppose even when I had the first book and then the second book published, although in one sense I was the author of those books, I still hesitated. I suppose one doesn't want to set oneself up to be in the position that one perhaps has longed to be in. One is a bit afraid of the knife in the back. Mind, everyone's been most affectionate and loving towards me, I don't know why I worry. I suppose it's just lack of confidence. One is terribly afraid of people saying, "Oh, calls herself a writer, does she? And that's all she's done." Because, of course, this is part of the cruelty of the world, that people are cruel about each other, especially in a competitive world, aren't they? And maybe you shrink from putting yourself forward, because if you do that then somebody else can knock you down. I think there's a famous line: "He that is down can fall no further", or something like that.

*   *   *

A lot of the central relationships in your books are about women. Can you tell me about the importance of women in your work?

Yes. I'm very interested in women, overbearing women, and the kind of headmistress type of woman, the matron type, the secretary who's in a muddle. I suppose I've seen these people in operation in different organisations and institutions, and I suppose I'm interested to explore what's behind the white blouse and the jacket. And of course in the world of nursing you meet a great many women, and a nurses home is a hotbed, in a sense. At the age of seventeen I left school and I did training in two different places. It must be that I became aware of large numbers of women and their relationships and their interests, and my imagination just got off on them. I was at a mixed boarding school. We had masters and mistresses. Even then, I was aware of relationships between males and females in the school, and between women staff.

Is there any guiding principle behind your work?

I'm not trying to reform or judge. I'd like to interest people. I would like to entertain people, and I would like people perhaps to go with me in the exploration of human beings, but one can only explore really, and put one's exploration forward. If anything in my writing should inadvertently hurt someone, I would feel terrible. There would be no point in writing and being published. And if anyone thought I was cruel in my writing, that would upset me too. I don't intend to be cruel. I do see a ridiculous side in human nature because I don't think we can live without it; and if I've portrayed that, it isn't out of cruelty, it is just that I think it helps us to get through. I don't ever want to write anything cheap or sensational. I would hate to do that, and sometimes in my first writing I do just that, and I hope that some of that doesn't get left in by mistake. But I suppose you put things down in the quickest, most cliché-ridden way that you can, to get it down, and I'm sometimes horrified at some of the scenes that I might write. And then I rewrite, and craft that. In *Miss Peabody*, you see, I did really quite a terrible scene between Edgely and Thorne before Gwenda comes around and knocks on the door, and then I do a very slight picture there, and at one book club where I was a woman said, "How could you write such a filthy scene?" What she's done is to see what I wrote in my early writing, but I only imply something, you see. There's nothing really filthy written there at all. So I thought that was very interesting, that even though I had removed the whole thing, but just made an implication, it still was there.

*   *   *

Do you think that writers, by their craft or their profession, transcend issues like gender and perhaps also nationality, that there is an international community or unity?

Yes, a sort of universal thing, yes. I think of writers as people, and it doesn't worry me, man or woman writer. The thing is that it's quite true that in some feminist writing there's a tremendous gushing of the menstruation, as it were. But I think that a man writer could write the same thing, if he wanted to. A man writer would have the same awareness and perceptions and imagination that a woman writer will have, and he will know certain things. A man watching his wife in childbirth will see more of the childbirth than the woman will. He will even experience with his own imagination and awareness, and his own tenderness if he has it, her feelings, I think. Certainly he'll see the colour of the amniotic fluid, and the placenta, which the woman who is giving birth won't see. Many women like to write about childbirth, when they've experienced it. Others write about it without experience. I don't think you need to experience — you can make the implications, or you can leave it. You can leave what I call a sophisticated space on the page, and the reader will create for himself, or herself.

I really do think that to get emotional about women writers is a mistake. It's well-intentioned, but I think that a writer should be a writer, and a perceptive man is as perceptive as a perceptive woman. Somebody who is unaware, man or woman, will remain unaware. I think a man can be aware of a woman's sexuality, very much so, because after all there isn't all that much difference between male and female sexuality. Resentment can be felt equally. Suppose it's an unsatisfactory sexual relationship: both can feel resentment, and it would be the same sort of feeling. Why should a woman feel that her resentment is the thing that matters, when a man might be feeling that his is, do you see?

Have you been particularly involved in, or affected by, feminism?

Well, I can see the cause. A woman married to the wrong man, submitting to sexual caresses that she doesn't like and that she wants to get away from but doesn't know how — I think she needs liberating. But I don't know whether the feminist movement, as such, will ever reach that particular woman in a suburb.

This kind of thing has gone on forever. Some men really prefer not to be married, but were expected to marry. They're breadwinners, and they've got to caress their woman when they don't really want to. I think the sexual side of the unhappiness of people marrying when they shouldn't be married will go on. Not many people are brave enough to withstand marriage and children if they're under pressure for this conventional social behaviour, you see. I think it's better than it was, but it still does exist, and I don't know what the answer to that is. I'm glad if women have their movement, and I'm sorry if I disappoint them by not being a feminist writer.

Do you have any theories about the increasing number of women writers being published?

I think that the women writers are writing well now, and if they're writing well then they deserve to be published; and I don't know that they were kept down. I felt when I was being rejected that I was being kept down, but that may just have been a personal paranoia, you see. It never occurred to me that it was because I was a woman. I don't think it was. I think it would be because some of the stuff wasn't quite ready, and that it is just very hard to break into publishing anyway, whether you are a man or a woman, isn't it? I mean, I meet as many men that would like to get published and aren't.

Do you find reviews of your work helpful to your writing?

Yes, they should be, they should be. I find them painful and difficult. I worry about a review very much, you know, and I think reviewing is very hard to do. I've done some myself, and I think it is one of the hardest things in writing, to read someone's book and then, in a short space, deal with it. I think reviewers can be helpful if they pick on some fault. The only trouble is that no two reviewers pick on the same fault, or very rarely.

So you could end up thinking you've got a very faulty book!

Well, yes, you could, and that would be the devastating thing. I can get very distressed reading reviews — reviews about anybody's work, not just about my own. It's a kind of writing that bothers me, you know.

Why does it bother you?

It has to be written in a particular kind of style. It's clinical, and has to be efficient, and the reviewer can't use his imagination. It's factual, it's direct, it's got a bit of authority, you know, and it's all the things that one might be afraid of in life, really, like a dental examination or a medical test or something. I think that I'm a bit afraid. I'm frightened of writing a review, and frightened of reading one.

What do you think makes a good review, though?

Well, I think the reviewer needs to give a little picture of what the book is, and if he finds a fault I think he should be able to substantiate the fault, with a quotation, or something like that. When I'm reviewing, I take the idea that when I write the review I would like to make somebody feel they want to read the book, so that if I can find phrases that show how the writer makes pictures, or captures something, I would like to quote them. If I find there's some grave fault in the book that I really can't take, then I have to bear in mind that somebody else might not think that was a fault, but at the same time I may want to draw attention to it in some way. Of course, a severe criticism, if it's done in a particular way, can still encourage a reader to have a look for himself. But I think any statement should be supported. And, of course, a reviewer is quite free to give his personal opinion. That is the whole idea. It is his personal opinion. And that is important too.

What about literary awards? Do you think they serve a useful purpose?

Oh yes, I do. I think even if you don't win one you might think, oh, it would have been nice to win that, all that money slipped through my fingers, you know. But I do think prizes help because we live in this competitive world and, after all, publishing is a business. Anything that will help the sale of books I think is a good thing. I think if people are generous enough to present prizes, then we should be grateful. However much you dislike publicity, and you don't regard yourself as a public person, you understand that you've simply got to go along with certain things. You sign a contract to that effect, in a way, with the publishers, that you will do things, you won't object to publicity and so on. They've got to make their living, and employ their people.

Are you happy being a writer?

I'm just about to say I'm never happy. Put it this way: I can forget all the worries of family life, and the world, except for the bit of world I'm dealing with in my novel. When I'm writing I go into the world of the novel, and the characters, and I like that. It is happy in a way. It's fascinating. Happiness is a difficult thing. I'm almost the kind of person who doesn't know she's been happy till she's unhappy. No, that's not true. I'm a very optimistic person, and I try to make the best of things. I like to write, though I find it terribly hard. Put it this way, if I wasn't writing I don't know what I would do.

The thing about writing is that you do several things alongside, and that writing is only one part of your life. If you made it your whole life, you might go entirely mad, especially if you didn't succeed, because it would be so devastating. I have my orchard and my goose farm, the family, and the teaching, and of course I was nursing before, and I also did things like door-to-door selling. I've done lots of different things. And I was writing all the time. I took the writing alongside, and I really did make a conscious decision that I would never just do writing and nothing else, because I could see that, if it was not good, and if I never got published, then the disappointment would be so devastating. So, you see, I love the orchard, and that's very soothing, and even if a book doesn't get accepted, well I've got my fruit trees and I've got my poultry, and the slope of the land and all that. You know, I think that's important.

I wonder, now that you have had nine books published, and you've been to lots of places and experienced lots of emotions through your work, do you feel wise?

Oh, I don't think I'll ever be wise. I'm the biggest fool on earth. I'm capable of making the same mistakes over and over again. You know this thing, the rite of passage, where you go through a little private ceremony of awareness, so that you are a changed person. It seems as if I have to keep going through these little enlightenments. I make the same mistakes over and over again. Isn't it strange? I don't know that I have any wisdom, but this is where I think perhaps Something may watch over me. They say God watches over drunks and little children. Well, I'm not a drunk and I'm not a child, but perhaps He also looks after people who blunder through things.

But you must feel that you've learned an incredible amount.

Yes, but it seems to run off me, you know, like water off a duck's back. What an awful cliché. Miss Thorne is wincing . . .

Helen Garner

EDITOR'S NOTE

Helen Garner's award-winning first novel, *Monkey Grip* (McPhee Gribble, 1977), was highly successful and established her as one of Australia's foremost contemporary writers. A feature film based on the novel was released in 1982. She later published *Honour and Other People's Children: Two Stories* (McPhee Gribble, 1980) and a novella, *The Children's Bach* (McPhee Gribble, 1984). *Postcards from Surfers* (McPhee Gribble/Penguin, 1985) is her first collection of short stories, and won the New South Wales Premier's Literary Award for fiction in 1986. Her screenplay, "Two Friends", directed by Jane Campion, was shown on ABC TV in 1986, and she has recently finished a second screenplay.

"Postcards from Surfers" and "Civilisation and its Discontents" were published in *Postcards from Surfers* (Fitzroy & Ringwood: McPhee Gribble/Penguin Books, 1985), pp.3-16, 93-101; "What We Say" was published in the *Sydney Morning Herald*, 6 January 1987; "A Woman's Word" was published in the *National Times*, 24-30 October 1982; "Someone should make this into a film" was published in the *National Times*, 17-23 October 1982, p.22; "Dazzling Writing" was published as the introduction to Eleanor Dark, *Lantana Lane* (London: Virago, 1986); the extracts from "Elizabeth Jolley: An Appreciation" were taken from *Meanjin* 42, ii (June 1983), pp.153-57, and the postscript was published in *Sydney Morning Herald*, 19 January 1985; and "Showing the Flipside" is an extract from an interview with Jennifer Ellison, in *Rooms of their Own*, ed. Ellison (Ringwood: Penguin, 1986), pp.140-45.

Postcards from Surfers

> One night I dreamed that I did not love, and that night, released from all bonds, I lay as though in a kind of soothing death.
>
> *Colette*

We are driving north from Coolangatta airport. Beside the road the ocean heaves and heaves into waves which do not break. The swells are dotted with boardriders in black wetsuits, grim as sharks.

"Look at those idiots," says my father.

"They must be freezing," says my mother.

"But what about the principle of the wetsuit?" I say. "Isn't there a thin layer of water between your skin and the suit, and your body heat . . ."

"Could be," says my father.

The road takes a sudden swing round a rocky outcrop. Miles ahead of us, blurred in the milky air, I see a dream city: its cream, its silver, its turquoise towers thrust in a cluster from a distant spit.

"What — is that Brisbane?" I say.

"No," says my mother. "That's Surfers."

My father's car has a built-in computer. If he exceeds the speed limit, the dashboard emits a discreet but insistent pinging. Lights flash, and the pressure of his right foot lessens. He controls the windows from a panel between the two front seats. We cruise past a Valiant parked by the highway with a FOR SALE sign propped in its back window.

"Look at that," says my mother. "A WA numberplate. Probably thrashed it across the Nullarbor and now they reckon they'll flog it."

"Pro'ly stolen," says my father. "See the sticker? ALL YOU

VIRGINS, THANKS FOR NOTHING. You can just see what sort of a pin'ead he'd be. Brain the size of a pea."

Close up, many of the turquoise towers are not yet sold. "Every conceivable feature," the sign says. They have names like Capricornia, Biarritz, The Breakers, Acapulco, Rio.

I had a Brazilian friend when I lived in Paris. He showed me a postcard, once, of Rio where he was born and brought up. The card bore an aerial shot of a splendid, curved tropical beach, fringed with palms, its sand pure as snow.

"Why don't you live in Brazil," I said, "if it's as beautiful as this?"

"Because," said my friend, "right behind that beach there is a huge military base."

In my turn I showed him a postcard of my country. It was a reproduction of that Streeton painting called *The Land of the Golden Fleece* which in my homesickness I kept standing on the heater in my bedroom. He studied it carefully. At last he turned his currant-coloured eyes to me and said,

"*Les arbres sont rouges?*" Are the trees red?

Several years later, six months ago, I was rummaging through a box of old postcards in a junk shop in Rathdowne Street. Among the photos of damp cottages in Galway, of Raj hotels crumbling in bicycle-thronged Colombo, of glassy Canadian lakes flawed by the wake of a single canoe, I found two cards that I bought for a dollar each. One was a picture of downtown Rio, in black-and-white. The other, crudely tinted, showed Geelong, the town where I was born. The photographer must have stood on the high grassy bank that overlooks the Eastern Beach. He lined up his shot through the never-flowing fountain with its quartet of concrete wading birds (storks? cranes? I never asked my father: they have long orange beaks and each bird holds one leg bent, as if about to take a step); through the fountain and out over the curving wooden promenade, from which we dived all summer, unsupervised, into the flat water; and across the bay to the You Yangs, the double-humped, low, volcanic cones, the only disturbance in the great basalt plains that lie between Geelong and Melbourne. These two cards in the same box! And I find them!

Imagine! *"Cher Rubens,"* I wrote. *"Je t'envoie ces deux cartes postales, de nos deux villes natales . . ."*

Auntie Lorna has gone for a walk on the beach. My mother unlocks the door and slides open the flywire screen. She goes out into the bright air to tell her friend of my arrival. The ocean is right in front of the unit, only a hundred and fifty yards away. How can people be so sure of the boundary between land and sea that they have the confidence to build houses on it? The white doorsteps of the ocean travel and travel.

"Twelve o'clock," says my father.

"Getting on for lunchtime," I say.

"Getting towards it. Specially with that nice cold corned beef sitting there, and fresh brown bread. Think I'll have to try some of that choko relish. Ever eaten a choko?"

"I wouldn't know a choko if I fell over it," I say.

"Nor would I."

He selects a serrated knife from the magnetised holder on the kitchen wall and quickly and skilfully, at the bench, makes himself a thick sandwich. He works with powerful concentration: when the meat flaps off the slice of bread, he rounds it up with a large, dramatic scooping movement and a sympathetic grimace of the lower lip. He picks up the sandwich in two hands, raises it to his mouth and takes a large bite. While he chews he breathes heavily through his nose.

"Want to make yourself something?" he says with his mouth full.

I stand up. He pushes the loaf of bread towards me with the back of his hand. He puts the other half of his sandwich on a green bread and butter plate and carries it to the table. He sits with his elbows on the pine wood, his knees wide apart, his belly relaxing on to his thighs, his high-arched, long-boned feet planted on the tiled floor. He eats, and gazes out to sea. The noise of his eating fills the room.

My mother and Auntie Lorna come up from the beach. I stand inside the wall of glass and watch them stop at the tap to hose the sand off their feet before they cross the grass to the door. They are two old women: they have to keep one hand on the tap in order to balance on the left foot and wash the right. I see that they are two

old women, and yet they are neither young nor old. They are my
mother and Auntie Lorna, two institutions. They slide back the
wire door, smiling.

"Don't tramp sand everywhere," says my father from the table.

They take no notice. Auntie Lorna kisses me, and holds me at
arms' length with her head on one side. My mother prepares food
and we eat, looking out at the water.

"You've missed the coronary brigade," says my father. "They
get out on the beach about nine in the morning. You can pick 'em.
They swing their arms up really high when they walk." He laughs,
looking down.

"Do you go for a walk every day too?" I ask.

"Six point six kilometres," says my father.

"Got a pedometer, have you?"

"I just nutted it out," says my father. "We walk as far as a big
white building, down that way, then we turn round and come
back. Six point six altogether, there and back."

"I might come with you."

"You can if you like," he says. He picks up his plate and carries
it to the sink. "We go after breakfast. You've missed today's."

He goes to the couch and opens the newspaper on the low coffee table. He reads with his glasses down his nose and his hands
loosely linked between his spread knees. The women wash up.

"Is there a shop nearby?" I ask my mother. "I have to get some
tampons."

"Caught short, are you?" she says. "I think they sell them at the
shopping centre, along Sunbrite Avenue there near the bowling
club. Want me to come with you?"

"I can find it."

"I never could use those things," says my mother, lowering her
voice and glancing across the room at my father. "Hazel told me
about a terrible thing that happened to her. For days she kept
noticing this revolting smell that was . . . emanating from her.
She washed and washed, and couldn't get rid of it. Finally she was
about to go to the doctor, but first she got down and had a look
with the mirror. She saw this bit of thread and pulled it. The thing
was *green*. She must've forgotten to take it out — it'd been there
for days and days and *days*."

We laugh with the teatowels up to our mouths. My father, on the other side of the room, looks up from the paper with the bent smile of someone not sure what the others are laughing at. I am always surprised when my mother comes out with a word like "emanating". At home I have a book called *An Outline of English Verse* which my mother used in her matriculation year. In the margins of *The Rape of the Lock* she has made notations: "bathos; reminiscent of Virgil; parody of Homer". Her handwriting in these pencilled jottings, made forty-five years ago, is exactly as it is today: this makes me suspect, when I am not with her, that she is a closet intellectual.

Once or twice, on my way from the unit to the shopping centre, I think to see roses along a fence and run to look, but I find them to be some scentless, fleshy flower. I fall back. Beside a patch of yellow grass, pretty trees in a row are bearing and dropping white blossom-like flowers, but they look wrong to me, I do not recognise them: the blossoms too large, the branches too flat. I am dizzy from the flight. In Melbourne it is still winter, everything is bare.

I buy the tampons and look for the postcards. There they are, displayed in a tall revolving rack. There is a great deal of blue. Closer, I find colour photos of white beaches, duneless, palmless, on which half-naked people lie on their backs with their knees raised. The frequency of this posture, at random through the crowd, makes me feel like laughing. Most of the cards have GREETINGS FROM THE GOLD COAST or BROADBEACH or SURFERS PARADISE embossed in gold in one corner: I search for pictures without words. Another card, in several slightly differing versions, shows a graceful big-breasted young girl lying in a seductive pose against some rocks: she is wearing a bikini and her whole head is covered by one of those latex masks that are sold in trick shops, the ones you pull on as a bandit pulls on a stocking. The mask represents the hideous, raddled, grinning face of an old woman, a witch. I stare at this photo for a long time. Is it simple, or does it hide some more mysterious signs and symbols?

I buy twelve GREETINGS FROM cards with views, some aerial, some from the ground. They cost twenty-five cents each.

"Want the envelopes?" says the girl. She is dressed in a flowered garment which is drawn up between her thighs like a nappy.

"Yes please." The envelopes are so covered with coloured maps, logos and drawings of Australian fauna that there is barely room to write an address, but something about them attracts me. I buy a packet of Licorice Chews and eat them all on the way home: I stuff them in two at a time: my mouth floods with saliva. There are no rubbish bins so I put the papers in my pocket. Now that I have spent money here, now that I have rubbish to dispose of, I am no longer a stranger. In Paris there used to be signs in the streets that said, 'Le commerce, c'est la vie de la ville.' Any traveller knows this to be the truth.

The women are knitting. They murmur and murmur. What they say never requires an answer. My father sharpens a pencil stub with his pocket knife, and folds the paper into a pad one-eighth the size of a broadsheet page.

"Five down, spicy meat jelly. ASPIC. Three across, counterfeit. BOGUS! Howzat."

"You're in good nick," I say. "I would've had to rack my brains for BOGUS. Why don't you do harder ones?"

"Oh, I can't do those other ones, the cryptic."

"You have to know Shakespeare and the Bible off by heart to do those," I say.

"Yairs. Course, if you got hold of the answer and filled it out looking at that, with a lot of practice you would come round to their way of thinking. They used to have good ones in the Weekly Times. But I s'pose they had so many complaints from cockies who couldn't do 'em that they had to ease off."

I do not feel comfortable yet about writing the postcards. It would seem graceless. I flip through my mother's pattern book.

"There's some nice ones there," she says. "What about the one with the floppy collar?"

"Want to buy some wool?" says my father. He tosses the finished crossword on to the coffee table and stands up with a vast yawn. "Oh-ee-oh-ooh. Come on, Miss. I'll drive you over to Pacific Fair."

I choose the wool and count out the number of balls specified by the pattern. My father rears back to look at it: this movement struck terror into me when I was a teenager but I now recognise it as long-sightedness.

"Pure wool, is it?" he says. As soon as he touches it he will know. He fingers it, and looks at me.

"No," I say. "Got a bit of synthetic in it. It's what the pattern says to use."

"Why don't you —" He stops. Once he would have tried to prevent me from buying it. His big blunt hands used to fling out the fleeces, still warm, on to the greasy table. His hands looked as if they had no feeling in them but they teased out the wool, judged it, classed it, assigned it a fineness and a destination: Italy, Switzerland, Japan. He came home with thorns embedded deep in the flesh of his palms, and stood patiently while my mother gouged away at them with a needle. He drove away at shearing time in a yellow car with running boards, up to the big sheds in the country; we rode on the running boards as far as the corner of our street, then skipped home. He went to the Melbourne Show for work, not pleasure, and once he brought me home a plastic trumpet. "Fordie," he called me, and took me to the wharves and said, "See that rope? It's not a rope. It's a hawser." "Hawser," I repeated, wanting him to think I was a serious person. We walked along Strachan Avenue, Manifold Heights, hand in hand. "Listen," he said. "Listen to the wind in the wires." I must have been very little then, for the wires were so high I can't remember seeing them.

He turns away from the fluffy pink balls and waits with his hands in his pockets for me to pay.

"What do you do all day, up here?" I say on the way home.

"Oh . . . play bowls. Follow the real estate. I ring up the firms that advertise these flash units and I ask 'em questions. I let 'em lower and lower their price. See how low they'll go. How many more discounts they can dream up." He drives like a farmer in a ute, leaning forward with his arms curved round the wheel, always about to squint up through the windscreen at the sky, checking the weather.

"Don't they ask your name?"

"Yep."

"What do you call yourself?"

"Oh, Jackson or anything." He flicks a glance at me. We begin to laugh, looking away from each other.

"It's bloody crook up here," he says. "Jerry-built. Sad. 'Every conceivable luxury'! They can't get rid of it. They're desperate. Come on. We'll go up and you can have a look."

The lift in Biarritz is lined with mushroom-coloured carpet. We brace our backs against its wall and it rushes us upwards. The salesman in the display unit has a moustache, several gold bracelets, a beige suit, and a clipboard against his chest. He is engaged with an elderly couple and we are able to slip past him into the living room.

"Did you see that peanut?" hisses my father.

"A gilded youth," I say. " 'Their eyes are dull, their heads are flat, they have no brains at all.' "

He looks impressed, as if he thinks I have made it up·on the spot. "*The Man from Ironbark*," I add.

"I only remember *The Geebung Polo Club*," he says. He mimes leaning off a horse and swinging a heavy implement. We snort with laughter. Just inside the living room door stand five Ionic pillars in a half-moon curve. Beyond them, through the glass, are views of a river and some mountains. The river winds in a plain, the mountains are sudden, lumpy and crooked.

"From the other side you can see the sea," says my father.

"Would you live up here?"

"Not on your life. Not with those flaming pillars."

From the bedroom window he points out another high-rise building closer to the sea. Its name is Chelsea. It is battle-ship grey with a red trim. Its windows face away from the ocean. It is tall and narrow, of mean proportions, almost prison-like. "I wouldn't mind living in that one," he says. I look at it in silence. He has unerringly chosen the ugliest one. It is so ugly that I can find nothing to say.

It is Saturday afternoon. My father is waiting for the Victorian football to start on TV. He rereads the paper.

"Look at this," he says. "Mum, remember that seminar we went to about investments in diamonds?"

"Up here?" I say. "A *seminar*?"

"S'posed to be an investment that would double its value in six days. We went along one afternoon. They were obviously con-men. Ooh, setting up a big con, you could tell. They had sherry and sandwiches."

"That's all we went for, actually," says my mother.

"What sort of people went?" I ask.

"Oh . . . people like ourselves," says my father.

"Do you think anybody bought any?"

"Sure. Some idiots. Anyway, look at this in today's *Age*. 'The Diamond Dreamtime. World diamond market plummets.' Haw haw haw."

He turns on the TV in time for the bounce. I cast on stitches as instructed by the pattern and begin to knit. My mother and Auntie Lorna, well advanced in complicated garments for my sister's teenage children, conduct their monologues which cross, coincide and run parallel. My father mumbles advice to the foot-ballers and emits bursts of contemptuous laughter. "Bloody idiot," he says.

I go to the room I am to share with Auntie Lorna and come back with the packet of postcards. When I get out my pen and the stamps and set myself up at the table my father looks up and shouts to me over the roar of the crowd,

"Given up on the knitting?"

"No. Just knocking off a few postcards. People expect a postcard when you go to Queensland."

"Have to keep up your correspondence, Father," says my mother.

"I'll knit later," I say.

"How much have you done?" asks my father.

"This much." I separate thumb and forefinger.

"Dear Philip," I write. I make my writing as thin and small as I can: the back of the postcard, not the front, is the art form. "Look where I am. A big red setter wet from the surf shambles up the side way of the unit, looking lost and anxious as setters always do. My parents send it packing with curses in an inarticulate tongue. Go orn, get orf, gorn!"

"Dear Philip. THE IDENTIFICATION OF THE BIRDS AND FISHES. *My father*: 'Look at those albatross. They must have eyes that can see for a hundred miles. As soon as one dives, they come from everywhere. Look at 'em dive! Bang! Down they go.' *Me*: 'What sort of fish would they be diving for?' *My father*: 'Whiting. They only eat whiting.' *Me*: 'They do not!' *My father*: 'How the hell would *I* know what sort of fish they are.' "

"Dear Philip. My father says they are albatross, but my mother (in the bathroom, later) remarks to me that albatross have shorter, more hunched necks."

"Dear Philip. I share a room with Auntie Lorna. She also is writing postcards and has just asked me how to spell TOO. I like her very much and *she likes me*. 'I'll keep the stickybeaks in the Woomelang post office guessing,' she says. 'I won't put my name on the back of the envelope.' "

"Dear Philip. OUTSIDE THE POST OFFICE. My father, Auntie Lorna and I wait in the car for my mother to go in and pick up the mail from the locked box. *My father*: 'Gawd, amazing, isn't it, what people do. See that sign there, ENTER, with the arrow pointing upwards? What sort of a thing is that? Is it a joke, or just some no-hoper foolin' around? That woman's been in the phone box for half an hour, I bet. How'd you be, outside the public phone waiting for some silly coot to finish yackin' on about everything under the sun, while you had something important to say. That happened to us, once, up at —' My mother opens the door and gets in. 'Three letters,' she says. 'All for me.' "

Sometimes my little story overflows the available space and I have to run over on to a second postcard. This means I must find a smaller, secondary tale, or some disconnected remark, to fill up card number two.

"*Me*: (opening cupboard), 'Hey! Scrabble! We can have a game of Scrabble after tea!' *My father*: (with a scornful laugh) 'I can't wait.' "

"Dear Philip. I know you won't write back. I don't even know whether you are still at this address."

"Dear Philip. One Saturday morning I went to Coles and bought a scarf. It cost four and sixpence and I was happy with my purchase. He whisked it out of my hand and looked at the label. 'Made in China. Is it real silk? Let's test it.' He flicked on his cigarette lighter. We all screamed and my mother said, 'Don't *bite*! He's only teasing you.' "

"Dear Philip. Once, when I was fourteen, I gave cheek to him at the dinner table. He hit me across the head with his open hand. There was silence. My little brother gave a high, hysterical giggle and when I laughed too, in shock, he hit me again. After the washing up I was sent for. He was sitting in an armchair, looking down. 'The reason why we don't get on any more,' he said, 'is because we're so much alike.' This idea filled me with such revulsion that I turned my swollen face away. It was swollen from crying, not from the blows, whose force had been more symbolic than physical."

"Dear Philip. Years later he read my mail. He found the contraceptive pills. He drove up to Melbourne and found me and made me come home. He told me I was letting men use my body. He told me I ought to see a psychiatrist. I was in the front seat and my mother was in the back. I thought, 'If I open the door and jump out, I won't have to listen to this any more.' My mother tried to stick up for me. He shouted at her. 'It's your fault,' he said. 'You were too soft on her.' "

"Dear Philip. I know you've heard all this before. I also know it's no worse than anyone else's story."

"Dear Philip. And again years later he asked me a personal question. He was driving, I was in the suicide seat. 'What went wrong,' he said, 'between you and Philip?' Again I turned my face away. 'I don't want to talk about it,' I said. There was silence. He never asked again. And years after *that*, in a cafe in Paris on my way to work, far enough away from him to be able to, I thought of that question and began to cry. Dear Philip. I forgive you for everything."

Late in the afternoon my mother and Auntie Lorna and I walk along the beach to Surfers. The tide is out: our bare feet scarcely mark the firm sand. Their two voices run on, one high, one low. If I speak they pretend to listen, just as I feign attention to their endless, looping discourses: these are our courtesies: this is love. Everything is spoken, nothing is said. On the way back I point out to them the smoky orange clouds that are massing far out to sea, low over the horizon. Obedient, they stop and face the water. We stand in a row, Auntie Lorna in a pretty frock with sandals dangling from her finger, my mother and I with our trousers rolled up.

Once I asked my Brazilian friend a stupid question. He was listening to a conversation between me and a Frenchman about our
countries' electoral systems. He was not speaking and, thinking to
include him, I said, "And how do people vote *chez toi*, Rubens?"
He looked at me with a small smile. "We don't have elections," he
said. Where's Rio from here? "Look at those clouds!" I say.
"You'd think there was another city out there, wouldn't you,
burning."

Just at dark the air takes on the colour and dampness of the sub-
tropics. I walk out the screen door and stand my gin on a fence
post. I lean on the fence and look at the ocean. Soon the moon
will thrust itself over the line. If I did a painting of a horizon, I
think, I would make it look like a row of rocking, inverted Vs,
because that's what I see when I look at it. The flatness of a
horizon is intellectual. A cork pops on the first floor balcony
behind me. I glance up. In the half dark two men with moustaches
are smiling down at me.

"Drinking champagne tonight?" I say.

"Wonderful sound, isn't it," says the one holding the bottle.

I turn back to the moonless horizon. Last year I went camping
on the Murray River. I bought the cards at Tocumwal. I had to
write fast for the light was dropping and spooky noises were coming from the trees. "Dear Dad," I wrote. "I am up on the Murray,
sitting by the camp fire. It's nearly dark now but earlier it was
beautiful, when the sun was going down and the dew was rising."
Two weeks later, at home, I received a letter from him written in
his hard, rapid, slanting hand, each word ending in a sharp
upward flick. The letter itself concerned a small financial matter,
and consisted of two sentences on half a sheet of quarto, but on
the back of the envelope he had dashed off a personal message:
"P.S. Dew does not rise. It *forms*."

The moon does rise, as fat as an orange, out of the sea straight
in front of the unit. A child upstairs sees it too and utters long
werewolf howls. My mother makes a meal and we eat it. "Going
to help Mum with the dishes, are you, Miss?" says my father from
his armchair. My shoulders stiffen. I am, I do. I lie on the couch
and read an old *Woman's Day*. Princess Caroline of Monaco
wears a black dress and a wide white hat. The knitting needles

make their mild clicking. Auntie Lorna and my father come from the same town, Hopetoun in the Mallee, and when the news is over they begin again.

"I always remember the cars of people," says my father. "There was an old four-cylinder Dodge, belonging to Whatsisname. It had —"

"Would that have been one of the O'Lachlans?" says Auntie Lorna.

"Jim O'Lachlan. It had a great big exhaust pipe coming out the back. And I remember stuffing a potato up it."

"A *potato*?" I say.

"The bloke was a councillor," says my father. "He came out of the Council chambers and got into the Dodge and started her up. He only got fifty yards up the street when BA — BANG! This damn thing shot out the back — I reckon it's still going!" He closes his lips and drops his head back against the couch to hold in his laughter.

I walk past Biarritz, where globes of light float among shrubbery, and the odd balcony on the half-empty tower holds rich people out into the creamy air. A bare-foot man steps out of the take-away food shop with a hamburger in his hand. He leans against the wall to unwrap it, and sees me hesitating at the slot of the letterbox, holding up the postcards and reading them over and over in the weak light from the public phone. "Too late to change it now," he calls. I look up. He grins and nods and takes his first bite of the hamburger. Beside the letterbox stands a deep rubbish bin with a swing lid. I punch open the bin and drop the postcards in.

All night I sleep safely in my bed. The waves roar and hiss, and slam like doors. Auntie Lorna snores, but when I tug at the corner of her blanket she sighs and turns over and breathes more quietly. In the morning the rising sun hits the front windows and floods the place with a light so intense that the white curtains can hardly net it. Everything is pink and golden. In the sink a cockroach lurks. I try to swill it down the drain with a cup of water but it resists strongly. The air is bright, is milky with spray. My father is already up: while the kettle boils he stands out on the edge of the grass, the edge of his property, looking at the sea.

Civilisation and its Discontents

Philip came. I went to his hotel: I couldn't get there fast enough. He stepped up to me when I came through the door, and took hold of me.

"Hullo," he said, "my dear."

People here don't talk like that. My hair was still damp.

"Did you drive?" he said.

"No. I came on the bus."

"The *bus*?"

"There's never anywhere to park in the city."

"You've had your hair cut. You look like a boy."

"I know. I do it on purpose. I dress like a boy and I have my hair cut like a boy. I want to *be* a boy. So I can have a homosexual affair with *you*."

He laughed. "Good girl!" he said. At these words I was so flooded with well-being that I could hardly get my breath. "If you were a boy some of the time and a girl the rest," he said, "I'd be luckier. Because I could have both."

"No," I said. "I'd be luckier. Because I could *be* both."

I scrambled out of my clothes.

"You're so thin," he said.

"I don't eat. I'm sick."

"Sick? Are you?" He put his two hands on my shoulders and looked into my eyes like a doctor.

"Sick with love."

"Your eyes are healthy. Lustrous. Are mine?"

His room was on the top floor. Opposite, past some roofs and a deep street, was the old-fashioned tower of the building in which a dentist I used to go to had his rooms. That dentist was so gentle with the drill that I never needed an injection. I used to breathe slowly, as I had been taught at yoga: the pain was brief. I didn't flinch. But he made his pile and moved to Queensland.

The building had a flagpole. Philip and I stood at the window with no clothes on and looked out. The tinted glass made the cloud masses more detailed, richer, more spectacular than they were.

"Look at those," I said. "Real boilers. Coming in from somewhere."

"Just passing through," said Philip. He was looking at the building with the tower. "I love the Australian flag," he said. "Every time I see it I get a shiver."

"I'm like that about the map." Once I worked in a convent school in East London. I used to go to the library at lunchtime, when the nuns were locked away in their dining room being read to, and take down the atlas and gaze at the page with Australia on it: I loved its upper points, its vast inlets, its fat sides, the might of it, the mass from whose south-eastern corner my small life had sprung. I used to crouch between the stacks and rest the heavy book on the edge of the shelf: I could hardly support its weight. I looked at the map and my eyes filled with tears.

"Did I tell you she's talking about coming back to me?" said Philip.

"Do you want her to?"

"Of course I do."

I sat down on the bed.

"We'll have to start behaving like adults," he said. "Any idea how it's done?"

"Well," I said, "it must be a matter of transformation. We have to turn what's happening now into something else."

"You sound experienced."

"I am."

"What can we turn it into?"

"Brother and sister? A lifelong friendship?"

"Oh," he said, "I don't know anything about that. Can't people just go on having a secret affair?"

"I don't like lying."

"You don't have to. I'm the liar."

"What makes you so sure she won't find out? People always

know. She'll take one look at you and know. That's what wives are for."

"We'll see."

"How can you stand it?" I said. "It's dishonourable. How can you lie to someone and still love her?"

"Forced to. Forced by love to be a hypocrite."

I thought for a second he was joking.

"We could drop it now," I said.

"What are you *saying*?"

"I don't mean it."

Not yet. The sheets in those hotels are silky, but crisp. How do they get them like that? A lot of starch, and ironing, things no housewife in her right mind could be bothered doing. The bed was wide enough for another two people to have lain in it, and still none of us would have had to touch sides. I don't usually go to bed in the daylight. And as if the daylight were not enough, the room was full of lamps. I started to switch them off, one after another, and thinking of the phrase "full of lamps" I remembered something my husband said to me, long after we split up, about a Shakespeare medley he had seen performed by doddering remnants of a famous British company that was touring Australia. "The stage," he said, "was covered in *thrones*," and his knees bent with laughter. He was the only man I have ever known who would rejoice with you over the petty triumphs of the day. I got under the sheet. I couldn't help laughing to myself, but it was too complicated to explain why.

Philip had a way of holding me, when we lay down: he made small rocking movements, so small that I sometimes wondered if I were imagining them, if the comfort of being held were translating itself into an imaginary cradling.

"I've never told anyone I loved them, before," said Philip.

"Don't be silly," I said.

"You don't know anything about me."

"At your age?" I said. "A married man? You've never loved anyone before?"

"I've never *said* it before."

"No wonder she went away," I said. "Men are really done over, aren't they. At an early age."

"Why do you want to fuck like a boy, then?"

"Just for play."

"Is it allowed?" he said.

"Who by?" I said. I was trying to be smart; but seriously, who says we can't? Isn't that why women and men make love? To bend the bars a little, just for a little; to let the bars dissolve? Philip pinched me. He took hold of the points of my breasts, between forefingers and thumbs. I could see his teeth. He pinched hard. It hurt. I liked it. And he bit me. He *bit* me. When I got home I looked in the mirror and my shoulders and arms were covered in small round bruises.

I went to his house, in the town where he lived. I told him I would be passing through on my way south, and he invited me, and I went, though I had plenty of friends I could have stayed with in that city.

There was a scandal in the papers as I passed through the airport that evening, about a woman who had made a contract to have a baby for a childless couple. The baby was born, she changed her mind, she would not give it up. Everyone was talking about her story.

I felt terrible at his house, for all I loved him, with his wife's forgotten dressing gown hanging behind the door like a witness. I couldn't fall asleep properly. I "lay broad waking" all night long, and the house was pierced by noises, as if its walls were too flimsy to protect it from the street: a woman's shoes striking the pavement, a gate clicking, a key sliding into a lock, stairs breathing in and out. It never gets truly dark in cities. Once I rolled over and looked at him. His face was sleeping, serene, smiling on the pillow next to mine like a cherub on a cloud.

He woke with a bright face. "I feel unblemished," he said, "when I've been with you." This is why I loved him, of course: because he talked like that, using words and phrases that most people wouldn't think of saying. "When I'm with you," he'd say, "I feel happy and free."

He made the breakfast and we read the papers in the garden.

"She should've stuck to her word," he said.

"Poor thing," I said. "How can anyone give a baby away?"

"But she promised. What about the couple? They must be dying to have a kid."

"Are you?"

"Yes," he said, and looked at me with the defiant expression of someone expecting to be crossed. "Yes. I am."

"I think in an ideal world everyone would have children," I said. "That's how people learn to love. Kids suck love out of your bones."

"I suppose you think that only mothers know how to love."

"No. I don't think that."

"Still," he said. "She signed a contract. She *signed*. She made a promise."

"Philip," I said, "have you ever smelled a baby's head?"

The phone started to ring inside the house, in the room I didn't go into because of the big painting of her that was hanging over the stereo. Thinking that he loved me, though I understood and believed I had accepted the futurelessness of it, I amused myself by secretly calling it The Room in Which the First Wife Raved, or Bluebeard's Bloody Chamber: it repelled me with an invisible force, though I stood at times outside its open door and saw its pleasantness, its calm, its white walls and wooden floor on which lay a bent pattern of sunlight like a child's drawing of a window.

He ran inside to answer the phone. He was away for quite a while. I thought about practising: how it is possible to learn with one person how to love, and then to apply the lesson learnt to somebody else: someone teaches you to sing, and then you wait for a part in the right opera. It was warm in the garden. I dozed in my chair. I had a small dream, one of those shockingly vivid dreams that occur when one sleeps at an unaccustomed time of day, or when one ought to be doing something other than sleeping. I dreamed that I was squatting naked with my vagina close to the ground, in the posture we are told primitive women adopt for childbearing ("They just squat down in the fields, drop the baby, and go on working"). But someone was operating on me, using sharp medical instruments on my cunt. Bloody flesh was issuing from it in clumps and clots. I could watch it, and see it, as if it were somebody else's cunt, while at the same time experiencing it being done to me. It was not painful. It didn't hurt at all.

I woke up as he came down the steps smiling. He crouched down in front of me, between my knees, and spoke right into my face.

"You want me to behave like a married man, and have kids, don't you?"

"*Want* you to?"

"I mean you think I should. You think everyone should, you said."

"Sure — if that's what you want. Why?"

"Well, on the phone just now I went a bit further towards it."

"You mean you *lined* it *up*?"

"Not exactly — but that's the direction I'm going in."

I looked down at him. His forearms were resting across my knees and he was crouching lightly on the balls of his feet. He was smiling at me, smiling right into my eyes. He was waiting for me to say, *Good boy!*

"Say something reassuring," he said. "Say something close, before I go."

I took a breath, but already he was not listening. He was ready to work. Philip loved his work. He took on more than he could comfortably handle. Every evening he came home with his pockets sprouting contracts. He never wasted anything: I'd hear him whistling in the car, a tiny phrase, a little run of notes climbing and falling as we drove across the bridges, and then next morning from the room with the synthesiser in it would issue the same phrase but bigger, fuller, linked with other ideas, becoming a song: and a couple of months after that I'd hear it through the open doors of every cafe, record shop and idling car in town. "Know what I used to dream?" he said to me once. "I used to dream that when I pulled up at the lights I'd look into the cars on either side of me and in front and behind, and everyone would be singing along with the radio, and they'd all be singing the same song. Even if the windows were wound up and we'd read each other's lips, and everyone would laugh, and wave."

I made my own long distance call. "I'll be home tonight, Matty," I said.

His voice was full of sleep. "They rang up from the shop," he said. "I told them you were sick. Have you seen that man yet?"

"Yes. I'm on my way. Get rid of the pizza boxes."

"I need money, Mum."

"When I get there."

Philip took me to the airport. I was afraid someone would see us, someone he knew. For me it didn't matter. Nothing was secret, I had no-one to hide anything from, and I would have been proud to be seen with him. But for him I was worried. I worried enough for both of us. I kept my head down. He laughed. He would not let me go. He tried to make me lift my chin; he gave it soft butts with his forehead. My cheeks were red.

"I'm always getting on planes with tears in my eyes," I said.

"They'll be getting to know you," he said. "Are you too shy to kiss me properly?"

I bolted past the check-in desk. I looked back and he was watching me, still laughing, standing by himself on the shining floor.

On the plane I was careful with myself. I concentrated on the ingenuity of the food tray, its ability to remain undisturbed by the alterations in position of the seatback to which it was attached. I called for a scotch and drank it. My mistake was to look inside a book of poems, the only reading matter I had on me. They were poems so charged with sex and death and longing that it was indecent to read them in public: I was afraid that their power might leak out and scandalise the onlookers. Even as I slammed the book shut I saw *I want to know, once more,/how it feels/to be peeled and eaten whole, time after time.* I kept the book turned away from two men who were sitting between me and the window. They were drinking German beer and talking in a European language of which I did not recognise a single word. One of them turned his head and caught my eye. I expected him to look away hastily, for I felt myself to be ugly and stiff with sadness; but his face opened into a dazzling smile.

My son was waiting for the plane. He had come out on the airport bus. He saw how pleased I was, and looked down with an embarrassed smile, but he permitted me to hug him, and patted my shoulder with little rapid pats.

"Your face is different," he said. "All sort of emotional."

"Why do you always pat me when you hug me?" I said.

"Pro'ly 'cause you're nearly always in a state," he said.

He asked me to wait while he had a quick go on the machines. His fingers swarmed on the buttons. *Death by Acne* was the title of a thriller he had invented to make me laugh: but his face in concentration lost its awkwardness and became beautiful. I leaned on the wall of the terminal and watched the people passing.

A tall young man came by. He was carrying a tiny baby in a sling against his chest. The mother walked behind, smooth-faced and long-haired, holding by the hand a fat-nappied toddler. But the man was the one in love with the baby. He walked slowly, with his arms curved round its small bulk. His head was bowed so he could gaze into its face. His whole being was adoring it.

I watched the young family go by in its peaceful procession, each one moving quietly and contentedly in place, and I heard the high-pitched death wails of the space creatures my son was murdering with his fast and delicate tapping of buttons, and suddenly I remembered walking across the street the day after I brought him home from hospital. The birth was long and I lost my rhythm and made too much noise and they drugged me, and when it was over I felt that now I knew what the prayerbook meant when it said *the pains of death gat hold upon me*. But crossing the road that day, still sore from knives and needles, I saw a pregnant woman lumbering towards me, a woman in the final stages of waiting, putting one heavy foot in front of the other. Her face as she passed me was as calm and as full as an animal's: "a face that had not yet received the fist". And I envied her. I was stabbed, pierced with envy, with longing for what was about to happen to her, for what she was ignorantly about to enter. I could have cried out, Oh, let me do it again! Give me another chance! Let me meet the mighty forces again and struggle with them! Let me be rocked again, let me lie helpless in that huge cradle of pain!

"Another twenty cents down the drain," said my son. We set out together towards the automatic doors. He was carrying my bag. I wanted to say to him, to someone, "Listen. Listen. I am *hopelessly in love*." But I hung on. I knew I had brought it on myself, and I hung on until the spasm passed. And then I began to recreate from memory the contents of the fridge.

What We Say

I was kneeling at the open door, with the cloth in my right hand and the glass shelf balanced on the palm of my left. She came past at a fast clip, wearing my black shoes and pretending I wasn't there. I spoke sharply to her, from my supplicant's posture.

"Death to mother. Death," she replied, and clapped the gate to behind her.

It had once been a kind of family joke, but I lost the knack of the shelf for a moment and though it didn't break there was quite a bit of blood. After I had cleaned up and put the apron in a bucket to soak, I went to the phone and began to make arrangements.

In Sydney my friend, the old-fashioned sort of friend who works on your visit and wants you to be happy, gave me two tickets to the morning dress rehearsal of *Rigoletto*. I went with Natalie. She knew how to get there and which door to go in. "At your age, you've never been inside the *Opera* House?" Great things and small forged through the blinding water. We hurried, we ran.

At the first interval we went outside. A man I knew said, "I like your shirt. What would you call that colour — hyacinth?" At the second interval we stayed in our seats so we could keep up our conversation which is no more I suppose than exalted gossip but which seems, because of her oblique perceptions, a most delicate, hilarious and ephemeral tissue of mind.

At lunchtime we dashed, puffy-eyed and red-cheeked, into the kitchen of my thoughtful friend. He was standing at the stove, looking up at us over his shoulder and smiling: he likes to teach me things, he likes to see me learning.

"How was it?"

"Fabulous! We cried *buckets*!"

Another man was leaning against the window frame with his arms crossed and his hair standing on end. His skin was pale, as if he had crept out from some burrow where he had lain for a long time in a cramped and twisted position.

"You cried?" he said. "You mean you actually shed tears?"

Look out, I thought; one of these. I was still having to blow my nose, and was ready to ride rough-shod. My friend put the spaghetti on the table and we all sat down.

"I'm starving," said Natalie.

"What a plot," I raved. "So tight you couldn't stick a pin in it."

"What was your worst moment?" said Natalie.

"Oh, when he bends over the sack to gloat, and then from off-stage comes the Duke's voice, singing his song. The way he freezes, in that bent-over posture, over the sack."

The sack, in a sack. I had a best friend once, my intellectual companion of ten years, on paper from land to land and then in person: she was the one who first told me the story of *Rigoletto* and I will never forget the way her voice sank to a thread of horror: "and the murderer gives him his daughter's body on the river-bank, *in a sack*." A river flows: that is its nature. Its sluggish water can work any discarded object loose from the bank and carry it further, lump it lengthwise, nudge it and roll it and shift it, bear it away and along and out of sight.

"Yes, that was bad all right," said Natalie, "but mine was when he realised that his daughter was in the bedchamber with Duke."

We picked up our forks and began to eat. The back door opened on to a narrow concrete yard, but light was bouncing down the grey walls and the air was warm, and as I ate I thought, Why don't I live here? In the sun?

"Also," I said, "I *love* what it's about. About the impossibility of shielding your children from the evil of the world."

There was a pause.

"Well, yes, it is about that," said my tactful friend, "but it's also about the greatest fear men have. Which is the fear of losing their daughters. Of losing them to younger men. Into the world of sex."

We sat at the table quietly eating. Words which people use and pretend to understand floated in silence and bumped among our heads: virgin; treasure; perfect; clean; my darling; anima; soul.

Natalie spoke in her light, courteous voice. "If that's what it's about," she said, "what do you think the women in the audience were responding to?" — for in our bags were two sodden handkerchiefs.

The salad went round.

"I don't know," said my friend. "You tell me."

We said nothing. We looked into our plates.

"That fear men have," said my friend. "Literature and art are full of it."

My skin gave a mutinous prickle. *Your* literature.

"*Do* women have a fundamental fear?" said my friend.

Natalie and I glanced at each other and back to the tabletop.

"A fear of violation, maybe?" he said. He got up and filled the kettle. The silence was not a silence but a quietness of thinking. I knew what Natalie was thinking. She was wishing the conversation had not taken this particular turn. I was wishing the same thing. Stumped, struck dumb: failed again, failed to think and talk in that pattern they use. I had nothing to say. Nothing came to my mind that had any bearing on the matter.

Should I say "But violation is our destiny?" Or should I say "*Nothing can be sole or whole/That has not been rent*"? But before I could open my mouth, a worst moment came to me: the letter arrives from my best friend on the road in a far country: "He was wearing mirror sunglasses which he did not take off, I tried to plead but I could not speak his language, he tore out handfuls of my hair, he kicked me and pushed me out of the car, I crawled to the river, I could smell the water, it was dirty but I washed myself, a farm girl found me, her family is looking after me, I think I will be all right, please answer, above all don't tell my father, love." I got down on my elbows in the yard and put my face into the dirt, I wept, I groaned. That night I went as usual to the lesson. *All I can do is try to make something perfect for you, for your poor body, with my clumsy and ignorant one*: I breathed and moved as the teacher showed us, and she came past me in the class and touched me on the head and said, "This must mean a lot to you — you are doing it so beautifully."

"Violation," said Natalie, as if to gain time.

"It would be necessary," I said, "to examine all of women's writing, to see if the fear of violation is the major theme of it."

"Some feminist theoretician somewhere has probably already done it," said the stranger who had been surprised that *Rigoletto* could draw tears.

"Barbara Baynton, for instance," said my friend. "Have you read that story of hers called 'The Chosen Vessel'? The woman knows the man is outside waiting for dark. She puts the brooch on the table. It's the only valuable thing she owns. She puts it there as an offering — to appease him. She wants to buy him off."

The brooch. The mirror sunglasses. The feeble lock. The weakened wall that gives. What stops these conversations is shame, and grief.

"We don't have a tradition in the way you blokes do," I said.

Everybody laughed, with relief.

"There must be a line of women's writing," said Natalie, "running from the beginning till now."

"It's a shadow tradition," I said. "It's there, but nobody knows what it is."

"We've been trained in *your* tradition," said Natalie. "We're honorary men."

She was not looking at me, nor I at her.

The coffee was ready, and we drank it. Natalie went to pick up her children from school. My friend put in the plug and began to wash the dishes. The stranger tilted his chair back against the wall, and I leaned on the bench.

"What happened to your hand?" he said.

"I cut it on the glass shelf yesterday," I said, "when I was defrosting the fridge."

"There's a packet of bandaids in the fruit bowl," said my friend from the sink.

I stripped off the old plaster and took a fresh one from the dish. But before I could yank its little ripcord and pull it out of its wrapper, the stranger got up from his chair, walked all the way round the table and across the room, and stopped in front of me. He took the bandaid and said,

"Do you want me to put it on for you?"

I drew a breath to say *what we say*: "Oh, it's all right, thanks —
I can do it myself."

But instead, I don't know why, I let out my independent breath,
and took another. I gave him my hand.

"Do you like dressing wounds?" I said, in a smart tone to cover
my surprise.

He did not answer this, but spread out my palm and had a good
look at the cut. It was deep and precise, like a freshly dug trench,
bloody still at the bottom but with nasty white soggy edges where
the plaster had prevented the skin from drying.

"You've made a mess of yourself, haven't you," he said.

"Oh, it's nothing much," I said airily. "It only hurt while it was
actually happening."

He was not listening. He was concentrating on the thing. His
fingers were pale, square and clean. He peeled off the two protective flaps and laid the sticky bandage across the cut. He pressed
one side of it, and then the other, against my skin, smoothed them
flat with his thumbs, and let go.

Dazzling Writing

Introduction to the Virago Edition of Eleanor Dark's *Lantana Lane*

Lantana Lane is Eleanor Dark's last novel. It appeared in 1959. Until I was asked to write this introduction I had never heard of it. To most Australians who were at high school in the 1950s, Dark was known as the author of the fattish historical novel *The Timeless Land* (1941: part of a trilogy) which we studied in fifth or sixth form. The strongest memory I had of this book is an early scene in which an Aborigine stands on the cliffs of Sydney Harbour (which bore for him, of course, a different name) and watches the approach of the sailing ships carrying the first European settlers to his land. It is a scene that the subsequent near-destruction of the Aboriginal race makes into an image of piercing irony.

Eleanor Dark's name returned briefly to public notice several years ago when a television series was made of *The Timeless Land*. Writers are accustomed to being passed over in the hooha that launches TV events, and Dark was no exception; but it is hard to imagine this old woman, living in the Blue Mountains, being much interested more than forty years after its publication in yet another interpretation of her most popular novel as little more than a colonial costume drama.

The TV series, using alcohol as the metaphor for racial destruction, touched lightly on the fatal impact of white settlement on the Aborigines, but paid little or no attention to the damage which, as Dark points out in her novel, greed and plunder did to the ancient land with which the Aborigines had lived in harmony. She uses the image of rape — but rape, it seems to me, within an already established relationship — when she says of her character based on Governor Phillip:

He heard them crying out to her insatiably, "Give! Give!" and was aware of her silent inviolability which would never give until they had ceased to rob.

If this strikes us as modern, we may be equally struck by this account, also from *The Timeless Land*, of Carangarang, elder sister of the main Aboriginal character Bennilong and a maker of songs; she sings,

> . . . but the words faded as swiftly as they had been born; smitten with fear of her own temerity, she glanced round apprehensively upon a ring of startled, hostile faces. They said nothing, but she understood their condemnation.

Her younger sister, too, made songs that "were not such as men might make . . . To the men she was like a faintly pricking thorn in the foot which they could not discover."

The women novelists of Australia between the 1920s and the end of the Second World War were no "faintly pricking thorns". They dominated the country's fiction output: Dark, Katharine Susannah Prichard, Barnard and Eldershaw, Dymphna Cusack, Kylie Tennant, and the two most brilliant, Christina Stead and Henry Handel Richardson, both of whom worked abroad for virtually their entire careers. It is the mark of the ability of Australians to distort our own cultural history that a novelist like Eleanor Dark, a critical and popular success for twenty years and twice a winner of the Australian Literary Society's Gold Medal, should now be someone whose name produces blank looks, whose books have almost all been out of print for years, and who is omitted from *The Oxford Anthology of Australian Literature* (published 1985 and by any standards a conservative selection).

Drusilla Modjeska's important book *Exiles at Home* (Angus and Robertson, 1981) has brought fresh attention to the women writers, solidly on the left and subsequently all but forgotten, who dominated the Australian novel of their time. Dark is one of these writers, but even in Modjeska's book she remains a shadowy figure.

In her early novels (*Prelude to Christopher*, 1934; *Return to Coolami*, 1936; *Sun Across the Sky*, 1937; *Waterway*, 1938) Dark was stylistically some way in advance of her resident female contemporaries. In my fossicking among the rare personal reports about Dark, I have picked up an impression that her early technical adventurousness (time compression, flashback, etc) and in particular her interest in psychology did not endear her to certain influential supporters of social realism who were devoted to the establishment and consolidation of a nationalistic Australian literary culture.

She may not have found congenial the heavy stress laid on social realism by Nettie and Vance Palmer and their network of commentators and writers, but her novels make it abundantly clear that her political sympathies lay with the left. In *The Little Company* (1945), the most explicitly political of her novels, written during the Second World War and reissued now by Virago with a rich and knowledgable introduction by Drusilla Modjeska, Dark tackled crucial questions about the meaning of war and the role of the radical and the writer in a world whose social and political fabric was being torn apart. She was never an activist, however, and rarely went to literary or political functions; it was her husband's name that appeared on the Council for Civil Liberties masthead.

A Melbourne historian who interviewed Eleanor Dark ten years ago in his research for a biography of one of her contemporaries on the left remarked to me that she was "reflective, and not opinionated, unlike most of the people I interviewed from the old left whose responses tended to the automatic. She was easily the most impressive person I interviewed. She was a person who was still thinking, and who was prepared, if she had no grounds for opinion, to say nothing at all." He described her, in her middle seventies at that time, as "well preserved, fine-boned, without make-up, very attractive, sitting up there in her beautiful house on the edge of the escarpment, chain-smoking and looking out the window and thinking before she spoke".

But Dark and her husband were branded fellow travellers in a period when any criticism of Australian society could bring accusations of communism. They were so harassed for their politics in the fifties that Dr Dark's medical practice suffered, and they were obliged to leave Katoomba where they had long lived and worked, and move for a time to a small farming community in Queensland.

Then, for most of that decade, Dark's silence.

Then, in 1959, *Lantana Lane*, a novel so strikingly different from her other works as to "make one gasp and stretch one's eyes".

It is impertinent to make ignorant guesses about an artist's state of mind, but *Lantana Lane* strikes me as a novel written by a happy woman. Its tone is light, lively and benevolent. Its humour is benign. Its observations of human behaviour, while razor sharp, are affectionately knowing, and informed with an attractive, amused tolerance. Its wit is without malice, blackness or strain. Its feminism is no more vitriolic than a firm but gentle chiacking of men in their self-importance and laconicism. It is not a novel of conflict, of character development, of strain and resolution: it is a contemplation of a particular microcosmic isolated little farming community "round the corner from the world". It is a book written with pleasure by a mature artist in calm command of her craft.

The Timeless Land, Dark has said, "necessitated a fearful lot of study and research, and not being a scholar, I was very tired of that". *Lantana Lane*, on the other hand, clearly springs from personal experience. The only evidence of scholarliness here, apart from Dark's superb handling of syntax, is the easy familiarity the unnamed narrator (who employs a god-like and gender-hiding "we") demonstrates with certain Great Works of our culture: The Old and New Testaments, the Arthurian legends, Dr Johnson, Tennyson, Freud and the works of Richard Wagner. These learned references are bandied about with a breathtakingly light-handed cool, and give rise to some of the book's most hilarious sequences.

It's a "slow read", as they say, a leisurely piece of writing, as if the easeful sub-tropical climate in which the farming community lives had affected the prose and structure of the book itself. Into her language of syntactic formality and wide vocabulary Dark slings sudden colloquialisms which blast the seriousness sky-high. The loveliest example of this is the chapter called "SOME REMARKS UPON THE NATURE OF CONTRAST with Special Reference to the Habits and Characteristics of Ananas cosmosus and Lantana camara and an Examination of their Economic and Psychological Effect upon Homo Sapiens". This dissertation on the uncontrollable weed, the bushy and massive lantana, in which the scientist's calm detachment keeps giving way to outbursts of cursing by the tormented farmer, is perhaps the showpiece of the book, not only for its sparkling language ("the feckless and slovenly lantana", "the stiff, tough, soldierly pineapples" — this woman is a mistress of anthropomorphism) but because it is also a dissertation on the epic struggle of humankind against nature, and because of the tremendous possibilities of lantana as an image for the human unconscious.

This last I find specially satisfying and entertaining because of Dark's early difficulties with the Australian social realist school who turned their backs on what it no doubt saw as the side alley of Freudianism.

The beauty of this symbol did not strike me until a friend remarked to me, while I was reading the book, that her husband had dismissed his own unconscious by describing it as "a deep dark hole where I throw things I don't want to think about, and I never see them again". Dark's phrase "Throw it Down in the Lantana" sprang to my mind. The lantana, this pestiferous spreading plant, Australia's version of Brer Rabbit's briar patch, is the hiding place for many an unwanted object:

> What would *you* do with tins and dead marines? What would *you* do with the old iron bedstead, the rust-consumed tank, the roll of useless wire netting, the ancient pram, the buckled bicycle wheel, the kettles, saucepans, egg-beaters and frying pans which have earned an honourable discharge? What would *you* do with the broken vases, medicine bottles, crockery and looking-glasses; the half-used bag of cement, now set like a rock; the worn-out gumboots, and the mouldering remains of your late grandmother's buggy? True, an incredible amount of junk will go under the house, but there comes a time when space there is exhausted — and then how thankfully we turn to the lantana! With a soft crash, and a sound of splitting twigs, discarded objects of all kinds, shapes and sizes fall through the green leaves, and discreetly vanish into the twilit world below.

And what is revealed when the mass of lantana is thinned or bulldozed or poisoned or destroyed will be, we imagine with a shiver, as momentous as the discoveries in store on the day when the sea shall give up its dead. It delights me to think of Eleanor Dark slyly slipping this image under the social realist rabbit-proof fence.

Dark's attitudes to the relationships between women and men are, in *Lantana Lane*, at their most benevolent. In earlier works she showed women frustrated and even driven mad by the contradictions forced on them, but the little community of Lantana Lane is so tightly knit and its people so interdependent that their situation is almost tribal: women's work is highly valued. Dark writes about the habits and roles of men and women in a pre-women's liberation movement way: without a political message, she presents the matter as a fact of nature, but oddly this enables her to point out with apparent innocence of motive things which any woman writer today could barely draw attention to without being accused of rampant man-hating.

The sequence in which "a youth named Barry James" carves a new road with a bulldozer, besides being a piece of writing of the most inspired brilliance, delicacy and strength, handles with controlled humour the fact that "the types of construction which most excite (men's) enthusiasm are those which demand, as a preliminary, excavation or demolition on a massive scale".

Bulldozed, with its paean to the machine and its sceptical respect for and witty sallies on many skills and concerns, is beautifully counterbalanced by an earlier chapter called "Gwinny on Meat-day". This sequence is a *tour de force* of another order. Here Dark gives us what is perhaps the book's greatest creation, the character of Gwinny Bell.

> And when you see her working down in the pines, or pegging out her vast quantity of vast garments on the line, or striding along the Lane to visit one of the neighbours, you seem to hear Wagnerian music, and lo! — the scene dissolves. Fade out the serviceable working clothes, or the best frock of gay, floral rayon; fade out the felt slippers, or the patent leather shoes; fade out the battered, weekday hat, or the Sunday straw with its purple flowers, and its little pink veil. Fade in accomplished draperies which reveal the limbs they should be covering, and shining breastplates which proclaim the curves they guard; fade in gold sandals laced about the ankles; fade in a horned helmet over blond, wind-driven hair. Fade out the timber cottage sitting on high stumps, crowned with corrugated iron, and surrounded by pineapples; fade in an abode of gods, resting on legend, crowned by clouds, and surrounded by enchanted air. Fade out, Lantana Lane . . . and fade in, Asgard!

Although I long to quote further from this wonderful chapter, I refrain out of reluctance to pre-empt others' pleasure. Suffice it to say that Gwinny Bell and the feats of her "fabulous memory" brought tears of laughter, admiration and envy to my eyes. It is dazzling writing, and the purest tribute to the working lives, the teeming brains and the splendid competence of ordinary women everywhere.

Elizabeth Jolley: An Appreciation

I first came across Elizabeth Jolley's writing in *Meanjin* in 1979. A story called *The Bench* (now retitled *Adam's Bride* in her Penguin collection *Woman in a Lampshade*) opens with these sentences:

> All small towns in the country have some sort of blessing. In one there is a stretch of river which manages to retain enough water for swimming in the summer; in another, the wife of the policeman is able to make dresses for bridesmaids, and in yet another, the cook at the hotel turns hairdresser on Saturday afternoons.

This is a perfect introduction to one of Jolley's dominant modes: the confident, attractive generalisation, the use of the word "blessing", the easy feeling for the detail, both natural and human, of life in the country, and respect for the minor skills and generosities of ordinary people.

*　　*　　*

The order of writing [of Jolley's books], without consulting Jolley herself, would be hard to establish, for the world of her imagination is so unified, and her themes and images have been so thoroughly worked and reworked, re-examined, re-arranged and re-used, that one could dive in at any point in any of the six books and not be able to say with confidence, "This is early Jolley" or "This is late".

Jolley operates with an inspired thrift. She returns unabashed to what she finds evocative and rich and not yet properly understood or exorcised. It's not just a matter of recurring characters, though that's part of it. Certain images, phrases, whole sentences, whole paragraphs, whole trains of events emerge again and again, in a manner which at first unnerves, like a half-remembered dream or a flicker of *déjà vu*, but which finally produces an unusual cumulative effect. She will take a situation, a relationship, a moment of insight, a particular longing, and work on it half a dozen different versions, making the characters older or younger, changing their gender or their class, gaoling or releasing a father, adding or subtracting a murder or a suicide; and these repetitions and re-usings, conscious but not to the point of being orchestrated, set up a pattern of echoes which unifies the world, and is most seductive and comforting.

What are these images, so industrious but never threadbare? The timbered valley, the rooster which has just lost a cockfight and is too ashamed to peck at its food, the old man who designs his wine labels before he has even bought the land, the brick path made by the nine-year-old boy, unexpected rain coming into an open shed, the ribbed pattern of a vineyard, the old man whose "freshly combed white hair looked like a bandage", the child's mouth "all square with crying", the dream-like "lawns made of water", "the great ship with a knowledge not entirely her own", the half-eaten pizzas discarded in the laundry after a party, the person who crushes herbs in the palm of one hand and sniffs at them, the pile of firewood that the old husband lovingly maintains so that the housewife "only had to reach out an arm for it", the father who, when his small daughter writes a sentence, "kissed the page", the observation that "water is the last thing to get dark". These things are some of Jolley's icons.

Her characters, too, are part of this strange net of familiarity, and are held in it: that weird trio, always in paroxysms of laughter or rage, the mother who cleans houses for a living to support her feckless son and her anxious daughter — the daughter as often as not the narrator; mother as landlady or vice versa; pairs of sisters; pairs of lesbians, one much older than the other; migrants humiliating themselves to earn a living as salesmen; crazed European aunts who sob with homesickness and knit "wild cardigans"; harmless impostors, simpletons and idiots; couples ill-matched intellectually; savage nurses with vast bosoms and shameful pasts. And running through all six books is the strong connecting tissue of land, land, land: the obsession with the ownership of land, the toiling and the self-denial and the saving for it with such passion that denial itself becomes the pleasure;

land that people bargain for and marry for and swindle for; land with strings attached; land to be deprived of which can drive people mad; land that flourishes, land that is sour and barren; land that is stolen from ageing parents by children and sold; land with healing properties, land without which life has neither meaning nor purpose. "All land", say her characters over and over, "is somebody's land".

But how can I have got this far without mentioning that Elizabeth Jolley is a very *funny* writer? The novel *Palomino* is the only one of the six books which is devoid of her weird humour, and this is one of the reasons for its failure. Her humour is not cruel, though some people have used this word to describe the novel *Mr Scobie's Riddle*. The bottom line, for Jolley, is love. What makes us laugh in her books is the friction between humour and pathos. She is droll, sly, often delicate: not averse to the throwaway line ("Matron Price, while she had her scissors handy, bent down and cut off what remained of Mrs Murphy's hair"; a baby "dressed with simplicity in a grimy napkin"); she is offhand, with a batty sideways slip that I find hilarious: and she is capable of the most skilful construction and priming, as in the first nine pages of *Mr Scobie's Riddle* which set out the whole ghastly, frantic moral sink of St Christopher and St Jude's Hospital for the Aged in a brilliantly comic exchange of official reports between Night Sister Shady (Unregistered) and the dreadful Matron Price.

*   *   *

Pathos is a risky mode. If the humour doesn't come off, the pathetic thing can be left stranded, wet and dripping. This happens: a little slide that's too easy, a too blatant twanging of the heart strings, a too convenient car crash. Sometimes she is a bit heavy-handed with the adverbs, or one of the family's comic brawls loses its rhythm and collapses. But even a clumsy, flustered, amateurish story will have a nugget of sense at its centre, an image that surprises, a simple — even a crude — stroke that comes off and almost saves it; or else she'll strike a note that only a woman of her age would have the nerve or the knowledge to go for: some low-toned remark that will flip a situation over or make a sudden quiet of acceptance.

*   *   *

She is not quite at home with contemporary idiom. There is something irredeemably between-wars about the feckless son "the Doll", Mr Scobie's racy nephew Hartley, and their ilk: you can't help seeing them in two-tone shoes and brilliantine, their slang is dance-hall, and she doesn't seem to be doing it on purpose. Sometimes these anachronisms jar; sometimes they have a shock effect that makes your head spin. This slight sense of uncertainty is compensated for, however, by her ability to make an unerring choice of detail:

> Like yesterday I had only two people in all day, just two little boys who looked at everything . . . spilled all the marbles . . . and then in the end they just bought themselves a plastic dagger each.

"A plastic dagger each": bullseye.

Because *Mr Scobie's Riddle* is about an old people's home, some critics have taken a sociological approach to it, as if Jolley were making an impassioned plea to the general public to soften its heart towards the aged. She's much tougher than that and much more of an artist. What she says about old people reminds me that one day I shall be one of them: she provokes not condescending sympathy but rushes of "pity and terror":

> His hand, flapping, caught the door post on the way back. The frail skin, brown mottled and paper thin, was grazed and broken . . . Quickly she tore up a piece of old rag kept for padding up the old women and bound up the bleeding hand.

An expression like "kept for padding up the old women" has the same effect as the half-understood references to adult sexual life that one reads as an eight-year-old: revulsion and fear, coupled with a sense of fate.

Life is pretty grim, in Elizabeth Jolley. People are disappointed, weak, frightened for their children, ill with homesickness, struggling against hostile circumstance, skating close to chasms — and some of them are right over the edge, dispossessed, helpless, deregistered, blackmailed, incontinent. But they are all battlers.

Even if fantasy is the best they can do, they keep going. There is the possibility of love, of communion with land if no human being wants you; the regenerative power of land and of nature.

> In the quiet moments of soft rustling between the bursts of singing, a noisy crow, flying over the neglected gardens of St Christopher and St Jude, cried the tragedy and the gift of half-remembered places, of distant towns and villages, of mountains and rivers and of wharves and railway stations. The crow, swooping closer, still crying, brought to the doors and windows of St Christopher and St Jude the sound of wind rushing across endless paddocks, the steady hopeful clicking of windmills and long country roads leading to serene crossroads. Another crow, in another garden, crying loneliness, seemed to answer the first one. When the crows were silent, the voices of the doves could be heard; a contented sound, perhaps a language of reason and of acceptance and resignation.

And in the last chapter of *Mr Scobie's Riddle*, when the old men have died and the mad woman has not been able to escape Matron's clutches, there is still the symbol of the tents, fragile, optimistic, temporary structures, clumsily erected in hope.

Postscript

Elizabeth Jolley's novel *Palomino*, now reissued in hardcover by UQP, was first published in 1980. Eighteen months ago I read her entire output (since then she has published *Miss Peabody's Inheritance* and *Milk and Honey* — does this women ever get up from the desk?) and wrote an appreciation of it for *Meanjin*, in which I passed over *Palomino* in a high-handed fashion, saying that it was a "failure" because it was "devoid of her weird humour".

I would now like publicly to withdraw this remark. Re-reading *Palomino* I take off my hat to Elizabeth Jolley once again: the long-running, commaless sentences, the tender warmth she creates between her women characters, the way she wears her wisdom so lightly, the intensity of feeling for land and landscape, and the presence of music in her world: Jolley is one of our older women writers at whose feet I would willingly cast myself.

Somebody Ought to Make this Book into a Movie

Extract from Review of Thea Astley's *An Item from the Late News*

Thea Astley uses in this novel the flexible, cheeky device used by (among others) F. Scott Fitzgerald in his unfinished book *The Last Tycoon* and which he sets out in his notes for that book:

> By making Cecilia, at the moment of her telling the story, an intelligent and observant woman, I shall grant myself that privilege, as Conrad did, of letting her imagine the action of the character. Thus, I hope to get the versimilitude of a first person narrative, combined with a God-like knowledge of all events that happen to my characters.

Gabby, Astley's narrator, says late in the book, "I am the omniscient narrator. I am a bearer of knowns and almost-knowns. I translate. I paraphrase. It's all legal in a *confessio amantis*."

Fitzgerald's Cecilia makes a remark which also applies to Astley's narrator. "What people are ashamed of usually makes a good story."

Great story, great characters. Stylistically, however, this book is like a very handsome, strong and fit woman with too much make-up on. On page one, Gabby tells about Christmas in Allbut: "And why barbaric? Always barbaric? Not always, I suppose, though the beer-gut belchings and the rattle of schooner glasses that always discover the Christmas crib and soothe the infant with whack yoicks, seem to me to have a much worn style."

This kind of writing drives me berserk, and not because I'm against messing with sound, but because the way Astley does it here is heavy-handed, layered-on, inorganic, self-conscious, hectic and distracting.

It gives the prose a sense of strain which is terribly irritating and bothersome, a layer of force and twist on something that needs no fancy treatment, for always present, under the maddening flourishes of decoration, is an utter assurance at making character and telling a story.

When she stops trying so hard to be a stylist, Astley shows that she already is one, in a much less flashy way. She writes a driving narrative, she makes landscape and weather unforgettable, she'll tackle big themes and symbols with the gloves off. She's got ease and power: she doesn't need to pump iron.

The long sequence which is the book's climax, the townsmen's stupid, stubborn search for the sapphires, is marvellous: sustained, clear, relentless, with the underlying notes of betrayal and doom sounding away there so that the reader is practically in a sweat.

Somebody ought to make this book into a movie.

A Woman's Word

Do women, must women, can women, should women write differently from men? Not just what they write about, but how they use language? Can a reader judge a writer's gender from a tiny excerpt, or are clues to be found only in larger elements — structure, plot or not, characters or not, narrative or not, or what?

Gillian Beer, in an essay "Women Writing and Writing About Women", says: "Virginia Woolf does not tell about women's bodies but in *The Waves*, having driven out authoritarian narrative, she uses women's special experience of time as one of the two underlying orders of the book. The book accepts the common human condition of growth and ageing, while relying for its particular order on recurrence and cycle. The menstrual relationship to time is implicit in the tides, the recurring waves, the stilled episodes of reunion and dissolution."

*　　*　　*

Computer studies have been done which show that there are certain words used more frequently by female writers than by male. I do not know what these words are.

*　　*　　*

English novelist Sara Maitland writes: "We must demand and respond to more and better novels, but we cannot demand that any one novel be simultaneously: (a) satisfying to our sense of the complexity of our lives; (b) a paradigm of orthodox feminism; (c) an evangelical document to convert the unconverted; (d) the bearer of a whole new language and symbol structure and world model; (e) a good read — witty, inspiring, identifiable with; (f) able to provide us with mythological heroines; and (g) an exposition of the fullness of women's oppression."

Perhaps it is the reader, and not the writer, who makes a book a feminist book.

*   *   *

Last summer at Writers' Week in Adelaide, Maxine Hong Kingston mentioned in passing that she was trying to get beyond female first-person narrative (of the kind where the author and the "I" are very closely related, if not the same person), and that in retrospect she felt "selfish" for having written *The Woman Warrior* from this perspective.

I happen to think that this is one of the strengths of that book, and I took her use of the word "selfish" as ironic, but some of the women in the audience took it literally and grumbled among themselves, " 'Selfish'? Where does that leave women's writing? Is she heading towards just 'the artist'?" "Limited" may be a better word than "selfish".

It's easier, at least in terms of craft, to write a first-person narrative, to "self-express", than to do the broader thing, to split your imagination and spread yourself and go in a dozen directions at once. Easier in terms of craft, but it's not necessarily emotionally easier, as many men writers might admit.

*   *   *

"Literature is a making, not an out-pouring. 'Self-expression' leads too quickly to self-indulgence; writing fiction is the verbal counterpart of self-control, self-determination." — US novelist Janet Burroway, in *The Writer on Her Work*.

There is such a thing as a distancing between teller and tale which, when the events served raw or medium rare would have been unbearable, enables the reader to bear, to understand, to contemplate without boredom or despair, and finally in some sense to master, as the writer has done, the matter in question.

*   *   *

In 1961 at Melbourne University, Professor A.D. Hope read to a first-year English class Tolstoy's description (in *Anna Karenina*) of Kitty's preparation for an evening which would decide the direction of her life.

How wonderful, said Hope, is Tolstoy's ability to understand and portray the working of the female mind.

I was nineteen and believed everything I was told. I now find this account of Kitty's attitude toward her own appearance a rather obvious, even superficial piece of observation. This does not mean I don't think Tolstoy is a wonderful artist.

*   *   *

Three Chinese women were guests at the Women Writers' Week: two writers, one interpreter.

The interpreter, translating the brief life story of the older woman writer, Han Zi, said, "the feet of her grandmother and her mother were bounded. Very sma' size. Because of feudalist ideas their feet were bounded."

A woman in the audience asked two questions of Han Zi, famous writer of children's books.

"Are there, in Chinese fairy tales, evil female archetypes — the wicked witch, the wicked stepmother? And is there clearly differentiated male and female behaviour, in fairy tales?"

The Chinese woman did not seem to understand these questions, or the concepts underlying them.

Perhaps there were not words in Chinese for the concepts. They murmured among themselves for a length of time disproportionate to the simplicity (it seemed to us) of the questions. Finally the interpreter spoke. "There are some stories which are about boys, and some stories about girls."

She looked about her helplessly, hands out, palms up. "Is this . . .?"

*   *   *

Novelist and biographer Barbara Jefferis, talking at the festival about biography: "Male biography is about historical achievement. Men tend to set up heroes and try to emulate them. You can tell this from the hilarious terms of reverence they have devised: 'Your Holiness', 'Your Serene Highness'.

"Ask a woman who her heroes are and she won't have any. Heroines? Certainly not Joan of Arc, Boadicea, the Virgin Mary. Women are less envious, thus less likely to want reflected glory from the subjects of their biographies."

*   *   *

Conversation between two women writers at the festival:

A: "How do you write men characters?"

B: "I go right into the male part of myself and I start inventing. I never thought of that till this very minute. Does it sound like bullshit?"

A: "On the contrary. You've given me the green light. Thanks."

Showing the Flipside

Extract from Interview by Jennifer Ellison

Within the broader theme of domesticity which seems to inform all your work, there seem to be two recurring motifs: children and music. Are you conscious of these?

Children are terribly important. Gerard Windsor said in his review of *The Children's Bach* that the characters are judged by their attitudes towards children. This is true but I hadn't done it consciously. Children are wondrous; they strike me with awe. And they're so tough, and funny.

Music is always there too. I never thought about it, until *The Children's Bach* — it was just there, like air, as it is in everyone's life in the modern world.

In *The Children's Bach* the music works as some kind of moral or ordering principle. It's a cliché but nevertheless true that art tries to impose order on experience which is not orderly, on a universe full of terrifying and demoralising things. I've tried to make music do that job.

Are you then addressing explicitly "moral" issues in your writing?

Yes. I suppose so. Two things got me out of a big mess at a certain point in my life. One was feminism and the other one was the whole ethos of collective households. That's the sort of thing that people who don't live like that were attracted to in *Monkey Grip* — the fact that there were those open households where people actually cared about each other and tried to create some kind of alternative to a family, some social organisation that would contain the good things about a family and minimise the bad things, the awful neurotic thing that happens in families. It certainly happened in mine.

"Honour" has a moral title and it's a moral story. It's about people trying to behave in ways that are open and generous. The two women are trying to learn to confront each other, and to confront the fact that one's the first wife and the other's the second wife; they're not going to let themselves get slotted into social roles that have been created for them. They're going to try and approach it in some more open way. I think you could say that was a moral story. And *The Children's Bach* is a moral story because the woman comes back — and by that I don't mean that all women should go back to marriage. I think a lot of people probably interpreted it that way, you know; they thought, here's Helen Garner recanting. Of course, I think it is possible for people to walk out of a marriage. There's a period of sadness and suffering and so forth, but some of the kids I know who are products of broken marriages are the most extraordinary children. They're children who've got resilience and knowledge and sense. People talk about kids of broken marriages being traumatised, but how many people are traumatised by marriages that *don't* break up?

Would you say you are very conscious of the female characters and the whole issue of feminism in your work?

Of course. Some people think my men characters are drips; they don't know how the women in the stories can be bothered with the men. But I think that's a function of the fact that the women are centre stage and the men are slightly to one side. It might also be because my work shows the flip side of what feminists have grumbled about for all those years, that women weren't very well observed, that male writers didn't know what they thought or how they felt. I always feel conscious of taking a risk when I say "This is what this man's thinking", because I don't know. But then I don't know what other women are thinking either! I'm only guessing. You can only guess and go by hints and try to listen carefully.

Are you particularly interested in finding out more about male characters? Would you like to write more about male characters?

Yes, yes, I would, and in fact am doing so now. I've always had a very difficult relationship with my father. I think a lot of amateur psychologists would have spotted this already in my work. My relat: nship with my father has been the chief drama in my life and still is. It's going to be a job for me to understand my relationship with my father. He rejected me for many years and I behaved in such a way that he could only reject me. It was a tremendous battle and it's only now, in my forties, that I'm starting to be able to see him as separate from me, and not this force of nature breathing down my neck and saying "No, no, no." The other thing that happens to women like me, who have had such a difficult relationship with their fathers, is that you tend to be attracted to men who aren't going to love you as much as you want them to; it's because you've got unfinished business with your father. You want to recreate that situation with other men. Why would someone like me fall in love with a junkie? Because he's the sort of person who's unable to express love and so I can continue this battle to get him to love me, which is what the whole thing is with my father. That might seem a rather crude analysis but I think it's true.

It's taken me a long time to understand this about the male characters in my work, how many of them are unable to love. People have said they're weak or they're boring, but that's not the point. The point about them is that they're incapable of love. That's why for me, this character of Dexter is such a huge advance: Dexter can *love*. He may be slightly clownish still and a lot of people have written to me and said "What a dill this Dexter is, I really couldn't stand him", but to me Dexter is a wonderful character. In terms of my personal emotional development separately from my work (if the two can be separated, which I doubt) that's a bit of an advance.

How did feminism directly influence your writing?

It directly influenced my writing in the sense that I felt that it was all right for me to be writing in the first place. I still have trouble even now with the thought that I'm not as worthy as a man. I have to put on a bit of bravado sometimes to get past that. I mean as a writer. It's the kind of female cringe that we recognised in ourselves when feminism gave us a way of looking at ourselves usefully. An act of will isn't enough to break out of female conditioning. You can't just bounce on the sofa drawing attention to yourself, saying "Look at me! I'm terrific!" You have to believe it, quite quietly, right inside you. That's a lifelong process.

But the reception that *The Children's Bach* got certainly helped. After Don Anderson's review in the *National Times*, the first one that came out, I thought, Phew — nothing can touch me now.

The idea of feeling less worthy is a hard one to examine. It's hard to distinguish between some form of not wanting to be up oneself, and the objective nature of people's responses to you. Every time somebody in a magazine or a newspaper says "Australian writers, like . . ." and then gives a list of names, if I'm not on that list I feel mortified. And when I feel like this I stop and I think, now what's happening here? I think, is this just my screaming ego wanting to be among the top of the class, or am I really looking out to see if I'm being excluded from some sort of category because I'm a woman? If you really wanted to answer that question in a specific case you'd have to go and read everything that critic's ever written, and why bother?

Also, I think that even people who like my work, and who think it's good, are probably waiting for me to write about something else. They seem, almost in spite of themselves, still to think of it as small beer because it's about domesticity and what happens in kitchens and bedrooms. I used to think, why can't I have a war or a revolution or something? And then I'd think, but I don't know anything about those things, and I won't be able to write about them until I do, and I may not ever, and I can't go out and look for them. There's a lot of that in it, the feeling that women's concerns are small or less important or secondary in some way. I don't think that myself. I think they're very crucial. I love novels about families. I suppose everybody does. Look at *War and Peace* — that's about a family as well as being about war. When I was writing *The Children's Bach* I felt very strange and anxious from time to time because the scope of it was so small and domestic. And one day I was walking home from my room where I'd been working, and I went past a print shop. In the window of the shop was a print of a Van Gogh painting, that famous one of the chair in his bedroom. I looked at it and I thought, this is a wonderful painting, a painting that fills you with hope and life. And I thought, what is it? It's a painting of the inside of his bedroom and there's not even a person in it!

Do you think generally women writers do need to fight for recognition in Australia in a way that men don't?

That's a hard question to answer. I don't have the chip on my shoulder that I would have once had about this sort of thing. And, besides, I haven't had to deal with men in the business because I've got women publishers.

Has that been important to you?

Oh God, it's been crucial. If I'd had to take *Monkey Grip* to a male publishing company, either it would have been thrown out immediately as being too emotional, et cetera, or I would have had to hack at it and change it in lots of ways. It may be that the structure of it wouldn't have been acceptable to male publishers. I'm not saying that this is definitely the case — it may not be true — but I think it probably is.

Hilary McPhee and Diana Gribble are wonderful to work with. They're the sort of people whose opinions I really care about. When they came to Paris and told me my second novel was shit I knew it was shit because I trusted their judgment. They're the sort of people I can take something to when it's only half done and say, "Am I on the right track here?" and they'll say yes or no; I trust them to that extent. I don't really trust anyone else to that extent. *Anyone.*

Select Bibliography

Adelaide, Debra. *Australian Women Writers: A Bibliographic Guide*. Sydney: Pandora, 1988.

Ahearne, Kate. "Exploring Life's Lonely Struggle". *National Times*, 9-15 December 1983, p.27. (An interview with Beverley Farmer.)

Barry, Elaine. "The Expatriate Vision of Jessica Anderson". *Meridian* 3, i (May 1984): 3–11.

Bird, Delys. "Australian Woman: A National Joke?" *Australian Journal of Cultural Studies* 1, i (May 1983): 111–14.

_____ . "Towards an Aesthetics of Australian Women's Fiction: *My Brilliant Career* and *The Getting of Wisdom*". *Australian Literary Studies* 11, ii (October 1983): 171–81.

Blair, Ruth. "Jessica Anderson's Mysteries". *Island Magazine* 31 (1987): 10–15.

Brett, Judith. "Cultural Politics and Australian Literary Magazines". *Meanjin* 43, iii (September 1984): 423–28.

Brydon, Diana. "Barbara Hanrahan's Fantastic Fiction". *Westerly* 3 (September 1982): 41–49.

Carroll, Alison. *Barbara Hanrahan: Printmaker*. Adelaide: Wakefield Press, 1987.

Clancy, Laurie. "Love, Longing and Loneliness: The Fiction of Elizabeth Jolley". *Australian Book Review* 56 (November 1983): 8–12.

_____ . "The Fiction of Thea Astley". *Meridian* 5, i (May 1986): 43–52.

Couani, Anna, & Sneja Gunew, eds. *Telling Ways: Australian Women's Experimental Writing*. Adelaide: Australian Feminist Studies, 1988.

Craven, Peter. "Of War and Needlework: The Fiction of Helen Garner". *Meanjin* 44, ii (June 1985): 209–19.

Craney, Jan, & Esther Caldwell, eds. *The true life story of . . .* St Lucia: UQP, 1981.

Daniel, Helen. "Elizabeth Jolley: Variations on a Theme". *Westerly* 31, ii (June 1986): 50–63.

Falkiner, Suzanne, ed. *Room to Move: Redress Press Anthology of Australian Women's Short Stories*. Sydney: Allen & Unwin, 1985.

Ferrier, Carole, ed. *Gender, Politics and Fiction: Twentieth Century Australian Women's Novels*. St Lucia: UQP, 1985.

_____ . "Problems in Feminist Criticism". *Australian Book Review* 104 (September 1988): 24-27.

Gallagher, Donat. "Tirra Lirra by the Brisbane River". *LINQ* 10, i (1981): 101-10.

Gibbs, Anna, & Alison Tilson, eds. *Frictions: An Anthology of Fiction by Women*. 2nd ed. Melbourne: Sybylla Co-operative Press, 1983.

Gilbert, Pam. *Coming Out From Under: Contemporary Australian Women Writers*. Sydney: Pandora, 1988.

Goldsworthy, Kerryn. "Dense Clouds of Language". *Island Magazine* 27 (1986): 24–27.

_____ . "Female Culture in a Small Town". *Island Magazine* 25/6 (1986): 116–17.

_____ . "Feminist Readings, Feminist Writings: Recent Australian Writing by Women". *Meanjin* 44 iv (December 1985): 506–15.

_____ . "Thea Astley's Writing: Magnetic North". *Meanjin* 42, iv (December 1983): 478–85.

_____ . "Voices in Time: *A Kindness Cup* and *Miss Peabody's Inheritance*". *Australian Literary Studies* 12, iv (October 1986): 471–81.

Gunew, Sneja. "Feminist Criticism: Positions and Questions". *Southern Review* 16 (1983): 151–61.

_____ . "Framing Marginality: Distinguishing the Textual Politics of the Marginal Voice". *Southern Review* 18, ii (July 1985): 142–57.

_____ . "Migrant Women Writers: Who's on Whose Margins?"

In *Gender, Politics and Fiction*, ed. Carole Ferrier, pp.163–78.

_____ . "What Does Woman Mean?: Reading, Writing and Reproduction". *Hecate* 9, i & ii (1983): 111–22.

Gunew, Sneja, & Jan Mahyuddin, eds. *Beyond the Echo: Australian Multicultural Women's Writing*. St Lucia: UQP, 1988.

Gunew, Sneja, & Louise Adler. "Method and Madness in Female Writing". *Hecate* 7, ii (1981): 20–33.

Hall, James. "Why Women Writers Crowd the Best Sellers List". *The Bulletin*, 27 May 1986, pp. 72–77.

Haynes, Roslynn D. "Art as Reflection in Jessica Anderson's *Tirra Lirra by the River*". *Australian Literary Studies* 12, iii (May 1986): 316–23.

Jones, Dorothy. "Drama's Vitallest Expression: The Fiction of Olga Masters". *Australian Literary Studies* 13, i (May 1987): 3–14.

_____ . "The Goddess, The Artist and the Spinster". *Westerly* 29, iv (1984): 77–88.

_____ . " 'Which hend you hev?' Elizabeth Jolley's *Milk and Honey*". *Westerly* 31, ii (June 1986): 35–39.

Levy, Bronwen. "Constructing the Woman Writer: The Reviewing Reception of Hazzard's *The Transit of Venus*". In *Gender, Politics and Fiction*, ed. Carole Ferrier, pp.179–99.

_____ . "Women and the Literary Pages: Some Recent Examples". *Hecate* 21, i (1985): 5–11.

_____ . "Paterson's Curse or Salvation Jane? The Impact of Women's Studies with Australian Studies". Unpublished paper presented at ASAL 1987.

Lohrey, Amanda. "The Dead Hand of Orthodoxy". *Island Magazine* 27 (1986): 19–21.

Lord, Mary. "Celebrating Olga Masters". *Australian Book Review* 103 (August 1988): 32–33.

Mercer, Gina. "Little Women: Helen Garner, Sold by Weight". *Australian Book Review* 81 (June 1986): 26–28.

_____ . "Interview with Kate Grenville". *Southerly* 45, iii (1985): 295–300.

Mott, Julie. "Interview with Barbara Hanrahan". *Australian Literary Studies* 11, i (May 1983): 38–46.

Parker, David. "Re-mapping Our Suburbs". *Quadrant* (July-August 1986): 126–30.

Perkins, Elizabeth. "A Life of its Own: A Deconstructive Reading of Astley's *A Kindness Cup*". *Hecate* 21, i (1985): 1–18.

Riemer, A.P. "Displaced Persons — Some Preoccupations in Elizabeth Jolley's Fiction". *Westerly* 31, ii (June 1986): 64–79.

Salzman, Paul. "Elizabeth Jolley: Fiction and Desire". *Meridian* 5, i (May 1986): 53–62.

Schaffer, Kay. *Women and the Bush: Forces of Desire in the Australian Cultural Tradition.* Cambridge: Cambridge University Press, 1988.

Shapcott, Thomas. "Five Acre Hell". *Westerly* 25, iv (December 1980): 73–75.

Spender, Dale. *The Penguin Anthology of Australian Women's Writing.* Ringwood: Penguin, 1988.

_____ . *Writing a New World: Two Centuries of Australian Women Writers.* Sydney: Pandora Press, 1988.

Stewart, Annette. "Barbara Hanrahan's Grotesquerie". *Quadrant* 32, i & ii (January-February 1988): 59–65.

Sykes, Alrene. "Barbara Hanrahan's Novels". *Australian Literary Studies* 11, i (May 1983): 47–57.

_____ . "Jessica Anderson: Arrivals and Places". *Southerly* 46, i (1986): 57–71.

Trigg, Stephanie. "Elizabeth Jolley: Something Remarkable Every Time". *Scripsi* 4, i (July 1986): 265–67.

_____ . "Postcards from Helen". *Scripsi* 4, ii (November 1986): 197–201.

Walker, Shirley. *Who Is She? Images of Women in Australian Fiction.* St Lucia: UQP, 1983.

Webby, Elizabeth. "The Long March of Short Fiction: A Seventies Retrospective". *Meanjin* 39, i (April 1980): 127–33.

_____ . "Short Fiction in the Eighties: White Anglo-Celtic Male No More?" *Meanjin* 42, i (March 1983): 34–41.

Willbanks, Ray. "A Conversation with Jessica Anderson". *Antipodes* 2, i (1988): 49–51.

Windsor, Gerard. "Writers and Reviewers". *Island Magazine* 27 (1986): 15–18.

UQP AUSTRALIAN AUTHORS

The Australian Short Story
edited by Laurie Hergenhan
Outstanding contemporary short stories alongside some of the best from
the past. This volume encompasses the short story in Australia from its
Bulletin beginnings in the 1890s to its vigorous revival in the 1970s and
1980s.

Writings of the 1890s
edited by Leon Cantrell
A retrospective collection, bringing together the work of 32 Australian
poets, storytellers and essayists. The anthology challenges previous
assumptions about this romantic period of galloping ballads and bush
yarns, bohemianism and creative giants.

Catherine Helen Spence
edited by Helen Thomson
An important early feminist writer, Catherine Helen Spence was one of
the first women in Australia to break through the constraints of gender
and class and enter public life. This selection contains her most highly
regarded novel, *Clara Morison*, her triumphant autobiography, and
much of her political and social reformist writing.

Henry Lawson
edited by Brian Kiernan
A complete profile of Henry Lawson, the finest and most original writer
in the bush yarn tradition. This selection includes sketches, letters, autobiography and verse, with outspoken journalism and the best of his comic
and tragic stories.

Christopher Brennan
edited by Terry Sturm
Christopher Brennan was a legend in his own time, and his art was an
unusual amalgam of Victorian, symbolist and modernist tendencies. This
selection draws on the whole range of Brennan's work: poetry, literary
criticism and theory, autobiographical writing, and letters.

Robert D. FitzGerald
edited by Julian Croft

FitzGerald's long and distinguished literary career is reflected in this selection of his poetry and prose. There is poetry from the 1920s to the 1980s, samples from his lectures on poetics and essays on family origins and philosophical pre-occupations, a short story, and his views on Australian poetry.

Australian Science Fiction
edited by Van Ikin

An exotic blend of exciting recent works with a selection from Australia's long science fiction tradition. Classics by Erle Cox, M. Barnard Eldershaw and others are followed by stories from major contemporary writers Damien Broderick, Frank Byrning, Peter Carey, A. Bertram Chandler, Lee Harding, David J. Lake, Philippa C. Maddern, Dal Stivens, George Turner, Wynne N. Whiteford, Michael Wilding and Jack Wodhams.

Barbara Baynton
edited by Sally Krimmer and Alan Lawson

Bush writing of the 1890s, but very different from Henry Lawson. Baynton's stories are often macabre and horrific, and her bush women express a sense of outrage. The revised text of the brilliant *Bush Studies*, the novel *Human Toll*, poems, articles and an interview, all reveal Baynton's disconcertingly independent viewpoint.

Joseph Furphy
edited by John Barnes

Such is Life is an Australian classic. Written by ex-bullock driver, half-bushman and half bookworm, it is an extraordinary achievement. The accompanying selection of novel extracts, stories, verse, *Bulletin* articles and letters illustrates the astounding range of Furphy's talent, and John Barnes's notes reveal the intellectual and linguistic richness of his prose.

James McAuley
edited by Leonie Kramer

James McAuley was a poet, intellectual, and leading critic of his time. This volume represents the whole range of his poetry and prose, including the Ern Malley hoax that caused such a sensation in the 1940s, and some new prose pieces published for the first time. Leonie Kramer's introduction offers new critical perspectives on his work.

Rolf Boldrewood
edited by Alan Brissenden
Australia's most famous bushranging novel, *Robbery Under Arms*, together with extracts from the original serial version. The best of Boldrewood's essays and short stories are also included; some are autobiographical, most deal with life in the bush.

Marcus Clarke
edited by Michael Wilding
The convict classic *For the Term of His Natural Life*, and a varied selection of short stories, critical essays and journalism. Autobiographical stories provide vivid insights into the life of this prolific and provocative man of letters.

Nettie Palmer
edited by Vivian Smith
Nettie Palmer was a distinguished poet, biographer, literary critic, diarist, letter-writer, editor and translator, who played a vital role in the development and appreciation of Australian literature. Her warm and informative diary, *Fourteen Years*, is reproduced as a facsimile of the original illustrated edition, along with a rich selection of her poems, reviews and literary journalism.

Colonial Voices
edited by Elizabeth Webby
The first anthology to draw on the fascinating variety of letters, diaries, journalism and other prose accounts of nineteenth-century Australia. These colonial voices belong to adults and children, some famous or infamous, others unknown, whose accounts reveal unusual aspects of Australia's colourful past.